The Drama of Ideas

THE DRAMA OF IDEAS

Platonic Provocations in Theater and Philosophy

Martin Puchner

OXFORD
UNIVERSITY PRESS
2010

OXFORD
UNIVERSITY PRESS

Oxford University Press, Inc., publishes works that further
Oxford University's objective of excellence
in research, scholarship, and education.

Oxford   New York
Auckland   Cape Town   Dar es Salaam   Hong Kong   Karachi
Kuala Lumpur   Madrid   Melbourne   Mexico City   Nairobi
New Delhi   Shanghai   Taipei   Toronto

With offices in
Argentina   Austria   Brazil   Chile   Czech Republic   France   Greece
Guatemala   Hungary   Italy   Japan   Poland   Portugal   Singapore
South Korea   Switzerland   Thailand   Turkey   Ukraine   Vietnam

Published by Oxford University Press, Inc.
198 Madison Avenue, New York, New York 10016

www.oup.com

Oxford is a registered trademark of Oxford University Press

Library of Congress Cataloging-in-Publication Data

Puchner, Martin, 1969–
The drama of ideas : platonic provocations in theater and philosophy
/ Martin Puchner.
p. cm.
Includes index.
ISBN 978-0-19-973032-2
1. Drama—20th century—History and criticism. 2. Philosophy in
literature. 3. Plato—Influence. 4. Drama—Greek influences. I.
Title.
PN1861.P83 2010
809.2—dc22   2009026990

1 3 5 7 9 8 6 4 2

Printed in the United States of America
on acid-free paper

For Amanda Claybaugh

Preface

When I went through some old papers recently, I came across a theater review I had written for the college newspaper in 1991. The show in question had been conceived by two assistant professors of philosophy and revolved around various philosophical characters. My review applauds the attempt to combine philosophy and theater, and ends with a somewhat snarky complaint about the conspicuous absence in the audience of the "ladies and gentlemen philosophy professors," and more generally the lack of contact between philosophy and theater. At the time I was majoring in philosophy, but I also spent a lot of time doing theater. Our black box theater happened to be located directly below one of the largest lecture halls on campus, in the space left by the ascending auditorium, an arrangement that echoed Plato's parable of the cave with its shadow theater below and philosophy above. Attending philosophy lectures upstairs by day and doing theater in the black box downstairs by night seemed unrelated activities—except that for me they weren't. Ever since then, I have been trying to figure out what the relation between those two activities, between those two spaces, might be.

In my previous books, this question has played an important but ultimately secondary role. In *Stage Fright: Modernism, Anti-Theatricality, and Drama* and other publications connected to it, I articulated why the dramatic experiments of modernism could not be described in Aristotelian terms and instead turned to Plato's notion of diegesis to capture modernism's conflicted relation to the stage. In *Poetry of the Revolution: Marx, Manifestos, and the Avant-Gardes*, I touched on the relation between theater and philosophy in another way, by trying to explain the move from theory to action as it occurs in the genre of the manifesto. But it is only now that I have come to realize that the relation between theater and philosophy is what I have been trying to write about all along—that I have been driven by the sense, first articulated in my theater review, that theater and philosophy are intimately, if contentiously, related. I do not know whether this book will encourage the "ladies and gentlemen philosophy professors" to take the theater more seriously or theater people (and professors) to delve more deeply into philosophy. But I think I have been able to explain to myself why I never could decide whether to remain upstairs with the philosophers or downstairs in the theater.

It remains to be seen whether it will be possible to establish a new relation between theater and philosophy. Even now, after having written this book, I am not certain whether my subject matter, a truly philosophical drama and a truly dramatic philosophy, actually exists. I have looked for this idea in many places and found an astonishing variety of instances that participate in it one way or another. They include dramatic adaptations of Plato's dialogues, modern dramatists inspired by Plato, nineteenth- and twentieth-century philosophers interested in drama and theater, and finally contemporary Platonists attuned to Plato's literary form. But the idea of the coincidence of drama and philosophy itself seems to have retreated whenever I thought I was getting close. At first this filled me with dismay. But more and more I have come to the conclusion that this is a fitting predicament for an inquiry that takes Plato as its point of departure. The question of how an abstract construct can ever be fully materialized, after all, is the Platonic dilemma par excellence. So be it: I have been chasing a shadow up and down the histories of theater and philosophy. The glimpses of this shadow I was able to catch compose the substance of this book.

Catching these glimpses would have been impossible without the generous help of many friends, colleagues, and institutions. First, I would like to thank Freddie Rokem and the three anonymous readers for Oxford University Press, whose sharp eyes and minds not only saved me from many embarrassments but also helped me to sharpen my argument considerably. Over the many years that this book project has been percolating through my mind, I was invited to present pieces of it at American University, Columbia, Cornell, Dartmouth, Duke, Freie Universität Berlin, Harvard, Johns Hopkins, University of California at Irvine, University of Wisconsin at Madison, University of Mainz, New York University, Northwestern, University of Pennsylvania, Rutgers, Yale, and York University, and I found helpful audiences at several conferences, including those of the American Comparative Literature Association and the Modern Language Association. Inspiring conversations with the following people helped me develop my argument: Alan Ackerman, Arnold Aronson, Alain Badiou, Christopher Balme, Akeel Bilgrami, Svetlana Boym, Matthew Buckley, Lawrence Buell, Efe Cakmak, Marvin Carlson, Tracy Davis, Elin Diamond, Kathy Eden, Erika Fischer-Lichte, Philip Fisher, Deborah Fisk, Helene Foley, Elinor Fuchs, Ellen Gainor, Darren Gobert, Alexander Goehr, Lydia Goehr, Seth Harrison, Ursula Heise, David Kornhaber, Friedemann Kreuder, Karl Kroeber, Douglas Mao, Sharon Marcus, Peter Marx, Christoph Menke, Bernadette Meyler, Klaus Mladek, Toril Moi, Sara Monoson, Bryan Reynolds, Joseph Roach, Bruce Robbins, Marc Robinson, Freddie Rokem, Elaine Scarry, Laurence Senelick, Matthew Smith, Joanna Stalnaker, Henry

Turner, Rebecca Walkowitz, Christopher Wild, Emily Wilson, and Mary Ann Witt, as well as the students in my graduate seminars on theater and philosophy at Harvard and Columbia. Also, I would like to thank my research assistants Meagan Michelson, Amy Ramsey, and Ruth McCann. At Oxford University Press, I feel extraordinarily lucky to have in Shannon McLachlan a truly exceptional editor who not only supported the book from the beginning but also helped me think through its arguments in great detail. Brendan O'Neill was of great assistance at many moments in the process, and for copyediting I am indebted to Sue Warga. I put finishing touches on this book while a fellow at the Institute for Advanced Study in Berlin and would like that thank that institution for its generous support. I would also like to thank my brothers, Stephan and Elias, as well as my mother, who patiently listened to different versions of this project during the many years of its conception and realization. Finally, I wish to thank the person whom I will never learn to thank enough, so all-encompassing is her contribution to everything I think and write—and to my happiness: Amanda Claybaugh, to whom this book is dedicated.

A few brief sections and lectures were published in different form elsewhere: "Kenneth Burke: Theatre, Philosophy, and the Limits of Performance," in *Staging Philosophy*, edited by David Krasner and David Saltz (Ann Arbor: University of Michigan Press, 2006); "Kierkegaard's Shadow Figures," in *Image and Imagination*, edited by Bernd Hüppauf and Christoph Wulf (Munich: Finck Verlag, 2007); "The Theater of Alain Badiou," *Theatre Research International* 34, 3 (2009); "Shaw and the Comedy of Ideas," in *Performing the Matrix*, edited by Meike Wagner and Wolf-Dieter Ernst (Munich: Podium, 2008). I thank the editors and publishers for their kind permission to use these pieces here. Alain Badiou's "Rhapsody for the Theatre" was published under my editorship in *Theatre Survey* 49, 2 (2008).

Contents

The Drama of Ideas

1

The Poetics of the Platonic Dialogue

Plato, Dramatist

Sometime during the fifth century BCE, a young playwright submitted his tragedy to the annual theater competition at Athens. Despite his youth, he was already quite experienced in the theater. He had secured the financial backing of a patron, Dion, and so acquired one of the most desirable posts in the Athenian theater world: leader of the chorus (*choregus*). This was apparently not enough for the young man, for there was one higher honor to be had: winning first prize as playwright. The competition was fierce. Everyone would be there, assembled in the huge open-air Dionysius Theater, holding more than fifteen thousand, to witness triumph or humiliation. If his play won, it would be the making of his career. He would be feted for days on end and become an instant celebrity; surely he would stop going to school and quit wrestling, his other two occupations. But as he made his way to the theater to submit his play, something unexpected happened. He ran into a small group of people who were listening to a disheveled, stub-nosed creature whom he recognized as the notorious public speaker Socrates. He started to listen and was strangely compelled by Socrates' witty and ironic phrases, which cut like razors through the incoherent speeches put forward by various bystanders. He decided to become a student of this man. And then, on the steps of the great Dionysius Theater of Athens, he burned his play.

The playwright, of course, was Plato, and the scene is transmitted to us by Plato's first biographer, Diogenes Laertius, who even has Plato exclaim melodramatically, "Come hither, O fire-god, Plato now has need of thee," as his play goes up in flames.[1] But why did Plato burn his tragedy? Much is at stake in the answer, for Western philosophy has tended to construe a history according to which Plato had to consign to the flames his ambition as a playwright in order to be reborn as a philosopher.

Nothing could be further from the truth. Plato continued to write in a dramatic mode throughout his life. The conflagration on the steps was not an end but merely a change in direction that would give rise to one of the most unusual careers in drama. When Plato started to write again, he did so with a strange type of drama, the Socratic dialogue.[2] These dialogues were richly conceived scenarios paying minute attention to setting, character, and plot even as they deviated from all known forms of drama, combining characters and ideas, actions and arguments in curiously meandering, labyrinthine plots. With those dialogues Plato found his true calling, developing a most powerful philosophical character and a most unusual form of philosophical drama. Plato had managed to transform himself from leader of the chorus and author of juvenile tragedies to an entirely new kind of writer.

Plato's innovation has not been fully recognized, although we can find glimpses of such recognition everywhere. A number of Greek commentators considered Plato's Socratic dialogues within the theatrical context of the time, even though they did not always know what to make of them. This was certainly the case with the greatest ancient authority on drama, Aristotle. Aristotle developed the first taxonomy of ancient drama, which included the established forms of tragedy, comedy, and satyr play, but he added two minor, recent creations, both rather eccentric in their use of prose, a mode usually reserved for medical or scientific treatises. The first of those minor genres was the mime, short, vulgar sketches that had recently been given some literary prestige by a writer from Syracuse, Sophron. The second minor genre was the Socratic dialogue, a new form introduced by a number of former students of Socrates.[3] Aristotle was not alone in associating Plato with drama. Diogenes Laertius' biography portrays Plato as someone who was fully involved in the theater of Athens throughout his life, even after having burned his tragedy. Plato traveled with the famous tragedian Euripides, we learn; he received much help from the comic playwright Epicharmus; and he composed his dialogues in tetralogies, just like the tragic playwrights.[4] Perhaps thinking of Aristotle's comparison of the Socratic dialogues and Sophron's mimes, Diogenes Laertius even reports that it was Plato who had first introduced those mimes to Athens.[5]

By the same token, Diogenes Laertius' biography of Socrates gives us no reason to think Socrates would have convinced Plato to give up drama entirely. Instead we learn that Socrates was writing tragedies himself, in collaboration with Euripides, and that he frequented the Dionysius Theater.[6] One anecdote has him standing up in the theater during Aristophanes' *Clouds* so that the audience could compare Aristophanes' comic portrayal of Socrates with the real thing.[7] The two philosophers socialized with playwrights, traveled with them, learned from them, collaborated with them, and even attended and worked in the great theatrical arena of the city. Perhaps Socrates was on his way to watch one of the tragedies he had cowritten with Euripides when he encountered the eager young playwright Plato at that fateful moment. Plato, in any case, responded in kind.

He abandoned tragedy, but in place of it he perfected a new philosophical drama with Socrates as the main character, thus returning Socrates to the theater.

Even though it is unclear what evidence Diogenes used for his biographies, written several centuries after Plato's death, what matters is the very ease with which he considered both philosophers as full participants in the theatrical life of Athens. It was precisely the rich and deep relation between these two philosophers and theatrical culture that got lost with subsequent interpreters, who tended to consider philosophy as the sworn enemy of theater. The basis for this belief was scattered arguments made by Plato's character Socrates, who speaks critically of various aspects of Greek theater, including actors (in the *Republic* and the *Ion*), the characters and plots taken from Homeric myths (*Republic*), the ridiculing of authority in comedy (*Republic*), and first and foremost the presence of large crowds (*Laws*); finally, Socrates banishes tragedians and other poets from the ideal city in the extended thought experiment of the *Republic*. It is true that Plato was extremely critical of the entire theater system just as he sought to dislodge Homer and the poets more generally from their cultural position as educators. His critique, however, must be understood not as that of an outsider but as that of a rival; he was not an enemy of theater but a radical reformer. Attacking many features of Athenian theater, he sought to create an alternative form of drama, the Socratic dialogue, which avoided all of these features: it was mostly read aloud by one person in front of small audiences; it was based on a new subject matter, philosophy; and it lacked the spectacular effects of choral dancing.

Throughout his dialogues, Plato writes with the theater in mind, and nowhere is this as clear as in the famous cave parable, which imagines an elaborate shadow theater that is also described as the work of a puppet master who is creating astonishing spectacles.[8] The captive audience knows nothing of the world outside this cave, nor of the elaborate setup by which the puppet master achieves his effects: a fire is the source of light, and a low wall conceals the assistants who hold up different shapes that cast shadows onto the back of the cave, which the shackled prisoners, who cannot even move their heads, are forced to behold. The cave echoes with sounds and noises. The drama of the parable begins when a prisoner escapes, turns around, and recognizes the theatrical setup of fire, wall, puppeteers, and shapes. But this is only the first step. He leaves the cave and must go through the painful process of getting used to a new source of light, much stronger than the first one: the sun. At first he contents himself with looking at its reflection; finally he is able to look at it directly. But this acclimatization to the sun is not the end of his pain. He now must go down into the cave again and give his fellow prisoners the good news of the world above, freeing them of their illusions. This news is not welcome, however, and our protagonist first is ridiculed and finally fears for his life. Thus ends the scenario envisioned by Plato, who of course is thinking of none other than his teacher Socrates, killed by his fellow citizens in the year 399 BCE.

To be sure, Plato develops this dramatic parable with its elaborate shadow theater for a single purpose: to illustrate a point about education. But many commentators, especially later dramatists, recognized that the parable, with its gothic setting in the cave, puppet players, echoing sounds, dramatic escape, and travails in the upper world, was simply too spectacular not to take on some life of its own, in particular a theatrical life. In such theatrical readings of the parable, it quickly became important that the prisoner does not, in fact, leave the theater for good. After he has escaped and learned to look at the sun, he returns to the cave in order to report on his new insight to a hostile audience. At least within the space of the parable, the theater is not closed down or abandoned for good. On the contrary, the cave represents a world to which even the most enlightened philosophers must return; it remains their field of operations. Indeed, the very word *theater* points to a close alliance between theater and philosophy. The Greek root *thea* is to be found in the word *theorein*, which denotes theoretical contemplation, but also in the word *theatron*, where it identifies the theater as a place of seeing.[9] In the cave parable, Plato uses precisely this root when he speaks about the drama of sight, thus superimposing seeing and contemplation, theater and theory to form a single activity.

The origin of the terms *theater* and *theory* in a common root was not something many subsequent philosophers and dramatists knew or cared much about. The history of philosophy fixated on the reputation of its principal founder as an enemy of the theatrical and then followed his putative example, giving rise to centuries of philosophical attacks on the theater. Many philosophers who thought they were following in the footsteps of Plato did not understand the distinction between an attack that seeks to annihilate its object—to close all theaters—and an attack that seeks to reform its object so radically that it seems to change it beyond recognition. Plato's attack on the theater was of the latter sort, a critique that sought to change the theater in fundamental ways. At the same time, most philosophers abandoned Plato's dramatic form, preferring instead the lecture, the treatise, or the monograph. The dominance of the monologue as philosophy's preferred mode has lasted until today. Only on occasion has it been broken by philosophers trying their hand at the philosophical dialogue—with varying degrees of success. Often they produced dry exchanges devoid of almost everything that was dramatic about Plato's dialogues, including characterization, attention to diction, setting, and the progression of action; nor were these dialogues meant for public recitation. With notable exceptions, including Lucian, Denis Diderot, and Oscar Wilde, they are devoid of everything that made Plato an inspired dramatist. This antitheatrical and undramatic tendency of philosophy has on occasion led editors to turn Plato's own dialogues into treatises, cutting everything except for Socrates' pronouncements.[10]

While philosophy attacked the theater in the name of Plato, the theater world by and large agreed with this understanding of Plato, only here this same diagnosis appears with different values attached: Plato's attacks on the theater are called "antitheatrical prejudice," a term that implies that attacking the theater is a moral failing, a "prejudice" to be overcome.[11] More generally, theater historians have tended to take any critique of the theater as a threat to their very existence.[12] The self-appointed champions of theater thus reacted to Plato and Platonism in a defensive mode, unwilling to examine Plato's actual statements about theater or his own dramatic practice. Using their tendentious language of prejudice, I am tempted here to speak of an anti-antitheatrical prejudice, that is, a knee-jerk reaction to anything that smacks of critique. As a consequence, dramatists and directors failed to recognize Plato as a radical theater reformer, the prescient inventor of a form of drama that is closer to modern drama as we know it than to anything known in the classical world.

In the face of this double misrecognition, Plato must be rescued from the friends and enemies of the theater alike. For this rescue operation, fortunately, I can rely on a minor and mostly underground tradition that saw in Plato's Socratic dialogues a new approach to drama. From the seventeenth century onward, playwrights encountering Plato's dialogues were struck by their unique dramatic form and followed suit. Their plays—what I call Socrates plays—range from educational dialogues and closet dramas to tragedies, comedies, operas, and philosophical plays written for audiences large and small. Often these playwrights labored in obscurity, without knowledge of one another, outside the philosophical and theatrical establishments, and only rarely did they manage to capture audiences for their work on the great and small stages of their time. But whatever else may be their merits or faults, their now mostly forgotten creations kept alive the idea of Plato as a dramatist. A brief history of the Socrates play composes the second chapter of the book.

In the third chapter, I describe the emergence of a newly ambitious drama first called "new drama" and then "modern drama," which broke with all established rules and sought to endow theater with a new sense of intellectual ambition. Playwrights such as Oscar Wilde and George Bernard Shaw in Great Britain, August Strindberg in Sweden, Luigi Pirandello in Italy, and Georg Kaiser and Bertolt Brecht in Germany infused their plays with philosophical themes, creating a new drama of ideas. For this project, they turned to Plato as a source of inspiration and as an alternative to Aristotelian drama. Modern playwrights even continued the tradition of the Socrates play, resulting in an upsurge in the number of plays centered on the philosopher. More important, Plato's own dialogues were now routinely performed in theaters, not just in educational settings, as they had been perhaps since the foundation of Plato's Academy. More and more dramatists and directors considered Plato to be a playwright, or to put it another way, the theater establishment finally caught up with his radical reforms. This development is crucial for the argument of my book, since it describes the process through which Plato came to be seen as a playwright.

Over the course of the nineteenth and twentieth centuries, the consensus between the theater establishment and philosophy that Plato should be considered an enemy of the theater thus began to crumble. This was true not only of dramatists but also of philosophers, some of whom finally came around to accepting Plato as a playwright, as I will detail in chapter 4. For this to occur, philosophy needed to develop a new relation to drama and theater, to overcome its so-called antitheatrical prejudice. This overcoming might be called the "theatrical turn" or "dramatic turn" of philosophy, the moment when philosophy returned to its dramatic origin in Plato and discovered the rich resources drama and theater offer to the philosopher who knows how to use them. The theatrical turn thus implies not an uncritical praise of the theater (a mere reversal of the earlier dismissal) but rather the strategic use of drama and theater by philosophers. The result is a theatrical history of modern philosophy—a history of philosophy from the point of view of drama and theater. The most important episodes in this theatrical history of philosophy include Søren Kierkegaard, Friedrich Nietzsche, Jean-Paul Sartre, and Albert Camus. All of them were inspired by Plato to use dramatic and theatrical forms and concepts. In proposing a theatrical history of philosophy, I rely on two thinkers who themselves worked toward writing such a history, the American theorist Kenneth Burke and the French philosopher Gilles Deleuze; both were keenly attuned to the ways in which drama and theater had come to shape philosophy.

The significance of Plato for these various theatrical philosophers is surprising, since several of them were professed anti-Platonists, including Nietzsche and Deleuze. Indeed, the history of modern philosophy, from Kierkegaard and Nietzsche to Deleuze, is a history of repeated critiques of Platonic idealism. However, the Plato I am after is not an idealist but rather a dramatist, and this means someone acutely engaged with conditions of materiality. These various theatrical philosophers had an inkling of this other, dramatic Plato even as they attacked the theory of forms, and my discussion of them can therefore serve as a point of departure for rethinking the tradition of modern anti-Platonism.

Despite the overwhelming strain of anti-Platonism in modern philosophy, there are a number of contemporary philosophers who resist this trend and instead develop different forms of modern Platonism. It so happens that some of these Platonists also exhibit a lively interest in Plato's drama, as is the case with Iris Murdoch, Martha Nussbaum, and Alain Badiou, who therefore stand at the center of the fifth chapter. Their work will allow me to highlight the critical role a dramatic understanding of Platonism can play in our current intellectual climate. The approach developed in this book, that of a focus on dramatic philosophy as well as philosophical drama, thus proceeds on several tracks. It offers a dramatic and theatrical perspective on Plato (chapter 1); it is a tool for excavating the more or less forgotten history of the Socrates play (chapter 2); it is a frame for understanding the modern drama of ideas (chapter 3); it presents a history of modern philosophy from the point of view of theater (chapter 4); and finally it suggests a way of rethinking

Plato for our own time through a discussion of contemporary Platonism (chapter 5).

Plato's Genres: Tragedy, Comedy, Satyr Play

Tragedy

Aristotle's *Poetics* was the first philosophical account of Greek theater. I will endeavor to supply its complement: a *Poetics* of Plato's Socratic dialogues. Such a poetics must begin by relating the Socratic dialogue to the dominant theatrical genres of the time, and this means, first of all, tragedy. As Diogenes Laertius' emphasis on Plato's and Socrates' collaborations with tragedians suggests, tragedy can be seen as an important source of inspiration and foil for the Socratic dialogues.[13] For all his protestations to the contrary, Plato continued writing tragedies in some manner even after burning his earliest one. In his very last work, the *Laws*, he compares the creation of a perfect city-state, such as the one this dialogue describes, to tragedy: "we ourselves, to the best of our ability, are the authors of a tragedy at once superlatively fair and good; at least, all our polity is framed as a representation of the fairest and best life, which is in reality, as we assert, the truest tragedy. Thus we are composers of the same things as yourselves, rivals of yours as artists and actors of the fairest drama."[14] His city is the "truest" tragedy and the most beautiful "drama," outshining the creations of all other "artists." Not only are the creators of the perfect city-state poets themselves, they are actors, too, acting as "antagonists" in this most perfect drama. After being critical of tragedy in a number of dialogues, most famously so in his demand to banish tragedians from his ideal city in the *Republic*, Plato perhaps remembers here, in his last work, his early occupations as chorus leader and tragedian, his early desire to engage in a competition with other tragedians. He identifies himself as a rival to the tragic poets, a rival who is outdoing them on their home turf.

Tragedy remained a foil for Plato in a more concrete sense as well: Socrates' death casts a shadow over every single one of Plato's dialogues. Even though Socrates' death is not mentioned in many dialogues, author and readers cannot but be painfully aware of it. Indeed, those dialogues that mention Socrates' trial and death have often been seen as Plato's masterworks. The *Apology*, in which the fateful death sentence against Socrates is depicted, is Plato's first work. A number of dialogues make reference to the impending court proceedings, while a second group is set after the verdict itself. As we let ourselves be drawn into arguments with Socrates, examining hypotheses, watching arguments being decimated and common beliefs reduced to absurd conclusions, we are reminded again and again that all these activities will end with death. Finally, in his middle period, Plato writes his masterpiece, the *Phaedo*, in which the death of his protagonist is depicted in excruciating detail. In the *Phaedo*, Plato famously has Socrates describe philosophers as those who practice dying.[15] Plato's decision to devote the rest of his working life to writing about Socrates, to center his own original philosophy around his dead teacher, was clearly some kind of working through of a traumatic event that shaped his entire life, including the very conception and practice of his philosophy. In and through his dialogues, Plato's mind remained fixed on Socrates' death, even as these vivid and compelling dialogues brought the dead teacher to life again. Such is the magic of the theater: conjuring up the shadows from the underworld, bringing the dead back to life even if they are also made to die, again and again, in front of our very eyes every time the dialogue is read or performed.

Certainly, Plato was recognized as some kind of a tragedian by subsequent authors of Socrates plays. Beginning in the seventeenth century, playwrights wrote tragedies, often entitled *Death of Socrates*, in which they adapted Plato's death cycle to their own contemporary conventions, be they Elizabethan revenge tragedy, Miltonian tragedy, classicist tragedy, bourgeois tragedy, or modern tragedy.[16] Often they synthesized the four dialogues depicting the trial and death of Socrates—the *Euthyphro*, *Apology*, *Crito*, and *Phaedo*. At other times, they created more wide-ranging plays that incorporated material from other dialogues, for example, the *Symposium*, but framed them with reference to the trial and death of Socrates, so that even Plato's most lighthearted scenes are tainted by the anticipation of death. These playwrights, more so than many philosophical commentators, sensed the presence of death in all of Plato's Socratic dialogues, and they translated this into their own tragic idioms.

At the same time, many Greek commentators as well as subsequent authors of Socrates plays recognized profound differences between Plato's dialogues and tragedy, both classical and modern. Plato's dialogues drew their characters and plots not from Greek mythology as transmitted by Homer but from contemporary Athens. Instead of poetry, they were written in prose, and they did not compete at the seasonal theater festivals of Athens. Aristotle cast only a passing glance in the direction of the Socratic dialogues before moving on to the glorious topic of tragedy. Diogenes Laertius likewise had trouble conceiving of Plato's dialogues fully as dramas because they were so very different from tragedy, the most central of the dramatic genres.[17] Plato's dialogues, in short, were an unusual form of drama conceived for a particular purpose: expressing Plato's philosophy. For this purpose, they hijacked tragedy, using the form to new ends. Plato's rivalry with tragedy, it turns out, was not a competition among tragedians seeking to outdo one another within the same genre. Rather, it was a rivalry between a standard form of tragedy and Plato's own drama. Plato takes certain features from tragedy only to turn them into something new and better. By claiming to outdo tragedy, Plato was aiming at a central genre of the political, social, and ritual life of Athens. Earlier in the *Laws*, Plato had constructed a hierarchy of the arts, in which puppet shows and comedies were at the bottom and tragedy at the top, to be exceeded only by epic poetry.[18] In attacking tragedy, Plato was seeking to change nothing less than the entire value system of Athenian culture, including Athenian democracy, with which tragedy had come to be closely associated.[19]

The play in which Plato highlighted his difference from tragedy most clearly is also the one that is closest to it: the *Phaedo*. In this dialogue, Plato trains his readers or audiences to react differently to events that otherwise they would tend to view through a tragic lens. The scene is set in prison. Socrates, the philosophical protagonist, has been sentenced to death, and the sentence should have been carried out already but has been temporarily delayed. Socrates thus lives on borrowed time, which creates a sense of urgency that shapes the dialogue throughout. The *Phaedo* observes the unity of time, the rule that plays should depict events that take up no more time than the play itself, to the letter. The feeling of suspense is heightened once the prison guard enters and provides the hemlock. Things are now rushing toward the cruel ending of the play with increasing speed. Far from seeking further delay, Socrates speeds things up even more, drinking the poison sooner than necessary, over the objections of his assembled friends, who want him to wait until the last moment. Once the cup is emptied, the whole scene shifts into a different temporality: from suspense we move to a slower but no less heart-wrenching pace, dictated now by the circulation of Socrates' blood as it delivers the poison first to his legs and then, slowly but steadily, to the rest of the body. We are learning the effects of the poison live, from Socrates' own lips; he describes its progress blow by blow, limb by limb, until finally it reaches his head and Socrates, now lying on the bed, is incapable of speech. He is dead.

It is difficult to conceive of a drama more calculated to cause the kind of fear and suffering in the audience that is the hallmark of Greek tragedy. And since we look at this scene through a tragic lens, it is not surprising that the audience onstage, Socrates' assembled friends, react to this scene the way the audience of a tragedy would. The drama describes intense suffering: as Socrates drinks the poison, one friend curses the bad luck that is striking down his philosopher, and tries to hide his grief by covering his face with a cloak; another starts to wail openly and uncontrollably, at which point the entire assembly breaks down, with everyone giving vent to their agony. The *Phaedo* depicts and incites tragic suffering, and it also uses a typical tragic vocabulary, such as "luck" (*tyche*), to describe the downward trajectory of its protagonist.[20] As the moment of death comes closer and closer, Socrates himself characterizes the scene in terms of tragedy, observing that he is "being called, as a tragedian would put it, by fate."[21]

At the same time, the dialogue does everything to instruct both the audience onstage and the audience—or readers—offstage that these tragic reactions are wrong. The bulk of the dialogue is devoted to a philosophical discussion that aims to convince the audience that death is not a calamity. Through many rounds of testing and exploring this hypothesis, Socrates seeks to convince his friends that death is the best thing that could possibly happen to him. To this end, Socrates claims that the soul is immortal, and death is but the liberation of the soul from the body. He then proceeds to provide a whole host of arguments to support this view. First he suggests that things are born from their opposite and that therefore death must give rise to some kind of life again. Then, in what is for many the central argument, he says that learning is remembrance of things known to the soul in a previous life. But Socrates does not stop there. He observes that the swan sings most beautifully before dying and concludes that this anticipates the impending liberation of the soul from the body. Finally, and most poetically, Socrates invents an elaborate myth of a layered world with various subterranean caverns into which the soul proceeds after death, reminiscent of the famous cave parable in the *Republic*.

The only problem with all these wonderful arguments, images, and myths is that they fail to convince his friends that they should in fact be happy about Socrates' rapidly approaching death. They cry, wail, and curse all the same. Early on, Socrates is visibly exasperated by his failure to convince Simmias that dying is a wonderful thing, and when he is faced with more and more tears from his other friends, he does not know what to do except repeat his arguments and demonstrate their validity through his own comportment.[22] While Socrates' own stoic conduct is in keeping with his view on death, the project of convincing his friends to abandon their tragic reactions seems to have failed. Having raised objections throughout, they are either still unconvinced by Socrates' argument or they fail to put their newly acquired belief in the immortality of the soul into practice. The *Phaedo* is a divided dialogue: on one hand we have Socrates, who is leading an exemplary philosophical life (and death) in which his arguments and his conduct are in complete agreement, and on the other hand we have his disciples, who are resistant to his reasoning and, even when they accept it, fail to live up to it.

But there is another, more troubling side to Socrates' attempt to integrate thought and action, one of the reasons he has such trouble convincing his friends: his entire antitragic argument about the immortality of the soul is a case of special pleading. It is advanced by someone faced with certain death. All the beautiful arguments and images Socrates creates—aren't they simply an attempt to make himself, and perhaps also his friends, feel better about the inevitable? More than anyone else in the room, Socrates has a personal interest in his own argument. Socrates and his friends become aware of this dilemma, but they don't quite know what to make of it. After some hesitation, they admit that they feel uncomfortable arguing against Socrates for fear that their skepticism might make him feel bad "in his present misfortune."[23] Later on, Socrates himself concedes that his interest in the argument is "selfish," that he is eager to believe it himself, and that in fact he is not in a purely "philosophical" frame of mind just now, because of his impending death.[24] When seen in this light, we also wonder why Socrates keeps piling argument upon argument. One striking argument might convince us, but Socrates moves from one argument to the next in a way that might be construed—or misconstrued—as desperation. This is not to say that Plato wants to undermine his wonderful arguments for the immortality of the soul, some of which he also makes elsewhere. But here these arguments are, if not entirely undermined, at least affected by the dramatic situation in which they are made. Socrates' stoic conduct might well be exemplary, as befits the philosophical protagonist of a Socratic dialogue. At the same time, the very focus on the figure of the exemplary philosopher and his situation in prison, awaiting death, turns out to be a problem: it interferes with the argument itself, adding to it self-interest, fear of death, and a desire to believe that death is in fact a good thing.

Plato carefully entangles the argument with the dramatic situation in prison in other, more indirect ways as well. Time and again, Socrates uses words associated with prison to describe the situation of the soul and the body; he speaks of souls being imprisoned in the body, of souls regarding the world as if through prison bars, and of the soul being tied to the body.[25] Even when Socrates or his friends are not explicitly drawing attention to the fact that they have a special interest in the outcome of the argument, Plato never lets us forget that the whole discussion occurs behind prison bars, that Socrates has until recently been in shackles and has only been allowed to take them off for the time being; there is, at this point, no more escape for him.

The only solution to this conundrum is, as Socrates realizes, that his friends, and perhaps even he himself, must not think of his present situation but instead consider the arguments purely on their own merits. We must entirely abstract ourselves from the scene, from the prison, from our admiration and love for Socrates, even from our hope that he might be right after all, despite his selfish interest, in his argument that the soul really is immortal and that his soul in particular, the soul of a philosopher, will henceforth enjoy a new and better life freed from the body. The command to disregard scene and character, to move away from them and toward abstract considerations free from selfish interest and fear, resonates powerfully with the most fundamental tenets of what is usually called philosophical Platonism: a disregard of the concrete, embodied, lived experience and a desire, instead, to ascend to some realm of abstract forms or ideas, pure and simple. Indeed, the *Phaedo* is one of the first dialogues, and perhaps the very first, in which Plato articulates this theory of forms.

The scene in prison that gives rise to this theory shows, however, that the theory of forms is something of a countermeasure, an attempt to solve the problem introduced by the fateful implication of the character Socrates and the scene in the argument. The theory of forms justifies Socrates' desire to disregard his person, his situation, his certain death—to disregard precisely the drama of the *Phaedo*. Once we are attentive to this dramatic dimension of the dialogue, however, we can no longer take the theory of forms as an end in and of itself: we recognize its function within the dramatic structure of the dialogue. Usually, the standard understanding of the theory of forms ignores the fact that Plato chose to articulate this theory in a dramatic form, that is, in a form that would pull this theory in the other direction, the direction of the concrete, embodied, lived experience. This form required him to create characters and place them in situations that would render any argument about ideas necessarily impure, imbuing the characters with particular motivations that would skew the discussion, create distracting circumstances, and suggest vested interests everywhere. Why would Plato choose the Socratic dialogue as a genre to articulate an abstract theory of forms when this genre is clearly the worst possible choice for such a purpose? Yet this choice was not a mistake. Abstract, philosophical arguments about death need to be connected to and charged by the desires and fears of three-dimensional characters; in any case, this is what happens in his dialogue, and it has larger implications for the relationship between forms and matter, idealism and materialism. Plato never lets us forget the scene, the situation, the character, the drama of the *Phaedo*. Every turn in the argument changes the interaction among Socrates and his friends: when the argument in favor of the immortality of the soul seems to be winning, there is a sense of relief in the room, but when convincing counterarguments are put forward, the anxiety level rises and things get extremely awkward. How could one not think that this situatedness, this entanglement of the theory of forms in the scene, is precisely what Plato intended?

The conclusion to be drawn from Plato's dramatic technique is that abstraction from people and scenes as demanded by Socrates and explained by the theory of forms happens in response to the overwhelming drama of the scene Plato has created expressly for this purpose. In fact, the relation between drama and form is exactly parallel to Socrates' argument about body and soul. Just as he hopes that the soul will be able to leave behind the prison of the body, so he hopes that he and his friends will be able to leave behind, forget and disregard, the dramatic prison and the prisoner, turning their minds instead to pure arguments. The end result is a kind of tug-of-war: scene and character pull in one direction, the command to disregard them and consider forms in the other.[26] But perhaps the image of the tug-of-war is not entirely right, for it presumes that we can or should isolate the dramatic scene on one hand and abstract argument on the other. Everything that happens in the *Phaedo* suggests that this cannot be done. Socrates cannot do it; his friends certainly cannot do it; and we cannot do it, either. Instead of a tug-of-war, we must think of the result as a carefully constructed mixture of interest, philosophy, preparation for death, anticipation of mourning, and the hope for better things to come. Indeed, the framing idea of the entire text is that of the mixture of pleasure and pain. Socrates has been allowed to shed his shackles and observes the strange mixture of pleasure and pain he experiences as his blood returns to his numb limbs. It is this concrete observation that gives rise to the first argument about the immortality of the soul, namely, that things are born from their opposite, that pleasure and pain, life and death, are not neatly separated but entangled in each other.

The mixture of pleasure and pain is also what characterizes the final reaction of the audience to the scene in prison. Like many of Plato's middle dialogues, the *Phaedo* is, strictly speaking, not a pure drama but a narration of the discussion and the events surrounding Socrates' last hours. This narration occurs within an outer drama, a dialogue between Echecrates and Phaedo, with the latter describing the events he himself has witnessed. Echecrates then asks Phaedo what he felt during Socrates' final hour, and Phaedo answers that, strangely, he did not feel pity, as one might expect. The word he disavows, *eleos* (pity), is precisely one that Aristotle would soon use to describe one of the central affects evoked by tragedy.[27] For all their tears and fears, it seems that Socrates' argument did have an effect on his friends after all. While the friends could not control themselves right there and then, in retrospect they (or at least Phaedo) experienced a strange mixture of pleasure and pain. Socrates did not manage to get his friends to disregard his present plight, but his argument, informed as it may have been by self-interest, met its goal halfway: besides weeping, his friends were also laughing, and in the end they did not feel pity for him. Tragedy is vanquished or at least fundamentally changed.

Comedy

The laughter incited among Socrates' friends in the *Phaedo* points to the other major dramatic genre known to classical Athens: comedy. Indeed, Plato's Socratic dialogues are at least as reminiscent of comedy as they are of tragedy. Like the Socratic dialogues (and unlike tragedy), comedy took its characters from contemporary Athens and put them in contemporary settings, allowing them to speak something closer to everyday speech than what could be heard in tragedy, despite Euripides' efforts to move tragedy closer to an everyday idiom. For all his admirable qualities, Socrates is not one of the mythic heroes depicted in Homer or in the tragedies derived from his epics. As the son of a sculptor and a midwife, Socrates' social position would be too low to make him a good candidate for being a tragic hero, but it makes him a perfect candidate for comedy. His peculiar dress, speech, and behavior, his habit of walking around barefoot and in shabby clothes, and the fact that he is ugly clearly destine him, according to the generic conventions of classical Greece, for comedy. Indeed, the relation between Socrates and comedy is not merely a question of analogy or distant kinship. Socrates actually became a character in several comedies, of which the most prominent, Aristophanes' *Clouds*, survives. If Socrates' death casts a tragic shadow over Plato's dramatic oeuvre, Aristophanes' depiction of Socrates in *Clouds* reminds us that Plato's second great resource was comedy.

The affinity between Socrates and comedy was something that subsequent authors of Socrates plays recognized even if it was ignored by many philosophical commentators, who considered Plato's use of comedy even more unseemly than his use of tragedy.[28] A significant number of playwrights found in Plato's dialogues ample material to furnish various styles of comedy, from opera buffa to twentieth-century Broadway comedy. Often, the relation between Socrates and his wife (or several wives, according to Diogenes Laertius' biography) is a source of domestic comedy, even as many modern authors of Socrates comedies wrest Xanthippe from her traditional role of shrew, embellished during the Middle Ages, and turn her into a more complex character. These playwrights recognized other comic elements in Plato's dialogues as well. Small bodily gestures and poses interrupting elevated philosophical arguments, seemingly irrelevant details of everyday life acquiring great importance—these techniques have always been part of the comic repertory, and they can be found in a significant number of comic adaptations of Plato's dialogues. Another group of playwrights combined comic and tragic elements, thus coloring tragic set pieces such as Socrates' death with comedy.

The importance of comedy for the Socratic dialogue is most clearly visible in the depiction of Socrates as what I call a comic stage philosopher. When philosophers such as Socrates are allowed onstage at all, invariably they turn out to be comic: concerned only with ideas, they keep stumbling over concrete reality. One fragment about the first known philosopher, Thales, has him looking at the stars and stumbling into a ditch with a Thracian maid looking on and laughing. The grounds for such laughter were explained in the early twentieth century by the philosopher Henri Bergson. He singled out as a surefire subject for comedy any character in the grip of an idea: comedy happens when a fixed idea determines a character's actions, turning complex individuals into puppets controlled by an abstract principle, thus making them incapable of reacting to changing circumstances.[29] The historian Hans Blumenberg even turned the many retellings of the Thales anecdote into a cultural history of theoretical inquiry, showing just how much the history of philosophy is part of the history of laughter at philosophers.[30] The fact that philosophers tend to become laughable does not necessarily mean that their philosophy is discredited, although that is sometimes the case. But it explains why any dramatic depiction of philosophers and ideas invariably needs to grapple with comedy.

Plato did not seek to emulate comedy any more than he sought to emulate tragedy. He clearly regarded Aristophanes' *Clouds* as a competitor to be engaged, not as a model to be imitated. Plato makes this adversarial relation to that play clear in his very first text, the *Apology*, in which he has Socrates accuse Aristophanes, somewhat implausibly, of fueling public resentment against Socrates and thus helping bring about his trial and death.[31] *Clouds*, Plato suggests, is no mere laughing matter: there is clearly something wrong with the play's depiction of Socrates and perhaps comedy more generally. Indeed, many of Plato's harsh sentences against drama are directed first and foremost at comedy, specifically at its depiction of the laughable, corporeal, and inane. Yet Plato aligned himself with comedy for important, strategic reasons, because, like the comic dramatists, he was aiming to dislodge the cultural prestige of Homer and Greek tragedy. Socrates is not simply a comic figure but a new type of everyday protagonist, almost a modern antihero who stands his ground against the cultural elite by means of his own wits, despite his ragged clothes, unheroic ugliness, and awkward social manner.[32]

If the *Phaedo* is the dialogue in which Plato reuses pieces of tragedy, the *Symposium* (together with the *Phaedrus*) is the dialogue in which he reuses pieces of comedy. The *Phaedo* and the *Symposium* are also the most theatrical dialogues and therefore the ones most often adapted by later playwrights or even staged without any alteration.[33] The stage history of the *Symposium* is even less surprising than that of the *Phaedo*. Plato pays constant attention to the physical interaction among the characters, and the play culminates with the noisy entrance of the most spectacular figure of Athens: Alcibiades. Alcibiades was known to Plato's audience as someone larger than life, a celebrity who led Athens to victory but who also betrayed the city when it tried to restrain his increasingly unruly behavior, his sheer expenditure of action and will. In having Alcibiades enter in a state of inebriation toward the end of the play, Plato was allowing onto the stage a character who was likely to steal the show.

Plato is pulling out all the theatrical stops because the *Symposium* is the dialogue in which he takes on the theater most directly. The symposium that gives the dialogue its name is a celebration to honor Agathon, a tragedian who has just won first prize with his tragedy. If we believe Diogenes' claim that Plato once had harbored similar hopes, it is difficult not to read the *Symposium* as Plato's way of examining what could have been, of measuring his early aspiration against his present one. But Agathon is not the only playwright at the symposium. The second one is none other than Aristophanes, Plato's archrival in dramatizing Socrates and also in writing what one might call, at least in retrospect, Socrates comedies. Clearly, Plato wanted to set himself a dramatic challenge: how could he compete with the likes of Agathon, Aristophanes, and Alcibiades when it comes to holding the interest of readers or an audience? Plato sought to measure his protagonist and his type of drama against the theatrical establishment of Athens.[34]

Plato shows in the *Phaedo* that the philosophical attitude toward death differs from the tragic one, and in the *Symposium* that the philosophical attitude toward love differs from the one presented in comedy. The *Symposium* gestures toward comedy in its attention to the follies of love, corporeal details, and how the body gets in the way of philosophy. At the outset, Aristodemus has encountered Socrates and makes fun of him for being freshly bathed and wearing a good pair of slippers, in contrast to his usual disheveled look.[35] Socrates invites him to come along to Agathon's victory celebration but then falls behind, so Aristodemus finds himself in the awkward position of arriving as an uninvited guest without Socrates. These and other peculiarities of Socrates are a source of good humor and laughter. They set the tone for the ensuing competition of the evening, encomia on love, which include much lighthearted and sportive banter in between the individual presentations and sometimes even during the performances, as when a speech heavily dependent on medical language is accompanied by a competitor's hiccups. This way, the set pieces of rhetoric, alternately poetic and abstruse, are constantly brought down to the scenic context in which they are performed and confronted with an audience that comments on them, praises them, and laughs about them. The sequence of speeches, and thus the plot of the dialogue, obeys a scenic and hence theatrical logic: the participants have decided to go around the table, so we see the dialogue move from character to character, only infrequently skipping a person. The seating order is also an occasion for erotic ado, especially once Alcibiades has entered and wants to sit next to Socrates. The dialogue thus plays abstract theory off against bodily realities, and rhetorical set pieces against a sometimes unruly audience even as it derives its forward thrust in part from the arrangement of bodies in space.

In the middle of this scenically organized plot, Plato places a version of the immortality argument from the *Phaedo*, namely, the theory of what has come to be known as Platonic love. Reporting a conversation between himself and Diotima, Socrates recounts Diotima's theory of ascending steps through which love is gradually detached from bodies and redirected toward beauty and truth. Like the immortality argument of the *Phaedo*, Diotima's theory of love is often extracted from its context and presented as Plato's theory of forms. The result is an understanding of Plato, or rather, of Platonism, as a rejection of the body and an embrace instead of forms. But this invocation of forms does not have the last word. Just as *Phaedo* implicates Socrates in the argument about the immortality of the soul, so the *Symposium* implicates him in Diotima's theory of love. The speech is followed by the theatrical climax of the dialogue, Alcibiades' entrance and ensuing declaration of love for Socrates. Alcibiades then presents an encomium not on love in general but on Socrates in particular, or more precisely on his own entanglement with Socrates, including how he and Socrates ended up sleeping in the same bed, but not as lovers.[36] This surely is not a form but an action, a scene shaped by Diotima's idea of love, but also the confrontation of this form or idea with chastely inter-locking bodies. The two types of love, the love of bodies (*erotike*) and the love of wisdom (*philia*), are laid side by side; they interact and get entan-gled without canceling each other out. In a more programmatic manner, a similar account of the two types of love is given in the *Gorgias*, a dialogue written sometime before the *Symposium*. Here Socrates has declared his two loves to be Alcibiades and wisdom. To be sure, he describes his love for Alcibiades, like all love of bodies and people, as fickle, and the other, the love of wisdom, as constant. But there is no reason to think that the love for Alcibiades has to be given up entirely in order for the love of wis-dom to be possible. They can exist side by side; more important, they affect each other, leading the love of bodies to moderation and making the love of wisdom more tangible.[37] In the *Symposium*, Plato's dramatic tech-nique means that the actual embrace, and more generally the interaction between Socrates and Alcibiades, is what remains most vividly in one's mind, although it is filtered through Diotima's image of the ascent.

Once we consider Diotima's theory of ideal love in the context of the entire dialogue, and as part of Plato's attempt to rewrite comedy, we can appreciate its specific function, one that runs parallel to the function of the immortality argument in the *Phaedo*. The theory of forms, with its turn away from bodies, is a strategy of keeping comedy at bay, just as it had been for keeping tragedy at bay in the *Phaedo*. Comedy deflates ideas or forms by confronting them with the material reality of the world. Plato conceived of an alternative to comedy by suspending it between a pull toward bodies and a pull toward forms, thus turning comedic materialism into philosophical drama. If extracted from its dramatic context, the theory of forms would lead one to contemplate a separate metaphysical realm of forms. It is not that this view of Plato's theory is wrong; Plato did articulate a theory of forms that posited their independent existence, even though he also spent a great deal of time worrying about the implications of this claim. But any such consideration of the theory of forms outside their dramatic context would be incomplete. Once the articulation of the theory of forms is seen within its dramatic contexts, it can be recognized as a powerful counterforce to comedy's—and, more generally, to drama's—material pull. It is a counterforce that does not leave bodies, scenes, and drama behind; it profoundly changes them and their dramatic function, rearranging them in a way that is then called philosophical. Bodies now no longer serve to prove forms or ideas wrong (or foolish). Instead, these bodies become part of a philosophical drama that immerses them in forms, a drama that shows bodies to be shaped by forms that are in turn affected by the material incarnations to which they give rise.

Satyr Play

The new drama Plato created works off comedy, just as it works off tragedy, but in the end it is neither; it is a third genre that draws on the other two. Greek theater knew a third genre, the satyr play, a curious combination that treated the mythological subject matter of tragedy but in a farcical manner closer to comedy. Indeed, Alcibiades associates Socrates with a satyr in the *Symposium*, and this association confirms that Socrates is a creature neither of tragedy nor of comedy, holding his ground against the tragedian Agathon and the comedian Aristophanes.[38] At the same time it is clear that Plato's dialogues are not in any simple sense satyr plays. What they share with the satyr play is only that they, too, participate in tragedy and comedy without being either. The most programmatic, if also enigmatic, pronouncement about this question of genre comes from Socrates at the very end of the *Symposium*. Everybody is drunk, with the exception of Socrates and the two dramatists, and Socrates tries to convince them that tragedy and comedy derive from the same source and that the same person therefore should be able to write both. Again we are encouraged to envision a mixture between the two genres, without knowing what that mixture might be. The *Symposium* thus ends with the enigma of genre mixing, and in this sense, too, it mirrors the *Phaedo*, which is framed with the acknowledgment that Socrates' friends responded to their master's death with a mixture of tears and laughter.

While the *Phaedo* and the *Symposium* leave open the question of crying and laughing, of mixing tragedy and comedy, Plato elaborates it to some extent in the *Philebus*. Here Socrates argues that what tragedy and comedy share is that they cause mixtures of pleasure and pain in the audience.[39] The mixture of pleasure and pain in tragedy is relatively easy to understand: Socrates points out, as Aristotle would after him, that people apparently enjoy watching tragedies, even if they are moved to weep. (In book ten of the *Republic*, Socrates also attacks the particular types of emotion incited by tragedy.) The argument for the existence of pain in comedy is somewhat more counterintuitive. Here, Plato claims that laughter at the ridiculous is mixed with envy, which is a negative and therefore painful emotion, a "pain of the soul."[40] What matters about this argument is not so much its theory of envy but the theme of mixture itself, which turns out to be central for both comedy and tragedy. Indeed, the importance of mixture for Plato has tended to be underestimated, in part because it goes against the common misperception of Plato as an absolutist who liked to keep things pure and simple rather than mixed and muddled. But in fact it is the other way around. Plato mixes comedy and tragedy, weeping and laughter, but what is most important is that he mixes abstraction and embodiment. It is this mixture that sets his drama apart from its competitors.

Many subsequent authors of Socrates plays have taken Socrates' speculation about the ultimate similarity of tragedy and comedy, along with the mixed nature of the Socratic dialogue, as a guiding principle of their own Socrates plays, which often include tragic and comic scenes and elements in equal measure.[41] To be sure, many Socrates plays also incorporated a wider range of styles and modes, not just borrowings from comedy and tragedy. In this, too, they followed Plato, who drew on virtually all literary and nonliterary modes of the time, including funeral orations, rhetorical set pieces, myths, and proverbs.[42] Like Plato's own dialogues, subsequent Socrates plays are thus not neat combinations of two genres, but more like sponges that absorb different modes of literature, creating a new—and inherently mixed—genre in the process.

How to identify this new genre has been a much-debated issue. In a widely influential theory, Mikhail Bakhtin took the mixture of tragedy and comedy, together with Plato's insistence on prose and his construction of Socrates as a kind of modern antihero, to be a major source for a newer genre: the novel. Like Plato's dialogues, novels thrive on mixing other genres, creating an unruly hodgepodge that presents itself as an upstart genre out to challenge its more established rivals.[43] As powerful as this reading is, it removes Plato's dialogues from the domain of drama, which remained Plato's most important reference point. While Plato may well have been a point of origin for the novel, he was also the origin of a new drama that anticipates modern drama. Plato forged his drama by means of an entirely new use of the different dimensions of drama and theater: a Platonic dramaturgy.

Plato's Dramaturgy

In order to understand Plato's dramaturgy, we can go back to the scattered remarks of ancient commentators. In his brief remark on the Socratic dialogue, Aristotle takes note of its choice of prose, a deviation from the elaborate forms of poetry governing Greek drama. After this remark, he abandons the Socratic dialogue, not knowing what to make of it except to classify it formally with other prose plays such as the mimes of Sophron. Diogenes Laertius also notices Plato's prose as an anomaly but proceeds to grapple with Plato's use of dialogue much more thoroughly, praising Plato for having perfected the form.[44] Diogenes Laertius goes on to emphasize that Plato invented imaginary characters even though they sometimes resembled actual existing Athenians.[45] This is particularly important when it comes to Socrates himself. Certainly a philosopher named Socrates really existed and was executed in Athens in the year 399 BCE. But Plato's Socrates is a unique creature, very different from portraits given by other sources, such as Xenophon.[46]

After discussing Plato's prose and his construction of character, Diogenes hazards something of a definition of the Socratic dialogue: "a conversation consisting of questions and answers on philosophical or political topics grounded in particular characters and their speech patterns."[47] A form consisting of invented characters in conversation about philosophical or political topics is of course familiar to us from the subsequent history of drama. But this form was more unfamiliar to the classical world, since both Greek tragedy and comedy were dominated by the chorus and by exchanges between the chorus and one character; true dialogue among individuals only gradually increased in importance. Diogenes Laertius also mentions that Plato read his dialogues aloud; while they were not meant to be performed in the large open-air arena of Athens, they were written to be recited to small, select groups of listeners.[48] From Aristotle and Diogenes Laertius, we can thus gather the outlines of a classical understanding of the Socratic dialogue: a dialogue in prose (rather than poetry) to be read aloud to small groups of listeners (rather than a large audience) based on the speech of individual characters (rather than a chorus) who engage in conversations on philosophical topics for the purpose of either giving instruction or accumulating knowledge.

In order to pinpoint Plato's dramatic form in more detail, it is useful to consider as a foil those aspects of drama that Aristotle would identify as the primary dimensions of Greek tragedy.[49] Among them are precisely the features mentioned by Diogenes Laertius: character, action, and the relation to the audience. In comparing Plato's dramatic practice to Aristotle's *Poetics*, we can arrive at a poetics of Plato's Socratic dialogues.

Character

Aristotle spent a good deal of time thinking about the nature and status of tragic protagonists, demanding, for example, that they be of an elevated social and moral position so that their eventual downfall will incite fear and pity, not relief. He goes so far as to define tragedy as a play based on characters "who are superior to us," thus giving character an important place in the conception of the genre.[50] Character is important because it is the site of moral choice. At the same time, character is also the bearer of cognitive insight, a dimension often neglected in neo-Aristotelian conceptions of character, what Aristotle calls "thought" (*dianoia*). Plato, too, carefully constructs his principal protagonist: Socrates. Alcibiades' adulation, the description of Socrates' prowess in battle, his readiness to suffer pain and deprivation, and also his ability to drink without getting drunk are all examples of the care with which Plato builds up his main character. But Socrates is not simply a Greek hero who exceeds the abilities of common Athenians. He is someone whose conduct sets him apart from the social conventions governing life in the city. His dress and social habits are different, almost deranged. He is a critic, constantly attacking the cultural, political, and religious beliefs and values of Athenian society (including Homer), the anthropomorphic gods of mythology, and democracy. In forging a character both exemplary and strange, Plato borrowed once more from tragedy and comedy. From comedy he took the violation of social norms; from tragedy, mythic exemplarity and uniqueness. On the level of character, we thus encounter the formula from the end of the *Symposium* in a different form: Socrates is derived from the protagonists of both tragedy and comedy, but he is more than a simple combination of the two. Out of the mixture of tragedy and comedy, Plato forged a strange new philosophical hero, at once laughable and admirable, exemplary and ordinary.

The main reason for Plato to have his dialogues revolve around a carefully constructed philosophical protagonist is to show the extent to which philosophy is a matter of character, something that manifests itself in the personality. Philosophy, in other words, is embodied and lived; it cannot be abstracted from the exemplary philosopher. Socrates' equanimity in the face of death, for example, is a direct consequence of his philosophical insight into the nature of death and the immortality of the soul.[51] This unique construction of character was part of a Greek understanding of philosophy as something that manifests itself in the conduct of one's life as much as in philosophical works.[52] Only a handful of modern philosophers, such as Ludwig Wittgenstein and Michel Foucault, have continued this theme of demanding that philosophy be understood not so much as a system of thought but as a way of life.[53] This is yet another reason why any conception of a Platonist metaphysics that entirely dismisses the corporeal is false; it disregards precisely this classical conception of philosophy, whose emphasis on the actions of a person is best captured in dramatic form, where they can be represented as the actions of a character.

Even though Plato's dialogues are centered in its eponymous protagonist, Socrates does not embody philosophy and the philosophical life all by himself. In order for philosophy to take place, he needs at least one interlocutor to engage with. The range of interlocutors is quite remarkable. Of course, they tend to be young men from the better families of Athens, and the Socratic dialogues can seem rather enclosed and rarified as a consequence. But when one surveys Plato's entire dramatic oeuvre, a much larger range of participants comes into view, including politicians, rhetoricians, sophists, and dramatists, as well as foreign visitors. Plato also breaks with social exclusivity when he engages a slave in a dialogue, at least temporarily, and when he invokes Diotima in the *Symposium*, thus letting a woman enter a Socratic dialogue. Sometimes the interlocutors are reduced to a simple "Yes, Socrates" that has often been mocked and that has led some editors to cut Plato's dialogues down to Socrates' speeches. But even in those extreme cases when Socrates develops long arguments and myths (complete with imaginary cities and alternative worlds) on his own, occasional reminders that Socrates is in fact speaking to another person, that even the most elaborate mental edifices emerge from the interaction among at least two people talking and thinking together, crucially ground those dialogues in a dramatic situation. Plato stages these exchanges in different ways, embedding Socrates in different situations and allowing him to distract us from these situations for different lengths of time. In the end, we are always brought back down to the dramatic situation, even by so inconspicuous an interjection as "Yes, Socrates." The role of Socrates' interlocutors is crucial because Plato does not want to suggest that philosophy is invariably tied to his protagonist. While Socrates retains the central role, philosophy is an activity, rare and rarified as it may seem, that can be taken up by anyone, even a slave. Socrates is exemplary, but he also is, and must be, replaceable. This is perhaps the reason why Plato's last dialogue, the *Laws*, does without him entirely: a Socratic dialogue without Socrates.

The other dialogues also have built into them mechanisms suggesting that philosophy can be detached from Socrates—de-Socratized. The most important of these mechanisms is role switching. In the *Symposium* characters take turns praising Eros. More common is a form of role switching that frequently occurs in the course of a philosophical argument. Plato's Socratic dialogues typically start with an exchange between Socrates and one other character. Soon enough, however, other characters join in, and often they take turns, picking up the argument where their predecessors left it. Some dialogues even discuss the principle of role switching quite explicitly. The *Statesman*, which continues where the *Sophist* had ended, begins with a proposal of role switching. The Stranger suggests that his previous interlocutor, Theaetetus, should now rest and that his friend, the young Socrates, should take his place, continuing the argument on his behalf.[54] After Thrasymachus, in the first book of the *Republic*, gets too angry to be of any use, Glaucon takes his place for the remainder of that long dialogue.[55]

The taking of turns even includes Socrates. Sometimes Socrates encourages others to defend his position, thus inducting them into his mode of doing philosophy. The most unusual example of this occurs when he conjures Diotima, in the *Symposium*, and places her in the privileged position of presenting the theory of forms. Of course, Diotima is not present directly and is only invoked by Socrates in what is quite overtly a literary device. No one present asks who this unusual and remarkable woman is and whether Socrates really met with her. Socrates' interlocutors accept Diotima as a figure, which is perhaps not surprising since the whole evening has been devoted to invoking different gods and personages in the course of praising love. Seen from this perspective, Plato's dialogues train their readers or audiences to follow the example of Socrates, but they also teach them to proceed without him. This, of course, is yet another approach to the hidden center of all Socratic dialogues, the trauma of Socrates' death. The Socratic dialogue brings Socrates back to life; it revives him for the purpose of continuing philosophy. At the same time, this project is successful only if philosophy can in fact take place without him either as an actual person or as a character. In this way, Plato's dialogues repeat the central experience of Plato's life: finding a way of doing philosophy in the name of but also ultimately without the person of Socrates. This project, to which role switching centrally contributes, could thus be called de-Socratization, which is at the same time a special case of the more general depersonalization at work in Plato's philosophy, the move toward abstracting from concrete individuals and scenes. Plato creates a powerful character, but at the same time he develops strategies for making this character dispensable.

Plato's use of character, including his technique of role switching and the back-and-forth between a fixation on Socrates and a detachment from him, is thrown into relief when we compare Plato to his closest competitor, Xenophon. Xenophon, too, is concerned with building up Socrates as a character, but it is a very different kind of character indeed. Xenophon's version of the *Symposium*, for example, delights in the loving exchanges that characterize the relation between Alcibiades and Socrates in Plato's *Symposium*. But Socrates is a very different kind of philosopher, primarily a source of good advice to his friends, counseling them in everything from how to lead an army to trivial matters of everyday life. The main reason for the difference between Plato and Xenophon is the purpose of their respective texts. Xenophon's *Memorabilia* is dominated by the goal of demonstrating the injustice of Socrates' trial and execution. Everything Xenophon reports about Socrates, whether it is actual conversations with friends or summaries of his advice, is meant as a repost to Melitus' accusation. The result is not Socrates the gadfly, the searcher for truth, but Socrates the harmless counselor.[56] More important, Xenophon's Socratic dialogues are all personalization and do nothing to depersonalize philosophy by confronting it with forms. To be sure, Plato, too, wrote in the shadow of the judgment against his teacher, and his oeuvre, too, can be seen as a long defense. This defense, however, took the form of turning Socrates into an unusual philosopher via an unusual use of drama.

Action

Plato's construction of character and his technique of role switching have consequences for the plot and the action of his dialogues. Once more the comparison to Aristotle is instructive. For Aristotle, the most important element of drama is action, and it is to the depiction of a unified action that a play must be devoted. All other components, including character, are in the service of this overriding goal. As a consequence, Aristotle offered a detailed account, almost a formula, for tragic action. Unlike epic poetry, tragedy needed to present a unified and complete action, which meant a single action with a clear beginning, middle, and end.[57] Much of his efforts were devoted to detailing the trajectory of tragic action. For Greek tragedy, Aristotle offered two categories: reversal (*peripeteia*) and recognition (*anagnorisis*). Reversal describes an abrupt change in the action, a reversal of fortunes. Such a reversal can, but does not necessarily need to, coincide with the second category, recognition. Recognition is primarily an internal change, the moment when a character must come to terms with the world, when adversarial circumstances force themselves onto the consciousness of a hitherto oblivious or resistant protagonist: a change from ignorance to knowledge. In the best tragedies, Aristotle says, the external change in the action and the internal recognition coincide, as they do in Sophocles' *King Oedipus*. Instead of exonerating Oedipus, the messenger indicts him, thus forcing Oedipus to recognize who he really is. This also marks the external reversal in the action: the murderer of the former king has been found and will now be punished.[58]

Plato's dialogues are likewise centered in a single unifying principle; however, this principle is not action but argument. More precisely, Plato's dialogues interlace the interaction among the characters with argumentative exchanges so that action and argument feed on each other—or differ. The banter between Socrates and Aristophanes in the *Symposium*, for example, clearly adds an important element of physical interaction to Diotima's abstract argument, and in the *Phaedo*, the interaction between the condemned Socrates and his friends adds urgency to the argument about the immortality of the soul and also implicates the philosopher in the argument. The drama of interaction and the drama of argument thus complement each other in complicated ways.

But what kinds of plots do these combinations of argument and action produce? Plato employs the dramaturgy of reversal and recognition that Aristotle would later identify in Greek tragedy, but he uses it in a completely different manner. While Plato's dialogues have a clear beginning, carefully setting the scene and introducing the characters, they don't proceed from a single reversal to a moment of recognition and then to a conclusion. Instead they veer off in different directions, circle back to start over again, or find themselves interrupted and forced to change course entirely. These meandering plots still contain reversal and recognition, but one reversal after another, one recognition scene after another. This proliferation of reversals and recognitions creates the labyrinthine pattern out of which emerges the complex and confusing structure of Plato's dialogues. Often these dialogues don't come to a conclusion at all and end abruptly, without closure.

We can deduce from these strange plots important insights into Plato's notion of philosophy and truth. The standard plots of tragedy and comedy, Plato is suggesting here, are not conducive to novel insights. The testing of hypotheses, the exploration or critique of previously held opinions, the attack on a common enemy, or the elaborate construction of a mythologi-cal and argumentative edifice all require different rhythms, different ways of proceeding, and therefore different plots. For Plato the standard tragic and comic plots need to be interrupted and turned on their head by his own stop-and-go rhythm of questions and answers. Truth is something that must come as a surprise; it must come out of left field, unexpectedly and suddenly. This is why his dialogues need to be able to change course at any moment, turning around, inverting, and interrupting common opinion, coming at a familiar problem from an unexpected vantage point. They keep the characters and the readers off balance so that they cannot revert to familiar plots, familiar patterns of knowing. Plato's plots are so strange because truth itself is improbable, paradoxical, and counterintui-tive. Everywhere Plato sees false opinions, fostered by sophists, teachers of rhetoric, Homer, habit, and drama. His dialogues need to undo these familiar plots in order for truth to emerge.

Audience

The relation of the drama to the audience is the final theatrical category that gets revised in the Socratic dialogue. Here, too, Aristotle is a useful foil, since he spent some time thinking about the effects of tragedy on the audience. Fear and pity are the two emotions evoked by a good tragedy, and to this he adds that those emotions have to be purged or somehow released.[59] For the most part, however, Aristotle considered the audience, and hence live performance, with some ambivalence. This ambivalence is encoded in the word *opsis*, "visual representation," which he recognizes as a crucial element of theater. At the same time, however, he dismisses *opsis* as the most incidental component of drama, one that we can even do with-out: fear and pity would also work when a tragedy is being read rather than theatrically performed.[60]

Plato anticipates Aristotle's ambivalence with respect to the audience, but he feels it much more strongly. Here it should be remembered that the audience for Greek tragedy and comedy was an inclusive and democratic affair. The Dionysius Theater held at least fifteen thousand people, admit-tance was partially subsidized, and it is probable that women and slaves were allowed to attend. Moreover, the festival was partly in the hands of the audience: citizens presided over the competition, they were represent-ed in the chorus, and they could manifest their pleasure and displeasure right there. The playwright, actors, and producer were directly exposed to them, even though the prizes were given by a select group of judges. It was precisely this kind of audience that Plato rejected. In the *Laws*, he voices his most polemical invective against the theater, speaking of a veritable "theatrocracy," the rule of the audience over the production.[61] His own theater would not be subject to this rule.

While Plato rejected the rule of the audience, he did not want to do without an audience—that is, without performance—altogether. Plato's dialogues were probably performed in front of groups of students or even at competitions.[62] The best model for the type of performance originally intended by Plato is provided in one of his own dialogues, the *Theaetetus*. Like other Socratic dialogues, the *Theaetetus* opens with the encounter of two acquaintances sometime after Socrates' death. Theaetetus has just been wounded in battle, and the acquaintances speak of his prowess and how Socrates had predicted that Theaetetus would distinguish himself. So far, *Theaetetus* opens in a way that is not unusual for a Platonic dialogue, with several frames and scenes of narration: the encounter between the two friends, the report of what has been said, Socrates' actual conversations with the young Theaetetus. What is unusual is that we do not get a report from memory of Socrates' conversations with Theaetetus. Instead, our friend had written down Socrates' report and in fact checked its accuracy with Socrates himself during several visits to Athens. He holds a written account of the conversation and of the interaction among the characters, just the kind of written dialogue we ourselves are reading.[63] So in this opening scene of the dialogue, what we get is a performance. The two acquaintances are now the audience, and they are being read to aloud by a slave, who is doing the characters in different voices. This is not dissimilar to what Socrates, in the *Republic*, describes as happening when rhapsodes recite epic poetry. They don't read neutrally, but assume different roles and characters, and they can't help emulating the voices and gestures of the characters: they become actors.[64] In the same way, the slave boy here becomes a reader and actor, verbally enacting the scene of which the rest of the dialogue is composed.

But what about the audience of such performed readings? Plato's critique of theater contains a powerful critique of passive audiences. His ideal is closer to what one might describe as participant observers. Bystanders, in Plato's dialogues, often enter the argument, the action. This is why the technique of role switching is so central. Any audience member should, in principle, be able to participate in the argument, taking over from a character who is circling off. We can deduce further information about Plato's conception of an ideal audience from the internal audience—the interlocutors—of his dialogues. Many of Plato's dialogues include characters who have to be coaxed into argumentation, who are resistant, unwilling, or dismissive of the type of philosophical exchange Socrates favors. Often they get angry, even violent, and threaten to leave. Indeed, many of the philosophical exchanges in Plato's dialogues proceed under the constant fear that they may be abandoned abruptly.[65] Socrates often must bait his interlocutors and do everything in his power to keep them engaged in dialogue. The angry Thrasymachus, in the first book of the *Republic*, who is by turn aggressive and defensive and who can barely bring himself to play along, is perhaps the most famous example.[66] The *Lysis* ends prematurely because the young boys with whom Socrates has been talking are called by their tutors and told to go home.[67] The *Greater Hippias* proceeds under the constant threat of a premature end as well. Hippias gets frustrated when Socrates undermines his confident sense of what beauty is, and he declares that he will leave and meditate on the question of beauty himself. Socrates has to use all his rhetorical skill to coax him into staying in the dialogue, and almost fails.[68]

Plato's dialogues thus demonstrate over and over again how difficult, rare, and fragile a true philosophical exchange really is. Few of Socrates' interlocutors are ideal philosophers. Mostly the dialogues are devoted to the induction of a character into the mode of philosophy; dramatically, this means that these dialogues are instructions about how to participate in a philosophical conversation, how to become a character in a philo- sophical play. This also explains the relative exclusivity of these dialogues. They usually include a small set of characters who are educated and ca- pable of engaging in discussion and argument. This does not mean, however, that they are in any simple sense exclusive or elitist. These dia- logues always threaten to end prematurely even as they do their utmost to induct a large number of characters—young nobles, famous citizens, for- eign visitors, slaves—into philosophical discourse. Plato's dialogues were probably intended both for a readership outside the Academy and for highly controlled educational performance at the Academy; in any case, they were representations of the type of conversation Plato hoped would take place in his school and beyond it.

Plato's attack on tragedy and his view of theater also have a strong po- litical valence. Tragedy, with its emphasis on a chorus composed of citizens and its mode of presentation in front of a good portion of the citizenry of Athens, was closely associated with democracy. Hence Plato's critique of the democratic audience as a "theatrocracy," a kind of mob rule caused by playwrights who, without proper philosophical knowledge, incite the bas- er emotions of the audience. Plato's own choice of the dramatic dialogue with its avoidance of a chorus as well as large audiences thus also implies a political preference for small, select groups over large assemblies. In this sense, a literary and formal reading of the theatricality encoded in these dialogues confirms Plato's antidemocratic stance. But such a reading can also add nuance to Plato's critique of democracy, for we can now specify that Plato rejected Athenian democracy precisely to the extent that it pre- sented itself as a "theatrocracy." What he envisioned as an alternative, however, was not some kind of conspiratorial rule of the few, a class-based oligarchy that meets behind closed doors. Rather, the open but controlled form of the dialogue captures the ideal of a fragile educational process that is in principle open to anyone. This, at least, is the politics encoded in Plato's dramatic form.

The intimate and restrained performance of the Socratic dialogues and the preference for participant observers also shed light on Socrates' noto- rious critique of writing. In the *Phaedrus*, one worry about writing is the fear of a loss of memory: if we can write things down, we won't have to remember them and will therefore lose our ability to remember, which in turn will have adverse effects on our ability to think for ourselves. This critique has seemed paradoxical to many readers: while the historical Socrates famously did not write a single word, the authors of Socratic dialogues, Plato among them, made the deliberate choice in favor of writing. Why then should Plato include a critique of writing in one of his dialogues? Many authors of subsequent Socrates plays seized on this paradox by introducing Plato as a character who, contrary to Socrates' instructions, writes down what transpires in conversation around him.

In order to understand this paradox better, it is important to remember that the *Phaedrus* includes a second critique of writing: that the audience—the readers—cannot confront the speaker and ask follow-up questions or demand clarifications. Technically, this is true of Plato's written dialogues as well. However, the dialogues escape this problem in two ways. First, they model an interactive relation between actor and audience, with bystanders engaging Socrates or even, through role switching, taking part in the discussion.[69] More important, these dialogues, written though they are, demand to be performed in controlled and intimate settings, and this type of performance is actually encoded within them. Modifying Aristotle's remark that a good tragedy should work equally well for reading and for theatrical performance, one could say that the theatrical dimension of Plato's dialogues, their particular type of participatory performance, is activated whether they are actually performed or not.

The entanglement of writing and performance goes deeper still. Eric A. Havelock has argued that Plato's call to replace the wisdom literature of Homer and Greek tragedy with his own philosophical genre was tantamount to asserting the superiority of the values implied by the new literacy, such as reason and structured argument, as opposed to formulaic pieces of wisdom and poetic maxims that lent themselves to oral transmission.[70] This line of reasoning was further explored by Walter J. Ong, who pointed out the extent to which Plato's emphasis on abstraction and discursive argument was itself the product of the spread of writing and literacy in Athens.[71] With Havelock and Ong in mind, one might say that Plato rejected precisely those forms of theater that were rooted in orality, namely, the performance practices associated with Athenian theater and the recitation of Homeric rhapsodes. These he opposed with a new type of educational performance appropriate to his own rational and literary prose dramas.

This new understanding of drama, and the forms of theatrical performance it implies, is not only different from the Athenian theater system but also much closer to a modern conception of drama. Friedrich Nietzsche was one of those who recognize Plato as the inventor of a fully *literary* drama, a drama that has shed its reliance on song, dance, and ritual action and that subjects all other dimensions of drama, especially the category of stage action, to the dictates of its own prose discourse. This is precisely what, beginning in the eighteenth century, bourgeois reformers of the theater would demand: a literary drama ruling over all other dimensions of theatrical presentation, a drama that could be read as well as seen and that, even when seen, would remain fully literary. At the same time, Plato's investment in an active audience of participant observers is reminiscent of such forms as Brecht's teaching plays (*Lehrstücke*), which are likewise meant for a small audience of participants.[72] Plato here emerges as the precursor of modern literary drama, and in this sense he occupies an important place in the transition from an oral culture to prose literacy.

My approach, analyzing Plato's dialogues through their relation to modern drama, is in a sense anachronistic, but it is an anachronism that can shed new light on a familiar topic. In addition, the connection between Plato and modern drama is not only a matter of using the later formation as a lens through which to look at the earlier one. Once modern literary drama had emerged, ushering in a new conception of theatrical performance, more and more playwrights and philosophers began to recognize Plato, retrospectively, as a playwright ahead of his time. The subsequent history of Socrates plays, which were the first to identify Plato's dialogues as drama (and which later were joined by the works of modern dramatists inspired by Plato), confirms this interpretation. Plato's conception of theater was at once a break with Athenian theatricality, that holdover of an oral culture of performance, and a hesitant attempt to envision a mode of performance that would coexist with writing. Plato's dialogues are reformist texts that seek to change the very practice of theatrical performance, pointing the way to the theater of the future.

Plato's Purpose

Plato's antitragic and anticomic poetics was geared toward his own philosophical ends, and it should now be possible to say what those ends were. The first end was the undoing of false certainties, of commonly held opinions as they were articulated in the cultural, political, and religious canon of classical Athens. Often the undoing of false certainties is the explicit plot of Plato's dialogues: typically Socrates visits purported experts such as sophists or politicians in order to deflate their most cherished certainties. The same thing happens on the level of the dramatic form. His dialogues undo the certainties enshrined in tragedy, epic poetry, and other culturally privileged genres by rudely interrupting them, inverting them, quoting from them, and replacing them with a new and entirely different form of drama, one suited to the goal of deflating all other genres. Plato's dialogues have absorbed all the prevalent genres of literature, philosophy, and mythology, mixing them freely and cunningly into a new genre of drama, in which they cannot exert their usual influence. Now they are ruled by a different principle, truth, which is arrived at by testing arguments in reasoned prose dialogues conducted by witty, ironic characters.

If one function of Plato's dialogues is the undoing of false certainties, the other, equally important function is what at first looks like the opposite: defeating relativism, which is to say, undoing false uncertainties. This purpose is connected to the ramifications of one of the most successful philosophical paradigms, Heracleitus' claim that everything is in motion and always changing, which also means that nothing can be said with certainty about the world.[73] This paradigm could be seen as laying the groundwork for a new type of relativistic teaching by sophists such as

Protagoras, who coined the formula "man is the measure of all things." One consequence of this approach was that argumentative skill became an end in itself, a tool to be used in order to get an advantage. Since the sophists had forsworn the search for truth, they, too, seem to believe at least implicitly that no certainty can ever be reached and no true knowledge established; therefore, argumentation never leads to insight but can result only in victory or defeat in a battle of wits.

Heracleitus' philosophy of flux and the sophists' relativism are the main targets of Plato's philosophy. Indeed, Plato invented the philosophical drama as a vehicle for defeating them both. What his dialogues show is that the path toward knowledge may be difficult, meandering, and full of false starts, that it may take you in unexpected directions and be prone to lead you astray, but that despite all of these difficulties it is a path that is possible and in fact necessary. This is why Plato wrote dialogues in which little positive insight is achieved—the early aporetic dialogues—and then moved on to his middle and late periods with dialogues in which much is learned and gained.

Plato's most well-known and also most extreme measure for defeating the sophists, at least in his middle period, is the theory of forms. Plato is invested in this invention not because he is discontent with the actually existing world around him, unlike latter-day Christian Platonists who devalue this world in order to set their sights on the next. Rather, he invented the theory of forms as a way of keeping sophism at bay, since sophism for him meant replacing truth with power. The theory of forms allowed him to acknowledge Heracleitus' recognition that the world is changeable and shifting—always "becoming." It also allowed him to see that the reason why the sophists were so successful in teaching argumentation as a strategy for winning debates was that words themselves have shifting meanings and are often unreliable. Plato was able to acknowledge all of this, yet insist that there existed a reference point for true knowledge: the form. Only if we posit forms to be stable and unchangeable reference points can we overcome sophism. Forms allow us to look beyond the changing world and to try to reach true knowledge the way the philosopher, in the parable of the cave, turns around, ceases staring at shadows, and eventually leaves the cave, at least for the time being. Only if there is more to this world than changing shadows does it make sense to embark on a quest for truth. When seen from this vantage point, forms are a necessary corrective, an imperative: we must act as if forms really existed, otherwise we will be stuck with sophism forever.

The theory of forms came at a steep price, for they threatened to be treated as more than a means for defeating sophism: they were seen as actually existing things, residing somewhere beyond the cave or up in the clouds as supernatural, metaphysical entities. After establishing the theory of forms in a number of dialogues, Plato recognized the difficult implications of this metaphysics and responded to it in the *Parmenides*, which includes the most full-fledged critique of the theory of forms. In particular, the *Parmenides* questions whether it makes sense to think of forms always as independent entities, as he had suggested in the parable of the cave and in a number of other dialogues. Many self-declared Platonists and Platonist idealists have opted to ignore the *Parmenides* and continue to treat Plato as the inventor of a theory of forms as articulated by Diotima in the *Symposium* and Socrates in the *Phaedo* and the *Republic*, disregarding Plato's later critique. After arriving at its impasse, the *Parmenides* does not give up on the theory of forms but rather reformulates it precisely as a philosophical imperative: there must be forms, for if there weren't, the very project of philosophy would come to an end.

Once we recognize Plato's philosophical purpose as navigating between the undoing of false certainties and the undoing of false uncertainties, it is possible to assess more precisely the function of his dramatic form. To this end, it is necessary to revisit Plato's most notorious critique of drama, which no doubt was one reason why so many later commentators failed to recognize Plato's own dramatic technique. In books three and ten of the *Republic*, Plato launches several arguments against drama as a mimetic art. He first approaches this question through the distinction between mimesis and diegesis. Mimesis is the direct presentation of different voices and the types of impersonation that happen not just in theater but also when rhapsodes recite Homeric poetry, doing the lines in different voices (it is also what happens when the boy in the *Theaetetus* recites that dialogue). In contrast to this theatrical mode of presentation, Plato favors a more distanced one, namely, a narrative mode called diegesis. Even though this preference seems to do away with theater entirely, there exists in fact a whole theatrical tradition that can be said to be diegetic: a theater that is suspicious of mimesis and instead tries to frame and distance what happens onstage through narrators and other techniques.

In book ten of the *Republic*, Plato picks up this argument and generalizes it. Rather than talk about actors in particular, he speaks more generally of imitation, a rubric that includes all the arts. Plato's main worry now is epistemological: since artists are experts not in what they depict but only in techniques of imitation, their products cannot produce insight and truth, only falsehood. Again it looks as if this is a blanket attack on all arts whatsoever, but again this is not true. Any art would be permissible that was in fact driven by a genuine—and for Plato this means philosophical—desire for truth. His own dramatic dialogues are prime candidates for such a truth-seeking drama. If Plato did not entertain the possibility of such a good, philosophical mimesis, a mimesis of forms, his own dramatic form would be an obvious and blatant contradiction. Plato accepted the possibility of a good mimesis in the form of a drama of truth.

What such a drama of truth means can be specified by looking at the way in which Plato sought to use his particular dramatic technique to create a hovering between the physical and the metaphysical that is the hallmark of his philosophy. Whether it triggers an imaginary performance in the mind of the reader (or listener) or leads to an actual performance, dialogic drama uses all the elements that make up the physical world. Drama is, as Plato suggested in book three of the *Republic*, the most mimetic of the arts and also the art that depends for its mimesis on the physical presence of bodies and languages spoken in concrete situations. At the same time, drama—especially dialogic drama—uses these human beings, scenes, and actions selectively, taking them one by one, extracting them from the real world and placing them in this strange place called theater—whether real or imagined. There they are put together anew as if in a laboratory, forming a simpler and more controlled version of the world from which they were taken. They are matter still, but matter dislodged from the thickness of the world, uprooted and ready to be altered, redirected, or refurbished in a new and philosophical project of truth. Because it effects the unmaking of matter, drama is perfectly suited to presenting a scenario in which it is shown that matter does not rest in itself, content and undisturbed. Rather, matter here is shot through with ideas or forms; in Plato's parlance, matter participates in forms. These forms will never and can never appear by themselves; they manifest themselves by indicating that whatever and whoever is present onstage is connected to forms and thus cannot derive stability and identity from mere matter. This was Plato's greatest discovery: that if handled in a particular way (a way very different from the conventional one), dialogic drama could become the perfect medium for the contentious connection between matter and form that defines the core of his philosophy. All he had to do was invent a dramatic form that would both evoke and critique theater; make and unmake characters, scenes, and actions; conjure abstract forms; and rematerialize those forms in the provisional materiality of the theater.

Plato thus interrupts the different dimensions of drama in order to dislodge the materiality of the theater, turning that materiality into something much more detached, removed, mediated, and unstable. Only after the materiality of the theater has been dislodged can his dialogues be used to point to or invoke abstract forms. These abstract forms, in turn, are never presented by themselves. They arise from the materiality of the theater precisely when this materiality is drained of its solidity and stability. The process can be described the other way around as well: abstract forms effect the partial and incomplete dematerialization that is so characteristic of Plato's dialogues. His characters, scenes, and actions all seem to be in the service of forms. The metaphysical theory of forms affects the materiality of the theater, making it hover uneasily between the physical, on which it draws, and the metaphysical, to which it points.

This dramatic understanding of Plato—let's call it dramatic Platonism—could not be more different from what is generally associated with Plato and Platonic idealism. It is also the type of Platonism that I think is necessary in today's intellectual climate. As I will argue in more detail later on, for the past 150 years almost all philosophies of any wider cultural influence have been devoted to a rigorous and thorough undoing of Platonism, understood as a form of idealism. Whether they be the pragmatism of Ralph Waldo Emerson, the historical materialism of Karl Marx, the philosophy of the body developed by Friedrich Nietzsche, the language games of Ludwig Wittgenstein, the empiricism of Gilles Deleuze, or the historicism of Michel Foucault, these philosophies and their various followers have one thing in common: an implacable anti-Platonist stance. They have with predictable frequency taken what they understood as idealist tendencies and shown them to be wrong. Instead, they have pointed to material conditions, among them, experience, individual existence, the social system of production, the body, pragmatic uses of language in concrete situations, or state institutions. Always, the gesture has been to cut down vertical edifices of ideas and place them on the horizontal axis of matter. The rare exception of this anti-idealism is mathematics, in which a kind of intuitive idealism is prevalent among its practitioners, many of whom work with the assumption that mathematical entities, whose properties can be discovered, really exist; but even this mathematical idealism has been included in the anti-Platonist polemic of Wittgenstein.[74]

The anti-Platonist, anti-idealist gesture has become so prevalent that we hardly recognize it anymore. Anti-Platonism has become our belief, our common knowledge, dare I say our ideology. The only way in which anti-Platonists have had to acknowledge any discontents is by recognizing that it has been accompanied by the revival of its somewhat less popular twin, relativism. We are very happy to be ridiculing and undoing ideas left and right, but do we want to be thought of as relativists? Even the most influential form of relativism, cultural relativism, has come under new scrutiny since it has become clear that cultural relativism can be used with the greatest ease as a vehicle for conservative power politics. Plato, of course, knew all about that. He had seen relativism being used in the great game of power at the tail end of the Athenian empire. It was in response to this cynical relativism that he invented dramatic Platonism.

Today it is not a matter of reversing this repeated anti-Platonist reversal. Indeed, it is the very gesture of reversal that is part of the problem. As I understand it, dramatic Platonism is not something that can or needs to be reversed or that itself simply reverses materialism. Dramatic Platonism is an infinitely more dynamic construction, an oscillation or hovering that has incorporated some elements of which anti-Platonists are so proud. Dramatic Platonism includes materialism as one of its moments: it is a balancing act, and this is nowhere else as clear as when one observes the ways in which Plato constantly adjusted his philosophical drama over the course of his career. He began with a public and striking courtroom drama in the *Apology* and the early dramatic dialogues. Then gradually, as if he had recognized that he was veering too much toward embodiment, he embedded his scenes in multiple frames of narration, thus mediating direct drama with multiple layers of distancing devices. This is also the period when Plato invented his strongest antidote, the theory of forms. But then he reverted back to direct drama, although he controled drama by other means, by reducing character, scene, and action and instead giving more space to the speculative creation of edifices of argument and ideas. When seen from the perspective of dramatic Platonism, Plato's oeuvre appears as a careful balancing act between matter and form, which I therefore posit as Plato's true goal.

It was a goal that almost failed. The main culprit was Plato's self-appointed successors, the various schools of Platonism and Neoplatonism, which turned dramatic Platonism into idealism pure and simple, resulting eventually, through the logic of reactive critique, in our current crop of anti-Platonists. Fortunately, when Plato was rediscovered in the West, there emerged, hesitant and barely visible at first, a minor and disregarded tradition of authors who continued Plato's dramatic legacy by keeping alive the insight that Plato should be regarded as a dramatist, albeit a very peculiar one. Few of those dramatic followers of Plato—the authors of Socrates plays—recognized the full philosophical import of Plato's drama. And so they worked primarily, as Plato had done, by using the available dramatic modes of their time. What is striking about the tradition of the Socrates play is thus not its faithfulness to Plato but the very variety of modes and style used by authors seeking to follow Plato the dramatist. Through this variety shines the unique poetics of the Socratic dialogue.

2

A Brief History of the Socrates Play

On November 7, 1468, Lorenzo de' Medici arranged for an evening commemorating Plato's birthday to be held at a villa in Careggi, outside Florence. Such commemorations had been common in antiquity but had since fallen out of fashion; in fact, 1,200 years had passed since the last such celebration had taken place, and the evening was therefore meant as an important historical moment—a return to Plato. Nine guests were invited, including a bishop, a physician, a poet, and a rhetorician. The evening began with the rhetorician, Bernardo Nuzzi, reading aloud the entire text of Plato's *Symposium*. After this dramatic reading, Nuzzi asked each of the guests to give a lecture on one of the speeches. This second part of the evening thus mirrored Plato's text, with each of the participants taking turns delivering commentaries on Plato. The interpretation of the *Symposium* was itself a symposium, and the whole event both a reading of Plato's *Symposium* and a new version of it.

The (probably fictional) account of this evening can be found in *De Amore* by Marsilio Ficino, the person chiefly responsible for Plato's revival in Renaissance Europe.[1] With the encouragement of his patron, Cosimo de' Medici (grandfather of Lorenzo de' Medici), Ficino had immersed himself in Plato's original text and laboriously translated Plato's entire oeuvre, much of it for the first time, into Latin. It was this translation that catalyzed and shaped the breathtaking revival of Platonism in Western Europe. Ficino also created a network of Plato enthusiasts and called it Plato's Academy, named after the school founded by Plato outside the agora of Athens; this became the center of Platonism in Florence. Ficino's Academy and his celebration of Plato's birthday continued to be seen as a crucial scene even centuries later. In 1862, the Italian painter Luigi Mussini revisited this scene in a painting called *Celebration of Plato's Birthday at Lorenzo Il Magnifico's Villa in Careggi on November 7, 1474.*[2] The figure at the center, Ficino (or Nuzzi), is reading a speech taken from the *Symposium* or commenting on a particular passage, with his right hand resting on the open book and his

2.1. Luigi Mussini, *Celebration of Plato's Birthday at Lorenzo Il Magnifico's Villa in Careggi on November 7, 1474* (1862). Galleria d'Arte Moderna, Turin, Italy. Photo: Erich Lessing/Art Resource, New York.

left raised in an a declamatory gesture (figure 2.1). The painting captures the double nature of this celebration: the reading of Plato's text, to which the right hand points, and the performance to an audience, underlined by the raised left.

The revival of Plato in Florence was part of a long and varied history of Platonism through late antiquity and the Middle Ages. A relatively continuous, if not uninterrupted, Academy existed in Athens until 529, when Emperor Justinian closed the school, forcing the Platonists into exile in Persia and Syria. For a time, the works of Plato were preserved and commented upon mostly by Eastern scholars; as a result, during much of the Middle Ages, Western philosophers and theologians knew of several dialogues only secondhand. Even though Platonist elements can be found among many Christian theologians of this and later periods, not all the works of Plato were known, notable exceptions being the *Timaeus* and the *Phaedo*. But even this muted influence could lead to significant effects, for example, the Platonic strain in Dante, who echoed the *Symposium* in his *Il Convito* (1314). The full corpus of Plato's dialogues reached the West only in 1428 via Greek scholars working in Constantinople, at a time when that city was increasingly asking the West for help defending itself against the Ottoman Empire. The West did not provide the necessary aid, leaving Constantinople to be conquered by Sultan Mehmet II in 1453. The increasing pressure brought on Constantinople, however, did have the side effect of forcing more intellectual contact between Byzantine scholars and the city-states of Italy, especially Venice and Florence. Byzantine scholars brought Plato's original Greek oeuvre, and a whole tradition of commentary, to Italy, where it captured the imagination of Cosimo de' Medici, who in turn supported the first complete translation to be undertaken into Latin by Ficino.

After Ficino, the Western history of thought—and, as I will argue, the history of literature and art—witnessed a number of revivals of Platonism, including the one that occurred in seventeenth-century Cambridge, and these revivals were part of a more general renewal of interest in classical Greece in the latter part of the eighteenth century. This led not only to a new classicism but also to Romantic idealism in the early nineteenth century. Despite the dominance of positivism and materialism through much of the nineteenth century, Platonism remained a significant undercurrent, especially as an aesthetic doctrine. Even though this aesthetic idealism was attacked by incipient modernism, various forms of Platonism continued to exist into the late twentieth century. Given how inextricably Western thought is bound up with Plato's heritage, it's not surprising that Alfred North Whitehead could claim that the history of philosophy is nothing but a series of footnotes to Plato.[3]

Ficino did more than make Plato available to readers of Latin. He also recognized how intimately Plato's philosophy was bound to its dramatic form. Ficino is not only the beginning of Platonism in the Renaissance but also the beginning of dramatic Platonism—something captured in Mussini's depiction of Ficino's theatrical declamation. Indeed, painters were keenly aware of the scenic potential of Plato's dialogues and were drawn

2.2. Jacques-Louis David, *Death of Socrates* (1787). Catharine Lorillard Wolfe Collection, Wolfe Fund, 1931, The Metropolitan Museum of Art.

to their most theatrical set pieces, such as Socrates' death or Alcibiades' entrance toward the end of the *Symposium*. The most famous example of the former is undoubtedly Jacques-Louis David's 1787 work *Death of Socrates* (figure 2.2), which captures Socrates' suffering companions, many of whom have averted their eyes as Socrates seizes the cup, and contrasts their behavior with Socrates' own stern equanimity in the face of death.

As for Alcibiades' noisy entrance, this was a scene nicely captured in 1869 by Anselm Feuerbach's *Plato's Symposium* (figure 2.3), which renders the sudden shift in tone effected by Alcibiades: while Socrates is still deep in conversation, several of the guests are already turning to the appetizing appearance of the famous Athenian, whose tunic comes threateningly close to exposing his private parts. Painters agreed with dramatists as to the theatrical potential of Plato's dialogues.

Socrates on the Stage

Dramatic Platonism can be found in many places, but in this chapter I will trace its development in what I call the Socrates play.[4] Socrates plays follow Plato in presenting Socrates' thoughts as well as his actions in dramatic form. Many Socrates plays use material presented in Plato's own dialogues, while others avail themselves of sources such as Xenophon's Socratic dialogues or Diogenes Laertius' *Life of Socrates*. What they have in common is the conviction that the most adequate way to present Socrates is in the form of drama. This conviction was all the more remarkable since most Platonist and Neoplatonist schools had abandoned Plato's dramatic form and instead opted for the commentary—or, indeed, Whitehead's footnote—as their chief philosophical genre. It was thus left to dramatists to keep the idea of Plato's drama alive, or even to create it in the first place. Many of the authors writing Socrates plays worked in relative obscurity

2.3.   Anselm Feuerbach, *Plato's Symposium* (1869). Staatliche Kunsthalle, Karlsruhe, Germany. Photo: W. Pankoke.

and without knowledge of one another. This means that the history of the Socrates play does not proceed in a linear fashion, with each writer knowing and deliberately revising the works inherited from predecessors. Instead, this history proceeds by fits and starts, forming clusters and gaps; in many ways, the authors of Socrates plays had to invent their dramatic form each time from scratch (see the appendix for a list of Socrates plays and a graph tracking the genre's development).

The sheer diversity of these plays demonstrates Plato's profound influence on modern Europe and North America, including its drama. This influence has been obscured by the distorted image of Plato as the enemy of drama and theater and, more generally, by the lack of interest in the conjunction of drama and philosophy on the part of both theater scholars and philosophers. But authors of Socrates plays recognized Plato's dramatic genius, seeing at work in his Socratic dialogues a new and startling use of prose drama ahead of its time. It is through this tradition that we can retrospectively identify Plato as a dramatist. Put a different way, this chapter tells the story of how Plato became a playwright.

While authors of Socrates plays were attuned to the dramatic dimension of Plato's dialogues, they often failed to recognize the particular use to which Plato had put drama—his distinct dramaturgy. Their chief interest was in character, the assumption that philosophy is tied to a philosophical protagonist whose every action acquires philosophical significance. But unlike Plato, they did not simultaneously detach philosophy from its dependence on Socrates, and more generally they showed little interest either in Plato's intricate double move of both personalizing and depersonalizing philosophy or in his interweaving of scene and action with abstraction and argument. In a sense, they can be accused of partially de-Platonizing the Socratic dialogue. This is perhaps not surprising, since they rarely presented themselves as faithful adherents of Plato and instead used his drama to address their own problems and concerns, just as they translated Plato's dramatic technique into forms and genres of their own time.

While the challenge of the dramatic form remained a live issue for these authors, equally important were the philosophical questions raised by Plato's oeuvre and its chief protagonist. Of particular importance to many writers of Socrates plays from the seventeenth to the nineteenth century was the relation between Plato and Christianity. Many religious writers were drawn to Plato because they, like Christian theologians, saw in Plato a precursor of Christian monotheism. Here the Socrates play continues one of the most important intellectual events in late antiquity, the fusion of Platonism and early Christianity, which led to the first proper Christian theology; it is a history that includes Origen and reaches an initial high point with St. Augustine. Socrates, in this reading, anticipates Christianity and therefore, of all the Greek pagans, he deserves the most serious attention. *Socrates, A Dramatic Poem* (1758) is a case in point. It is a play written by Amyas Bushe, a member of a prominent family in Kilkenny, Ireland, and a fellow of the Royal Society. Unlike many other Socrates plays, this one is relatively dreary, expressing Plato's idealism, the coincidence of beauty and the good, in a memorable jingle: "Beauty and virtue are the same; / They differ, only in the name."[5] The play is prefaced by a poem, allegedly written by an anonymous fan, stating the play's Christianizing mission in its very first lines: "The half-evangeliz'd, inspired store / Of sacred Socrates—his heaven-taught lore / Informs with dignity divine your lays; / There pagan truths with christian fervor blaze, / The gospel's harbinger, who shone so bright, / With more than ethic rays, than nature's light / His lamp was rais'd."[6] The image of Socrates as holding the supernatural lamp that blazes the way for Christianity is representative of the need felt by many writers of Socrates plays to apologize for turning the pagan, yet already half-evangelized, Socrates into an ethical hero.

Henry Montague Grover of St. Peter's College sounded a very similar note in a play authored in 1828 also called *Socrates: A Dramatic Poem*. A young man preparing for the clergy, Grover was especially invested in presenting Plato as a proto-Christian, finding in his dialogues "emanations of prophetic doctrines."[7] Grover brings to Plato the same kind of reading Christian commentators bring to the Hebrew Bible, interpreting it as a prefiguration of Christ. Grover even engages in the wild speculation that Plato traveled to Judea and modeled his Socrates on his experience there.[8] Grover declares that Plato's philosophy anticipates the coming of Christ, showing "in her glass the form of things, which be / In embryo yet; but in that fashioning, / Doth gender a new birth for future minds, / Whose soil shall bring them forth in magnitudes. / Such as appointed."[9] Socrates represents Christ in embryonic form and thus can be assimilated into the Christian canon.

For others, Plato's critique of the anthropomorphic deities of Homer identified him as a very different theological thinker, namely, an advocate of the abstract god of eighteenth-century Enlightenment philosophers. A Socrates play by a radical member of the French Revolution, Jean-Marie Collot, is a representative example. *The Trial of Socrates, or, the Regime of Ancient Times* was performed in Paris at the Théâtre de Monsieur in 1790, at the height of the French Revolution. Collot's Socrates preaches a "God of reason," even (and fatefully so) during his trial; in other words, Socrates is being executed for proposing Enlightenment deism in the face of religious orthodoxy.[10] Both pious Christians and revolutionary deists thus turned Socrates into a martyr for their respective theological causes.

Another aspect of Plato's dialogues proved more difficult for Christian writers to stomach: the erotic banter between older men and younger boys. An underground tradition of erotic Plato literature had formed, advocating a modern version of such love. In 1630, an influential Venetian philosopher and teacher of rhetoric, Antonio Rocco, wrote an erotic response to Plato's *Symposium* entitled *The Young Alcibiades at School*.[11] In this text, a narrative mostly based on dialogic exchanges, Socrates eloquently convinces his young pupil of the pleasures of intercourse in a manner rich in parable and graphic in description. From Rocco a line extends to the Marquis de Sade, in whose play *Philosophy in the Boudoir* (1795) Socrates is

2.4.   Jean Delville, *The School of Plato* (1898). Musée d'Orsay, Paris,
France. Photo: Hervé Lewandowski/Art Resource, New York. Printed
with permission of the Artists Rights Association.

turned into a verb, "to socratize," describing anal intercourse.[12] Homoerotic circles, such as the ones that existed at the Oxford of Plato translator
Benjamin Jowett and Oscar Wilde in the late nineteenth century, but also
around the early twentieth-century German poet Stefan George (who was
an admirer of Wilde), frequently read or staged the *Symposium* for their
own pleasure. George even had a special room outfitted for these stagings.
The Belgian symbolist artist Jean Delville captured the homoerotic tradition of Plato in a painting called *The School of Plato* (1898), which portrays
muscular, nude students lounging in the grass around their teacher, whose
white robe and beard make him look strikingly similar to Jesus
(figure 2.4). The history of the Socrates play is part of a history of homosexuality.

In most cases, however, Socrates was deliberately and systematically
weaned of his love for young boys and turned into a heterosexual husband, however negligent he might have been in filling this role. During
Socrates' life, as one could learn from Diogenes Laertius, Athens had
encouraged its men to take more than one wife due to the shortage of
Athenian males at the end of the Peloponnesian War.[13] Many writers of
Socrates plays, especially those veering toward comedy, eagerly seized on
this opportunity. Indeed, giving Socrates two wives solved two problems
at once: it allowed for many dramatic possibilities, and it downplayed the
erotic dimension of Socrates' relation to his male pupils. In much the
same way, Socrates is often given female students as well.

The *Symposium* posed a particular problem. Aristophanes' speech,
with its myth of homosexual as well as heterosexual love, was mostly left
unchanged due to its prominence, but the erotic adulations of Alcibiades
were often cut or defanged through alteration or commentary. When Mary
Shelley published Percy Shelley's complete translation of the *Symposium*
in 1840, after her husband's death, she had to leave out Alcibiades and his
testimony about Socrates and their (chaste) night together; the full text
did not appear until 1931.[14] Another solution to the "Alcibiades problem"

2.5.   Jean Baptiste Regnault, *Socrates Dragging Alcibiades from the Breast of Voluptuous Pleasure* (1791). Louvre, Paris, France. Photo: Erich Lessing/Art Resource, New York.

was to turn Alcibiades into a womanizer. But this solution brings with it another set of problems. Socrates' influence, after all, was supposed to distract from sensual pleasures, or at least gradually abstract from them. Having Alcibiades enjoy himself with women is therefore not something that can be unconditionally endorsed, least of all by Socrates. It is for this reason, perhaps, that the painter Jean-Baptiste Regnault has "Socrates dragging Alcibiades from the breast of voluptuous pleasure," as the title of his 1797 painting has it (figure 2.5). In light of both Socrates' and Alcibiades' history, however, this act retains an ambiguity. Since the "voluptuous pleasure" from which Alcibiades is torn away is that afforded by women, one is left wondering whether Socrates necessarily disapproves of all forms of pleasure or only those involving the other sex.

Be this as it may, most plays—like most paintings—need to work hard to downplay anything smacking of homoeroticism. A television drama based on the *Symposium* produced in 1966 still censors Alcibiades' speech and even eliminates from Aristophanes' myth all references to same-sex love.[15] Only in the gender-bending 1990s did Aristophanes finally come into his own with the punk-rock transvestite musical *Hedwig and the Angry Inch*, whose song "The Origin of Love" is an inspired version of Aristophanes' speech.[16]

Equally thorny for many authors of Socrates plays from the eighteenth to the twentieth centuries was another dimension of Plato's dialogues: their open dismissal of democracy. Although critical of the tyranny of "the thirty," an oligarchy imposed on Athens by Sparta, Plato has Socrates be even more critical of the democracy that followed when the rule of the thirty was overturned. More unfortunate still for democratic adapters, it is not at the hands of the thirty that Socrates dies but at those of the reestablished democratic city-state. While some writers of Socrates plays have no qualms repeating Socrates' dismissal of the rule of the many, others struggle to turn Socrates into a political hero who can be redeemed for democracy. Often the solution is to accuse Plato of antidemocratic sentiments while presenting Socrates as a proto-democratic figure: thus the character is played off against the author on the presumption that it is possible to separate the historical Socrates from Plato's own agenda. (One of the consequences of my dramatic reading of Plato's dialogues is that such a separation is impossible: the Socrates in Plato's dialogues is not the historical Socrates but a fictional character, and we must credit Plato for his creation.)

Despite these difficulties, postrevolutionary American and French writers turn Socrates into a political rebel who stands up to all forms of tyranny, whether in the form of monarchy, oligarchy, or democracy. Collot's Socrates is a good example, an outspoken archenemy of aristocracy, a lone individual bravely opposing an oppressive state. In such presentations, Plato's antidemocratic political philosophy is simply ignored; to justify omitting this thorny issue, authors of Socrates plays often defend their decisions in prefaces or footnotes by claiming that antidemocratic speeches attributed to Socrates were in fact Plato's later inventions and had little to do with Socrates' own views of the matter. Nevertheless, some Enlightenment philosophers shied away from Socrates because of his association with the antidemocratic Plato and instead used other classical figures, such as Antigone, as projection screens for their revolutionary fantasies. But in general, Socrates was a central figure for Enlightenment philosophy, a position registered in an enthusiastic article on Socrates in the *Encyclopedia* (the article probably was penned by Diderot), in addition to a somewhat more ambivalent article on Platonism. At the same time, Rousseau used Socrates' bold stance against the status quo as inspiration against what he perceived to be the new dogmatism of Enlightenment thought. As an oppositional philosopher, Socrates thus proved to be remarkably malleable.

The political opinions of Plato were even more of a problem for Cold War writers, who tended to associate Sparta with the Soviet Union and Athens with the democratic West. In doing so, they had to face the problem that it was free and democratic Athens, not totalitarian Sparta, that chose to kill our nonconformist hero. They solved this problem by having Socrates refuse exile in Sparta, remaining a lover of Athens despite the city's violence against him. Maxwell Anderson's 1951 *Barefoot in Athens* was a typical creation of this sort, and notable because of its Broadway success, which was aided, perhaps, by the fact that the role of Xanthippe was played by Lotte Lenya, wife of Kurt Weill, the composer and erstwhile collaborator of Bertolt Brecht.[17] In Anderson's version, Sparta has defeated Athens, and the Spartan king, Pausanias, imposes a dictatorship by using the thirty as a proxy to impose his will on the city. Early on, Socrates is shown to be a political dissident against the new dictatorship of the thirty. So far, so good: Socrates is safely on the side of democracy.

But then things get complicated. Sparta withdraws and Athens returns to democracy. Socrates remains a political dissident and is declared an enemy of democracy, accused, and finally imprisoned. Like other writers since the French Enlightenment such as Collot, Anderson wants to preserve Socrates as a democratic subject. He tries to achieve this goal by presenting Socrates as the most ardent lover of Athens and Athenian democracy; so much, in fact, does Socrates love Athens that he prefers to die unjustly at its hands rather than seek refuge in undemocratic Sparta, which has offered him exile. Only in Athens, Socrates observes, can he be who he really is—a gadfly and dissident—even if he will die for it: Athens is freedom and Sparta dictatorship.

In the political terms of the early 1950s, *Barefoot in Athens* is a critique of McCarthyism and the restrictions on civil liberties in the United States of that era, but also an anti-Soviet play that does not want to use Socrates' trial as an argument on behalf of the Soviet Union. If there is a totalitarian in this cast of characters, it is not Socrates but Plato, as Anderson makes clear in his preface. Here Anderson is influenced by Karl Popper, whose 1945 classic *Open Society and Its Enemies* had presented Plato as a proto-totalitarian thinker.[18] While Plato becomes persona non grata, Socrates is all the more welcomed as the unruly gadfly who, while often critical of democracy, embodies the democratic spirit through his constant questioning of authority. This division between Socrates and Plato worked so well that a German-French contemporary of Anderson, Manès Sperber, used it for his own Socrates play written around the same time.[19] To his credit, there is an aspect of Anderson's play that betrays unease about this solution: Socrates gets along extremely well with Pausanias, the king of Sparta. The two become friends, and it is because of this friendship that Socrates escapes his enemies during the rule of the thirty and is offered exile in Sparta after Sparta's retreat. On the level of personal friendship, then, Anderson can acknowledge what his political agenda forbids him to face: that Plato's Socrates had spent a lot of time admiring the political system of Sparta and attacking that of Athens. The affinity of Socrates for Sparta is there, but only in such a way that Socrates can ultimately reject Pausanias and his offer and die in Athens, which he never ceases to love even in this, its darkest hour.

Authors of Socrates plays were drawn to Plato for political, religious, and erotic reasons, but also because they recognized Plato to be as much a playwright as a philosopher. More important, they tell a history of their own: how Plato became a dramatist. They knew that they were up against the most ingrained traditions of conventional drama and conventional philosophy, neither of which wanted to admit to the kind of convergence of the two that Plato had undertaken. Against the image of Plato as the philosophical enemy of theater, these authors insisted that Plato was a poet and playwright. In order to claim Plato as a poet, authors of Socrates plays had to contend with the fact that Plato famously had spoken of a long-standing quarrel between poetry and philosophy.[20] In response, they praised Plato's elaborate and beautiful myths, from the cave parable to the detailed creation of the world in the *Timaeus*, as the work of an inspired poet, in whose footsteps they were now following. To be sure, some Socrates plays conceive of the relation between poetry and philosophy in quite traditional terms. In 1731, George Stubbes, an aspiring writer, wrote a witty Socratic dialogue entitled *A Dialogue on Beauty in the Manner of Plato*, intended to win the patronage of the Duchess of Dorset.[21] Stubbes envisions as the primary advantage of this dramatic form that it would be "enlivening Philosophy with the Charms of Poesy."[22] He also claims that "nothing of this Kind has been attempted in our Language," demonstrating how fragmented and discontinuous the history of dramatic adaptations of Plato's dialogues really is, with few writers being able to draw on the experiments of their predecessors.

Others, however, had a more sophisticated understanding of the role of poetry in Plato's oeuvre, pointing to moments when Plato's Socrates admits to being a poet or else describes the project of philosophy in terms that resonate with poetry. Most famous is the scene toward the beginning of the *Phaedo* in which Socrates reports, to the astonishment of his friends, that he has been writing poetry himself: a hymn to Apollo as well as an adaptation of Aesop's fables into verse.[23] Francis Foster Barham (1808–1871) was one of the writers who drew on this passage when composing his drama. In many ways he was a typical author of a Socrates play. Not a member of the literary establishment, Barham was a lawyer working in London who spent all his free time obsessively reading, collecting, and later writing books. It is in his *Socrates: A Tragedy in Five Acts* (1842) that he elaborates on this passage. In response to Crito's astonished remark, "You talk / As if you were a poet," Socrates says: "So I am; / The true philosopher is the true poet."[24] He then goes on to tell his companions, who are visiting him in his prison cell, of the dream in which he has been told to compose poetry.

Other passages from Plato also served as inspiration for a poetic perspective on Socrates and Plato. In the *Phaedrus*, Socrates convinces his interlocutor that the greatest good is the madness inspired by love and that philosophy itself should participate in this madness.[25] While one might expect madness to be associated with prophecy or poetry, as Socrates acknowledges, here it becomes an attribute of philosophy as well. This conversation takes place while the two interlocutors are reclining in the shade among the trees outside Athens, a scene that is as unusual as a setting for a Socrates play as it is common for love literature.[26] It is not surprising that some writers of Socrates plays have been drawn to the *Phaedrus*, for example, the French modernist composer Erik Satie, whose work *Socrate* (1918), later adapted by John Cage, is based on the lush scenic description from the *Phaedrus* before it moves into a tragic mode by switching to passages taken from the *Phaedo*.[27]

By attending to Plato as a poet, these authors recover the full meaning of Plato's claim, made in his seventh letter, that philosophy is expressed not directly but in "veiled terms."[28] Neoplatonists had taken this declaration as an invitation to parse Plato's dialogues for hidden, mystical meaning. Plato's texts, they argued, may have overt meanings, but their true meaning is hidden, accessible only to initiates.[29] Where the Neoplatonists took Plato's statement as a license to look for coded meanings, authors of Socrates plays recognized in it an imperative to look at Plato's form: if Plato expressed himself indirectly, he did so by literary means.

Particularly perceptive with respect to Plato's relation to poetry is *The Death of Socrates* (1808), a play by Jacques-Henri Bernardin de Saint-Pierre. Bernardin led a remarkable life at a tumultuous time, which included the French Revolution and its Napoleonic aftermath. After serving in the army, he moved around in Eastern Europe, probably became a secret agent, and also worked on the Indian Ocean island of Mauritius. His literary career started with a travel book that caught the attention of Jean-Jacques Rousseau, with whom he struck up a literary friendship. Around the turn of the century, he rose to the highest ranks of the French literary world, becoming a professor of rhetoric at the École Normale Supérieure, then a member of the French Academy, and finally its president in 1807, exerting significant cultural influence on public affairs (by supporting Napoleon, for example).[30]

Like many authors of Socrates plays, Bernardin introduces Plato as a character in the play, something Plato himself had never done (in fact, Plato mentioned himself in only two dialogues, the *Phaedo* and the *Apology*).[31] When Socrates' death approaches, Plato tells Socrates that he owes him everything, since it was Socrates who made him give up poetry and embrace philosophy, referring, no doubt, to the opening scene from Diogenes Laertius' *Life* in which Plato burns his tragedy. Socrates, however, does not let this opposition between poetry and philosophy stand. Instead, he replies: "To each his own: one day you will be the Homer of the philosophers."[32] Among the many remarks made by authors of Socrates plays about Plato's relation to poetry, and indeed among the many literary interpretations of Plato as a poet, this formulation has always struck me as particularly insightful: Plato did not, in fact, give up poetry in order to become a philosopher, but he also did not continue writing poetry in the usual ways. Rather, he created a particular and unique position for himself as a poet among the philosophers, or a philosophical poet—the Homer of the philosophers.

Another group of authors saw Plato not only as a poet but specifically as a playwright. Here the cave parable, with its ominous shadow theater and the drama of ascent and descent, proved to be a particular inspiration. The cave parable is perhaps the most palpable way in which Plato's critique of theater burrowed its way deep into the heart of drama. Yes, Plato seeks to expose the theater as nothing other than a false world of shadows that must be abandoned for the real world above ground. But dramatists quickly figured out that Plato's parable was itself a brilliant piece of theatrical imagination—that the best form for denouncing the theater as nothing but a shadow world was indeed a theatrical one. The cave thus became the matrix for what the American critic Lionel Abel would later call metatheater, theater about theater.[33] Sometimes such metatheater is actually set in a darkened cave, as is the case with Pierre Corneille's *L'Illusion Comique* (1636), in which a father in search of his long-lost prodigal son visits the cavern of a magician, who proceeds to show him his son's life through theatrical magic.

Given how central the cave parable proved to be for Western drama, it is small wonder that some dramatists not only included scenes set in caves but also actually incorporated the cave parable itself into their dramas. One example is Howard Brenton's *Bloody Poetry* (1985), a play set among the British Romantics on Lake Geneva. Lord Byron, Mary and Percy Shelley, and their entourage decide to "do" the cave parable, that is, to perform it for their own amusement.[34] After some debate over roles—the overbearing Lord Byron is demoted to playing Glaucon, while Mary Shelley plays Socrates—they tie Byron's pedantic biographer, Polidori, to a chair, forcing him into the position of the prisoner. The distribution of roles is one problem, but the more interesting one is the theatrical setup of the entire scene. A chandelier is placed in the front of the stage, near the footlights, so that the actors' shadows are cast onto the backdrop of the stage; the chandelier, which stands in for the fire, is thus aligned with the footlights, and we, the audience, find ourselves in Plato's shadow cave. This play-within-a-play is followed by a series of interpretations in which Mary Shelley recognizes the gothic atmosphere of Plato's scenario and, anticipating her later novel *Frankenstein; or, The Modern Prometheus* (1818), imagines a shadow coming to life as a monster.

The most full-fledged staging of the cave parable occurred some years earlier, in a chamber opera by the British composer Alexander Goehr. *Shadowplay* (1970) features a narrator, a tenor who sings Socrates' description of the parable, taken more or less directly from Plato. The tenor is joined by an actor who plays the prisoner who leaves the cave, experiences the pain of light, and finally learns to behold the sun.[35] As a composer, Goehr is attuned to a dimension of the parable that is often neglected: the cave produces not only shadows but also the echo of voices. In the end, however, the primary dimension of the cave parable is that of sight, and the translation of sight into sound is among the many intriguing dimensions of this opera. The climax is a sunrise, captured in a musical interlude that proceeds by accelerating repetitions of five instruments: an alto flute, an alto saxophone, a horn, a cello, and a piano. The opera veers toward descriptive program music here, but not quite, since it is embedded in an intricate composition that asserts its own musical logic through several autonomous interludes, passages that are detached from the drama enacted in front of us. Significantly, Goehr not only uses a narrator but also lets the prisoner speak in his own voice. It is this choice that completes the translation of the cave parable into theater: we now follow the drama of sight by hearing the actor's report on his travails, pains, and joy of discovery. But Goehr does not end on a hopeful note: the piece concludes with the lights dimmed and the prisoner, now accustomed to the light, groping about blindly. The narrator takes over again and leaves us with the ominous speculation that if the prisoner returns to the cave, he will be ridiculed by his fellow prisoners and eventually—the opera ends with this word—killed.

Even when they did not engage the cave parable directly, writers of Socrates plays found other ways of appreciating Plato's engagement with theater and drama. Central here was the construction of Socrates as a character—one of the pillars of Plato's own dramaturgy. This interest in character dovetailed with the classical understanding of philosophy: what matters is not so much what Socrates says but what he does, the conduct of his life.[36] If philosophy is primarily a question of life and of acts, then drama is the perfect form for capturing this philosophy. The work that became central for this focus on Socrates as a character was the *Life of Socrates*, written in 1650 by François Charpentier, a French archeologist and man of letters. In this biographical work, which was translated into English in the early eighteenth century, Charpentier explains, in keeping with his emphasis on character, that "all the actions of his [Socrates'] life had . . . clearly discover'd what his Opinions were."[37] Here, too, the assumption that Plato revealed his true meaning not in direct statements but in his actions gave support to dramatists interested in turning this figure into a dramatic character.

Even though the writers of Socrates plays recognized Plato as a poet and dramatist, they did not follow Plato's complicated system of characterization. Plato may have focalized his philosophy through Socrates, but he also suggested, through role switching and abstraction, that philosophy could be undertaken by other people in other places. He personalized philosophy, but he also depersonalized it. In this way, he distinguished characters from ideas. These dramatists, by contrast, turned Socrates and all the other characters populating Plato's dialogues into full-fledged, stable characters thoroughly rooted in their everyday world. And so they were willing to augment Plato's account of Socrates with other sources, such as Diogenes Laertius' *Life* and the Socratic dialogues of Xenophon, which presented Socrates as exemplary, but also, and more important, as ordinary.

Equally interesting are the ways in which these authors treat other characters in the dialogues. Melitus and Anytus, the two accusers of Socrates, are given more elaborate roles, with many plays supplying personal motives. They are envious of Socrates, or in love with his daughter, or deceived, or scheming politicians out for their own reward. More important and interesting is the prominence of Socrates' wife, Xanthippe. Often she is given the role accorded to her by tradition (mostly a medieval tradition), namely, that of a shrew who drives Socrates into the streets and thus to philosophy because he cannot stand to be at home with her. At the same time, dramatists summon quite a bit of sympathy for Xanthippe and fashion her, for the first time, into a complex character; in fact, some of the writers almost side with her against her otherworldly, uncouth, and difficult husband. The reasons for this shift are interesting to contemplate. Of course there is the desire to lessen the misogynist characterization of Xanthippe. Also, dramatists have to invent rich contexts, settings, and personal interaction in addition to those already provided by Plato. This means almost invariably that Plato's balancing act between concrete, everyday detail and abstract idea is being skewed toward the everyday. And Xanthippe is precisely the person charged with the everyday, with running Socrates' life while he is out and about pursuing philosophy. In a way, these dramatists are in the same position as Xanthippe: they, too, have to chase after Socrates, taking care of the everyday life neglected in the dialogues. No wonder they become sympathetic to Xanthippe's plight.

Another figure who is accorded prominence in many Socrates plays is Alcibiades. Here the authors often draw on Plutarch's *Life of Alcibiades*, which describes the extraordinary path of this young Athenian from precocious youth and friend of Socrates to a military genius who finally betrays Athens and dies ingloriously in exile. A good number of Socrates plays use the two men as a pair of contrasting protagonists. While Socrates is the philosophical hero, Alcibiades is the dramatic one, providing his audience with good looks, high rank, adventurous daring, and the luster of the Athenian warrior and rogue. Sometimes the balance shifts toward Alcibiades altogether, and the Socrates play turns into an Alcibiades play, with Socrates as the contrasting minor character. This second role, however, often still serves to accentuate the relation between philosophy and politics, or philosophy and war.[38] In their use of Socrates as a foil for Alcibiades, these plays echo once more Plutarch's *Life of Alcibiades*, which opens with the assertion that Alcibiades became famous only because of his association with Socrates, thus foregrounding the fact that Athens' most famous—and notorious—son could not be adequately understood outside his early association with the eccentric philosopher.[39] Only rarely do we find Alcibiades without Socrates, one exception being *Alcibiades: A Tragedy* (1675) by the Restoration playwright Thomas Otway, in which Alcibiades is shown to be the victim of revenge.[40]

Be this as it may, just as the dramatists elaborate and embellish characters rather than follow Plato's attempt to contrast characters with ideas, so they emphasize dramatic action over philosophical argument. We get domestic interludes with Xanthippe, behind-the-scenes plotting and scheming by Anytus and Melitus, and dramatic conflicts with Alcibiades, such as when Alcibiades reports how Socrates saved him in battle.[41] This scene was taken up by many dramatists, including the modernists Georg Kaiser and Bertolt Brecht, and it also inspired visual artists, including Antonio Canova, who in 1797 created a relief based on this scene called *Socrates Saves Alcibiades at Potidea* (figure 2.6). Dramatists seized on the rare occasion of presenting Socrates as a war hero through a sequence that could claim its origin in Plato's oeuvre.

If the authors of Socrates plays can be distinguished from Plato himself in their handling of character, they can be distinguished even more clearly in their handling of genre. While Plato had used the available genres of his time as a foil against which to establish his own unique form of drama, many of the dramatists following him sought to assimilate Plato's dialogues to existing genres. There are instructional dialogues, meant as

2.6.   Antonio Canova, *Socrates Saves Alcibiades at Potidea* (1797).
Archivio Accademia San Luca.

teaching tools, and closet dramas, plays written without the intention of being performed. There are seventeenth- and eighteenth-century opere buffe, singspiels, and twentieth-century chamber operas. There are tragedies, comedies, tragicomedies, and philosophical plays of all kind. In assimilating Plato's unique dramatic form to the genres and tastes of their times, the authors of Socrates plays could be accused of diluting and even betraying Plato's peculiar dramaturgy. But Plato's dialogues themselves had borrowed freely from all available dramatic and nondramatic genres. This eclectic borrowing turned his plays into a veritable hodgepodge of styles, which laid the groundwork for the equally varied mixtures adopted by later authors of Socrates plays.

Despite the variety, two genres emerge as the most important touchstones for Socrates plays: tragedy and comedy. This is no surprise, since those two genres were the ones with and against which Plato himself had constructed his philosophical plays. It is therefore in relation to tragedy and to comedy that the contours of the Socrates play come most clearly into view.

The Death of Socrates

Tragedy is the most frequent genre used by authors of Socrates plays; a majority of those plays clearly identify themselves as tragedies, with titles such as *Death of Socrates: A Tragedy*. The trial, Socrates' defense, and his behavior in the face of death are the events routinely depicted in such plays (and echoed by painters devoted to the subject).[42] Even as these playwrights transformed Plato into whatever tragic modes were available to them, they encountered resistance: Plato had deliberately veered away from tragedy, repurposing the genre for his own ends. Thus ensued a generic struggle that all authors of Socrates plays had to face. In a sense, these Socrates tragedies provide us with a short history of tragedy, the dramatic genre that has been the most revered and therefore the most hotly debated since antiquity. In particular, they throw into relief the struggle between different forms of tragedy, chiefly the distinction between the more freewheeling Renaissance tragedy most closely associated with Shakespeare, which mixed tragic and comic elements and otherwise blithely ignored just about every Aristotelian rule, and various attempts at classicist or neoclassicist tragedies, attempts to return tragedy to its Greek origin. At the same time, these tragic renderings were also engaged in an uphill struggle. Plato had toyed with the figure of the tragic hero but ultimately opted to turn Socrates into an antitragic protagonist, combining features of comedy and tragedy. Tragic authors had to ignore this mixture or else assimilate their conception of tragedy to the hybrid form created by Plato.

In trying to adapt Plato's dialogues to changing conceptions of theater, these authors often emphasized Plato's theatrical context, which Diogenes Laertius and other Greek commentators had alluded to in their discussions of Socrates and Plato. Here, too, dramatists proved to be more astute readers of Plato than many philosophers and philologists, who usually ignored this theatrical context. An example of this interest in Plato's relation to the theater is John Gilbert Cooper, the author of an influential biography of Socrates, who repeats and underlines Diogenes Laertius' claim that Socrates had a hand in the tragedies of Euripides.[43] Many authors show Socrates spending time with the tragedian Agathon, whom Socrates encounters in Plato's *Symposium*, as well as with Euripides.

One of the earliest Socrates tragedies was by the translator, writer, and minister George Adams, *The Heathen Martyr: or, the Death of Socrates, An Historical Tragedy. In which is shewn, That the Plague which infested the People of Athens was stay'd by the Destruction of the Enemies of that Divine Philosopher* (1746).[44] His approach to Socrates was via Greek tragedy, especially Sophocles. Adams was the first to offer a complete prose translation of Sophocles' seven extant tragedies "with notes historical, moral, and critical" (1729), a translation that sought to benefit learners of Greek but that was also attacked (by another translator, of course) for violating the beauty of Sophocles' poetry.[45] Adams attempts to turn Socrates into a tragic hero. The first three of the play's five acts are unsurprising. The play opens with Critias and Lysias talking about Socrates and Athens when they hear that Socrates has been accused and that his death has been sought but not yet pronounced. In various ways, Socrates' friends try to dissuade Socrates' accusers, who won't give in, and during the trial Socrates refuses to give the speech his friends have prepared for him and instead delivers the speech we know from Plato's *Apology*. Plato, who is a character in the play, and other students plead on Socrates' behalf, but to no avail. Socrates is imprisoned (we are now in the third act) and refuses the escape plot arranged by Crito; Xanthippe comes, cries, and is sent away. Socrates dies foretelling Plato's fame and demanding that his doctrines be "planted" in his blood.[46] He is a martyr of philosophy.

Such an ending, which favors the future of philosophy over the tragic fate of one of its practitioners, was more than Adams could endure. And so he added two more acts of properly tragic material; it is in those two acts that his immersion in Sophocles' tragedies, in particular *King Oedipus*, becomes visible. After Socrates has been executed, a plague befalls Athens, just like the one that wrecks Thebes in *King Oedipus* (but also like the plague that befalls Athens during the Peloponnesian War, as famously described in Thucydides' history). As in Sophocles' play, Athens consults the oracle at Delphi only to get the reply that there has been "innocent blood in Athens lately shed."[47] The plague is punishment for this crime, and the only question now is who the culprit is. At this point, Adams shifts into a different mode and, with a nod to *Hamlet*, introduces a play-within-the-play. It is the latest play of Euripides that is being performed in order to distract the court from the misery of the plague. But distraction is not what they get in their time of trouble, for the play happens to fit the situation in Athens all too well: it's a mousetrap. Euripides' play-within-the-play represents Nauplius, a Greek who had forced Ulysses to participate in the Trojan War against his will, and whom Ulysses later wrongly accused in order to get his revenge, causing Nauplius to be unjustly stoned to death. In other words, the play is about false accusation. Like Claudius in *Hamlet*, King Theseus of Athens quickly gets the reference: "That Line, 'tis plain, relates to *Socrates*," he shouts.[48] Thus his conscience is caught and he must admit that he had presided over an unjust trial and execution. For those who are still in doubt, Euripides, who is in attendance at the performance, spells it out: "'Tis well, my Lords, now that you've sadly felt / Such sad Calamities, you seek the Cause: / 'Tis well that sad Experience makes you believe / What you before would not believe was true. / You put to Death the guiltless *Socrates*: / Therefore the righteous Gods thus visit you / With Multiplicity of diverse Plagues."[49] Now that the true cause of the plague has been presented both by the oracle and by Euripides, the tide turns and the accusers become the accused. Themselves threatened with death, they act quite differently than Socrates did: they are not philosophers. Anytus falls ingloriously, Melitus and Prophirius fight with each other, and they all find their various unseemly deaths. Theseus concludes the play with the summary: "We now have done all that is in our Power / T'avenge the guiltless Blood of *Socrates*."[50] The excising of the guilty party, however, is presented not as a religious purification driven by a divine oracle, as in *King Oedipus*, but as a matter of revenge visited on Socrates' accusers, as in *Hamlet* and the tradition of revenge tragedy on which it is based.

Ancient Greek and Shakespearean tragedy continued to be the two main models for British writers of Socrates plays. In 1806 the dramatist, poet, and librarian Andrew Becket published *Socrates: A Dramatic Poem*, subtitled *Written on the Model of the Ancient Greek Tragedy*.[51] Becket, too, was a relatively unknown writer. The son of a bookseller, he was in training to follow in his father's footsteps when he was inspired to become a writer himself. He did not earn a living by his pen but managed to make ends meet when David Garrick, the famous actor and producer, arranged for him to work as assistant librarian for the Prince of Wales.[52] In addition to his *Socrates*, Becket composed a number of literary works, including several works on Shakespeare, among them a concordance and a work on Shakespeare's language. In the preface to his *Socrates*, Becket takes part in the debate about the value of Shakespeare's language, defending Shakespeare against those who attacked him for his irregularity and his violation of Aristotelian rules. In defending Shakespeare, Becket revealed why he would be quick to appreciate Plato as a dramatist. Like Shakespeare, Plato had freely mixed the various genres of the time, including tragedy and comedy.

Like so many of his colleagues, Becket claims that he knows of no other dramatization of Socrates and that he must invent the form from scratch.[53] Despite this false claim (innocently made, no doubt, given the obscurity of the other Socrates plays), his play shows interesting similarities to and differences from several others. In contrast to Adams's play, Becket's begins in prison, with Socrates rejecting the escape plan. Where Adams focuses on revenge and the purging of Athens, Becket sets his play, which is an intensely moralizing one, in a different register: temptation, specifically, the temptation to escape. Like many other Socrates plays, this one goes out of its way to Christianize Socrates and to present him as a prefiguration of Christ, with Socrates declaring "that the Deity I so fervently adore, / Has not been nam'd."[54] Becket adds another component: pressure is exerted on Socrates to disclose the whereabouts of Alcibiades, who has fallen into disrepute. But the main innovation, in terms of plot, is a third temptation. Like many other authors of Socrates plays, Becket works hard to provide Socrates' accuser Melitus with a motive. And again, as so many authors do, Becket chooses a love interest. Socrates has a daughter, Chelonis, with whom Melitus is in love. The question of what Chelonis will do is the true dramatic conflict in the play. Even at the moment of highest tension, after Socrates has been declared guilty and the only remaining question is the severity of the punishment, Melitus offers to have the sentence converted to a nominal fine if Socrates will give him Chelonis in marriage. The offer is rejected and Socrates is condemned; Chelonis dies of grief when she learns that Socrates will be executed. But after turning his Socrates play into a morality tale, Becket cannot quite do without a bit of revenge after all. In the end, Socrates' supporters kill Melitus and Anitus (Anytus), even though—and this is important— Socrates tries to hold them back and bids them to abide by the laws. Becket gives his audience the revenge it wants while also saying that the philosophical principle defended here is set against such a base emotion.

Becket's play is Christianized, but it is also, as the subtitle promises, made classical. This is mainly achieved by means of the dramatic element most closely associated with Greek tragedy, the chorus, here composed of Socrates' students and friends. Plato's own dialogues had studiously avoided the Greek chorus, along with so many other features of Greek theater. Everywhere Socrates dislikes collective judgments and large crowds; most important, he feared "theatrocracy," the rule of the audience. And since the chorus, often representing the citizens or a portion thereof, is the stand-in for the audience, it is safe to conclude that Plato disliked the chorus as well and deliberately forged a drama that made no use of it. Instead, Plato favored participants who would take turns speaking and listening. Yet the *Phaedo* is the dialogue that comes closest to presenting something like a chorus. Socrates often addresses his assembled friends collectively, chiding them for crying and for not celebrating his impending death as a liberation of the soul from the prison of the body. They all react the same way, and in the end they are passive onlookers rather than active participants in this unusual dialogue.

Becket's dramatic model is a composite of a Christian morality play based on temptation and Greek tragedy. For Becket, this combination adds up to a single name and model: John Milton. As Becket states in his preface, his own tragedy is an imitation of Milton's *Samson Agonistes*.[55] In that work Milton had attempted to return to Greek tragedy and defended his choice on aesthetic and moral grounds. At the same time, Milton showed that a return to Greek tragedy was compatible with a mode of poetry immersed in Christian theology and moral thought. This was just the combination Becket was looking for. While Adams had written a revenge tragedy combining Sophocles and Shakespeare, Becket wrote a Miltonian tragedy of temptation. Milton's *Samson Agonistes* was also the best example of a classicist tragedy as closet drama. Becket was under no illusions that his Socrates play would ever be performed (and indeed, to the best of my knowledge, it never has been). Becket called his play a "poetical performance," sounding almost like a late twentieth-century theorist of textual performance.[56] While not written for the stage, his work was fully theatrical, aiming at the imagination of the reader in the manner of Milton. In a sense, Milton and Becket here continue Plato's own worries about large audiences and cast Plato retrospectively as the precursor of the modern closet drama, which is to be read rather than staged in front of large audiences.

When they did want to bring Socrates onto the stage, however, most writers of Socrates plays worried about whether Socrates was a sufficiently theatrical character. This worry went right to the heart of Plato's own dramatic project: to reform the theatrical system of Athens by confronting it with an entirely new protagonist and an entirely new type of drama. Many of Plato's dramatic adapters were caught between the demands of the existing theatrical system and Plato's legacy. One of them, Louis Billardon de Sauvigny, a dramatist associated with the French Enlightenment, wrote in a variety of genres, including opera, comedy, and vaudeville, but above all bombastic tragedy. Like many Enlightenment writers, Sauvigny was an admirer of the early Republic and would go on to compose a tragedy celebrating the American Revolution in a play called *Vashington* [sic], *ou, La Liberté du nouveau monde* (1791).

When turning to Socrates as his subject matter, he immediately felt the need to apologize for his choice of protagonist. First, he claims that he never expected his tragedy to be performed in the first place, sounding like Milton or Becket. Then, however, he switches from defense to offense: "Many claim that this subject [Socrates] is not sufficiently theatrical. I believe that this is more the fault of the work than of the subject, which can incite fear and pity."[57] Invoking Aristotle's definition of tragedy as inciting fear and pity, Sauvigny shores up the tragic credentials of his subject. But he also admits that he had to make certain changes to the material. The first was that he could not always stick to the sources, obeying the acknowledged principle that history has to be sacrificed to "theatrical effect." Despite these changes, Sauvigny claims to have stayed close to Plato. He describes his play's relation to Plato in an intriguing formulation: "My lack of experience in theater made me risk many things excellent in Plato, but out of place [*déplacées*] in a tragedy." Sauvigny found himself mediating between the theater and Plato, who himself might be said to have "displaced" theater. Sauvigny recognized the affinity of Plato to the theater, but also the differences. His own attempt to write a Socrates play made it necessary to return to the theater, to place Socrates on the stage from which Plato had originally wrested him. Sauvigny's strategy worked. Unlike Becket's closet drama, his Socrates play made it to the stage, and to one of the important stages of Paris at that: it premiered at the Théâtre François in May 1763.

The anonymous Italian author of the tragedy *Socrate* (1796) also recognizes the particular requirements necessary for bringing onto the stage a character whom he identifies as "philosophy personified," and he admits that the result was a "new path" in the theater.[58] But he, too, insists on the necessity of treating Socrates in the tragic mode. In fact, he considers his own tragedy to be a late response to Aristophanes' *Clouds*. Like Plato in the *Apology*, he feels that Aristophanes disgraced Socrates in making him the protagonist of a comedy, and ends his preface with the following address: "Socrates, if only you were still alive! You already had the displeasure of seeing yourself being dragged onto the stage by an insolent comedian. Now you would see your apotheosis by the phoenix of the tragic authors."[59] For this author there is a direct battle between the comedians and the tragedians over Socrates' legacy. First came irreverent comedy, but now, finally, Socrates is being redeemed by tragedy.

Both Sauvigny and the anonymous Italian wrote their Socrates tragedies in the shadow of the single most famous author of such a play: Voltaire. Voltaire's name in the history of the Socrates play is particularly significant since his oeuvre spans the gamut from literature to philosophy. His *Candide* (1759) is perhaps the most famous work of literature devoted to refuting a philosophical position, Leibniz's doctrine that we live in the best of all possible worlds. Several of Voltaire's dramatic works are infused with Enlightenment positions and philosophy, including the play *Mohammed* (1741), where he uses the founder of Islam as a stand-in for all religious doctrines, which are denounced as opium for the masses. It is difficult to find, in the English-speaking world, a figure with equal dramatic facility and an equal determination to infuse drama with thought. The closest relative of Voltaire is perhaps George Bernard Shaw, who will appear in the next chapter, although Shaw, while sharing Voltaire's passion for propaganda, did not share his philosophical precision and originality.

It is not surprising that Voltaire would have been drawn to Plato's dramatic dialogues and to their main protagonist, Socrates. Although his *Socrates: A Tragedy in Three Acts* (1759) is not among his most well-known works, it exerted significant influence on a number of authors of Socrates plays, including the anonymous Italian author, who admits to following Voltaire's model. This author may be following Voltaire in another way as well, namely, by concealing himself and claiming to have found the manuscript of *Socrate* without revealing the identity of the author. In the preface to the first edition of his Socrates play, Voltaire had claimed to be merely the translator of the play, which allegedly had been penned by the playwright James Thomson (*Candide* was also published anonymously).[60]

All writers of Socrates plays have to contend with the problems already discussed with respect to Adams, Becket, and Sauvigny: the decision to write a Socrates tragedy implies a return to classical tragedy. However, the death of Socrates, as conceived of by Plato, violates Greek tragedy. It has no chorus; Socrates instructs his friends not to experience fear and pity; and Socrates' relatively low social status, emphasizing the importance of everyday life in contemporary Athens, is irreconcilable with the high style of Greek tragedy. For French and English writers of the seventeenth and eighteenth centuries, this tension can be expressed in competing, contemporary models of tragedy: on one hand is the classicist tragedy of Racine, Corneille, and Milton, and on the other hand is Shakespeare, with his irreverent mixture of high and low and his willingness to introduce comic characters into his tragedy.[61]

Voltaire, like most authors of Socrates plays, found himself in a position of having to mediate between those two traditions, Shakespearean and neoclassical. His biography helped, since he had spent more than three years in England in exile, bringing back a nuanced understanding of English tragedy, in particular of Shakespeare. In his *Letters Concerning the English Nation* (1733), an influential conduit for English political thought, philosophy, and culture to France, Voltaire writes: "Shakespeare boasted a strong fruitful genius. He was natural and sublime, but had not so much as a single spark of good taste, or knew one rule of the drama."[62] This sentiment is common: it acknowledges Shakespeare's genius but chides him for violating the classical (Aristotelian) rules on which the French tradition, exemplified by Racine, prided itself.

Voltaire had frequently returned to classical subjects, both Roman (with his tragedies *Brutus* and *The Death of Caesar*) and Greek (with *Oedipus*). When he tried his hand at Socrates, however, he clearly felt that such a subject could not be dealt with within the strictures of classical tragedy. What it required, instead, was precisely Shakespeare's unruly mixture. In his preface, Voltaire says as much. His fiction of the English writer James Thomson as the author is introduced so that Voltaire can present his own play as a Shakespearean tragedy. Thomson, he claims, undertook this Socrates tragedy (in the language of the first translation into English) to "renew the method of Shakespear, by introducing into the tragedy characters from among the people." This meant to "make this piece into one of those naive representations of human life, one of those pictures that include all walks of life." Introducing "the people" into a tragedy requires a Shakespearean approach, one that Voltaire associates with the "naive" genius of Shakespeare, a characterization that sounds more patronizing today than it did in the vocabulary of the time. Voltaire is also among those who recognize the significance of Xanthippe as a character in capturing the relation between tragedy and everyday life: "He [Thomson] painted Xantippe, Socrates' wife, as in fact she was, a bourgeois shrew, always scolding her husband, yet fond of him."[63] Voltaire's cunning strategy, attributing his most Shakespearean drama to an English author, was not lost on his contemporaries—especially the English ones. Only one year after the publication of the (putatively translated) French original, an English translation appeared whose author sets the matter of the play's authorship straight. He attributes the play to Voltaire and gives as the probable reason for Voltaire's shenanigans his debt to the English style: "It is not improbable, that in this case, he might think the licence and irregularity of the *English* theatre, might authorize so singular a kind of Drama as this."[64] The translator, too, recognizes the generic entanglements of a play based on Socrates. Elevated classical tragedy cannot serve as a model for such a "singular" play; only the irregularity of Shakespeare can.

There is one problem with this attempt to authorize Socrates plays with reference to Shakespeare: Shakespeare never wrote anything close to a play based on a philosopher (even though *Hamlet* was sometimes turned into one)—and for good reason, some might add. Once he came close to writing such a play, with *Timon of Athens* (1605), which features both Alcibiades and a philosopher. This philosopher, a comic figure who keeps expressing his disgust with the world, is not Socrates but someone closer to the cynic Diogenes (not to be confused with the biographer Diogenes Laertius), although the cynics, like other ancient schools that reject the world, are ultimately derived from partial interpretations of Socrates. I admit that I have always read *Timon* with some regret: somehow Shakespeare came within striking distance of writing a Socrates play, but instead wrote a play in which a philosophical relative of Socrates is contrasted with Socrates' friend Alcibiades.[65]

What the writers of the eighteenth century needed, in any case, was a more contemporary model for bringing the philosopher Socrates and his entourage onto the tragic stage. Fortunately, there was such an author and such a play: Joseph Addison and his immensely popular *Cato* (1713). With this play, Addison attempted to reorient English tragedy away from the revival of Shakespeare promoted by such writers as Thomas Otway and more toward classicism. He thus insisted on the importance of reason, order, and form. At the same time, Addison was by no means a blind follower of French classicism. Indeed, one of his primary influences was none other than Milton, to whom he devoted many pages of literary criticism. Addison could be described as an eclectic author with strong classicist leanings. He was, for example, the translator of Virgil's *Georgics*, which was an influential text for the early eighteenth-century classical revival. This flexible classicism made him a touchstone for a new, non-Shakespearean English style, a classicized Shakespeare. Dr. Johnson conceded: "Whoever wishes to attain an English style, familiar but not coarse, and elegant but not ostentatious, must give his days and nights to the study of Addison."[66]

Addison's fascination with Roman antiquity made him turn to Cato, the Roman senator who kills himself rather than submit to the tyranny of Caesar. It is a subject without much inherent drama, devoted instead to the character and the philosophy of the patriotic Roman who is ready to die for his beliefs. Even when Cato addresses his soldiers in a last-ditch attempt to rouse them to fight, philosophy is never far from his mind. His enemy, Sempronius, calls Cato's speech derisively, though not inaccurately, a "Medly of Philosophy and War."[67] The philosophy that Cato espouses is none other than that of Plato. Toward the end of the play, we see him read Plato's *Phaedo* before deciding to follow Socrates and commit suicide. Alexander Pope, who added a prologue to the play, also emphasizes the affinity between Socrates and Cato: "Virtue confess'd in human Shape he draws, / What Plato thought, and God-like Cato was." In his *Letters Concerning the English Nation*, Voltaire praises Addison's *Cato* as a "masterpiece" and writes that Cato was the "greatest character that was ever brought upon any stage."[68] The comparison between (Addison's) Cato and Socrates was quite well established. Jean-Jacques Rousseau's unpublished manuscripts, for example, include a sketch for a comparison between the two moral heroes.[69] If there was need for a model that combined Milton with a more expansive, if not outright Shakespearean, notion of tragedy, Addison's *Cato* fit the bill. Apparently, Addison had even thought about writing a play on Socrates before he decided on the Roman hero instead.[70]

The fascination with Addison's *Cato*, with its heroic speeches on patriotism and resistance to tyranny, was particularly strong in the North American colonies. Benjamin Franklin used a passage from *Cato* for the first page motto of his *Virtue Book*; George Washington had *Cato* performed for the Continental army while encamped at Valley Forge; and many revolutionary texts, phrases, and bon mots can be traced back to Addison's *Cato*, which was widely performed before, during, and after the Revolutionary War, including by Walter Murray and Thomas Kean's important acting company during the 1749–50 season.[71] Patrick Henry's "Give me liberty, or give me death" comes from *Cato,* as does Nathan Hale's "I regret that I have but one life to lose for my country." *Cato* quickly became a revolutionary classic par excellence.

Given the play's significance in North America, it is perhaps not surprising that an early play written in the American colonies was indeed a Socrates play: *The Death of Socrates,* by Thomas Cradock. An Anglican minister at St. Thomas' Parish in western Baltimore, Thomas Cradock is primarily known for his sermons, although he wrote rather extensive poetry, ranging from devotional poetry to the *Maryland Eclogues,* modeled, in the taste of the time, on Virgil. Cradock also mingled with the lively literary scene in the Chesapeake Bay area, including the "Baltimore Bards."[72] Addison would finally inspire Cradock to write a play based on Socrates, but Socrates and Plato had been on Cradock's mind for some time. Like so many devout admirers of the pre-Christian classical world, he took pains to Christianize them both. In 1753, he even declared that both Socrates and Plato, had they had the choice, would have been Christians, indeed Anglicans.[73] It is in this spirit that Cradock approached the life of Socrates. His main innovation is the introduction of a young woman, Agape, a follower of Socrates and, to add dramatic tension, the sister of Melitus, one of Socrates' accusers. It is through Agape that Cradock presents the doctrine of (heterosexual) Platonic love: Agape is scolding Phaedon, who is in love with her, to take to heart the message of moderation propounded by their teacher. The original instigator of the trial, a footnote helpfully explains, is Anytus, who did not want to kill Socrates but who honestly believed Socrates to be a danger to the populace and therefore wanted him exiled. Unfortunately, Anytus enlisted Melitus, who turned out to be, as another footnote explains, a "religious fanatic."[74] One might see in Melitus a kind of radical Puritan of the kind Cradock and the Anglican Church more generally feared and dismissed in the sister colonies of New England. Socrates thus becomes many things at once: a political hero who, like the Cato beloved by independence-minded colonists, stands up to tyranny; a proto-Christian (and proto-Anglican) in his belief in the authority of the state and his rejection of religious fanaticism (Puritanism); and finally a proponent of moderation and abstinence in matters of love.

The set of dilemmas and formulas used by writers of Socrates plays in the seventeenth and eighteenth centuries—Greek tragedy plus Shakespeare, Milton and/or Addison—proved surprisingly influential even in the nineteenth century. One example is Francis Foster Barham (1808–1871). He was another isolated writer and thinker with an intensely personal philosophy and religious sense that led him to formulate his own version of transcendentalism, a reconciliation of religious, philosophical, and natural truths. For a time, he added to his name the title "Alist," to mark his own peculiar faith, which also included sexual abstinence and asceticism. Although he broke his vow of chastity at age thirty-six, he remained devoted to his faith and kept working on a large number of unfinished projects, including translations of the Hebrew Bible and the New Testament. When he died of a heart attack, he left 116 pounds of manuscript in minuscule handwriting on such varied topics as pacifism, vegetarianism, and animal welfare, in addition to philosophical and theological treatises, poems, and plays.[75]

Barham's *Socrates: A Tragedy in Five Acts* (1842) is in many ways representative of the nineteenth-century Socrates tragedy. It is introduced with an epigraph from Milton; it rejects French classicist tragedy as unsuitable to Plato; and it settles on Shakespeare as the model of tragedy that offers the greatest flexibility and that might encompass as idiosyncratic a tragic hero as Socrates. Barham is also aware of some episodes in the history of the Socrates play, or at least one of its original sources, Charpentier's *Life of Socrates*.[76] For the most part, though, Barham advocates for a revival of Greek tragedy. Like so many of his predecessors, he had been rejected by the theaters of his time. But unlike other writers of closet dramas, he did not want to cede the theater to the fashion of the day and insisted that his tragedy was written to be performed—if only the theater would have it. Barham knew that the middle of the nineteenth century was a moment in theater history when there was especially little space for serious drama. New stage machinery, the developments of sensationalist melodramas, and other changes had led to a withering away of serious drama, pushing it in the direction of the closet or reading drama. Theaters had been significantly enlarged and needed to draw larger, often less discriminating crowds. Despite all this, however, Barham did not give up hope. He sensed that things could not go on in the same manner and felt that the theater was ripe for a change, declaring that "a new dramatic era is dawning on us."[77] This era would witness the revival of ancient Greek tragedy, he predicted, and his Socrates play would be a contribution to that revival, "a feeler of the public taste."[78] It should be added that at the time of Barham's writing, performances of Greek tragedy were relatively rare and became staples of the stage only in the twentieth century through efforts such as his.

These framing statements are borne out in Barham's actual play. His dedication to the theater is registered in the fact that he foregrounds everywhere Socrates' close relation to contemporary theater. We encounter Sophocles, Euripides, and Aristophanes and their respective rivalries, including Aristophanes' decision to write a play satirizing Socrates. Euripides tries to keep Socrates out of it but does not prevail. It turns out that Aristophanes used to love Socrates, a love that has now turned to hate. As a tragedian, Barham has the tragedian Euripides side with Socrates against the comedian Aristophanes. Only Euripides and Plato remain Socrates' valiant supporters to the end, though unable to prevent his death.

For all his insistence on the renewal of Greek theater, Barham was a child of his time, and he therefore includes many spectacular elements in his Socrates play. In particular, Barham leaves no opportunity untouched for mythical, ritualistic, mysterious, and supernatural scenes. He seizes on the fact that the oracle had uttered the ominous sentence that no one is wiser than Socrates, and he includes an elaborate scene in Pythia's cave (perhaps another reference to Plato's cave parable) depicting the seer's ecstasy. Socrates' daemon, the figure that allegedly tells him what to do, makes an apparition in the manner of Hamlet's father's ghost. There is a symposium, but it takes place at the house of Aspasia, the glamorous mistress of Pericles, with the jealous Xanthippe in attendance. Of course we also see Socrates in battle, saving Alcibiades. The ghost reappears at an opportune moment to foretell Socrates' future, and this after a wizard and a witch have already warned him of his fate. Even more far-fetched is a scene in which Socrates is initiated into a secret lodge, a kind of Freemasonry devoted to monotheism in the manner of Mozart's *Magic Flute*. Barham, in other words, pulls out all the stops, seeking to satisfy the tastes of the audience. Clearly, he did not agree with his predecessors who worried about the lack of theatricality contained in Plato's dialogues. Barham saw theatrical potential wherever he looked, and when he did not find it, he simply added it without qualms. Barham was right that mid-nineteenth-century theater was ripe for a renewal. But this assessment also applies to his own play: his *Socrates* was a symptom of, not a solution to, the problem of serious drama on a popular stage.

In the long run, however, Barham turned out to be right. A new drama emerged, and at the same time the revival of Greek tragedy became a reality. Both of these developments helped shape what is now called modern drama, as I will detail in the following chapter. Barham was also right that the Socrates play, and the theatrical vision of Plato as a dramatist implied therein, was somehow going to be part of this modern drama. For the fact is that modern drama significantly changed and enlarged the conception of drama, including tragedy. As a consequence, the twentieth century saw a steep rise in the number of Socrates plays. At the same time, it also saw a significant explosion of other dramatic genres. These two developments were linked because Socrates had never been a good fit for tragedy, no matter of what kind. Socrates plays were too unusual, too idiosyncratic, too intent on mixing tragedy with other genres, in particular comedy. Indeed alongside the dominant tradition of Socrates tragedies there had emerged a second tradition of Socrates comedies.

The Comic Stage Philosopher

A second group of authors recognized Plato as a dramatist, but one in a comic mode. These writers acknowledged what the tragedians did not want to admit: that Plato's dialogues veered at least as much toward comedy as toward tragedy, despite the overwhelming significance of Socrates' death. In fact, Plato had employed comedy precisely in order to cast Socrates' death in a nontragic manner, to ensure that what might be a scene of tragedy was instead a scene of philosophy. For this reason, much in Plato's dialogues points toward comedy: Socrates' relatively low social status; the significance of everyday life, including clothes, shoes, and habits of eating, drinking, and sleeping; the attention paid to hygiene; the more general importance of material facts of life; and finally the constant interest in matters of love. All this meant that Plato could be seen as an odd type of comedian.

There was one problem, though, that many comic adapters encountered in their attempt to continue Plato's legacy of philosophical comedy: Aristophanes. In the *Apology*, Plato has Socrates accuse Aristophanes of having contributed to the popular resentment against him, although later dialogues, such as the *Symposium*, depict Aristophanes as a friend of Socrates and show little sign of animosity between them. But even if one does not place Aristophanes in the camp of Socrates' accusers, the fact remains that *Clouds* portrays Socrates in an unflattering light. Or rather, it portrays Socrates as what I call a "comic stage philosopher." Such philosophers abound in comic drama. There is a line of descent from Aristophanes to the *dottore*, or doctor, in the Italian commedia dell'arte: hailing from Bologna, the seat of the oldest university, the *dottore* is a quintessential comic professor, using his abstract knowledge for personal gain of all sorts, mostly to no avail. Goldoni, who turned commedia dell'arte into a literary form, contributed *The Country Philosopher* (1754) to this tradition. The Marquis de Sade, even though he sought to integrate philosophy and drama in such plays as *Philosophy in the Boudoir* (1795), could not resist the temptation of writing a play based on the comic stage philosopher. *The Self-Proclaimed Philosopher* (1772) portrays a would-be philosopher who uses his status only to pursue his female pupils. When he is cruelly exposed by the end of the play, he concludes, with remorse: "O Socrates, O Plato! What has become of your disciples!"[79] But in a way, this philosopher is not so different from Socrates, at least as he is rendered in the comic tradition of the stage philosopher.

For comedies of almost any type or variety, philosophers proved a compelling target because their focus on metaphysics and abstract ideas could be contrasted, to comic effect, with the everyday reality of their lives. Many practitioners and theorists of comedy, from Aristophanes to Bergson, have used the collision of idea and matter as a quintessential comic technique. Nothing is more comic, they hold, than a character who pursues ideas and thereby disregards everyday life. In the case of *Clouds*, Aristophanes not only uses the collision of the metaphysical with the physical but also shows that the search for the metaphysical is imbued with worldly interests. Unlike Plato's Socrates, Aristophanes' Socrates takes money for his instruction, just as his students are driven to the study of philosophy in order to make a quick profit. Lofty ideas are brought down from the clouds.

Even though this portrayal of Socrates seems quite different from the one offered by Plato, the two are in fact much closer than one might think. True, the profit interest is being rejected, again and again, in Plato's dialogues. What remains the same, however, is the insistence on Socrates' disheveled looks, the fact that his life, clothes, and habits differ from the social norms of his class and therefore become an object of laughter. Even in Plato, his friends always laugh at Socrates despite the fact that they are also in awe of his intellect. In Plato, Socrates is still a comic stage philosopher, albeit one with a serious philosophical purpose.

Given the overwhelming prominence in Aristophanes for the comic tradition (which he is often seen as inaugurating), the comic playwrights seeking to follow Plato had to come to terms with Aristophanes whether they wanted to or not. But whereas the tragic playwrights wrote their plays in direct rebuttal of Aristophanes' comic slander, the comic writers had a more ambiguous relation to Aristophanes and his portrayal of Socrates. Should they acknowledge him as the inventor of the comic Socrates play and then somehow argue that Socrates' accusation in the *Apology* is wrong, or should they omit the accusation quietly and not draw attention to the fact that their own comic versions owe a debt to the comic writer? Robert Walter, in his early twentieth-century comedy *The Great Art of Midwifery* (1927), for example, turns Aristophanes' *Clouds* into an important plot element.[80] At the beginning of the play we see Aristophanes write *Clouds* and witness its popular success. Mischievously, Aristophanes even credits Socrates with having saved his career by being such a perfect subject matter for comedy. When it comes to the trial, however, Aristophanes does not play along with Socrates' enemies: he wants to give Socrates money for his defense, and during the trial he speaks out on Socrates' behalf and even becomes part of the group of friends in Socrates' prison cell. Walter, in other words, wants to rebut the accusation, launched by Plato in the *Apology*, that Aristophanes contributed to the sentiments against Socrates. Or rather, he shows that there is a world of difference between Socrates' hateful accusers and Aristophanes, who simply recognized Socrates as a figure particularly well suited to comedy.

A number of writers of Socrates plays likewise have Aristophanes regret the slanderous effects of *Clouds* or repudiate the play entirely. The American writer Charles Wharton Stork, for example, includes such a scene of repudiation in his play *Alcibiades: A Play of Athens in the Great Age* (1967), having Aristophanes admit that he didn't really know Socrates when he wrote *Clouds*.[81] This correction is all the more significant because Stork's play uses Socrates merely as a foil for its main subject matter, Alcibiades. Around the same time, the Canadian writer Lister Sinclair, a radio dramatist during the golden age of that form, wrote *Socrates: A Drama in Three Acts* (1957). Lister addresses the problem of Aristophanes head-on as well. In the preface, he acknowledges that "the easy explanation is to say that Aristophanes was obviously an enemy of Socrates," but then he proceeds to observe that "Aristophanes is prominent in Plato's dialogue *The Symposium*, and is unmistakably shown as Socrates' friend." It is the latter point that Sinclair wants to stress, adding in parentheses, "This is the basis on which he appears in my play."[82] The play proceeds to portray Aristophanes as a particularly unruly member of Socrates' entourage, always inclined to play pranks. Toward the beginning of the play, Aristophanes interrupts the assembly by holding up a large, dead octopus during a speech by the chief magistrate, Philip; the audience breaks out in laughter and the assembly has to be dissolved.[83] But all the way to the end,

Aristophanes remains a trusted friend and no one ever dreams of considering him an enemy of Socrates. Other writers of Socrates comedies were aware of Aristophanes—no writer of comedy could ever *not* be aware of him—but skirted the issue by avoiding in their own comedies any reference to their problematic predecessor.[84] Either way, the legacy of Aristophanes informs every Socrates comedy.

Even if the comic Socrates plays manage to avoid or solve the Aristophanes problem, they have to solve a more serious problem as well: the figure of the comic stage philosopher itself. While Plato's dialogues were immersed in comedy, they did not, for the most part, present philosophy as a laughing matter. The more general form of the Aristophanes problem was therefore how to create a comedy in which philosophy—and by extension the philosopher—is not undermined by comic laughter, or at least in which Socrates has the last laugh.

Of course, this was a problem only for those writers who wanted to avoid turning Socrates into a simple object of comedy in the first place. This was not the case with Philippe Poisson, who was eager to portray Socrates as a comic stage philosopher of the worst kind. Rather than softening the blow Aristophanes had dealt to Socrates, wittingly or unwittingly, Poisson reinforces it. A rather successful writer of both tragedies and comedies, Poisson turned to Socrates in his comedy in verse, *Alcibiades: A Comedy in Three Acts*, which premiered at the prestigious Théâtre François on February 23, 1731.[85] To call the plot of this play convoluted is a gross understatement. Socrates is guardian to a young woman, whom Alcibiades woos without knowing who she is. In fact, he confuses her with her much older governess, who in turn happens to find herself in love with him. Socrates, for his part, has fallen in love with his ward himself while giving her philosophy lessons. When Alcibiades boasts to Socrates that he has been catching glances of the well-protected ward, Socrates reprimands the governess, who reveals to him that she had pretended to be the ward to better guard her from Alcibiades' eyes. A friend of the ward tries to convince the governess that the stranger is in fact reciprocating her love, until the governess finally understands that the object of her own affection is Alcibiades, to whom she promptly sends a love letter. Alcibiades, who still takes the governess to be the ward, rejects the love letter on account of that confusion. Finally Alcibiades discovers that the governess had played a trick on him by pretending to be the ward, and manages to find access to the real object of his desire. Socrates discovers the lovers, and while the governess claims she had tried to guard the ward, she is exposed by her own love letter to Alcibiades. In the end, Socrates consents to give his ward to Alcibiades in marriage. This, I should add, is only a bare-bones outline of the plot, leaving out many intrigues, twists, turns, and minor characters with their own love interests and confusions.

What matters in this play is that the philosopher, Socrates, gets entangled in a love plot with all the pleasures but also all the humiliations that come with it. In fact, Mirto, Socrates' wife, suspects all along that

Socrates' high-minded philosophizing is just a front to better ensure success with his love interest.[86] The play may not side with this most cynical view of philosophy entirely, but for the duration of the play, at least, philosophy is used for romantic purposes and thus discredited. At one moment Alcibiades and Socrates talk putatively about philosophy, but all they have on their minds is their love for Socrates' ward. Even if the play may allow, in theory, for something like genuine philosophy to exist, it is everywhere undermined by its stronger rival, erotic love. Poisson here turns on its head Plato's doctrine that philosophical love conquers earthly love: in comedy, earthly love always wins. In this play, Socrates is portrayed in a manner that is familiar from the comic tradition: his philosophical study, putatively disinterested, is in fact a means of pursuing his love interest, even if he is not particularly adept at getting what he wants.

Louis-Sébastien Mercier's *The House of Socrates the Wise* (1809) is in many ways similar to Poisson's comedy. Mercier was a successful and influential playwright who wrote more than fifty plays. Even more influential was his treatise on drama, *On Theatre* (1773), in which he advocated a more realist but also moral drama, attacking the dominance of verse tragedy at the time. He also became an enthusiastic supporter of the French Revolution, serving in the National Convention. His opposition to Robespierre's radicalism landed him in prison, but he was liberated after the fall of Robespierre and returned to the Convention. His lasting legacy, perhaps, is the term *romantique*, which he suggested to his friend Pierre Félicien le Tourneur, who in turn used it, perhaps not surprisingly, in a text on Shakespeare.

The House of Socrates is not much less convoluted than Poisson's play. Again, Socrates gets entangled in a complicated love plot, falling in love with his ward, Myrthoe, and once again Alcibiades is his main rival. Other characters involved are the jealous Xanthippe and Myrthoe's maid. Mercier's play is a direct descendant of Poisson's, but at the same time he turns Poisson upside down: where the love plot in Poisson had been developed at least partially to discredit Socrates and his philosophical pretensions, Mercier redeems the philosopher in the end. It turns out that Socrates' love is just a ruse: in reality he wants to marry Myrthoe to Alcibiades. He is afraid that Myrthoe, who he knows is dearly attached to him and his philosophy, will dismiss Alcibiades as too fickle, too interested in worldly affairs and adventures, too different from Socrates himself, and also that Alcibiades for his part might harbor only a passing fancy for Myrthoe. It is for this reason that Socrates develops his elaborate ruse, the pretense of having fallen in love with Myrthoe himself, a strategy that, through a myriad of plots, finally arrives at its proper goal: Myrthoe is convinced of Alcibiades' love through the latter's constant pleading, and Alcibiades shows himself to be firm in his love for Socrates' ward.

The whole play is thus composed with the figure of the comic stage philosopher in mind, but only to prove it wrong. Socrates does not use philosophy to gain love, nor is his philosophy somehow disproved by his love. In fact, this willingness to play a ridiculous role enhances his philosophical reputation. He is presented as a stoic who does not get angry at Xanthippe's constant outrage. He is a true philosopher, but he also knows the ways of the world and can thus conceive of a plot such as the one that leads to the happy marriage of Myrthoe and Alcibiades. Mercier uses the comic stage philosopher in a careful balancing act that mobilizes all the possibilities of comedy without turning it against philosophy. He also knows that comedy has always been the genre most fully dependent on a shared cultural context. Comedies rarely work across time and place; they are much less portable than tragedies because they depend on shared social codes and norms of behavior and a shared language. In order to make a historical play such as *The House of Socrates* work for the Parisian audience, he turned Myrthoe's maid into a Gaul, an outspoken, comic character who frequently compares and contrasts the behavior of Athenians to how things are done at home in France.

Mercier's attempt to reconcile philosophy and comedy also emerges in how he handles the Aristophanes problem. When Socrates pretends to be in love with his ward, he recognizes that the role of eager lover will cast him in a light quite different from the expected one of philosophical gravity, turning him into something much closer to Aristophanes' portrayal. Socrates in fact starts to laugh about himself.[87] This Socrates is aware of Aristophanes and even agrees that the popular conception of the philosopher as grave and humorless is limited and false. While this Socrates does not claim that Aristophanes does justice to philosophy, he is more than happy to laugh with Aristophanes about himself, dismissing the earnest understanding of the philosopher to be had, presumably, in other noncomedic accounts.

The most interesting Socrates comedy was written at the end of the nineteenth century by Théodore de Banville.[88] His *Socrates and His Wife* (1885) also rescues Socrates from the role of a comic stage philosopher, though in a less convoluted manner than Mercier's play. Socrates manages to win not only Myrrhine's husband to the cause of philosophy but also Myrrhine herself. In a moment of conversion, she jumps up out of joy and kisses Socrates. Just at this moment, Xanthippe enters, sees the kiss, and immediately comes to the conclusion all audiences anticipate: Socrates' philosophy has been merely a pretense to make love to Myrrhine. Always quick on her feet, Xanthippe shouts sarcastically: "Bon appétit, Myrrhine."[89] *A typical stage philosopher, my husband*, she thinks, except, of course, she is wrong. She faints and seems to be dead. When she comes to again and sees Socrates genuinely grieving for her, she is reformed and promises not to distrust him anymore. Like Mercier, Banville uses the conventions of the comic stage philosopher only to rescue Socrates from them. His play was one of the most successful Plato adaptations, playing at the Comédie-Française in 1885, with Benoît Constant Coquelin, one of the most famous comic actors, in the role of Socrates. Banville wrote at the tail end of a tradition that includes Aristophanes, Shakespeare, and Milton, all of whom he mentions in his extensive work. He might be considered the culmination of the Socrates play before it moves into the period that will be the subject of the next chapter of this book: modern drama.

The comic tradition of the Socrates play found a second home in comic opera. This was not surprising, perhaps, since opera was invented in Renaissance Italy around the same time as the revival of Plato and since it was understood to be a return to the original integration in Greek theater of music, dance, and speech. More of a coterie art form, opera could also tolerate more eccentric topics if they were favored by the right patron.

The first Socrates opera I have been able to find was performed in 1680 in Prague, with a libretto by Nicolò Minato and music by Antonio Draghi. Titled *The Patient Socrates with Two Wives*, this opera revolves around doubles, a classical comic technique. Like a number of adapters, and in keeping with the musical form, Minato decided to introduce a chorus. The opera, or at least the libretto, was successful enough that it was adapted several decades later in Germany and set to music by the most famous composer associated with a Socrates opera: Georg Philipp Telemann. His librettist, Johann Ulrich König, left Minato's libretto relatively unaltered, using German recitatives and Italian arias; Telemann, one of the very prolific Baroque composers, added his own musical style. The opera, although not part of the regular repertoire, has been performed on occasion, due to Telemann's fame, and it was recorded in 1965.[90]

The libretto's point of departure is the law, reported by Diogenes Laertius and used in a number of comic adaptations, that Athenian men should take second wives. Socrates thus has two quarreling wives and is led, again and again, to the refrain "Fellow men, learn in time to be patient." While the Socrates plot revolves around moments of reconciliation and division among the two wives, Melito has the opposite problem: even though he is loved by two women, Edronica and Rodisette, he can have only one additional wife due to a promise given to the father of an earlier love interest. The dramatic situation is that he cannot make up his mind which of the two he should choose. This dilemma seems resolved when the father of the early love interest gives up the prior claim, but now one of the two women Melito loves, Rodisette, suddenly no longer wants to get married to him as one of many wives, and only the other one, Edronica, is ready to accept the deal. Socrates is called upon to decide and comes to the conclusion that Rodisette loves Melito more. These two sets of doubles, Socrates' two wives and Melito's choice between two women, are mirrored by a third constellation: Antippo loves two women, but his problem is that they both reject him. Here, too, though, a happy ending immediately suggests itself, resolving several problems at once: Edronica, rejected by Melito, is willing to marry Antippo, and the opera's ending is finally ensured.

The plot is quite removed from anything Plato wrote, to put it mildly. Melito (Melitus), for example, does not appear here at all as an enemy of Socrates. Even though the opera is comic, however, Socrates is not, or at least not simply, a comic stage philosopher. He is sought out for counsel, and he reacts with equanimity to pamphlets that have been distributed against him. More to the philosophical point is the moment when he sings his famous line "Quest' io so, che nulla so" (this I know, that I know nothing). Socrates knows that he does not know anything, and in keeping with the opera's title, he exercises superb patience. Thus Socrates' most cherished philosophical maxims find their unlikely operatic expression.

There is one more comic Socrates opera to be mentioned: *The Imaginary Socrates* by Giovanni Paisiello, which premiered in 1775 in Naples.[91] Paisiello was a prolific composer who had turned to classical themes before, for example, in his opera *Antigone*. *The Imaginary Socrates* is not so much a Socrates opera as a meta-Socrates opera, modeled, as the preface states, on *Don Quixote*. Just as in that novel Don Quixote is possessed by the idea of being a knight errant and spends the rest of the novel pursuing that idea to comic effect, so in the opera the protagonist thinks he is Socrates and spends the rest of the opera acting out this peculiar form of madness. Like Don Quixote, he imposes his obsession on the world and the people around him. He refuses to be called by his original name, and he also renames everyone around him after characters from Plato's dialogues; for example, he insists on calling his barber Plato. He decorates his house in Greek style and starts to live adventures somehow derived from Plato, including the consultation of the oracle.

Of all the Socrates operas, Paisiello's was one of the more successful. It met with applause during Paisiello's own time and has been revived since. His opera is a cautionary tale with serious implications for adapters of Plato. Many of those adapters, whether operating in the mode of tragedy or comedy, somehow tried to bring Plato's drama up to date, making it relevant for modern times. This, after all, is what drama does: it takes place in the present tense, in front of a live audience, and needs to address the concerns of that audience. Socrates dramas always imply that however distant Socrates may be, he remains relevant and alive for us. I don't know how aware Paisiello was of the tradition of the Socrates play, but in any case he recognized something crucial about that tradition: trying to revive Socrates easily verges on the comic.

Even though writers of Socrates plays spent much effort and ingenuity in turning Plato's dialogues into contemporary tragedies and comedies, they all felt that Plato's own dialogues were neither. Their reading of the *Phaedo* might have impressed on them the insight that Plato rejected the tragic reaction to Socrates' death, seeking to infuse it with comedy. And their reading of the *Symposium* and the *Phaedrus*—and of Aristophanes' *Clouds*—might have reminded them of Plato's ambivalence with respect to comedy. Both tragedians and comedians struggled to take into account Plato's critique of tragedy and comedy.

A few writers of Socrates plays, however, went further than this and sought to create genuine mixtures. One of them was the aforementioned Jean-Marie Collot, who had turned Socrates into a precursor of Enlightenment deism. Originally an actor and comedian, Collot was manager of a theater in Lyon until 1789. As soon as the French Revolution broke out, however, he threw himself wholeheartedly into the fray and became a leading figure in the most radical political association, Robespierre's

Jacobin Club. He advocated for the overthrow of the monarch in 1792 and other measures. Increasingly he became a rival to Robespierre himself and in fact brought about his downfall. When the entire Jacobin Club fell out of favor after a failed uprising, however, Collot was deported to Guyana, where he died of yellow fever.[92]

At first sight, his play *The Trial of Socrates* seems to resemble the many tragic adaptations of Socrates' death written by predecessors and contemporaries, including his revolutionary colleague Bernardin de Saint-Pierre. Like several other tragic adaptation of the time, this play made it onto the stage, premiering at the Théâtre de Monsieur on November 9, 1790. The only difference is that *The Trial of Socrates*, with its depiction of the trial and death of the philosopher, is not a tragedy at all. It is subtitled *A Comedy in Three Acts and in Prose*. Rather than looking for tragic models, such as Shakespeare, that would allow for the inclusion of comic elements, Collot went all the way and presented the death of Socrates as a comedy. Collot knew what he was doing. He was fully aware of the tragic adaptations and mentioned, for example, the one by Voltaire, but he recognized tragedy to be the wrong genre. As a consequence, his own play is a strange mixture of tragedy and comedy. Socrates' accuser, Anytus, is motivated, as in so many Socrates plays, by personal motives, in this case his belief that Socrates has turned the woman he loves against him. The female student is in fact persuaded to marry a poor fellow student, Agathon, who, it turns out, actually has a secret inheritance coming his way. The love plot is interlaced with the brewing conspiracy between Anytus and Melitus against Socrates. There is no sense of a majority vote against Socrates, only a conspiracy. Socrates, who has been uttering patriotic and deist opinions all along, ends the play in his prison cell with a speech against idolatry. His death is a calamity of some sort, but the cause of philosophy prevails through and after his death.

In presenting the death of Socrates in a nontragic light, *The Trial of Socrates* continues with other means what Plato had done in the *Phaedo*. Even though it was written at the end of the eighteenth century, this play anticipates what would become the norm in modern drama: the mixing of tragedy and comedy. Almost 140 years later, the playwright Robert Walter would do the exact same thing: write a comedy centered on the trial and death of Socrates. Collot and Walter recognized that in order to celebrate Socrates as a philosopher, his death must not be presented as tragedy. Even though numerous authors of Socrates plays got many things wrong about Plato's dramaturgy, many of them thus also got some things right.

Walter had a great advantage: by 1927, when his play *The Art of Midwifery* was written, the difference between tragedy and comedy had undergone a complete change. The new, modern drama invited the generic mixing toward which writers of Socrates plays had been veering all along. Or, to put it the other way around, in modern drama Plato finally had his way: writers of tragedies had become writers of comedies. In this sense, Plato and the writers of Socrates plays anticipated modern drama, and Plato therefore can be used as a lens through which to reexamine modern drama more generally.

3

The Drama of Ideas

odern drama is commonly characterized as non-Aristotelian. In this
chapter I will argue that it should be understood more specifically
as Platonic. Even though Plato is rarely used as a lens through which to
look at modern drama—or any drama—it is striking to contemplate how
many of the most salient features of modern drama can be found in Plato's
own dramatic practice. Plato's antitragic drama, for example, can be seen
as an anticipation of the widespread sense that the modern world, with its
belief in human agency, progress, and democracy, is fundamentally at
odds with the harsh worldview of tragedy. The modern tragicomedies that
resulted from this development are prefigured in Plato's own genre mixing.
Modern drama can be called Platonic also in its insistence that theater be
an intellectually serious undertaking, a theater of ideas. Not only were
modern dramatists deeply influenced by philosophy, they also believed that
the theater had something crucial to contribute to the formation of ideas.

Modern drama developed a widespread distrust of the more spectacular forms of theatricality, sometimes leading modern dramatists to outright
antitheatrical positions (such as demanding that actors be replaced with
marionettes) or even to write closet dramas not intended for performance.
A similar impulse led to forms of metatheater, which allowed modern dramatists to distance themselves from some forms of theater while adopting
others.[1] Metatheater, especially when it goes along with a critical reflection on different modes of theatricality, can be traced back to Plato's cave
and its distinction between two theatrical worlds, the confrontation of two
realities, two modes of existence.[2] Indeed, a majority of the plays I will be
discussing in this chapter participate in metatheater, including the dialogues of Wilde and Brecht (which are dialogues about theater), Shaw's
multilayered *Man and Superman*, and Pirandello's and Stoppard's overt
metaplays. Metatheater had always served as a way for the theater to
reflect upon itself, but in modern drama, this self-reflection developed a
critical edge that betrays Plato's influence.

Given these correspondences between Plato's drama and modern drama, it is not surprising that many modern dramatists turned to Plato as a source of inspiration, creating a Platonic drama in the process. In speaking of a Platonic modern drama, I do not refer to traditional Platonism as articulated in the theory of forms or ideas, although such a Platonism might well serve as a useful corrective to standard histories of modern drama, which have been in the thrall of various forms of materialism. Such materialisms have contributed to the well-nigh complete absence of Plato from the histories of the period. In the late nineteenth century, or so the story of modern drama is often told, playwrights adopted from Charles Darwin and other scientists and philosophers a worldview that insisted on the shaping power of the environment, inheritance, and other material circumstances. Their emphasis on matter and materiality also brought with it a complete overhaul of staging practices, since the physical ingredients of theater now represented those newly important material circumstances against which human protagonists rebelled in vain. Naturalist theaters, first in Paris and then in London, Berlin, and other European capitals, became obsessed with stage props and set design, outdoing one another in the race for an ever more cluttered stage. The Russian actor, director, and theorist Konstantin Stanislavski even imported Norwegian furniture to stage Ibsen. In this way, naturalism aspired to scientific objectivity and realized this aspiration in a theater of material objects.

Scientific naturalism was in turn superseded by even more radical playwrights and directors who found their materialism in the human body, turning to ancient and exotic rituals in order to infuse Western drama with a new sense of physical expression. The body and its movements became central for playwrights, directors, and visionaries of the theater as diverse as Max Reinhardt, who created stage spectacles of stunning beauty, and Antonin Artaud, who denounced all conventional drama and wanted to return to a ritual theater of screams and movement. The new emphasis on ritual and corporeality was taken up in the 1960s by directors and actors whose performances and happenings, in keeping with the spirit of the time, sought to liberate the body from the strictures of traditional drama and decorum, perhaps even from society at large. And like their predecessors of the early twentieth century, they turned to non-Western rituals and practices for inspiration. Finally, performance artists in the 1980s and 1990s broke the last taboos in their attempt to explore the final frontiers of corporeal theater, confronting audiences with the explicit body in performance. Theater scholarship has followed this materialist tendency, discussing theater in terms of corporeality, physical theater, the body, and ritual.[3]

While it would be tempting, and perhaps salutary, to confront this materialist history of modern drama with one attuned to the continuing influence of all kinds of idealism, such a confrontation would leave the polarization between materialism and idealism in place. Questioning this polarization is one of the goals of dramatic Platonism, which aims at the unsettling combination of idealist aspiration and material practice that characterizes Plato's dialogues and Platonic dramaturgy more generally.

In what follows I propose to take dramatic Platonism as my guiding principle, which means focusing on the ways in which playwrights fundamentally rethink the status of materiality in drama and theater. Dramatic Platonism pays attention to the intellectual aspirations of modern drama, but also to the way in which these aspirations are translated into the provisional materiality of the stage, into a new use of scene, character, and interaction. Worrying about the status of ideas in the theater inevitably results in a large-scale rethinking of theatricality, including the many self-critical forms of antitheater and metatheater that are typical of modern drama. In Plato's idiom, one might say that modern theater makers are keenly aware that they operate within a cave. However, the conclusion they draw from this insight is not to turn around and leave the theater behind. Rather, they turn around the theater itself, reorienting it so that it might serve as a vehicle for truth. The insistence on the part of so many dramatists and directors that what they produce are truths has largely been ignored as an embarrassing bit of rhetoric. Dramatic Platonism seeks to provide a frame within which such aspirations can be taken seriously.

The Modern Socrates Play: August Strindberg and Georg Kaiser

> Plato's drama . . . surpasses all other dramas.
>
> —Georg Kaiser

We can get a first sense of Plato's influence on modern drama by contemplating the contemporary resurgence of the Socrates play. To be sure, Socrates plays are often poor examples of Plato's own dramaturgy. While they tend to be attuned to Plato's mixing of genres, they often fail to recognize the subtle undercutting of character, action, and the deliberately restrained performance that is the hallmark of Plato's own dramatic form. But the very existence of a large number of modern Socrates plays registers the continuing significance of Plato for modern drama. After their emergence and first flowering in the second half of the eighteenth century, Socrates plays become significant again in the twentieth century, coinciding with the emergence of modern drama (see graph and the list of Socrates plays in the appendix). Some of these Socrates plays were familiar in form, either tragedies that took as their subject the death of Socrates or comedies focusing on Xanthippe. But there were new forms and genres as well. The literary theorist I. A. Richards created a synthetic version of the four dialogues depicting Socrates' death in simplified English, intended for use in schools and other pedagogical venues.[4] The German-French midcentury writer Manès Sperber wrote a Socrates play that becomes a novella halfway through.[5] In the wake of widespread experimentations with form, we encounter Socrates in chamber operas, musical theater, orchestral suites, Broadway shows, closet dramas, and TV shows.

3.1.   Target Margin Theater's production of *The Dinner Party* (i.e., Plato's *Symposium*) at the Kitchen, June 2007, directed by David Herskovits, with (clockwise from top left) Stephanie Weeks, Ian Wen, Han Nah Kim, Greig Sargeant, and Steven Rattazzi. Photo: Hilary McHone.

More important, Plato's dialogues themselves become part of official theater history. While they had always been the subject of dramatic readings in academies and schools, in the twentieth century they were actually performed in theaters and taken up by other media. The director Jonathan Miller staged Plato's *Symposium* for the BBC, and in the summer of 2007 the Off-Broadway theater company Target Margin Theater, under the direction of David Herskovits, staged the *Symposium* with considerable success (figure 3.1).[6] Herskovits cast Socrates, who is standing on the table, and several other participants as women, thus updating the participants in the symposium to reflect early twenty-first-century New York. The history of Plato's gradual emergence as a dramatist has now finally reached its endpoint: he has become a playwright, an author of Socrates plays that are being performed in theaters.

There were two authors of modern Socrates plays who had a particular influence on modern drama: August Strindberg and Georg Kaiser. In their work, the writing of Socrates plays coincided with the project of creating a new and modern drama. By examining their relation to Plato, we can get a first glimpse of the extent to which modern drama is a Platonic drama.

August Strindberg

Strindberg, it must be admitted, had only a dim understanding of the significance of Plato for modern drama. While the other modern dramatists

I will discuss in this chapter, from Wilde to Brecht, turned to Plato for his formal innovation and recognized in his dialogues a full-fledged dramaturgy that could be resuscitated and adapted, Strindberg was drawn to Plato primarily for his role in the history of ideas. For Strindberg, the dilemma of Western modernity was primarily a spiritual one: materialism and scientific positivism had caused the West to lose its way, eliminating all sense of the spiritual. Like many other writers and thinkers of the time, Strindberg therefore became fascinated with different forms of alternative spirituality and theosophy, leading his protagonists to speak in the exalted language of prophets and priests. His most influential work, *A Dream Play* (1901), turns to Hinduism and the god Indira to construct a spiritual framework through which a fallen world might find, if not redemption, at least the hope for it.

This interest in the world's religious and cultural traditions inspired Strindberg to write a play based on Socrates, which was part of a larger project meant to gauge the viability of Western philosophical and religious thought. Classical Athens had been on Strindberg's mind for many years. He had written an early play, *The Downfall of Athens* (1870), featuring Alcibiades, and it was this theme of the downfall of Athenian civilization to which Strindberg would return at the height of his dramatic powers in the first years of the twentieth century.[7] Like many contemporaries, he was convinced that examining the rise and fall of earlier empires, connecting the modern world to religious and philosophical figures of the past, might point the way out of the dead end at which the Western world had arrived. What drew Strindberg to return to Socrates was his fascination with world-historical personages, a history of epochs as represented in significant figures. Strindberg's 1903 play, sometimes called *Hellas* and sometimes *Socrates*, is part of a megacycle on world history that was never completed but of which significant parts exist, including a first play about Moses, a second one centered on Socrates, and a third on Jesus.[8] Strindberg considered his world-historical plays an important part of his oeuvre, so much so that upon recognizing that there was little chance of performance, he rewrote the three plays from the cycle as novellas and republished them in 1905 as prose works under the title *Historical Miniatures*.[9]

What the cycle of plays, called *World-Historical Plays*, tries to achieve is nothing less than a counterpart to the Hinduist *Dream Play*: a dramatic history of religious thought in the Hellenic and Judeo-Christian traditions. Throughout there is a sense that Greece is in decline; "I think Athens is in its death throes," Alcibiades opines, summing up the sense of demise.[10] A little later, Protagoras exclaims, "The gods are sleeping!" to which Euripides adds, "Or they have abandoned us," and it is left to Alcibiades to add a Nietzschean twist: "The gods are dead."[11] In keeping with Strindberg's search for representative figures, it is Pericles who embodies what is best about classical Greece, but also what it lacks; throughout the play Pericles suffers physically and spiritually from the decay of the civilization he embodies. When he dies at the end of the play, Greek civilization dies with him.

Socrates occupies a more ambiguous position. Of course he, too, dies by the end of the play, along with the culture that he represents, but Strindberg does not dwell on this death scene, the staple of other Socrates plays. The death sentence against Socrates follows on the heels of many similar sentences of an increasingly paranoid political regime; it is thus only the most recent, though also the most significant, manifestation of a civilization in decline. The other manifestation of this decline is the closing of the theaters: even Aristophanes, who had earlier called for the death of tragedy, cannot help weeping—the great comedian is weeping!—and now makes common cause with the philosopher (here Strindberg joins those writers who reconcile Socrates with Aristophanes).[12] In this way, Socrates becomes less a representative of Athens than a victim of its decadence and decline. At the same time, he also points beyond this decline, becoming a prophet of Judeo-Christian monotheism that will guarantee the spiritual revival of the West. In this also, Strindberg continues a tradition within the Socrates play, namely, a reading of Socrates as a harbinger of monotheistic Christianity. But Strindberg also revises this tradition by emphasizing a second alliance, one between Platonism and Jewish theology, a link historically grounded in the powerful writings of Hellenistic Jewish theologians such as Philo of Alexandria. In Strindberg's play, it is therefore a Jewish character who recognizes Socrates as a monotheist and who, like Socrates, dismisses the human-like Greek gods.[13] Socrates thus becomes a kindred spirit of Moses, to whom the first play in the cycle had been devoted, even as he anticipates Jesus, the protagonist of the subsequent play.

Like many of its predecessors (though probably Strindberg had no knowledge of them), *Socrates* embeds the philosopher in the theatrical context of Athens, emphasizing his friendship with Euripides and his rivalry with Aristophanes. Strindberg also makes good use of Socrates' relation with Alcibiades, whose rise to power, failure in the Sicilian campaign, betrayal of Athens to its rivals, and ultimate death in Persia provide the play with a vivid counterpart to Socrates. At the same time, the play suffers from some of the same obsessions that mar Strindberg's other works. The most jarring of them is probably his misogyny. Given Strindberg's attitude toward women in this and many other plays, it is not surprising that unlike many other playwrights who rescue Xanthippe from the role of shrew accorded to her by tradition, Strindberg seizes on this role, and in fact does everything possible to make Xanthippe even more unappealing and vicious than is usually the case. In Strindberg's play, she not only nags Socrates and dismisses his entire outlook on life but also conspires with his enemies, betraying Socrates and Alcibiades to Anytus, who will later bring suit against Socrates. Strindberg even thematizes—and defends—misogyny by having Euripides be accused of it early on in the play, a charge based on Euripides' *Hippolytus* and the title character's well-known hatred of women; clearly Strindberg here identifies with the accused Greek tragedian. Euripides' Hippolytus, whose misogyny is usually understood as ill-advised Puritanism and neurotic sexuality, provides

Strindberg with a welcome occasion to hold forth against women. His Euripides declares, for example, that his hatred of women enabled him to provide Hippolytus with effective speeches, though he adds that he only hates women in general and is capable of loving individual women (a sentiment that echoes Strindberg's). Besides misogyny, the second obsession of Strindberg's that informs this play is his homophobia. One reason for Athens' decay, we learn, is the love for boys; recognizing this truth, even the notorious Alcibiades renounces this preference and explains to the king of Sparta that homosexuality will surely lead to the demise of Athens.

Strindberg's *Socrates* is informed by his private obsessions but also by his philosophical and dramatic ambitions. It seeks to capture world-historical events in dramatic form and thus in the actions of a few significant characters. While this was not, in principle, a novel approach, the character-driven account of history had received an upgrade at the hands of Hegel as well as Nietzsche, with whom Strindberg had struck up an ill-fated correspondence.[14] Indeed, Strindberg may have partially adopted Nietzsche's view of Socrates when in his play Aristophanes holds Euripides and Socrates responsible for the death of tragedy. Strindberg follows Nietzsche, but without the latter's hatred of Christianity. Instead, he recognizes Socrates as a figure who points beyond the demise of classical Greece, a prophet of things to come.

Socrates is much less experimental in form than other plays by Strindberg, presenting the world-historical condition of modernity by drawing on Nietzsche's influential philosophy of theater. It stages a theater of ideas through the pronouncements and actions of exemplary figures, which are, in the course of the cycle, placed in relation to one another. It is a modern, or at least timely, play only in its attempt to embody a history of ideas in dramatic characters: these world-historical figures are conjured up in response to what Strindberg—and many of his contemporaries—perceived to be a crisis of civilization. *Socrates* was supposed to diagnose this crisis and also to point toward its resolution.

Georg Kaiser

Strindberg used Socrates as a personification of an age the way Hegel and Nietzsche had done, transforming their character-driven conceptions of philosophy into drama. Georg Kaiser went much further: not only did he embrace the figure of Socrates, but he also recognized Plato as a dramatist and created an entirely new dramaturgy based on Plato. Like Strindberg, Kaiser can be understood as a playwright deeply worried about the state of modernity. Kaiser devoted two plays to the dystopian depiction of a huge gasworks that, driven by capitalist greed, is destroyed in a gigantic explosion—reminiscent of Fritz Lang's film *Metropolis* and prescient of the growing recognition of modernity's destructive powers. Mechanical industrialization, the death of God, the rupture of social bonds, the horrors of World War I—these topics are central to Kaiser's work. Like other expressionists, Kaiser viewed the modern, material world with fascination, but also with repulsion. Whereas futurists hailed industrialization and mechanical modernity for their promise, Kaiser examined modernity in excruciating detail because he could not make his peace with it.

As was true of Strindberg's *Socrates*, Kaiser's Socrates play, *Alcibiades Delivered* (1917–19), has not received the recognition it deserves, despite the fact that Kaiser himself considered it a crucial play, nothing less than a model for a new Platonic drama.[15] Like several of his predecessors, Kaiser constructs the play's dramatic tension around the relation between Socrates and Alcibiades, which Kaiser establishes by means of a scene from the Peloponnesian War, in which Socrates saves Alcibiades in battle. But Kaiser is too irreverent (and too good a reader of Plato) to use this scene to prop up Socrates as a conventional hero. Instead he has him save Alcibiades through an accident: Socrates has a thorn in his foot and therefore falls behind as his comrades retreat from the advancing Spartan troops, only to find himself accidentally in a position to save Alcibiades, who is alone and surrounded by the enemy. The sudden, noisy appearance of Socrates leads them to flee, and Alcibiades is saved. Unlike Strindberg, Kaiser does not see Socrates as a world-historical personage who embodies the spirit of Athens and anticipates that of Judeo-Christian monotheism; rather, he sees him as a modern antihero who is driven by accidents, contingencies, and chaos.

Kaiser turns Socrates into a modern figure not only through the emphasis on contingency but also by turning him into an artist. In contrast to the portrait painted by Plato, who has Socrates declare, in the *Phaedrus*, that he almost never ventures outside Athens, here Socrates often flees his Athenian admirers and retreats to the countryside, since "an artist can only be creative in solitude."[16] Kaiser thus agrees with the poetic, "artistic" reading of Plato and Socrates, turning Socrates into a Romantic artist who seeks to escape the busy city in order to devote himself to his art. But when Socrates finds himself back in Athens, his well-known inquisitiveness comes to the fore in the mixture of comedy and philosophy that is the constant theme of this play. As in so many Socrates plays, genre mixing and the relation of philosophy to drama are Kaiser's main interests. The genre mixing is explored most fully in an act of the play that is based on the *Symposium*. Kaiser preserves that dialogue's most salient feature: Socrates' competition with the two playwrights Agathon and Aristophanes. But he heightens the proximity between Socrates and theater by incorporating into this one scene other famous remarks made by Socrates on the topic of theater, including his critique of theater in the *Republic*, thus condensing the rivalry between Plato and Greek theater.

By including Plato's notorious critique of theater in this play, Kaiser is also able to imply, correctly in my view, that this critique is not a simple rejection of theater but instead a way of creating a new, philosophical, and specifically Platonic theater. Once more, a playwright has a sharper eye for Plato's drama than many philosophers. Like so many authors of Socrates plays before him, Kaiser emphasizes the enigmatic ending of the *Symposium*, Socrates' declaration that tragedy and comedy derive from the same source. This genre mixing is what Plato himself had undertaken, and it is also what Kaiser now identifies as the core of his own drama. His Socrates play, after all, uses the comedic *Symposium* only to end, *Phaedo*-like, with Socrates' death.

Kaiser thus draws on the tradition of the Socrates play, but more important, he turns this tradition into the starting point for a new and modern drama. The principles behind this new drama are articulated in a short essay—almost a manifesto—called "Plato's Drama."[17] Here Kaiser explains that Plato's drama "surpasses all other dramas," even as he reiterates his dissatisfaction with conventional drama. In order to develop an alternative, Kaiser demands that dramatists learn from Plato to shun mindless spectacles and instead focus on ideas and their dramatic manifestation. The final sentence of the essay expresses this new Platonic aesthetics in Kaiser's succinct style: "Theater [*Schauspiel*] satisfies deeper desires: we have entered the play of thought [*Denkspiel*], having graduated from mere viewing pleasure [*Schaulust*] to the more satisfying thinking pleasure [*Denklust*]."[18] Guided by Plato, Kaiser seeks to transform theater, whose German term, *Schauspiel*, preserves the Greek emphasis on the act of seeing or viewing; more particularly, the passage transforms looking into thinking, thus arriving at a neologism that replaces what literally would mean "viewing play" (*Schauspiel*) with "thinking play" (*Denkspiel*). This new theater of ideas, Kaiser adds, should take its point of departure from Plato's two masterpieces, the *Phaedo* and the *Symposium*. These two dramatic works, and the play of thought more generally, are not simply nontheatrical. Indeed, Kaiser emphasizes the extent to which the character Alcibiades in the *Symposium* satisfied viewing pleasure (*Schaulust*), just as the *Phaedo*, with its prison, is based on the category of the scene. Platonic drama, in other words, is not the opposite of theater, but rather a transformed version of it.

Kaiser wrote this essay in 1917, when he was working on *Alcibiades Delivered*. But ten years later, long after having written the works for which he is now mostly known, including *Gas I* and *Gas II*, he still held on to his program of a Platonic renewal of theater. In an interview with Hermann Kasack conducted in 1928 but not published until 1952, Kaiser reiterates that Plato "created the greatest plays of world literature ever conceived, for example the *Symposium* and his *Death of Socrates*."[19] The gist of the interview is a profound ambivalence with respect to the theater, as one would expect from a dramatist inspired by Plato. Kaiser remains quite firm in his opposition to theatrical spectacles. For example, he says that he would be "embarrassed to be associated too closely with theater," and when asked whether he sometimes longs to see his plays performed, he admits to such a longing but immediately adds that he experiences a "bad conscience" (*Gewissensbisse*) once his plays are actually performed, especially after successful performances.[20] Like so many modern dramatists, Kaiser privileges the literary, purely dialogic dimension of drama and, as a consequence, dismisses other dimensions of theater, in particular the audience and its supposed demand for spectacle. But it is important to remember that such modernist antitheatricalism is rarely intent on leaving the theater behind; rather, it seeks to transform the theater. Kaiser demands precisely such a transformation through a return to Plato. Plato's dialogues can be a point of departure, an inspiration, even if they are not to be treated as a "recipe"; rather, they are a "goal."[21] At this point in the interview, Kaiser singles out his own Socrates play, *Alcibiades Delivered*, as a model. This play, he explains, was written as an attempt at a Platonic dialogue, yet it was written with "theatrical means"; like Plato's own texts, it is not just dialogue but a new type of drama.[22]

Kaiser was one of the most successful expressionist playwrights, and he influenced many later dramatists.[23] But few critics have taken up Kaiser's project or recognized the centrality of Plato for modern drama. Socrates plays, even Kaiser's formally ambitious one, failed to make a true mark on modern drama. They were destined to remain a minor, underground genre even in the twentieth century, and any account of Plato's dramatic legacy must take this fact into account. Yet I will take Kaiser, along with Strindberg, as a witness for the thesis that the modern drama is also, and importantly, Platonic drama. In the readings that follow, some of the most significant playwrights of the twentieth century—from Oscar Wilde and Bernard Shaw through Luigi Pirandello and Bertolt Brecht all the way to Tom Stoppard—are shown to participate in some kind of Platonic drama. All of them were keenly aware that they were inventing a new non-Aristotelian drama, and most recognized that their dramaturgy owed an important debt to Plato. But unlike Kaiser, few of them developed a full-fledged theory of Platonic drama. It will therefore be necessary to tease out and systematize their implied theories and practices of modern Platonic drama.

Identifying a Platonic impulse in modern drama is not to claim that there is a single, unified Platonism at work here. On the contrary, the sheer variety of Platonic strands in modern drama is remarkable. Besides Strindberg's world-historical figuration and Kaiser's play of thought, we have Wilde's renewal of the dramatic dialogue, coupled with an aesthetic theory based on Plato. There is Shaw's attempt to create a new play of ideas, authorized with reference to Plato, and Brecht's decision to recast his theory of drama in a series of dramatic dialogues that revolve around a philosopher. In Pirandello, the drama of ideas reaches its most identifiable form, a virtuoso confrontation of ideas with theatrical reality not to be reached again until Tom Stoppard's juggling of ideas onstage. The modern Socrates play thus testifies to a Platonic ambition among playwrights, but this ambition manifested itself fully only once it was translated into a series of dramatic experiments that had emancipated themselves from the figure of Socrates. The modern Socrates play gives way to modern Platonic drama.

Oscar Wilde

> In art I am Platonic, not Aristotelian, tho' I wear my Plato with a difference.
>
> —Oscar Wilde

Plato is everywhere in the writings of Oscar Wilde. The narrator of "The Portrait of Mr. W. H." (1889) even supplies us with a brief history of Platonism since the Renaissance, which harks back to Ficino's restaging of the *Symposium*. He writes: "In 1492 appeared Marsilio Ficino's translation of the 'Symposium' of Plato, and this wonderful dialogue, of all the Platonic dialogues perhaps the most perfect, as it is the most poetical, began to exercise a strange influence over men."[24] "The Portrait of Mr. W. H." is an unusual text, offering in the form of a murder mystery a theory of who the historical male addressee of some of Shakespeare's sonnets might have been. Whatever the merits of the rather far-fetched theory propounded by the main character—the addressee in question was a boy actor named Willie Hughes—"The Portrait of Mr. W. H." draws on the different stands of Platonism prevalent in the last decades of the nineteenth century. In what follows I will present a picture of Wilde that differs significantly from the dominant ones of Wilde as a decadent dandy, theatrical celebrity, or chronicler of late Victorian society through comedies of manners. Instead, Wilde should be understood as a pioneer in the formation of a modern Platonic drama.

Plato's influence on a given period tends to take different forms. In late Victorian England, one can identify three intertwined traditions of Platonism: pedagogical Platonism, homosexual Platonism, and aesthetic Platonism. The first emerges most clearly in the revival of Plato at Oxford leading to the great-books course called *literae humaniores*, in which the *Republic* featured prominently even as the whole course was based on the pedagogical ideal of the Socratic tutorial.[25] This pedagogical Platonism was intended to forge a new elite for Victorian England at the height of its empire. But when the narrator in "The Portrait of Mr. W. H." speaks of Plato's "strange" influence, he thinks not of the *literae humaniores* or the *Republic* but of the *Symposium* and, in keeping with a long tradition, the form of Platonism that takes the *Symposium* as a model, even as a code, for male friendship and love. In the letter from prison to his great and fateful love, Lord Alfred Douglas, which was to become *De Profundis*, Wilde mentions that an earlier letter to Douglas "can only be understood by those who have read the *Symposium* of Plato."[26] During his trial for indecency, Wilde famously brought this hidden meaning into the open, defending male love as a noble sentiment "such as Plato made the very basis of his philosophy."[27] This is the Platonism that has received the most critical attention in the last decades, an attention fueled by a wealth of insight into the history of homosexuality and its myriad influences on art and culture. Of primary importance here is the late work of Michel Foucault, whose thinking about Plato is still only beginning to emerge now that his last lectures at the Collège de France are finally being published in France.[28]

To pedagogical and homosexual Platonism, a third, related type should be added: aesthetic Platonism. Traditionally, aestheticism is seen as a reaction against nineteenth-century realism by harking back to a Romantic sensibility; indeed, John Keats was one of Wilde's heroes. Alternatively,

Wildean aestheticism, with its critique of nature, has been understood as a critique of normative heterosexuality, which by the late nineteenth century had come to be declared natural. Both of these interpretations of aestheticism are true enough, but they don't quite reach its philosophical foundation: this foundation is an aesthetic reinterpretation of Plato.

Wilde's aesthetic Platonism is articulated most clearly in his critical dialogue *The Decay of Lying* (1889), in which it reveals itself as the philosophical underpinning of his famous attack on nineteenth-century realism and naturalism. Émile Zola, Honoré de Balzac, and Charles Dickens get a beating, as do the philosophies on which they draw, such as Spenser's positivism and the more general reformist agenda of the realist novel.[29] The microscope and the parliamentary blue book, which Wilde associates with Victorian reformist impulses, emerge as the villains of Wilde's piece, convenient symbols of the spirit of scientism as applied to the natural and the social world. In order to come up with an alternative, Wilde initially turns to Kant, adopting a theory of art defined by it lack of social utility, or, in Kantian fashion, by it purposelessness. Where realism had justified itself through different forms of usefulness, art is now seen as fully itself only when it becomes its own purpose. On the face of it, the earnest Kant and the frivolous Wilde may seem opposites, but Wilde's overtly Kantian language of purposeless art helps us see that Kant himself privileged the ornamental, useless, and decorative, all qualities that would become central for late nineteenth-century aestheticism. The pedantic professor from Königsberg turns out to have paved the way for Wildean decadence.

Declaring art to be its own purpose is a good way of severing it from demands for social utility and making it fully autonomous. But autonomy is not enough for Wilde. He actually wants to assert the priority of art over nature, and it is for this project that Plato, or rather aesthetic Platonism, becomes crucial. Wilde, of course, was in the right place, for Oxford was the center of Platonism: in a century dominated by various forms of materialism and science, it took an Oxford graduate to develop a new, artistic understanding of Plato. The chief proponent of aesthetic Platonism at Oxford was Walter Pater, whose lectures, *Plato and Platonism*, celebrate art as the only way of giving shape to otherwise invisible ideas (like many aesthetic Platonists, Pater translates the Greek *idea* both as "form," something closer to its original meaning, and as "idea"). This tenet of aesthetic Platonism may at first seem like a counterintuitive proposition. After all, Plato had defined the search for forms in opposition to artistic representation, warning that if we want to approach the transcendent forms themselves, we should not get sidetracked by art. Pater and other proponents of aesthetic Platonism recognized the *Republic*'s polemic against art. At the same time, they also recognized Plato's own artistry: his invention of what I call dramatic Platonism, that is, his use of characters, scenes, and dialogue. At one point in his lectures, Pater says that the character Socrates himself comes close to being an *idolon theatri*, a "dramatic invention."[30] In addition to recognizing Plato as an artist, Pater goes one step further and claims that the only way of making ideas visible is through art, as Plato himself had demonstrated in his poetic dialogues. Plato's drama becomes the point of departure for formulating a full-blown theory of art as a privileged approach to ideas: invisible abstractions can become visible only when given poetic form. Plato had criticized art for good reasons, Pater and others were happy to concede. But when done right, art can embody ideas without weighing them down with the permanence and materiality of real things. The gamble of aesthetic Platonism is that, far from serving as a distraction, great art can give us an inkling of timeless forms.

In *The Decay of Lying*, Wilde appropriates this theory of aesthetic Platonism through Plato's most provocative term, which gives this dialogue its name: lying. First, Wilde slyly uses Plato to authorize his argument that it is morally acceptable for art to lie when it comes to educating the young. More important is a second argument, also taken from the *Republic*, that art is an imitation twice removed from the things themselves and therefore irredeemably stuck in the realm of falsehood: since nature is already an imitation, art imitating nature is the imitation of an imitation. In keeping with Pater, however, Wilde does not proceed to dismiss art as hopelessly removed from reality (let alone recommend censorship). Rather, he argues for a new, nonimitative art, an art that has wrested itself from a mimetic relation to nature and aspires instead to be an art of ideas. Nature still plays a role, but it is given an "ideal treatment," as Wilde puts it at one moment; he also echoes Kant once more in calling the result a "decorative" art.[31] Once it ceases to be imitative, art can circumvent nature, itself only an imitation, and relate directly to ideas.

Wilde's aesthetic Platonism undertakes a more surprising and at first sight implausible further step: not only does (should) art not imitate nature, but conversely, nature imitates art. The argument amounts to what we might now call radical constructivism of the kind more recently argued by Judith Butler and others: nature is not a given, but something perceived and hence constructed.[32] To the extent that art shapes perception, art comes first and our perception (or construction) of nature second. This part of Wilde's argument has rarely been taken seriously: the flippant tone in which it is presented makes it sound like one of those Wildean aphorisms that are too clever by half and should be appreciated exclusively as part of Wilde's outré art of deliberate provocation. But it is in fact not only an arguable position but also a direct consequence of his argument, the ultimate consequence of aesthetic Platonism: if art relates directly to ideas, it occupies a place prior to nature. This means that art imitates not nature but only ideas, leading to a play of thought, as Georg Kaiser put it in his vision of a Platonic drama of ideas.

It is significant that Wilde not only formulated a startling theory of aesthetic Platonism but adapted from Plato the form in which this theory had originally been formulated: the critical dialogue. Aesthetic Platonism here leads to a revival of dialogic drama. In order to understand the ramification of Wilde's aesthetic Platonism, we must reconstruct not only his doctrine but also his practice, his use of the Platonic dialogue. Indeed, his "nature imitates art" doctrine is presented not by Wilde but by a character, Vivian, whose theories are punctuated by the objections of an interlocutor, Cyril. While *The Decay of Lying* contains little explicit reflection on the dialogue form, this is not true of its companion piece, *The Critic as Artist* (1890). Here Wilde pauses to comment on this form with the following words:

> Dialogue, certainly, that wonderful literary form which, from Plato to Lucian . . . the creative critics of the world have always employed, can never lose for the thinker its attraction as a mode of expression. By its means he can both reveal and conceal himself, and give form to every fancy, and reality to every mood. By its means he can exhibit the object from each point of view, and show it to us in the round, as a sculptor shows us things, gaining in this manner all the richness and reality of effect that comes from those side issues that are suddenly suggested by the central idea in its progress, and really illumine the idea more completely, or from those felicitous after-thoughts that give a fuller completeness to the central scheme, and yet convey something of the delicate charm of chance.[33]

The first thing to note about the passage is that it directly relates the form of the dialogue to the doctrine of aesthetic Platonism: dialogue is capable of giving provisional reality to otherwise intangible entities. According to this passage, the dialogue (in contrast to the treatise) is able to express intangible ideas because it makes room for "side issues" and "after-thoughts" that create a reality effect that is further enhanced by an element of "chance." This sounds like an argument in favor of realism, but it isn't. Instead, art creates only an effect of reality while in fact being directed to what Wilde alternatively calls "fancy," "idea," and "scheme." In *The Picture of Dorian Gray* (1891), Wilde makes the Platonic resonances of these terms explicit: "the mere shapes and patterns of things [were] patterns of some other and more perfect form which shadow they made real . . . Was it not Plato, that artist in thought, who had first analyzed it?"[34]

Wilde's comment on the dialogue form is especially useful for understanding his view of character. The dialogue, Wilde writes, introduces one or several personae through which authors can both hide and reveal themselves. The question of how characters in philosophical dialogues relate to the opinions of the author has always disturbed—or intrigued—readers of such dialogues ever since Plato presented his philosophy through the persona of his teacher, Socrates. The question of impersonation, authorship, and mask also characterizes the passage itself, which is spoken by a character named Gilbert. The art of hiding behind a character is the feature of drama Wilde foregrounds in *The Decay of Lying*, in which Vivian reminds us that it wasn't Shakespeare who uttered the famous line about art holding up the mirror to nature but the character Hamlet, and as part of one of his supposedly mad fits. Nevertheless, much like Plato's dialogues, Wilde's dialogues invite the identification of one protagonist with Wilde, thus engaging the reader in a complicated back-and-forth between author and dramatic character. Wilde's dramatic dialogues depend on characters, but they also call the independence of these characters into question and instead use characters as devices through which to accomplish a set of intellectual goals. This is drama, but drama pressed into the service of ideas.

Just as the philosophical dialogue uses character in a peculiar manner, so it also uses the other dramatic categories such as setting and action. *The Decay of Lying* takes place indoors and thus sets the scene for the main argument with a denunciation of nature, located outside, and a praise of culture, inside. *The Critic as Artist*, likewise, is set in a place of leisure and reading: Gilbert's library. The contingencies of life are evoked but also pushed to the margin: at various moments the two interlocutors contemplate going out and their conversation is in fact interrupted by dinner. These activities, however, only frame the primary action of the dialogue, which is captured in the subtitle: *With Some Remarks upon the Importance of Doing Nothing*. Doing nothing also underpins the crucial distinction between the critic and the artist on which the argument of the dialogue is based: creating works of art is a form of doing and therefore debased, while criticism is a form of talking and therefore superior. Wilde here develops the opposite of a speech act theory of language by dissociating language from labor (doing and action) and associating it instead with leisurely talking, reading, and writing. Earlier in his life, Wilde had identified this same opposition of doing and doing nothing, of action and contemplation, with none other than Plato.[35] Indeed, inaction is Wilde's way of undermining and reusing the category of action—the traditional center of the dramatic form—for other purposes. It is also the explanation for Wilde's attempt to cultivate an air of effortlessness, indeed, his insistence on style in general, which he associates with a purposeless, decorative aesthetics. Wilde's Platonic drama turns characters into the author's personae, dramatic settings into scenes of explicit leisure, and dramatic action into studied inaction. Inaction also has an important political consequence, since Wilde's essay "The Soul of Man Under Socialism" hails socialism as the system under which a life of inaction will ultimately be brought about.[36]

Finally, Wilde's dialogues include a particular conception of theater; they are written, as Kaiser put it, with theatrical means. The critique of action, for example, implies a critique of actors, the agents of action. Even though Wilde never developed a theory of acting, we can derive such a theory from *Dorian Gray*, which presents the actress Sybil as a creature of the theater, an actor who fully inhabits all the characters she plays. The opposite of Diderot's calculating actor, Sybil cannot conceive of a split between herself and the role, because these roles are all she knows. When Dorian Gray is about to leave her, she looks back at her life as an actor, from which Dorian has rescued her. The language is taken straight from Plato's cave:

"Dorian, Dorian," she cried, "before I knew you, acting was the one reality of my life. It was only in the theatre that I lived. . . . The painted scenes were my world. I knew nothing but shadows, and I thought them real. You came—oh, my beautiful love!—and you freed my soul from prison. You taught me what reality really is. . . . You had brought me something higher, something of which all art is but a reflection."[37]

This is a critique of the theater articulated in a novella chiefly concerned with the tragic confusion of life and art. It is aimed particularly at actors, who are condemned to live in Plato's cave; once they leave it, as Sybil does when she comes under the sway of Dorian Gray, their art is over. Sibyl becomes self-conscious and suddenly finds herself incapable of good acting.

Wilde himself grew increasingly dismissive of actors, preferring puppets to actors, even though he continued to admire great actors such as Sarah Bernhardt, whom he had lined up to appear in *Salomé* before the play was censored. Wilde's critique of actors echoes the widespread polemic against actors among modernists, such as Edward Gordon Craig's call for marionettes instead of actors or Maurice Maeterlinck's preference for thinking of his works as "plays for marionettes."[38] From this perspective, Wilde's use of the dramatic dialogue is in line with a more traditional understanding of Plato: a form of literary drama that wants to do without actors. But like the dramatic Plato I am presenting here, Wilde resolves the question of theatricality not by shunning it but by creating a new conception of drama. This conception reverses some of drama's most central tenets, such as the emphasis on autonomous characters, action, and acting, replacing them with a dramaturgy based on authorial personae, inaction, and a critique of actors. Wilde was a Platonist, but he was also, and more important, a dramatic Platonist.

Wilde is a particularly good example of a Platonist who, far from abandoning the theater, in fact sought it out with an impressive array of plays, among them his two masterworks, *The Importance of Being Earnest* (1895) and *Salomé* (1893). These plays should be understood not as independent creations, disconnected from the dramaturgy and aesthetics of his dialogues, but as an alternative venue for expressing the same dramatic Platonism that informs his other works; these plays are deeply informed by Wilde's dramaturgy of authorial personae, inaction, and his critique of acting. *The Importance of Being Earnest*, with its focus on names, impersonation, the exchange of roles, as well as its language of paradoxical inversion, richly resonates with the dialogues. Indeed, it was with reference to *Importance* that Wilde wrote: "In art I am Platonic, not Aristotelian, tho' I wear my Plato with a difference."[39] One of the techniques *Importance* picks up from the critical dialogues is the manipulation of character; in fact, the title character, Ernest, had appeared in *The Critic as Artist* as Gilbert's interlocutor. The plot of *Importance* revolves around the fact that both leading male characters have invented doubles, a brother in one case, a good friend in the other, as an excuse to lead a double life. Behind the attraction of this illicit practice, called by the deliberately vague term "bunburying," stands also the forced double life of homosexuals: the confusions of character, in the theatrical sense, are charged with questions of "character" in the moral sense.[40] Only at the end of the play can the proper names be affixed to the proper people in a conclusion that belies the disruptive confusions deliberately created throughout the play.

If character is the primary focus of *Importance*, the secondary one is Wilde's other favorite category from the critical dialogues: inaction. The very title refers to it by echoing the subtitle of *The Critic as Artist: The Importance of Doing Nothing*. As in the critical dialogues, the protagonists in *Importance* do nothing but talk—in addition to their role playing. The quick-witted exchanges, non sequiturs, inversions, and unexpected conclusions form part of Wilde's signature repertoire and appear with equal frequency in both his critical dialogues and his stage plays. While it is true that most comedies of manners consist of nothing but talk, in the case of Wilde one should remember that, far from being a vehicle for comic action, talking is emphatically associated with comic inaction. Finally, the play can be said to illustrate Wilde's grand inversion of art and nature. At the end of the play it unexpectedly turns out that Jack is in fact called Ernest: life has imitated the art of deception.

If *Importance* is one way in which Wilde translates his dramatic Platonism from the critical dialogues into a stage play, the other, and perhaps more intriguing, translation can be found in a play that I consider the culmination of Wilde's dramatic oeuvre: *Salomé*. The first thing to note is its troubled stage history, which gives us an inkling of its complicated relation to the theater. The play was censored in England putatively by recourse to an old law prohibiting the representation of biblical characters onstage. Wilde shifted gears and produced an elegant print publication with drawings by Aubrey Beardsley. In 1896, however, just after Wilde's trials, the play was performed in France, a fitting location since Wilde had originally written it in French. Soon thereafter, the play served as the libretto for an opera by Richard Strauss, in which form it entered the opera repertory. The play itself, however, has maintained an ambiguous relation to the stage. Often it receives semistaged performances or staged readings (a recent one featured Al Pacino in the role of Herod); full-fledged productions are somewhat rarer and mostly reserved for the opera version.[41] Indeed, in his defense of the play, Douglas had written: "Artistically speaking the play would gain nothing by performance, to my mind it would lose much. To be appreciated it must be abstracted, and to be abstracted it must be read."[42]

This complicated relation to the theater lies at the heart of the play itself. *Salomé* is a showcase of Wilde's ornamental aesthetics of abstraction that does not imitate anything, least of all nature. It is also a test case of how this aesthetics can be translated into theater. On one hand, *Salomé* exploits the theater, culminating in Salomé's dance of the seven veils. On the other hand, the play also serves as a denunciation of the dance, as well as of the theater that makes it possible. One might say that *Salomé* is a play fully ensconced in Plato's cave, yet also highly aware that it can never be anything but an artificial world of shadows. In keeping with the play's uneasy relation to the theater—and Douglas' claim that *Salomé* needs to be read in order for its abstraction to work—the play is profoundly divided into a theatrical mode and a rhetorical one. It veers toward theater but also toward language, for like Wilde's dialogues, *Salomé* is also an intensely verbal play, thriving on different types of language. The two dimensions of this play, theatrical and verbal, do not exist easily side by side. Rather, it is from their competition and confrontation that the play derives its true drama.

In the domain of language, *Salomé* calls attention to itself through a relentless use of similes, extended comparisons that heap image upon image in an extravaganza of figuration. "Look at the moon! How strange the moon seems! She is like a woman rising from a tomb," the Page of Herodias exclaims, to be answered by the Young Syrian: "She has a strange look. She is like a little princess who wears a yellow veil, and whose feet are of silver."[43] The passage evokes a whole visual world that is not presented onstage but conjured by language. This figurative drive culminates in the encounter between Salomé and Jokanaan. In three extended arias, Salomé elaborates Jokanaan's body through chains of similes: "Thy body is white like the lilies of a field that the mower hath never mowed. Thy body is white like the snows that lie on the mountains, like the snows that lie on the mountains of Judea, and come down into the valleys." Soon, however, these images are deemed insufficient, and the comparisons turn negative. The passage continues: "The roses in the garden of the Queen of Arabia are not so white as thy body. Neither the roses in the garden of the Queen of Arabia, nor the feet of the dawn when they light on the leaves, nor the breast of the moon when she lies on the breast of the sea . . . There is nothing in the world so white as thy body."[44] Three times sequences of ever more extreme similes, followed by negative comparisons, inflame Salomé's desire. Salome is intoxicated by the visual world that is in part of her own making—by an excessively figurative language of the visible that will lead to the play's tragic ending.

Salome's figurative language is joined by the different, though no less figurative, language of Jokanaan (Wilde's version of John the Baptist). Throughout the play, he utters predictions in veiled phrases and prophecies that sound like this: "From the seed of the serpent shall come forth a basilisk, and that which is born of it shall devour the birds."[45] Not everything Jokanaan says is as difficult to understand, but his darkest pronouncements are dense and obscure and in need of interpretation. They are as figurative as the similes but are much harder to interpret. Figurative language does not always create pictures that add to or even compete with the stage. Sometimes, as in the case of Jokanaan, they cast a dark shadow over the whole project of figurative language, adding to it somber and ominous tones.

This excessive use of similes and omens leads to resistance. Herodiade is most adamant about rejecting any type of simile, and deadpans: "No;

the moon is like the moon."[46] Even Herod comes to a similar conclusion at one point, when he says: "It is not wise to find symbols in everything that one sees."[47] Instead of constructing similes, Herod's dominant use of language is that of speech acts, especially the speech act of the promise by which he grants Salomé any wish if she dances for him. Even though Herod is afraid of Jokanaan and loath to have him killed when Salomé demands it, he is bound to his oath and will not break his promise. Once the promise is fulfilled, however, he ends the play with another speech act, this time a command: "Kill that woman!" he instructs the soldiers, who promptly act it out, thus bringing the play to a close.[48]

Wilde's similes conjure a visual world that rivals and even outdoes the one we see onstage. They also exemplify his Platonic doctrine of a nonimitative, purely decorative art. The visual languages of the play don't imitate anything, but create a richly ornamental tapestry arranged in formal patters of repetition, echoes, and revisions that rival the world we see in the theater. From the point of view of dramatic structure, these languages are not necessary; there is no dramatic utility attached to them except their very excess. Since for Wilde art will adhere to Platonist ideas only if it abandons the task of representing nature, this artificial hall of mirrors of ornamental languages surely comes closest to achieving that goal. Wilde wrote his *Salomé* in French, the language of symbolism honed by such figures as Mallarmé and Maeterlinck. But in keeping with the cultural frame of reference of the time, Wilde associates the project of an ornamental language also with the biblical Orient. While the story of Salomé is based on the New Testament, especially on Mark, Wilde borrows his similes from the Song of Solomon: "Your hair is like a flock of goats, moving down the slopes of Gilead. Your teeth are like a flock of shorn ewes that have come up from the washing, all of which bear twins, and not one among them is bereaved. Your lips are like a crimson thread, and your mouth is lovely. Your cheeks are like halves of a pomegranate behind your veil."[49] Wilde's language is symbolist, and it is Platonist, but it is also part of what one might call ornamental orientalism.

Despite the play's obsession with language, *Salomé* is also a play that revels in theater, especially in the word's literal meaning as a place of seeing—and here we come to the second, theatrical dimension of the play. *Salomé* opens with a scene of seeing in which a page beholds Salomé and is immediately stricken with an infatuation that will end in suicide. Likewise, King Herod is prompted to swear his fateful oath because he desires to see Salomé perform the dance of the seven veils. Most important, Salomé insists on laying eyes on Jokanaan, and it is this act of perception that first stirs a desire that will eventually lead to Jokanaan's beheading and her own death.

In the midst of all these fateful scenes of seeing, however, Wilde introduces various forms of resistance to sight, thus betraying Plato's influence. There are, for example, the theological debates among Jewish characters about the invisibility of their God. While the other characters in the play dismiss such conceptions as patently absurd, we are free to come to different conclusions, admiring a religion that clearly seeks to escape the fateful entanglements of sight. The second rejection of sight emanates from Joka-naan. We hear his voice long before we see him until, by Salomé's prompting, he is finally dragged from the cistern into the open. Jokanaan knows all about the dangers of sight and does not want to be seen, nor does he want to see Salomé. This double rejection fuels Salomé's desire all the more. In keeping with this theme of sight and resistance to it, the play ends in utter darkness: we don't see Salomé kiss Jokanaan's severed head, but only hear her describe this act verbally. A last beam of light falls on Salomé; Herod catches sight of her and orders her killed.

Wilde cannot and does not want to escape the theater of the cave. At the same time, he subjects the theater to critical scrutiny. This is the conse-quence of aesthetic Platonism in the theater: the cave parable becomes the paradigm for a self-critical theatrical imagination. Wilde's meditation on sight needs the theater, uses the theater, and is about the theater: we want to see as much as the characters onstage do; we, too, are not content with the invisible nor with merely hearing Jokanaan's voice. When Salomé demands that Jokanaan be dragged from his prison, or when Herod en-tices Salomé to dance, we identify with this desire to see, since we find ourselves in a place of seeing as much as these characters. At the same time, this theatrical dimension is presented as leading to disaster. *Salomé* is a tragedy of sight, of the *theatron*: a tragedy of the theater itself.

George Bernard Shaw

Plato and Boswell, as the dramatists who invented Socrates and Dr. Johnson, impress me more deeply than the romantic playwrights.
—George Bernard Shaw

In many ways, Shaw is an odd mirror image of Wilde. The two London-based Irish dramatists closely watched each other's careers and sent each other their publications. Shaw's comedies, with their quick repartees and concise aphorisms, share much with Wilde's paradoxes. Even Shaw's peculiar outfits—his signature woolen suits were designed according to the specifications of a German theorist of organic clothing—and his con-spicuous vegetarianism could be seen as a version or inversion of Wilde's quintessential dandyism. All this, however, is beside my central point, which is that Shaw's theater of ideas emerges as a form of Platonic drama that toys with the techniques employed by Wilde, but ultimately rejects them in favor of a different model, a different conjunction of theater and philosophy, what he called the comedy of ideas.

Criticism on Shaw, especially recently, has not been sensitive to the project of a drama of ideas, probably because of the prevailing fascination with materiality, bodies, and objects. Earlier critics were more attuned to Shaw's idealism and even (though more hesitantly) to his Platonism. In

1909, the writer and philosopher G. K. Chesterton published what is still an intriguing book on Shaw. In the last section of the book, called "Philosopher," Chesterton highlighted Shaw's turn to Nietzsche and an evolutionary theory of breeding the Superman, and attributed these to Shaw's reading of Plato; he concludes, "Bernard Shaw has much affinity to Plato."[50] Chesterton also recognized that Shaw's project of combining theater and philosophy implied a radical overhaul of drama. Shaw "has brought back into English drama all the streams of fact or tendency which are commonly called undramatic," he wrote, but insisted that this quality of the undramatic merely meant that a new understanding of drama was afoot here, one at odds with traditional drama.[51] One critic to follow Chesterton in this assessment was Eric Bentley. His 1946 study *The Playwright as Thinker* discusses the role of ideas, noting how rarely they become a genuine part of drama:

> Seldom, however, have ideas been the lifeblood of drama. . . . Molière may be said to use ideas but not to make his drama out of them. . . . it may be suggested that Molière uses accepted ideas, lets his characters embody them and fight it out. The characters fight, the ideas lie still and unmolested. In a drama of ideas, on the other hand, the ideas are questioned, and it is by the questioning, and could only be by the questioning, that the idea becomes dramatic, for seldom or never is there drama without conflict.[52]

This definition neatly captures one side of Platonic drama: the effect drama has on ideas. It leaves out the other side: the effect ideas have on drama. Shaw's project was a combination of the two.

Shaw's drama is driven primarily by Shaw's own idiosyncratic form of socialism. In contrast to Wilde's aesthetic Platonism, Shaw developed a political and propagandistic Platonism premised on a half-baked concoction of Darwinism, Fabian-style socialism, and a belief in the shaping power of ideas. Indeed, Shaw sharply criticized Darwin for having taken the mind—and thus ideas—out of the evolutionary process. This is an idealist, or Platonist, evolutionary theory, one combined with an equally idiosyncratic form of Marxism, a dematerialized Marxism driven by a belief in theory, abstraction, discourse, and ideas as much as by a belief in acts, production, and labor. This peculiar combination, what one might call Platonic socialism, underpins Shaw's rarely performed eight-hour cycle *Back to Methuselah* (1922).[53] *Methuselah* combines two subgenres within the theater of ideas: the theater of science (Michael Frayn's *Copenhagen* would be a recent example) and the utopia, a genre that, perhaps due to Plato's influence, is often presented in dialogue form.[54] Extending from Adam and Eve to the year 31,920, the *Methuselah* cycle envisions a world in which humans have complete control over their external shapes and spend their increasingly long lives enjoying the pleasures of contemplation. Indeed, Shaw set the last and most futuristic play in the cycle, *As Far as Thought Can Reach*, in the costumes of Plato's Greece. This Greece, however, is actually located in Britain. Through a geographic inversion, the center of the British Empire has been moved to Baghdad, while the newly peripheral British Isles are occupied by long-lived sages who have outgrown their desire for the imitative arts and through an interest in mathematics have become philosophers interested only in Platonic forms. In *Methuselah*, Shaw's idealist socialism is translated more or less directly into the world of the play. Evolutionary socialism as Shaw conceived of it was poised against the hope for a single, revolutionary break. Shaw himself believed in a gradual evolution of humankind, an evolution driven by ideas, not material circumstances. This is why his evolution is teleological and why it reaches its apex, in *Methuselah*, in humans who have overcome their bodies and dwell in a realm of contemplation and ideas. Shaw here uses drama for the purpose of showing his evolutionary idealism in practice.

While Shaw's idealism in *Methuselah* does not need drama to be represented, the same is not true of his much more elaborate comedy of ideas, one that announces the ambition of combining drama and philosophy in its very subtitle: *Man and Superman: A Comedy and a Philosophy* (1903). With this work, Shaw undertakes a genuine integration of drama and idea. My discussion of this play will hinge on the nature of this conjunction, this "and" between comedy and philosophy.

At first it seems that the two terms of the subtitle—comedy and philosophy—refer to the two separate parts that make up the main body of this play: a regular framing comedy and an inner philosophical dialogue. The comedy revolves around the relation between the revolutionary pamphleteer John Tanner and his ward, Ann. Despite the objections of her other guardian and a swooning admirer, Ann is secretly out to marry Tanner, a goal she accomplishes despite Tanner's increasingly desperate acts of resistance. In the middle of this jolly comedy we are confronted, rather abruptly, with a philosophical dialogue, also known as *Don Juan in Hell*, a dream play in which all the figures from the outer comedy appear transformed into characters of the Don Juan plot. Shaw wittily called this middle section a "Shavio-Socratic dialogue."[55] He also imagined this part to be addressed to an audience of philosophers and, like Wilde and Kaiser, places it in the tradition of Plato.

The double bill of comedy and philosophy is framed by two more philosophical or theoretical texts: an extensive preface, one of Shaw's favorite genres, which tries to explain the relation between the outer comedy and the inner philosophy, and an appendix, the so-called *Revolutionist's Handbook*, written by the character John Tanner, which presents a theory of breeding the Superman that sounds like a combination of Darwin, Nietzsche, and Bergson put together by a scary fanatic. Fortunately, the significance of *Man and Superman* does not reside in the soundness of its philosophy. Rather, it is to be sought in Shaw's attempt to introduce philosophy into comedy and comedy into philosophy. Shaw's contemporaries recognized, but mostly rejected, such a project. Referring to the contrast between the delicious outer comedy, which audiences loved, and the dry discussions of the inner philosophy, which they ignored, Egon Friedell observed that it was clever of Shaw to sugarcoat his pill with comedy, but "even cleverer of the public to lick off the sugar and leave the pill alone."[56] Max Beerbohm observed of *Man and Superman*: "Treasure it, too, as a work of specific art, in line with your Plato." But he refused to accept it as drama: "a play it is not."[57]

The reviewers and commentators who recognized a division in Shaw between a proper drama (the outer comedy) and the inner Shavio-Socratic dialogue were half right, but they missed the fact that Shaw was attempting to fuse the two, creating a new drama of ideas in the tradition of Plato. When the play is seen from this angle, we can find several elements of Plato's dramaturgy at work, including the presentation and then undercutting of a philosophical character, a dialectic between action and inaction, and a critical use of metatheater. Like most authors intent on creating a new theater of ideas, Shaw found himself, wittingly or unwittingly, undertaking a reform of theater that resonated with Plato's dramatic dialogues—and their contemporary revival by Wilde.

As in the case of Plato and Wilde, a central component of the endeavor to create a theater of ideas was the use and manipulation of character, in particular, of the philosophical protagonist. Shaw introduces philosophy into the comedy through the figure of John Tanner, who takes every opportunity to hold forth on his crackpot theories, even as his masterpiece, the *Revolutionist's Handbook*, is thrown into the wastebasket in the very first scene of the play. To find a hapless philosopher such as Tanner in a comedy is not surprising. Tanner belongs to the tradition of the comic stage philosopher. By creating and then ridiculing a character who does nothing but expound philosophies, Shaw inoculates himself against the charge that his characters are mere mouthpieces for his own ideas. Shaw would return to the problem of authorial impersonation with similar irony in his greatest hit, *Pygmalion*, a play ultimately about the creation of a character and its manipulation.[58] Al Hirschfeld captured this view in his cover illustration for the *Playbill* for *My Fair Lady*, in which Shaw is the puppet master of Higgins, who in turn manipulates Eliza Doolittle. In the end, however, Eliza seeks independence from her creator, just as Shaw allowed his philosophizing creatures to become objects of laughter.

But Shaw does not only make fun of Tanner. He also uses him to stage a conflict between action and talking (i.e., inaction). Tanner is all talk, and he is similar to Wilde's Gilbert in his use of witty inversions and paradoxes. *Man and Superman* even parodies Wilde's famous list of aphorisms by having the dubious *Revolutionist's Handbook* end with a list of its own. However, talking is precisely not valued in Shaw's drama. Unlike Wilde, Shaw does not seek to create a drama of inaction—of doing nothing— and hence a drama of talk, but instead he wants to have comedy and philosophy occur simultaneously. Consequently, Tanner is not allowed to dwell in his natural habitat, the (Wildean) library, but is forced onto a collision course with the other characters populating the comedy. In other words, the philosophizing talker is confronted with dramatic action, including car chases and encounters with revolutionary bandits and crazy Americans.

The driving forces behind the play's action are women. Central to this conception of agency is something called the "life force," a concept Shaw frequently personifies and to which he ascribes superior agency. This life force acts principally through women, in this case, Ann, to bring about its ultimate purpose: a union between Tanner and Ann that will create offspring and hence advance evolution. Through the governing concept of the life force, Shaw's notion of female action is grounded in biology, in nature. This is why Shaw inverts the Don Juan plot by turning Ann (Doña Ana) into the hunter and Tanner (Don Juan) into the hunted. Against this female bio-action all philosophers are helpless, and the play ends with its triumph: Ann catches Tanner and the two will presumably have offspring. It turns out that even such a character as Tanner, who has theorized the life force and thus should be in a position to recognize and to avoid it, must succumb to it in the end. Ann, as the vehicle through which the life force does its work, becomes the motor with which Shaw animates the dramatic action of the entire comedy. However, even though Shaw undermines Tanner as a character, he simultaneously turns his philosophy of the life force into the animating principle of the comedy; the play could be considered a kind of laboratory of the life force hypothesis, very much the way *Methuselah* functions as a laboratory for the long-term effects of creative evolution. Shaw thus smuggles his philosophy back into the play, not as a talking character, but as the principle of (bio-)action. The philosopher (his action) is discredited, but the philosophy is proven right.

After bringing philosophy into the comedy through impersonation (the comic stage philosopher Tanner) and a particular conception of action (the life force acting through Ann), how does Shaw do the inverse and bring comedy into the philosophical dialogue? From the very outset, the philosophical dialogue, *Don Juan in Hell*, is determined by a completely different set of laws and forces. In particular, the bio-action animating the comedy is no longer operative since this section is set in the afterlife, in hell, where no one worries about reproduction, the life force, or marriage. Consequently, the entire logic of the comedy is brought to a temporary halt. It seems as if Shaw had decided that philosophy requires the suspension of comedy and of theatrical (and biological, evolutionary) action. In fact, Shaw wittily anticipated the complaints of his audience about the length of this dialogue by observing that the characters, being dead, have all the time in the world for their exchanges.[59] This is not something a theater producer wants to hear.

The interruption of comedy is most visible with respect to the category of setting. The play opens onto a library with books, including Tanner's own, serving as the main stage props in concert with statues of assorted philosophers and thinkers. Subsequently we move outside, and as soon as Tanner realizes that Ann is after him—and of course, as a foolish stage philosopher, he is the last one to realize this—the play turns into a car chase leading all the way to Spain, where it culminates with Tanner and his chauffeur being taken prisoner. The scenes in Spain are also central to the play's thematic interest in revolution. Tanner is an aristocratic socialist who knows nothing of revolutionary action, just as England more generally figures as a place where one can talk about revolution but never make one. If one wants to become an activist, one needs to go to Spain, where the guerrilla fighter Mendoza and his group of quarrelling socialists and communists waylay rich travelers, such as our group of English motorists.

It is at this moment that Shaw interrupts the action to begin the philosophical dream play. Both the (bio-)action of Ann and the revolutionary action of Mendoza are brought to an abrupt halt with a scene change described by an elaborate stage direction (one of Shaw's favorite genres): "Instead of the Sierra there is nothing; omnipresent nothing. No sky, no peaks, no light, no sound, no time nor space, utter void."[60] Philosophy, it seems, has to occur in an empty, abstract, negative space. But this negation is merely the beginning of something else: a thoroughly theatricalized stage. The scene continues: "Then somewhere the beginning of a pallor, and with it a faint throbbing buzz as of a ghostly violoncello . . . A couple of ghostly violins presently take advantage of this bass and therewith the pallor reveals a man in the void, an incorporeal but visible man seated, absurdly enough, on nothing. . . . [B]y the aid of certain sparkles of violet light in the pallor, the man's costume explains itself as that of a Spanish nobleman of the XV–XVI century." A little later, another ghostly figure appears: "Another pallor in the void, this time not violet, but a disagreeable smoky yellow."[61] All these spotlights are accompanied by musical passages from Mozart's *Don Giovanni*. The evacuated space is thus filled with extravagant costumes, fantastic light, and operatic music. During the rehearsals for the 1907 premiere of the play at the Court Theatre, Harley Granville-Barker, who played Tanner (but was made up to look suspiciously like Shaw), reproached the other actors for their flat performance: "Ladies and gentlemen, will you please remember that this is Italian opera!"[62] Shaw suspends action, but in its place he creates a theatrical extravaganza inspired by Mozart as if to prove that philosophy and theater can meet after all.

These spectacular, theatrical scenes also affect the characters. As Don Juan, aka John Tanner, informs us at the outset, bodies in hell are mere shadows, remnants of former lives. Their status as shadows, reminiscent of Plato's cave, allows Shaw to turn them into theatrical vehicles that can be manipulated at will. In the Don Juan plot, the statue of the dead commander, Ana's father, whom Don Juan has killed, appears at the end of the play to take revenge. Shaw preserves this set piece, but despite the Commander's putatively heavy and immobile form, the stage direction specifies that he "waives his majesty with infinite grace; walks with feather-like step."[63] As shadows, none of the characters have to bother about their bodies, even when they are statues; their shapes are entirely a matter of choice, of convention and habit. Indeed, these shadowy shapes can be changed at will. The old Doña Ana, for example, turns into a woman of twenty-seven in front of our very eyes by merely uttering a word. The stage direction indicates laconically, "Whisk! The old woman becomes a young one."[64] While in the framing comedy talking had been without consequence, here Shaw makes it clear that words can acquire supreme power. Shaw's Platonic dream play also draws on and anticipates a number of avant-garde techniques, from Strindberg to surrealism, in which words effect transformations of the theatrical space. In the outer comedy, action rules, but in *Don Juan in Hell* words and ideas reign supreme.

At the same time, *Don Juan in Hell* resembles a modernist metaplay, since its principal subject matter is the theater itself. Rather than setting his philosophical dialogue in a library, as Wilde had done, or in the Grecian England of *Methuselah*, Shaw sets it on a spectacular, operatic, and theatricalized stage. This means that the theater is not restricted to the outer comedy but returns, in a very different form, in the philosophical dream play. This dream play is not based on the conventions of comedy, with courtship, fast pursuits, and marriage—since everyone is dead and thus incapable of producing offspring, the life force has no power, or interest, here. Rather, this play-within-the-play presents a magical, derealized, and spectacular stage, a theater in which flesh-and-blood characters are turned into shadows, comedic action is suspended but also turned into stage magic, and empty speech becomes a potent force. Shaw recognized that Plato's cave is best understood as a modern stage equipped with electric light, sophisticated costumes, an orchestra pit, and trapdoors ready to effect sudden appearances, transformations, and vanishing acts, a stage capable of turning the actors and scenes of comedy into the shadow theater of philosophy.

This shadow theater is not completely cut off from the outer comedy. All the characters in the dream play are recognizable versions of characters from the comedy, and to emphasize these similarities, these pairs are played by the same actors: Tanner plays Don Juan; Ann, Doña Ana; Ann's guardian, Doña Ana's father; and the revolutionary rebel Mendoza, of course, plays the devil. If Wilde's Ernest led a double life in *The Importance of Being Earnest* and *The Critic as Artist*, Shaw brings his doubles into a single, if divided, play. Even though *Man and Superman* finally concludes with a return to comedy, bio-action, the stage philosopher, and the marriage of Tanner and Ann, the transformations and inversions of the dream play linger on, calling into question the distinction between empty talk and cunning action, ridiculous philosophy and serious biology. *Man and Superman* thus mixes idea and character, argument and action by forging a drama from their collision. This drama may be an acquired taste, but Shaw made it palpable enough to generate, together with Wilde, a genuine tradition of a theater of ideas in Britain.

In creating such a tradition, Shaw knew what he was up against. The center of the dramatic orthodoxy against which he had to fight was Shakespeare (even though Shakespeare had enabled earlier authors of Socrates plays to envision mixtures of tragedy and comedy), and it was against Shakespeare, therefore, that Shaw positioned his own drama of ideas.[65]

Platonic theaters always turn against the theatrical orthodoxy of their day, ever since Plato attacked Greek tragedy. Shaw's theater is a perfect example of this rule. On one hand, he used comedy to cut philosophers such as Tanner down to size, but on the other hand he invented a drama that thoroughly revises dramatic strictures either Aristotelian or Shakespearean. Toward the end of his long and productive life, Shaw wrote a puppet play—a form that itself echoes the puppet theater in Plato's cave. This play, entitled *Shakes Versus Shav* (1949), captures his ambition to overturn the acknowledged dramatic paradigm of Shakespeare. Shakespeare and Shaw squabble and hit each other on the head, as in a Punch and Judy show, to settle the question of who is the better playwright.[66] I like to think that the person pulling the strings here is Plato, that it was with Plato's help that Shaw managed to take on Shakespeare, creating a new Platonic drama in the process.

A Shavio-Wildean Socrates Play

One unlikely sign of success of Shaw's Platonic theater was its influence on a bona fide writer of a Socrates play, Laurence Housman. Originally Housman was a member of the Wilde circle. While working as an illustrator, he met Beardsley, the author of the famous woodcuts that accompany Wilde's publication of *Salomé*; Housman also illustrated a book by the Pre-Raphaelite Dante Gabriel Rossetti, and Beardsley had him work as an illustrator on the notorious *Yellow Book*. It is difficult to imagine assembling more credentials as a symbolist and aestheticist in turn-of-the-century London.

When it came to writing a Socrates play, however, Housman turned to Shaw. He had already coauthored a play with Shaw's collaborator Harley Granville-Barker and was therefore acquainted with Shaw's work and circle. His play, *The Death of Socrates* (1925), is a typical Socrates play, subtitled *A Dramatic Scene, Founded upon Two of Plato's Dialogues, the 'Crito' and the 'Phaedo'; Adapted for the Stage.*[67] As the subtitle promises, this is a rather faithful adaptation of Plato, depicting Socrates' refusal to escape from prison and a shortened account of his reasons for accepting death. Housman deviates from Plato only to praise Xanthippe's home economy and her way of raising the children—an echo of the Victorian doctrine of separate spheres. Housman also captures the stop-and-go rhythm of Plato's dialogue and the way the scene and the person of Socrates undermine his own insistence on the immortality of the soul.

Even though Housman thus teases out the dramatic elements and adds theatrics here and there with a light touch, he is unsure about the status of the play. In the preface, he worries, as so many of his predecessors did, whether there is enough "dramatic interest" in the play, "in spite of the lighter interludes which the action has enabled me to introduce."[68] Instead of action, there is much "discussion," which might turn out to be a problem with audiences. But then Housman takes heart when he remembers Shaw, the great champion of the discussion play, whose "genius" has made debate "not only tolerable but entertaining upon the stage." Encouraged by Shaw's example, he concludes his preface by insisting that Socrates' death is "so moving, so nobly dramatic," that it will work on the stage, and ends by regarding Socrates as a hero. Socrates, and with him Platonic drama, has been saved thanks to Shaw.

Luigi Pirandello

> Socrates has the *feeling of the opposite.*
>
> —Luigi Pirandello

When the critic and playwright Lionel Abel coined the term metatheater in 1961, he had in mind plays that were concerned not with the world, but only with the theater itself. No playwright fits this term better than Pirandello, whose mature dramas take the project of writing theater about theater to previously unheard-of extremes.[69] In these plays, directors, actors, authors, and audiences confront one another, leading us behind the scenes and into the rehearsal room to witness the ways in which this precarious art form—theater—achieves its peculiar power. At the same time, Pirandello's plays are known for the intellectual fireworks they set off, juggling such fundamental philosophical themes as reason and madness, appearance and reality, in new and ever more confusing constellations. Both of those features, metatheater and theater of ideas, point to Plato, whose philosophical plays often confront and thematize the theater, and nowhere as directly as in the famous cave parable. Like many writers in the Platonic tradition, Pirandello singled out Socrates as an important precursor in his theory of humor, identifying as essential Socrates' ability to maintain two points of view simultaneously: "Socrates has the *feeling of the opposite*," he writes, emphasizing the point by placing it in italics.[70] This feeling of opposition, contradiction, and division is at heart of Pirandello's drama.

Pirandello derived his feeling of the opposite, his keen sense for sudden reversals, from another source as well: his life. He was born into a well-to-do traditional Sicilian family that financed his studies in Rome and Berlin. Despite this relatively cosmopolitan experience, however, he agreed to an arranged marriage to the daughter of one of his father's business partners, in this and other ways accepting the traditional world of Sicily. This world was soon shattered when the sulfur mine on which the family fortune depended was flooded, wiping out his wife's dowry. Increasingly his wife exhibited pathological behaviors, including unfounded fits of jealousy, and was eventually sent to a mental institution. In response Pirandello took a teaching job, withdrew from social life, and started to work as a writer of short stories on the side, plunging himself into a world of his own making. Those stories are set in the deeply traditional, feudal world in which Pirandello grew up, a world dominated by arranged marriages, betrayals, and violence. Sicily also first sparked his interest in the theater, when he became acquainted with a theater group specializing in Sicilian dialect plays, using traditional commedia dell'arte masks and techniques. But for a long time Pirandello continued to consider theater as a secondary art form, and, like Wilde, he regarded actors as mere facilitators rather than artists, grouping them with book illustrators and translators.

From these unlikely resources, Pirandello forged one of the most influential oeuvres in modern drama. The traditional world of his upbringing and his short stories did not disappear entirely; rather, it became the very material and target for Pirandello's metatheatrical attack. Pirandello's metaplays derive their energy from the shattering of the traditional world that Pirandello himself had lost. Often he used a philosophizing character to develop the relativist arguments on which these metaplays thrive, even as he subjects these characters to ridicule in the tradition of the comic stage philosopher. The first of these metaplays was *It Is So! (If You Think So)* (1916), whose title announces the relativist outlook of the play with thesis-like clarity. The philosophical explicator comments on the action of the play, developing a skeptical position that is demonstrated in the play itself: there is no such thing as truth, for truth is only a product of make-believe.

Theater here is located entirely inside Plato's cave, dedicated to demonstrating over and over again that there is no firm ground we can trust; anything can happen, one never knows. If Pirandello thus belongs in the Platonic tradition, he does so in a peculiar manner: while Plato (and to some extent Shaw as well) sought to control the relativizing effects of theater, Pirandello emphasizes them. However, all writers of Platonic drama recognize that theater tends to relativize ideas; by embodying ideas in characters, the theater confronts these ideas with other people and with material circumstances, which often challenges their absolute dominance and validity. Pirandello's openly metatheatrical plays not only exploit this relativizing tendency of theatrical materialization but also constantly remind the audience that the theater is the perfect vehicle for manifesting relativism. In Pirandello's theater, multiple viewpoints collide without an authorial and authoritative conclusion; the very ground on which theater stands is hollow, full of trapdoors and other devices; you cannot trust what you see and hear. Pirandello invented a theater of ideas that exposes the theater as a medium prone to relativism.

The most successful example of this metatheatrical relativism is Pirandello's signature play, *Six Characters in Search of an Author* (1921). The play is based on the conflict between two groups of characters. One is a troupe of actors, plus a manager/director, who are engaged in a rehearsal of a play by the dramatist Pirandello. They are interrupted by a second group, characters who claim to be in search of an author. But in fact they do not need an author at all: their story is already there, inside them, and they are doomed to reenact it whenever the occasion arises. Throughout the play, they will fall into character and act out pieces of the drama to which they owe their existence, pieces of the story in which they are caught. This story is one of Pirandello's traditional, melodramatic plots, with betrayal, adultery, the threat of incest, heart-wrenching confrontations, conflict between stepsiblings, hatred, shame, and a death at the end.

The main plot of the play, then, is not about characters looking for an author, as the title suggests, but about characters looking for a chance to perform, to act out, the drama that is within them. The problem is that these characters aren't any good as actors because they are simply too caught up in their own drama to make good theater out of it; they are little more than raw material. For the story to become a successful play, they need the help of professional actors and a professional director who, more than an author, can whip the material into (theatrical) shape. These professionals quickly understand the outlines of the story (without the help of an author), but now they have to make it work on the stage by cutting, moving scenes, and changing the position of the actors. Characters must be arranged in groups, they have to be visible to the audience, and whispers have to be turned into stage whispers so that the audience will be able to understand what is going on. The characters are incapable of making these changes themselves; after all, these changes would mean altering and betraying the story that they are. In this way, the characters are trapped in the roles that give them their sole existence: they cannot alter them, because altering them would mean altering who they are, which is not within their own power. For this reason, and despite their protests, the professional actors have to take over, impersonating the characters as they see fit in order to ensure that the play will work for an audience. Throughout this painful process of adaptation, it is the father who functions as the spokesperson for the characters, acting as the person who explains the conceit of the play, its implications and conundrums, and who generally holds forth on all conceivable topics; he is reminiscent of the various comic stage philosophers trying to take control of the situation—without success.

The necessity of imposing artistic (theatrical) control onto the raw material of the characters speaks to a conviction located at the core of Pirandello's theatrical relativism. From his own biography, but also from Nietzsche and Bergson, Pirandello had absorbed a deeply skeptical understanding of the world as inherently changeable, prone to chaos, and ultimately uncontrollable by reason and understanding. It is in many ways a philosophical position not so different from the one Plato sought to confront and correct. The theater is the perfect vehicle for expressing such a view, and for this reason Pirandello chose it as the main medium and also as the subject matter of this drama—hence his predilection for meta-theater.

At the same time, Pirandello's very emphasis on theatrical relativism betrays an ultimate yearning for some kind of principle or force that would control all this theatrical, relativist chaos his plays unleash. Even as they seem to illustrate the inevitability of theatrical relativism, these plays actually show this relativism to be deeply troubling. Somehow, life and theater, both prone to relativist chaos, must be controlled. For Pirandello, they can be controlled through art. This conception of art as bringing a slippery world to order is derived from the critic and philosopher Adriano Tilgher. Not surprisingly, the rubric under which Tilgher undertook this exploration was none other than contemporary relativism; his crucial study is entitled *Contemporary Relativists*.[71] Here Tilgher formulated his dichotomy of changing life and eternal artistic forms, essentially a theory of aesthetic Platonism, with particular clarity: by means of artistic force, the artist and author must impose form onto ever-changing life. In *Six Characters*, form is imposed on chaos not by authors but by actors and a director.

This peculiar form of aesthetic Platonism fueled Pirandello's theory of drama throughout. Like Bergson, Pirandello realized that the contrast between ever-changing life and stable, abstract ideas is the source of comedy. He writes: "Life is a continual flux which we try to stop, to fix in stable and determined forms, both inside and outside ourselves . . . The forms in which we seek to stop, to fix in ourselves this constant flux are the concepts, the ideals which we constantly want to live up to, all the fictions we create for ourselves, the conditions, the state in which we tend to stabilize ourselves."[72] The passage speaks to the existential dimension of this relativism, the need for stability by means of forms, concepts, and ideals. When these attempts fail, the result is catastrophic—but also a source for humor. What Pirandello presents here is a form of existential humor, derived from a worldview shot through with the anxiety of relativism. While Shaw writes comedies of ideas with serious consequences, Pirandello writes tragedies of ideas with comic overtones.

It is important to recognize that Pirandello's conception of theatrical relativism and his yearning for artistic control, his own form of aesthetic Platonism, derive from another source as well: Italian fascism. Tilgher, who himself remained a liberal, was the first to identify Pirandello's aesthetics with the fascism of Mussolini.[73] Tilgher proved prescient, for Pirandello did in fact become one of the principal artistic representatives of Mussolini's regime. Indeed, Pirandello joined the Fascist Party not long after a particularly gruesome assassination, defying the antifascist forces that were trying to use that assassination to rein in Mussolini and keep him from seizing more power. Pirandello's fascism was certainly opportunistic: he wanted Mussolini to fund his theater. But, as Mary Ann Witt has shown, Pirandello's fascism was also a deeply held belief in what she calls "aesthetic fascism." In Italy (and elsewhere) fascism presented itself as being "above politics," as a movement that would unite the divided masses through the charismatic figure of Il Duce. The language of this postpolitical ideology was often aesthetic, arguing that the leader was "molding" the masses, the body politic, in the manner of an artist, giving shape to an otherwise shapeless and shiftless body.

It was this language of aesthetic fascism that Pirandello himself used when talking about Mussolini: Il Duce was the artist who was imposing form onto chaos; he was the author and authority Italy needed in order to become a functioning society. Mussolini achieved this not through a political process, especially not through a democratic, parliamentary process, which allegedly only bred chaos. Instead, he achieved this through action. Echoing his theory of humor, Pirandello now writes in the vein of aesthetic fascism:

> Since life is subject to continual change and motion, it feels itself imprisoned by form; it rages and storms and finally escapes from it. Mussolini has shown that he is aware of this double and tragic law of movement and form, and hopes to conciliate the two. Form must not be a vain and empty idol. It must receive life, pulsating and quivering, so that it should be for ever recreated. . . . The revolutionary movement inaugurated by Mussolini with the march on Rome and all the methods of his new government seem to me to be, in politics, the necessary realization of just this conception of life.[74]

Pirandello insists on a similarity between politics and art: the leader is like the artist, imposing form onto a chaotic world, like the missing author in *Six Characters* or the stage director who finally takes over.

Aesthetic fascism also explains one of the more puzzling features of Pirandello's metaplays: they all end, quite unexpectedly, with acts of violence. In *Six Characters*, the boy drowns at the end of the play. In *Henry IV*, the putatively mad Henry deliberately kills one of his attendants. In both of these cases, the ending turns metadrama into tragedy. At the same time, this violence serves to test, perhaps even to challenge, the theatrical relativism of these plays: "Is it pretense?" some ask at the end of *Six Characters*. "No, reality," others answer. The same confusion happens at the end of *Henry IV*. It is almost as if Pirandello is showing here that at the end of his complicated plays, where we don't know what is what, we need an act of violence, bloodshed, a pure act, to shatter the cabinet of mirrors so that the real can emerge. Aesthetic fascism favors deeds while dismissing words. Even though Pirandello's plays are intensely verbose and have been appreciated by audiences for their intellectual prowess, in fact they don't celebrate intellectual wit for its own sake. The way they end in acts of violence echoes the main fascist agenda: to stop the chatterings of parliament and return to a politics of pure acts. Such pure acts would cut though endless talk and create a reality of their own. The violence at the end of Pirandello's plays does not give us examples of acts that solve problems, but it registers the same desire to end the talking and start the action.

The sudden turn toward violence in metatheater may seem surprising, given that there is something undeniably playful when the theater takes itself as its chief subject. Leaving out comedy, Abel conceived of tragedy as a genre that refers to the harshness of the real world, whereas metatheater is a turn of the theater onto itself.[75] From this description, one might get the impression that metatheater is relieved from the pressures of the real world and delights in a kind of playful manner in the domain of theater: a celebration of theater by the theater. Yet sudden bursts of violence are a common feature of metatheater. *The Bacchae* of Euripides is perhaps the first play of metatheater, and it ends with a scene of perverse and seemingly gratuitous violence: Dionysius takes his revenge on Pentheus, who has come to spy on the Bacchae, by having Agave tear Pentheus, her own son, to pieces in a fit of madness. The other paradigmatic work of metatheater is Pedro Calderón's *Life is a Dream* (1638), a play in which we can surmise the structural reasons for the metatheater's tendency toward violence. The infant prince Segismundo grows up in prison—essentially another cave—cut off from the outside world. When he is temporarily given his rightful place, he takes it all to be a dream. In due course he becomes a violent tyrant who kills and rapes gratuitously, only to find himself transferred back to the prison whence he came. As Elinor Fuchs has observed in her essay on metatheater, the genre depends on the interaction of two ontological levels; in the case of *Life is a Dream*, one level is the prison tower, and the other is life at court.[76] Similar scenes of bloodshed occur in the subsequent history of metatheater, for example, in Jean Genet's *The Balcony*, with its juxtaposition of theatricality and revolutionary violence. Even the mousetrap, the other classical moment of metatheater, is in the service of a killing.

This predilection for violence begins to make sense once we trace metatheater back to its origin in the cave parable from the seventh book of Plato's *Republic*. As in so many other metaplays, this one begins in prison, and its drama consists of the prisoner's escape, the breaking of the shackles, and the turning around and recognition of the setup of the cave, with its fire, the objects, and the way in which they cast shadows onto the wall of the cave. Finally the prisoner is freed, escapes from the cave, and beholds the things themselves. Violence here happens upon his return to the cave, when his report from the outside is greeted with laughter and even threats of death.

While all metadramatists use violence to register the move from one level to another, Pirandello uses violence to answer, or to promise to answer, once and for all the question of which level has ontological priority. If Henry IV, in Pirandello's play, is stuck in time and does not know that the world in which he lives is a charade, he can take his revenge by killing one of the attendants. But it is not the case that metatheater merely licenses violence. There is also a desire for violence, the hope that acts of violence might become the means by which to test what is real. This is what happens in many of Pirandello's plays: the endless confusions between different realities must come to an end, and it is we, the audience, who want to know what is real and what isn't. The violent endings of Pirandello's most famous metaplays hold out this tantalizing hope, but they only partially realize it, maintaining the confusing play with different theatrical levels to the very end. We remain stuck in uncertainty, in the inability to adjudicate. This is what the theater is best at: confronting us with theatrical relativism without always telling us how to leave this relativism behind.

Bertolt Brecht

> In the epic theater . . . the actor sides with the philosopher.
>
> —Walter Benjamin

Brecht is readily acknowledged as one of the most influential reformers of twentieth-century theater. The dramatic text, acting, set design, music— Brecht overhauled each and every aspect of the theater, leaving nothing untouched. What is acknowledged much less is that this effort was driven by a deeply rooted "mistrust of the theater" that can be traced back to Plato.[77] Plato's influence is visible in a number of Brecht's most cherished beliefs. For example, he designed plays that were addressed to reason rather than to emotions; he wanted audiences to analyze rather than enjoy; and sometimes his plays seemed to preach to audiences, bombarding them with theoretical declarations and views. But even if there is something intellectual about Brecht's plays and theater productions, they nevertheless differ significantly from other examples of Platonic drama, although the theater of Shaw is sometimes recognized as an important precursor. Brecht's plays are dominated by action, not dialogue, and they use all the trappings and tricks of the theater. Few of his plays contain characters who present themselves as philosophers.

One of the few commentators to have nevertheless recognized a connection between Brecht and Plato was Brecht's friend Walter Benjamin, whose essay on epic theater, written in the early 1930s, concludes with an intriguing speculation about a Platonic tradition of drama.[78] Benjamin notes the affinity between Brecht's antitragic protagonists and Plato's Socrates, and singles out the *Phaedo* as a dialogue located "at the threshold of drama." This Platonic tradition, Benjamin goes on to say, is defined by its persistent distancing from tragedy, indeed from all conventional drama. But Benjamin warns us that this tradition is a strange one, hard to locate, a "badly marked street," although even this metaphor is then qualified when he adds that we are dealing not with a true street but with a secret path.[79] The somewhat unfamiliar view of Brecht I will present here can be taken as an elaboration of this Platonic genealogy, or path, indicated by Benjamin.

Brecht's most direct connection to dramatic Platonism is Georg Kaiser, who explicitly called for a renewal of drama in the name of Plato. Brecht's debt to Kaiser is well documented, although the skewed view most theater historians have of Kaiser, which generally does not include his Platonic project, has distorted the nature of this influence as well. But it was Kaiser's interest in Socrates and Plato that intrigued Brecht, who not only knew and admired Kaiser's Socrates play, *Alcibiades Delivered*, but also rewrote it as a short story. In the course of doing so, Brecht turned to Plato's *Symposium* to research the account of Socrates in battle given there. The Socrates theme emerges in several other texts as well, for example, in one of his Herr Keuner stories, but also in the play that comes closest to the kind of argument-driven, cerebral play one might more readily associate with the Platonic drama, *The Life of Galileo Galilei*, which in turn was inspired by Galileo's own dialogues. More generally, Brecht admired Socrates' critical edge, his dialectical reasoning, and his willingness to stand up to the powers that be even as he was skeptical about Plato's anti-democratic views. Still, it must be said that an interest in Socrates is one thing and a tendency toward dramatic Platonism is another. How did Brecht, the man of the theater, become associated with philosophical drama in the tradition of Plato?

Brecht's dramatic Platonism came to the fore when he was cut off from the actual theater during his years of exile, first in Scandinavia and then in the United States, in the 1930s and 1940s. By 1933, when he left Germany, Brecht had already formulated and put into practice most of the tenets of what he called epic theater. He had become famous for his estrangement effect, the desire to distance the audience from the theater by means of interruption, episodic plots, and other techniques of defamiliarization. Only by disturbing the basic, underlying familiarity with what happens onstage, Brecht argued, could theater makers induce audiences to consider events presented onstage critically, analytically, and in a new light. This new theory had become a theatrical success across Germany, turning Brecht and his group of collaborators into the most important new voice in the theater.

Brecht and his collaborators had to leave all this behind when they fled shortly after Hitler's rise to power, finding themselves cut off from the theater that had made them famous. It was during the following fifteen years in exile that Brecht wrote his most central plays, including *Life of Galileo Galilei* (1937–39), *Mother Courage and Her Children* (1939), *The Good Person of Sezuan* (1940), and *The Caucasian Chalk Circle* (1943–45). At the same time, he also experimented with other literary genres, including the novel, in the *Three Penny Novel* (1934) and *The Affairs of Mr. Julius Caesar* (1949), in addition to poetry. The man of the theater had become a writer.

Brecht used his distance from the theater for another, large project that would occupy him for the rest of his life: a reflection on and revision of the main elements of his theory of the theater. This effort took the form of a series of dialogues, oddly entitled *Messingkauf* (The Purchase of Brass).[80] The dialogues are all about the theater, and more particularly about Brecht's theater. Brecht himself is not referred to by name but is simply called, in keeping with his main occupation in exile, "the Playwright." The central components of Brecht's epic theater, including styles of acting, dramaturgy, use of music and set design, dramatic texts, and the role of the audience, are discussed among the participants, who are all theater people, including actors, a dramaturge, and a stagehand. These wide-ranging conversations also consider the political function of the theater, as well as its relation to science, and the question of whether the theater, in order to become a truly modern art form, must adhere to the tenets of Brecht's epic theater. The *Messingkauf* dialogues echo Brecht's immodest claim that the modern theater is the (that is to say, his) epic theater.

Even as the *Messingkauf* dialogues articulate the key elements of the epic theater, they do so with a crucial difference. The main character of the dialogues, the one around whom they are organized, is someone seemingly unconnected to the theater: a philosopher. *Messingkauf* is a series of dialogues in which Brecht revisits his entire theory of epic theater from the perspective of the philosopher. These dialogues can be seen as an attempt to view epic theater through a philosophical lens or, rather, to translate epic theater into philosophical theater. This translation takes place both on the level of content—the theory of theater—and on the level of form: Brecht chose to articulate this philosophical version of the epic theater in the form of a philosophical dialogue.

In the course of *Messingkauf*, it becomes clear that the philosopher who dominates the dialogue is in fact quite ignorant of the theater. He does not often go to the theater, does not especially value it, and is unfamiliar with its basic vocabulary; the theater professionals even have to explain to him the convention of the fourth wall. At the same time, he asks fundamental questions about how theater works, and he likes to peek behind the stage. In the process, the philosopher develops quite fundamental objections to the theater, in particular to the project of imitation. The theater professionals quickly assent to Aristotle's claim that the theater is based on the art of imitation. But instead of condoning imitation, the philosopher desires to go to the "things themselves," sounding just like Socrates in the *Republic*, with whom he also shares a scorn for actors.[81] He declares that he feels crowded, even "tyrannized," by actors who do not leave him "room to think."[82] Finally, he strongly disagrees with the other Aristotelian demand, quoted to him by the dramaturge, that theatrical imitation should incite the emotions of the audience, in particular fear and pity.

The objections raised by the philosopher tilt the dialogue: more and more the conversation revolves around satisfying the philosopher, and what gets developed in the ensuing conversations is an alternative to the theater as practiced by the theater professionals. Step by step, the philosopher unfolds the framework for a new and different theater, a theater suited specifically to his own philosophical purposes. The theater the philosopher demands is one that would be fully up-to-date, in keeping with the developments of the time. This means that the new theater would have to be scientific, addressed to the purpose of knowing, not feeling. The scientific theme brings the philosopher to one of his key concepts: that the theater should function like a laboratory, serving the purposes of knowledge and analysis. The philosopher here reiterates several components of Brecht's well-known estrangement effect: the emphasis on analysis rather than on empathy, the rule that audiences must not be drawn into the action of the play (their cigars must not go out), and that they should observe the events represented onstage acutely, with scientific interest. They must not merely look at the stage [*sehen*] but probe it critically [*prüfendes schauen*].[83] The philosopher, in other words, demands a particular kind of reception: science resides in the beholder. Scientific theater means a particular attitude toward the theater, the attitude a scientist brings to an experiment.

The main distinction used by the philosopher to illustrate this point is the distinction between a planetarium and a roller coaster. Riding a roller coaster means experiencing the ups and downs of the story viscerally, directly, emotionally, through the senses. The planetarium, by contrast, creates insight into the constellations.[84] It may still be impressive, pleasing, a sensory experience, but it does not stand in the way of understanding and analysis, as is the case with the roller coaster. The philosopher could ride the roller coaster (i.e., the regular theater that incites the emotions directly) and try, against all odds, to wrest pieces of insight from it; but this would be an uphill struggle, unlikely to succeed. So while in principle the analytic, scientific, and philosophical attitude can be brought to any theater, some theaters will make such an attitude all but impossible, while others will encourage it.

The main target of the philosopher's critique, however, is not emotionally heart-wrenching theater in the melodramatic tradition, nor the behavior of star actors who manage to ensnare an audience. Rather, it is the type of theater that at first sight might seem to be similar in kind to the scientific theater imagined by the philosopher, namely, naturalism. Naturalist theater, after all, began with a scientific impulse, derived from Darwin and others (as Wilde knew and objected to). Social life was to be presented without embellishment, as if under the microscope of the naturalists. While the naturalist novel and drama created an outcry because it meant dragging unpleasant facts of life—syphilis, corruption, adultery, incest—into art, the justification for this was mostly scientific rather than aesthetic: it was art's contribution to the understanding of the world.

But even the most unflinching, naturalist representation of unvarnished life is not yet scientific. In the words of the philosopher, not only must nature be represented, but also its laws must be revealed; nature must be "found out."[85] Here, the naturalists had only the vaguest idea or bandied-about pseudoscientific assumptions about inheritance and the shaping power of the environment on character. For this reason, the slice-of-life approach of naturalism, the ambition to render nature in all its complexity and texture, needed to be given up so that theater could become truly scientific and aspire to the condition of the laboratory. A laboratory is an artificial, controlled environment, not a fully rendered slice of life; in a laboratory, life situations are put together on a trial basis to see what kind of insight and what laws they might yield. Indeed, the insight that there are laws governing nature, and in particular the actions of humans, is itself the most important element of this new laboratory theater.

When it comes to detailing which kind of laws are supposed to be revealed by theatrical experiments, the philosopher has recourse to Marxism. In an important distinction, however, he cautions against using the theater as a mere illustration of Marxist theories or predictions.[86] Indeed, the philosopher recognizes that Marxism does not explain so much the behavior of individuals as that of masses, of large groups and classes—not something the theater is particularly good at. But the theater, when used experimentally, can aim at a kind of intermediary realm, one that demonstrates the interconnectedness of individuals. This is where the new theater can come in, showing, through careful selection of individuals and scenes, the hidden connections and dependencies of seemingly unconnected, far-flung agents. The dramaturge, who mediates between actors and the philosopher, bemoans the fact that it used to be the case that antagonists confronted one another in a single space, directly, scenically. But now a man in Chicago operates a machine that can kill twelve people in Ireland. The theater, he implies, must be changed in order for those connections, and the laws governing them, to become visible.[87]

The more the philosopher explains what he wants from the theater and how it might be changed, the more horrified the theater practitioners become. All their most cherished goals, including the accurate rendering of complex, psychological characters and the task of fascinating the audience, seem to have gone overboard. For this reason, they refuse to recognize as theater what the philosopher demands; instead they call it *thaeter*, inverting the letters *a* and *e*.[88] What is the status of this *thaeter*? First of all, it is driven by historical urgency, the struggle against fascism. From this perspective, the antitheatrical moment, the reduction and reorientation of theater, is a rebuke to fascism's full-blown theatricality, its exploitation of an emotional theater for political purposes. Hitler's political mass theater is based on emotion and identification; and political events such as the burning of the Reichstag, the crucial turning point of Hitler's increasing hold on power and the sidelining of democracy, can be seen as theater on a grand scale.[89] The philosopher acknowledges that his *thaeter* also presses theater into a political function, though in a different, critical manner. This politicization may not be an ideal, but it is a necessity. *Thaeter* is necessary right now; "it is not for eternity," but only for "dark times."[90] Once fascism in all of its guises is over, once socialism has won, we can all enjoy riding the roller coaster again.

Even more important than the content of the *Messingkauf* dialogues is their form. As a series of dialogues about the theater, *Messingkauf* belongs to a tradition that extends from Plato to Diderot's *Paradoxe*, Goethe's prologue to *Faust*, and Edward Gordon Craig's dialogues on the theater, not to speak of Wilde's critical dialogues. More important, they themselves are a kind of drama. The dialogues are arranged into different evenings, and they have been staged in various ways more than one hundred times since their premiere at the Theater am Schiffbauerdamm on October 12, 1963.[91] Brecht carefully calculated this theatrical dimension: while talking about theater (and *thaeter*), the participants, including the philosopher, sit on the stage. During the course of the discussion, the stage set, left over from another, regular show, is being slowly dismantled until the participants find themselves on an empty stage. This process epitomizes the philosopher's own dismantling of the theater. Emptying the theater, presumably, is what must happen in order for a *thaeter* to take place. At the same time, it is important to realize that the dialogues do not abandon the theater. This is perhaps the best indication that *thaeter*, despite its radical critique of the real existing theater, is not the theater's negation. Even though the philosopher is not particularly knowledgeable about the theater, and perhaps does not like it much, he does find himself, on this occasion, in the theater. He is interested in it, if only for its potential for philosophy.

This self-reflective dimension of the dialogues is not lost on the participants, and Brecht makes sure that it does not escape our attention, either. It is of course the philosopher who insists on this self-referential quality of the evening, claiming, "We too have made art for the past four nights."[92] To be sure, the *Messingkauf* dialogues are not the only form of *thaeter* the philosopher is calling for, but they are one possible example of it. They have not overwhelmed the audience with melodramatic stories; they have addressed reason, even when the discussion has become heated; and they have shown that the theater itself is not naturally given, but made and therefore changeable.

Brecht did not usually present himself as a thinker or philosopher. One of his more memorable lines is an advocacy of *"plumpes Denken"* (best translated as "crude thinking"), a predilection for simplicity rather than for needless complexity.[93] This attitude is also what gives the *Messingkauf* dialogues their title: the philosopher is like someone who wants to buy a trombone, not in order to make music, but merely for its brass. Boiling things down to essentials is certainly one aspect of Brecht's dramatic practice. Yet the *Messingkauf* dialogues are not all brass. They play music, they are art—albeit of a different type. Their music is one reminiscent of Platonic theater—perhaps this is the music made by Socrates in prison, something along the lines of Nietzsche's music-making Socrates. They rethink theater from a philosophical perspective, and they put this perspective into practice, as Plato and those writing in his tradition have done.

What happens if we take the philosopher's *thaeter* as a lens though which to look at Brecht's entire oeuvre? There is a set of plays that seems to be halfway between Brecht's great stage plays and the pared-down form of the *Messingkauf* dialogues, namely, his *Lehrstücke* or "teaching plays." They perhaps come closest to exemplifying the *thaeter* the philosopher calls for. They, more so than Brecht's other plays, are addressed to reason, presenting simple, experimental situations in which a character has to make a single, moral choice. The question of how this choice is made reveals much about social structures, about motivation, about society at large. In a pair of these plays, *The Yea-Sayer* and *The Nay-Sayer*, Brecht even creates two versions of the outcome in a way that is reminiscent of a laboratory experiment: it does not matter to the observer what the outcome is as long as we can observe the process that led to it.

Claiming that the *Messingkauf* dialogues, and through them Brecht's outlook on drama, should be placed in the tradition of Plato may seem counterintuitive given Brecht's dedication to historical materialism. Indeed, the philosopher's plea for a scientific theater is motivated by his belief in historical materialism. But it should be remembered that Platonic theater is not based on a metaphysical theory of abstract forms, what philosophers have extracted from Plato's dialogues and called philosophical idealism. Rather, it mediates between abstraction and a full immersion in the thick of life, a tug-of-war in which abstractions (ideas) are used strategically to uproot materiality and turn it into so many thought experiments. Like Brecht's *thaeter*, Platonic theater depends on the theater, uses the theater, takes place in the theater, and yet it subjects the theater to a crucial inversion. *Thaeter* is a good word for the "secret path" Walter Benjamin recognized, a path starting with Plato and extending to Brecht. Like Platonic theater, *thaeter* insists on using the theater for the purpose of knowledge, for the purposes of the philosopher. Brecht here articulates what Benjamin had recognized, but many have ignored: that Brecht's theater, too, can be described as a theater for philosophers, a theater uprooted from itself and turned to a new purpose.

Throughout his career, Brecht described his epic theater, and *thaeter*, as being directed against Aristotle and, more important, against the invocation of Aristotle as a way of defending dramatic and theatrical orthodoxies. Aristotle theorizes tragic action as caused primarily by fate and only secondarily by the actions of the protagonists, whereas in *thaeter* events can be changed by humans; Aristotelianism insists on the unities of space, time, and action, whereas *thaeter* wants to show the distanced interconnections of individuals. Insofar as *thaeter* is a philosophical rearticulation of epic theater, it presents what Brecht never tired of calling a non-Aristotelian theory of drama. This negative description has often been applied to modern drama more generally. What textbook does not revert to Aristotle as a foil against which to examine modernism's discontinuous and episodic plots?

But Brecht's theater can be described not only negatively as non-Aristotelian but also positively as Platonic. Plato of course wrote before Aristotle, but he defined his own dialogue, his own *thaeter*, one might say, against the dominant genres of Greek theater, subsequently theorized by Aristotle. In this sense Plato developed a theory and a practice of drama that is both pre-Aristotelian and non-Aristotelian. Throughout its history, Platonic drama has continued to battle Aristotelianism, and it has been able to flourish precisely at moments when Aristotelian drama was on the defensive. Modern drama is such a moment, the coincidence of a demise of Aristotelianism and a rise of Platonism. To the extent that a large number of dramatists—Wilde and Shaw, Strindberg and Kaiser, Pirandello and Brecht—participate in Platonic drama, it is possible to reformulate Brecht's claim that modern theater is non-Aristotelian as a claim that it is Platonic.

Tom Stoppard

> [*Jumpers*] goes against . . . all materialistic philosophy.
>   —Tom Stoppard

Despite Plato's particular prominence during the late nineteenth and the early twentieth centuries, his influence did not end with modern drama. It continues into the present, where it is visible in the work of Tom Stoppard, which becomes newly important in this context. Stoppard's plays have absorbed several of the key traditions in modern Platonic drama. First and most visible is perhaps Stoppard's tendency toward metatheater, most famously exercised in his breakthrough play, *Rosencrantz and Guildenstern Are Dead* (1966), which demonstrates his kinship to Luigi Pirandello. Like Pirandello, Stoppard uses the theater as a vehicle for destroying false certainties of all kinds. In his best plays, such as *Jumpers* (1972), the audience does not leave the theater thinking that they have learned something; this happens only in his lesser plays, such as *Coast of Utopia* (2002). Instead, they leave the theater confused, in particular about those certainties with which they had entered the theater.

Within the tradition of modern Platonic drama, the second influence on Stoppard is Oscar Wilde. This influence is perhaps the dominant one, for Stoppard has paid homage to Wilde in different ways throughout his life. Stoppard's plays take the verbal wit of Wilde's stage plays and combine it with the theoretical aspirations of the critical dialogues. This debt to Wilde comes to the fore in *Travesties* (1974), a witty homage to Wilde set among the exiled revolutionaries of Zurich, but also in his more recent *Invention of Love* (1997), which contrasts the poet and philologist A. E. Housman (the more famous brother of Laurence Housman, who authored a Socrates play) with the flamboyant Wilde.[94]

The third influence is George Bernard Shaw, who had demonstrated in a career spanning more than half a century his commitment to the drama of ideas. To this end, Shaw had made use of the comic stage philosopher but turned this figure to his own advantage, namely, to introduce philosophical dialogues and disputations, idées fixes, pet theories, and the like into his plays. Some of these ideas (and philosophers) echoed Shaw's own theories of creative evolution, but even when they didn't, what mattered was his insistence that drama needed to be suffused with argument, that it was a dialectical genre in the tradition of Plato. Shaw had formulated his Platonic theory and practice of drama as a program for dislodging Shakespeare from his position of unrivaled influence. Stoppard's metatheatrical commentary on Shakespeare in *Rosencrantz and Guildenstern Are Dead* belongs to this critique of Shakespearean drama as well.

While almost any play by Stoppard participates, in one way or another, in the tradition of Platonic drama, there is one play that aims at the fate of ideas in the theater with particular ingenuity: *Jumpers*. The play's main conflict unfolds between George E. Moore, professor of moral philosophy at Oxford, and his wife, Dotty, a former singer; even on the level of character, the play thus stages a conflict between philosophy and theater. Moore has many of the qualities one would associate with a comic stage philosopher: pages of the play are devoted to the composition of Moore's abstruse lecture on God, which culminates in the question "Are God?" As is the case with all comic stage philosophers since Socrates, Moore becomes an object of hilarity not only through his philosophical jargon but also through his erratic behavior. He is absentminded, gets sidetracked easily, and lives in a world of ideas while ignoring everything that happens around him. At the beginning of the play, he is interrupted in the composition of his lecture by cries of "help" and "murder" uttered by his wife. Indeed, a murder has occurred, and there is a dead body in the wife's bedroom. The philosopher, however, keeps entering the bedroom without seeing the dead body, busily doing philosophy when he is not looking for his pet hare. He soon loses track of this project and begins to shave, only to get caught up in something else, forgetting to remove the lather. He handles his other possessions, his pet tortoise and his bow and arrow, with equal absent-mindedness. When the door bell rings, his visitor will see, as the stage direction deliciously put it, taking the narrative viewpoint of the visitor: "The door is opened to him by a man holding a bow-and-arrow in one hand and a tortoise in the other, his face covered in shaving foam."[95] The visitor is taken aback, but when the madman cries, "I am a professor of moral philosophy," everything is clear.[96] Moore may as well have declared: *I am a comic stage philosopher.*[97]

Like Shaw, Stoppard uses the comic stage philosopher or professor not only as an object of fun but also as a starting point for a more ambitious entanglement of theater and philosophy. It turns out, for example, that the strange lecture "Are God?" is not really a parody, but part of a genuine philosophical question and approach. The confirmation for this reading of the play came not long after its London premiere, when A. J. Ayer, one of the philosophers spoofed in the play, wrote a short piece in the *Sunday Times* (London), entitled "Love Among the Logical Positivists," that begins: "It might have been thought that a play making fun of philosophers would offend a real live one. In fact, I enormously enjoyed Tom Stoppard's *Jumpers* at the National Theatre and came away feeling the greatest admiration of its author and for the actor, Michael Hordern, who takes the leading part."[98] Ayer continues:

> The characterization of the philosopher, both by the author and the actor, is exceedingly funny, it is also affectionate. I do not know how far it is based on any actual model. Some of Mr. Hordern's mannerisms reminds me strongly of one distinguished Cambridge philosopher—*not* G. E. Moore—and I thought perhaps conceitedly, that I occasionally caught echoes of my own intonations . . . But whatever sources they drew on, Mr. Stoppard and Mr. Hordern between them have created a character with his own distinct personality: unworldly, earnest, wryly humorous, subtle, intellectually honest, in some ways frustrated but not pathetic, and not at all ridiculous though sometimes absurd.

In identifying himself as part of the composite picture of the stage philosopher, Ayer may be said to continue here Socrates' own coup de théâtre, when he stood up during a performance of *Clouds* so that the audience could compare the Socrates created by Aristophanes to the real one. More important, Ayer recognizes that while Stoppard's stage philosopher is very funny, he is not "ridiculous"; the traits that we can readily recognize as those of a comic stage philosopher—unworldliness, absurdity—do not discredit his ideas. Intellectually honest and earnest, he is the primary vehicle through which ideas are introduced into the play.

When one explores ideas through a play, philosophical positions become a matter of character and are thus colored by personalities. We learn, for example, that Moore's lecture and the arguments presented there are bound up in rivalries, petty envies, and personal animosities with his colleagues at Oxford (one of whom had preempted Moore with the title of his book). We hear of his personal frustrations and marital problems, and we see him in action, which allows us to form a picture of him as a moral and social agent.

This, however, is not the main interest of Stoppard's play. Like Plato, Pirandello, and so many other representatives of Platonic drama, Stoppard uses theater to observe its relativizing effects. Once ideas are inflected by personalities and confronted with theatrical reality, they tend to be diminished, if not entirely discredited. Like Pirandello, Stoppard knows this relativizing effect of the theater, even invites and heightens it, but he also subjects it to critique. He does so by turning the question of relativism into the subject matter of the play. Moore's argument in his lecture "Are God?" is nothing less than a direct attack on moral relativism, against which he asserts his belief in God as an ultimate guarantor of the good. Within philosophy circles (not to speak of the world of politics), moral relativism is the reigning fashion and practice. Academic philosophy is dominated by different forms of language philosophy associated with Wittgenstein: there is no absolute good, but only different ways of using the word *good*. When we speak of a *good sandwich* in one context and in another condemn murder by calling it *bad*, we engage in different language games, different uses of the word *good*. There is nothing but the use of the word in different contexts, nothing outside language to which the word *good* refers, and therefore nothing by which it is endowed with an absolute, unchanging status.

The linguistic relativism of Moore's opponents is presented as a variant of cultural relativism. Proponents of cultural relativism make reference to different historical contexts and different cultures, often non-Western cultures, in which life and mores are premised on different value systems. How, in the face of so much cultural diversity, can we insist on a single, moral value of the good? In any case, neither linguistic nor cultural relativism is acceptable to Moore. He knows that the word *good* is used in different ways in different contexts and that values are not stable over time, but he nevertheless insists that values must make a claim toward an ultimate guarantor: values don't float free; we must think of them as grounded in authority. Like Plato's Socrates, Stoppard's Moore is engaged in a campaign against moral relativism.

Moral relativism is connected to epistemological relativism. Here, Moore takes on the argument that we cannot know for certain except what we know through our senses and that even our senses betray us. It does not make sense to hunt for absolute certainties; we have to content ourselves with provisional knowledge tied to particular situations and contexts. We are caught in a world of seeming in which nothing is for sure.

Stoppard backs up Moore's antirelativist position by thoroughly discrediting his philosophical adversaries, especially Archie Jumper, the highly credentialed and dandyish vice chancellor of the university, one of those who see Moore and his critique of relativism as a relic. Stoppard entangles the two in a kind of murder mystery, a genre he had flirted with in several other works. *Jumpers* opens with a murder, and the rest of the play is devoted to finding the culprit. One way in which Stoppard had established Moore as a comic stage philosopher was by having him be oblivious, throughout most of the play, to the murder; Moore thinks that the police are in his house because of a noise complaint, leading to many instances of dramatic irony in which Moore and various characters talk at cross purposes, with Moore making light of the inquiry, thinking it is a mere noise complaint, and the detective (as well as other characters) not recognizing the misunderstanding. This dramatic irony has a different purpose as well, for the discussion about murder is of course a good test case for different philosophical positions on morals. It serves to show different ethical philosophies in action.

Stoppard's main strategy, however, is to highlight the moral and epistemological relativism of Moore's opponents. It is here that the relativizing power of the theater can be put to use, dovetailing nicely with the relativism of the philosophers. The relativist vice chancellor engages in all kinds of dubious activities. He removes the dead body and makes it look like a suicide, with no qualms at all about manipulating evidence. Making things seem one way or another, after all, is his expertise. For this reason, it is difficult to tell whether he is, in fact, conducting a blatant love affair with Moore's wife. Here, he manipulates the evidence in such a way that it seems as though he is merely a doctor (an M.D. is among his many degrees) examining the skin of the patient. Wittgenstein's question is applied here: what would it look like if the vice chancellor were merely doing his job as a dermatologist? Of course—well, presumably—it would look the same.

From one perspective, then, things are clear: Moore may be comic and partially oblivious to what is going on, but he is a moral character, while his theatrical wife and the relativist vice chancellor seem complicit in the murder and in their love affair. Indeed, for all his smoothness and ability to manipulate people and scenes like a stage director, the vice chancellor is discredited also in the dimension of the play that gives it its name: he and his associates are amateur acrobats. Stoppard is here turning the common assumption that philosophy is nothing by mental acrobatics into stage reality.

Unmasking is a classical way for the theater to present itself as a vehicle for truth: the theater knows all about masks, after all. Under the right circumstances, this expertise can be put to good use; hence the predilection for theater to put itself in the service of unmasking. This, however, is not the only way in which Stoppard uses the theater.[99] In his most inspired move, Stoppard goes on to recognize a theatrical element in philosophy itself. When we encounter Moore, we find him preparing the lecture in which he is going to refute relativism in all of its forms. But with relativism on the rise, he has to make a particularly vivid impression on the audience. More important than the desire to make an effect is the means he intends to employ: a number of peculiar implements. Among them are his two pets, the hare and the tortoise, as well as his bow and arrow. It is with their help that Moore is going to do his philosophical demonstration. The implements, eccentric though they may seem, are not idiosyncratic; on the contrary, they are well known from the history of philosophy. The bow and arrow belong to Zeno's famous thought experiment that seeks to prove that change is an illusion. It may look as if the arrow leaves the bow and hits a target, but in fact such a thing is impossible: the arrow can never do more than cover half the distance, and then again half the distance, between the target and the bow. The tortoise and hare fulfill a similar purpose: give the slow tortoise a small lead, and the fast hare will only ever cut the lead in half, and then in half again, and so come closer and closer, but never actually overtake the tortoise. By equipping Moore with hares, tortoises, bows, and arrows, Stoppard does something quite cunning: he takes philosophical thought experiments such as Zeno's paradox and then turns them into theater. In doing so, he brings out the inherent, controlled theatricality of the philosophical thought experiment and turns it into a matter of stage props, transforming the theater, as Brecht's philosopher had demanded, into a philosophical laboratory.

Once the ingredients of a thought experiment are turned into theater, philosophers are bound to lose control of them. In any case, this is what happens to Moore almost immediately. His tortoise escapes, and he spends the opening scene looking for it in vain; the hare has disappeared entirely. All that remains of his equipment is the bow and arrow, which he fires off during the rehearsal of his lecture; but instead of hitting the target, the arrow goes astray and lands somewhere on a shelf. It is not until the end of the play that we learn what became of it. At that moment, we realize that it had accidentally hit and killed the hare, which was hiding there. Moore gets up on a stepping stool, retrieves it, and steps down only to crush his tortoise, which he had placed on the floor. If ever there was a philosopher who lost control over his thought experiment, it is Moore.

What Stoppard is dramatizing here is a process inherent in the nature of the thought experiment and the use of examples in philosophical arguments more generally. The status of the example has vexed philosophy throughout its history. Immanuel Kant famously called them the pushcarts (*Gängelwagen*) of philosophy. Philosophy needs those pushcarts, but this dependence harbors a danger. We never know which details are significant in an example or hypothetical situation evoked by a philosophical argument. How much contingency and detail should we admit? Where does the use of a single concrete example end? Examples, thought experiments—they invariably confront abstract argument with contingency.

Contingency is precisely what Stoppard has in mind when he pushes the logic of the thought experiment to its theatrical extreme. The reason Moore cannot control his tortoise and hare, his bow and arrow, is because he cannot control a concrete situation with concrete objects; there are too many variables, too many accidents waiting to happen—and Stoppard makes sure that they do happen. The play is full of accidents and coincidences: an early example occurs at the moment when Moore fires his arrow and we hear his wife call out "fire" from the next room. Coincidences are not philosophical; they are, by definition, accidental and therefore outside the purview of abstract argument and logic. They highlight the loss of (philosophical) control as soon as abstract arguments are placed in concrete situations. Coincidences and accidents—the ability to give those their proper place is what had appealed to Wilde in the use of the dialogue. They are also at the heart of Stoppard's theatrical attitude toward philosophy as presented in this play.

But does contingency have the last word? We are left with a discredited relativist, who delights in theatrical effects, and a discredited antirelativist, who has lost control over his philosophical props, if not of his argument. We feel that the discrediting of the vice chancellor is more damning, but we still laugh at Moore and his series of mishaps to the very end. The thrust of the play depends on how we understand our laughter. Are we amused by what happens when absolutes are brought down? I don't think so. For Stoppard does not celebrate the theater's supposedly relativizing effects. He recognizes these effects and exploits them, but he also redirects them. For him, theater ultimately must not be in the service of relativism even if it is also a perfect vehicle for demonstrating its reign. But when used in the right way, theater can show the relation between idea and its materialization. It is true that by being materialized, the idea loses its luster, its position of absolute authority, and must now contend with rival matter. At the same time, however, this drama of materialization can be looked at from the other side as well. Ideas begin to act in the world only once they are materialized; materialization is the moment of their greatest potency. In this sense, Stoppard's drama is not a celebration of the theater's relativizing materialism; *Jumpers*, as Stoppard himself said, "goes against . . . all materialistic philosophy."[100] This is the gamble and the project of all Platonic theater: to use the theater's precarious materiality, but to redirect its thrust; to use the comic stage philosopher, but not to discredit this figure. The result is not a materialist nor a relativist theater, but a new, critical theater of ideas.

But a play of ideas cannot simply end with the confrontation between Archie and Moore in the world of material objects and power. Stoppard adds a coda, which the stage direction calls a "symposium." This coda presents a condensed jumble of the various scenes and themes of the play. The jumpers are there; Dotty sings her song; Archie is in good form, as is the archbishop of Canterbury. But the putative theme of the coda is the philosophical symposium for which Moore had been preparing his lecture. Does this mean that now, finally, theater will become a platform for philosophy in its most unadulterated form? Hardly. This dream play takes an exceedingly "bizarre dream form," as the stage direction characterizes it.[101] And the philosophy doesn't fare all that well in it. Archie opens the coda with a philosophical rant that is reminiscent of Lucky's monologue in *Waiting for Godot*: "If goons in mood, by Gad is sin different or banned good, f'r'instance?"[102] Moore's lecture begins in a more promising manner, but all too soon he loses track of the argument, trails off, and begins to enlist hybrid figures in his argument that range from Zeno Evil to Jesus Moore as well as his hare, the late Herr Thumper. Even in this hallucinatory dream play, all this deranged philosophizing is confronted with action in its most consequential form: a murder. As in the opening scene, the jumpers form a pyramid, a shot is heard and the archbishop of Canterbury falls dead, bringing the whole pyramid down. By a strange coincidence, the last word uttered before the shot was *philosophy*.[103]

Stoppard's move to a dream play is not unusual. In fact, it is remarkable how often the drama of ideas seeks out alternative spaces in which to stage the spectacle of philosophy, be they the underworld, hell, heaven, or dream worlds. This tradition begins with Lucian's *Dialogues of the Dead*, which uses the underworld as a location from which to launch an attack on existing philosophy, but it can also be found in Shaw's dream play, *Don Juan in Hell*, as well as Sartre's *No Exit*. Even Kierkegaard and Nussbaum will revive the dead in their attempt to stage ideas, a desire that of course has its origin in Plato's revival of Socrates. This predilection to move away from the real world and into some alternative universe indicates how crucial it is for these writers to suspend mimesis and orient the theater towards other worlds in order to render ideas.

Platonic drama does not describe a single tradition within modern drama, but rather a cluster of playwrights who find different solutions and forms to the same question or problem: how to use ideas in the theater. Wilde's theater of language and inaction, Shaw's comedy of ideas, Pirandello's theatrical relativism, Brecht's *thaeter*, and Stoppard's antimaterialist comedy—they are all different versions of the conjunction of theater and philosophy first elaborated by Plato. These playwrights share a sense that theater can be used as an epistemological tool, a laboratory of truth, a thought experiment; that drama and theater can do something to philosophy, show something about philosophy that is difficult to perceive otherwise; that the conjunction of theater and philosophy allows for new possibilities in both theater and thought. This, more than anything else, is the insight and the provocation of Platonic drama.

4

Dramatic Philosophy

In the previous chapters, I approached the conjunction of drama and philosophy from the side of drama, showing how Plato's original invention of a dramatic philosophy gave rise to the Socrates play and then to an important Platonic strain in modern drama. In the two remaining chapters, I will approach the conjunction of drama and philosophy from the side of philosophy. When I began this project, I expected the philosophical inheritor of Plato's drama to be the philosophical dialogue itself. More and more, however, it has become clear to me that many philosophical dialogues lack Plato's dramatic imagination. For me, the test of whether a philosophical dialogue is Platonic is that it must be written with the theater in mind. Most philosophical dialogues since Plato fail this test. From Giordano Bruno and Galileo Galilei to George Berkeley and David Hume, philosophers use the dialogue merely to give voice to opposed positions, one of which is destined from the beginning to win (this is sometimes the case with Plato as well, though not the core of his dramatic technique). Naturally, there are exceptions to this rule, one being Lucian's *Dialogues of the Dead*, to which Wilde (another exception) refers in one of his own dialogues. Also noteworthy are the dialogues of Denis Diderot, who uses characters, situations, and the theatrical potential of the dialogue form to the fullest, creating parodies, imitations, and inversions in his satirical but also philosophical sketches. But Lucian and Diderot, as well as other practitioners of genuinely theatrical dialogues such as Wilde and Brecht, did not by themselves convince philosophers to write with the theater in mind.

It is hardly surprising that philosophers would not embrace the dramatic potential of the dialogue form given their long-standing distrust of the theater. Only gradually, over the course of the late eighteenth and nineteenth centuries, did influential philosophers rethink this distrust in fundamental ways and begin to use the theater as a privileged vehicle for thought. This development, the overcoming of what is sometimes called

the antitheatrical prejudice and the adoption of a more constructive relation to the theater, might be called, with some hesitation, the "dramatic
turn" or "theatrical turn" of philosophy. My hesitation is driven by the fact
that these philosophers by no means exchanged their earlier colleagues'
rejection of the theater for a simple enthusiasm for it. Much like Plato,
they did everything in their power to adapt the theater to their own uses,
to instrumentalize it for the purposes of philosophy. In the process they
sought to change the theater considerably, much as Brecht's philosopher
wanted to turn theater into *thaeter*. This transformation was the product
of an intense engagement with drama and theater that led to a variety
of ways in which Plato's dramatic legacy, largely buried throughout the
history of philosophy, manifested itself. In order to account for these
manifestations, it is necessary to write a new history of philosophy: a
history of philosophy from the point of view of its use of drama.

A history of philosophy from the point of view of drama must distinguish
between two principal interests. The first is an emphasis on the *theater* or
the *theatrical*. Both words are based on the Greek *theatron*, or place of seeing, and both aim at the act of seeing and visual representation more
generally. An interest in this dimension of theater is deeply rooted in Plato's
own philosophy, where it helps distinguish between (theatrical, onstage)
appearance and (nontheatrical, off-stage) essence. This distinction is captured most clearly in the parable of the cave with its shadow theater
of appearance inside and the world of essence outside the cave. In this
account, theater is relentlessly dedicated to the visible, to what we can see;
philosophy, by contrast, wants to look behind the visible façade of the world,
go beyond what we already know from everyday life and guide us toward
the first things, the fundamental entities that hold the world together.

Once philosophy abandoned the search for hidden essences, the cave
parable took on a new meaning. More and more the visible world seemed
a strange thing in and of itself, puzzling enough to warrant the attention of
philosophical ingenuity. Kierkegaard and Nietzsche, with whom I begin this
chapter, both play a primary role in this development. Kierkegaard based
his philosophy on subjective experiences and emotions, and Nietzsche
demanded that philosophy give up its obsession with metaphysics and
return to the study of life itself. In both cases, the attention to subjective experience and life also meant that the theater suddenly became
a viable and useful model for capturing aspects of these entities. This use
of theater is still premised on the cave: theater continues to stands for
appearance, only now appearance is no longer dismissed as a realm of
the false. It is not surprising that those philosophers who embraced the
theater in this way, beginning with Kierkegaard and Nietzsche, belong to
the prehistory of existentialism, later systematized by two more theatrical philosophers, Jean-Paul Sartre and Albert Camus. From this perspective,
existentialism acquires new importance as a philosophy that is fully,
though not uncritically, engaged with the theater.

There is a second approach to the conjunction between theater and
philosophy, namely, one focused on *drama* or the *dramatic* (based on the

root *dran*, "to act"). The dramatic impulse goes back to Plato's own dialogues and the tradition of Platonic drama more generally, and the approach captures the dramatic techniques through which Plato created philosophical characters, placed them in concrete scenes and situations, and had them engage in philosophically charged actions and interactions. Both Kierkegaard and Nietzsche, as well as Sartre and Camus, follow Plato in that they articulate their philosophies through invented characters born from this dramatic impulse and consider the actions of philosophical protagonists, their decisions, of primary philosophical importance. Everywhere, existentialism revolves around specific scenes, whose significance is then developed in philosophical form.

In principle the theatrical and the dramatic need to be kept apart; identifying them too closely would exclude, for example, all kinds of closet dramas, dialogues, and other dramatic forms originally not intended for stage performance. But the question of theatrical performance is nevertheless part of the genre of drama and of the dramatic. Rather than insisting that drama must be intended for performance, however, one should think of theatrical performance as a horizon of the dramatic, a possibility that must be grappled with. The awareness of this theatrical horizon, for example, is what separates untheatrical philosophical dialogues, which use drama only in a formal sense as the exchange of speeches among characters, from fully theatrical dialogues, such as the ones of Diderot, which are written with an eye toward theater. This theatrical horizon is visible in Plato not only when he envisions the reading aloud of a dialogue but also in his myriad references to and struggles with the theater. Indeed, not all dramatic philosophers simply embrace the theatrical. Plato himself is the best example of a bifurcation of the dramatic and the theatrical, embracing the one but critiquing the other. And even though one might speak of a dramatic or theatrical turn in philosophy, it remains true that many modern philosophers are much more ready to deploy select dramatic strategies than to fully embrace the theater (even as one can find dramatic and theatrical models and forms in the earlier history of philosophy). Rather than simply celebrating the theater, modern philosophers seek to appropriate it to their own purposes, as when Kierkegaard recommends particular techniques of going to the theater or when Nietzsche attacks Wagner's theatricality. This, then, is the definition of the dramatic I am working with: a form centrally based on character, scene, and action (including speech acts—the drama of speech) that operates within a theatrical horizon.

It is important to recognize that this dramatic impulse is not confined to drama in a narrow sense, that is, to playwriting. While some of the theatrical philosophers I discuss in this and the subsequent chapter, including Sartre, Camus, Iris Murdoch, and Alain Badiou, do indeed write plays, others, including Kierkegaard and Nietzsche, opt for different, more hybrid forms of representation, forms we would tend to call novelistic rather than dramatic. Furthermore, the nineteenth and twentieth centuries are filled with Socrates novels as well as Socrates plays. In some cases, a work is begun as a Socrates play only to change halfway through into a Socrates novel.[1] It is as if writers of Socrates plays, together with dramatic philosophers, were being pulled into the novel's gravitational field.

But should we accept this story of the novel absorbing Plato's dramatic legacy, a local instance of a broader history of the novel as the endlessly expansive genre? The problem here is an imbalance between the theory of the novel and the theory of drama. As soon as a writer abandons the strict dialogue form—characters conversing in direct, present-tense speech— the result is no longer called drama, or even dramatic, but novelistic, the genre in which hybrid forms are supposedly at home. Or so Mikhail Bakhtin has defined it. In Bakhtin's account, the flexibility of the novel, the porousness of its boundaries, enabled this upstart genre to triumph over its more established rivals. But this account of the novel has kept us from recognizing that the same claims could be made for drama. Indeed, it is from the drama that Bakhtin borrows his vocabulary for describing the novel's rise. When emphasizing that the novel incorporates many different registers of language, Bakhtin speaks of the presence of different voices, or "heteroglossia" and "dialogism."[2] All of these terms resonate very clearly with dialogue and drama, yet Bakhtin seeks to wrest them from this domain. Somehow, the novel turns out to be more dependent on different voices or tongues than the theater, in which we are confronted with actual voices and real tongues, just as the novel is presented as being more dialogic than the drama, even though drama is more fully and more exclusively based on actual dialogue.

To be sure, Bakhtin's argument is not entirely implausible. It is true, for example, that in a number of dramatic traditions the heterogeneity of voices and languages in a given play was restricted, while the novel tended to accommodate them more often and with greater ease. The reasons for this are varied, ranging from classicist traditions of drama to the tastes of theater audiences at particular times. By and large, however, Bakhtin's dramatic theory of the novel needs to be related back to drama, as some theater scholars have already begun to do.[3] Bakhtin's conception of drama was too narrow, too classicist, for him to recognize the many voices and languages in a Shakespeare play—or the remarkable expansion of drama in the modern period.

The Platonic genealogy I am tracing is a good point of departure for a critique of Bakhtin's genre theory. Given Bakhtin's celebration of hybridity, it is not surprising that he too considered Plato a central event in the prehistory of the novel. Following a remark made by Nietzsche, Bakhtin singles out the Socratic dialogues as a model for the novel. For this purpose, he makes much of the fact that Plato's dialogues are in prose, noting their proximity to spoken language, their interest in the lower spheres of life, and their mixing of different genres and styles, concluding: "We have before us therefore a multi-styled genre, as is the authentic novel."[4] This characterization is quite correct, but there is no reason to connect the dialogues exclusively or even primarily with the novel. Bakhtin should have followed Nietzsche, who, after suggesting that one might consider Plato's mixed mode as a precursor of the novel, went on to detail the more important genealogy connecting Plato to modern literary prose drama.

What is needed in this context is a new, expanded definition of drama. Rather than being narrowly defined as dialogue to be performed, drama—or, better, the dramatic—can be conceived of as a more expansive category that includes closet dramas, diegetic plays, dialogues, and other forms that foreground the category of action, placing characters in situations in order to have them act and interact. The dramatic is a category that insists on the primacy of character, direct speech, scene, and action, to the exclusion of narration and interiority. Equipped with this notion of the dramatic, we can even turn to the experimental novel and claim that the dramatic is realized not only in plays but also in certain novels. One group of novels that would lend themselves to such a dramatic analysis are those that explicitly drift toward drama, such as James Joyce's *Ulysses* (1922) with its 150-page Circe chapter as well as Herman Melville's *Moby Dick* (1851), Henry James' *The Outcry* (1911), or F. Scott Fitzgerald's *This Side of Paradise* (1920). Another group would include the novel of ideas, from Fyodor Dostoevsky to Thomas Mann, which depends heavily on dialogic scenes of intellectual discussion in the tradition of Plato. Rather than calling those moments examples of "typical" novelistic hybridity, it is more appropriate to think of them as dramatic moments in the novel, with the narrator, retreating into stage directions, giving over the scene to the pure action (and dialogue) of characters. If from one perspective this looks like the incorporation of drama by the stronger novel, from another it looks like the invasion of the novel by a newly resurgent drama.

Indeed, most, if not all, writers following Plato, from authors of Socrates plays to modern dramatists, have opted for drama as opposed to the novel. At the same time, dramatic and theatrical philosophers, even when they do not write straight plays, think of drama and theater as their primary categories. The genre drift they exemplify is not away from drama and toward the novel, but simply an expansion of the dramatic, the emergence of new and varied forms of drama that include all kinds of displaced dialogues, closet dramas, transformed plays, staged discussions, and other instantiations of a dramatic sensibility. And since Bakhtin located the origin of the novel in Plato, it is only fitting that I would suggest an alternative account of the drama and the novel as part of a larger project dedicated to Plato, one that restores the theory of the novel back to drama, whence it came in the first place.

Søren Kierkegaard

On June 2, 1841, a twenty-eight-year-old theology student at the University of Copenhagen wrote a letter to his sovereign, Christian VIII: "To the King! The undersigned hereby ventures to apply to Your Majesty with the most humble petition to submit his dissertation . . . in his native tongue."[5] In his great wisdom, Christian VIII granted the eccentric request from his subject, and after a defense that lasted more than seven hours and was conducted in Latin, the candidate received his degree. This request shows how much the student, Søren Kierkegaard, felt at odds with the requirements and rites of academia, and indeed it was the last business he would have with the university. But his objection was not just to the academic establishment as such. In the petition he explains his preference for Danish over Latin in terms of style: "I permit myself most humbly to call to the exalted attention of Your Majesty how difficult, indeed almost impossible, it would be to deal exhaustively with this subject in the language that has hitherto been that of the learned without causing the free, personal presentation to suffer unduly." Instead of identifying with the "learned," whose ranks he was never to join in any case, Kierkegaard strives toward something else: the "free" and the "personal." Indeed, a free and personal style is what would characterize all of his subsequent writings, which straddle different disciplines and modes from theology to philosophy and from theoretical reflection to literary expression. Kierkegaard's unique style turned him into one of the most unusual writers of intellectual prose in the nineteenth century.

It all began with Socrates, for the topic and title of the dissertation in question was *The Concept of Irony with Continual Reference to Socrates* (1841).[6] Like many of the authors of Socrates plays, Kierkegaard regarded Plato as a poet, admiring his elaborate myths and metaphors.[7] He savors the experience of reading Plato's prose, praising the rhythm of the dialogues, which unfold "slowly, solemnly," leaving the reader time to savor their scenes and characters.[8] Kierkegaard does not develop a full-fledged dramatic reading of Plato, but in his attempt to specify the form of irony at work in Plato's dialogues, he comes close to several of the main categories I identified as central to Plato's dramatic technique, including his use of scene, character, and action, as well as his strange relation to both tragedy and comedy. Together these reflections form a dramatic understanding of irony.

Kierkegaard is drawn to Plato as the inventor of a quintessentially ironic character, Socrates, a character fully consumed by this one quality.[9] Everything Socrates says and does is in the service of irony, to the point that he becomes its personification. This is the central assumption of the entire dissertation, the justification of why a work on irony would have to make "continual reference to Socrates," as the subtitle announces. In the course of teasing out the various dimensions of irony, Kierkegaard thus finds himself fully entangled in various dramatic categories. At one point, Kierkegaard even suggests that one might understand part of Socrates' irony as "dramatic irony."[10] By the same token, he turns to the tradition of the Socrates play in the form of its first practitioner, Aristophanes. What Kierkegaard admires in Aristophanes is the mobilization of the theatrical scene in relation to Socrates, and in particular the main scene in *Clouds*: Socrates suspended in a basket, halfway between heaven and earth. This scene, for Kierkegaard, becomes the perfect theatrical expression of Socratic irony: "The ironist, to be sure, is lighter than the world, but on the other hand he still belongs to the world," he writes.[11] There is something about irony that defies gravity, that detaches us from the ground on which we stand, that seeks out a state of "hovering," as it characterizes Socrates in the basket. The theater, it turns out, is the perfect vehicle for capturing this hovering, the essence of irony.

Irony, for Kierkegaard, is something bound to character and scene, but this does not mean that just any drama would be equipped to capture it. Irony is a particular use of drama, one shot through with negativity. Negative formulations therefore abound in the discussion of irony: irony has no purpose; it "turns against existence";[12] it expresses profound "uncertainty" and can be understood only as the "negative independence of everything."[13] Since Kierkegaard thinks of irony in dramatic terms—and recognizes that Plato did so as well—he argues that the form appropriate to irony is Plato's aporetic dialogue, that is, the dialogue without positive insight or outcome; these purely negative dialogues are fully "sustained by irony."[14] Irony is a peculiar use of negativity in drama. The aporetic dialogue works by "simplifying life's multifarious complexities by leading them back to an ever more abstract abbreviation."[15] Kierkegaard touches here on a central element of dramatic Platonism: Plato's dialogues capture the full complexity of life through their use of scene, multiple characters, and interactions. At the same time, they seek to simplify and abstract from those complexities by turning them into material for abstract arguments. The movement between the two, for Kierkegaard, is irony: irony abstracts from existence, which is to say life's messy complexity. Kierkegaard sees Plato's dialogues hover—much like Socrates in his basket—between the concrete and the abstract, offering a complex, material world but also reducing the complexity and materiality of this world through negative irony, or else through the positive power of ideas.

Once Plato's ironic form is associated with a particular use of drama, Kierkegaard begins to compare the dialogues with other dramatic genres of the time, including Greek tragedy and comedy. He recognizes, for example, that the ending of *Phaedo* importantly deviates from what one would expect in a tragedy.[16] At the same time, Kierkegaard emphasizes Plato's affinity to comedy—this is one reason why he considers Aristophanes' depiction of Socrates to be a basically accurate image of Socrates pushed to its comic, or ironic, extreme.[17] And, like many authors of Socrates plays, Kierkegaard is interested in Plato's mixture of comedy and tragedy. Indeed, he relates this mixture directly to Plato's own task as a writer: "Socrates may be said to constitute the unity of the comic and the tragic."[18]

Kierkegaard's dissertation proved to be a crucial point of departure for all of his subsequent writings. He stuck to Danish as his language of choice, pursuing his free and personal style. He kept referring to Socrates during the most crucial shifts and transitions—for example, turning Socrates into the prototype of the subjective, existentialist thinker in *Concluding Unscientific Postscript to Philosophical Fragments* (1846). And he ceased publishing under his own name, relying instead, as Plato had done, on a series of dramatic personae through which to present his philosophy, including Victor Eremita (the putative editor of *Either/Or*, 1843), Johannes Climacus (author of the *Unscientific Postscript*), Johannes de Silentio (from *Fear and Trembling*, 1843), and Constantin Constantius (from *Repetition*, 1843).[19] Throughout his character-driven philosophy, Kierkegaard kept using dramatic techniques, which acquired particular importance for his new style. Indeed, Kierkegaard ended up writing a version of the *Symposium* entitled "'In Vino Veritas': A Recollection" (1844). Devoted to drink and to giving speeches on love, Kierkegaard's symposium is populated by his philosophical personae, including Victor Eremita, Constantin Constantius, Johannes, and two unnamed friends.[20] With this text, Kierkegaard not only becomes part of the tradition of the Socrates play but also pays homage to its origin: Ficino's decision to conceive of his own commentary on the *Symposium* as an adaptation of it.

One important influence on Kierkegaard's dramatic conception of philosophy was Georg Friedrich Wilhelm Hegel. Some of Kierkegaard's contemporaries were drawn to Hegel because of his elevation of history, others for his account of religion or politics. For Kierkegaard, however, yet another feature stood out: Hegel's use of drama. There are four uses of drama that can be identified in Hegel's philosophy: the acknowledgment of drama as a central precursor to philosophy, the use of examples from the history of drama, the use of a theatrical language in describing history, and finally the role of drama for the dialectical method of philosophy. These four uses presented Kierkegaard with a model for a close affinity between drama and philosophy.

The first use of drama, as a precursor to philosophy, concerns Greek tragedy. The position Hegel accorded to tragedy was both central and limited. It was as part of his progressive history of the spirit that Hegel found a place for tragedy as an important stage in the development of consciousness. As important as it was, however, tragedy was superseded, and what was to inherit its place, complete its mission, and overcome its limitations was nothing other than philosophy. As the immediate precursor to philosophy, tragedy certainly occupied a kind of privileged position; it had the special honor of being superseded by the most glorious of all endeavors.

It was probably due to this privileged position as precursor that drama assumes its second function in Hegel's oeuvre: as an important source of examples, a reservoir of figures and scenes that capture important stages of historical progress. In this way, Hegel incorporated references to tragedy in his discussion of law or in *The Phenomenology of the Spirit*, in which he turns to *Antigone* to exemplify the conflict of two irreconcilable positions, laws, or moral codes.[21] Here philosophy does not supersede drama but incorporates drama as a privileged resource for philosophically relevant figures, scenes, and conflicts.

The third use of drama in Hegel's system can be found in the language through which he articulates his philosophy of history. One of the chief innovations of Hegel's philosophy is the fact that world history, as well as the history of philosophy, is not dismissed as so many errors that are now superseded by truth, but rather is considered as a series of necessary steps that culminate in the present. In his *Philosophy of History*, Hegel articulates this historical philosophy in theatrical terms, asserting that world history happens as if "in the theater," and speaks of the spirit in its various "theatrical presentations" (*Schauspiele*).[22] He also describes the spirit manifesting itself in different "stages," progressing always through some central "conflict," terms reminiscent of drama. Hegel's philosophy is thoroughly historical, and this history is articulated in distinctly dramatic and theatrical terms.

Finally, a fourth use of drama is visible in Hegel's philosophical method itself: dialectics. Dialectics, Socrates' key term for describing the philosophical dialogue, goes back, as Hegel knew, to the Greek verb *dialegestai*, which means "holding a conversation." In other words, dialectical philosophy is precisely the kind of philosophy that finds its most proper expression in Plato's philosophical drama. But Hegel takes this term, given a distinctly dramatic meaning by Plato and other writers of dialogues and plays, and drains it of its immediate dramatic valence, turning dialectics into an abstract method for doing philosophy. Philosophy no longer depends on dramatic form and instead becomes a process by which the transition from one stage to the next can be explained by the productive work of negation. As dialectics, the dramatic is reduced to an abstract mechanism for describing the dynamic of philosophy.

The persistence of theater in Hegel's philosophical writings shows that the theater has not, in fact, been fully superseded: drama continues to effect philosophy.[23] It was with some of these effects in mind that George Steiner wrote, in *Antigones*, "Only Hegel rivals Plato as a dramatist and self-dramatist of meaning."[24] Except, of course, that unlike Plato, Hegel was not a dramatist. Drama here is everywhere displaced, overcome, and incorporated; it is the last thing Hegel himself would write. Kierkegaard's entire career proceeds in the shadow of Hegel's system, or as Sarah Kofman put it, Kierkegaard writes in the "margins and gaps of the Hegelian system."[25] This is especially true with respect to drama. Kierkegaard recognizes the significance of drama for Hegel and then proceeds to return Hegel's philosophy to drama.

The first work Kierkegaard wrote after *The Concept of Irony* put this new dramatic theory of philosophy into practice; it is also his masterwork.[26] The title, *Either/Or*, originates in *Concept of Irony*, in which Kierkegaard had started to use the formulation "either/or" to describe a philosophy grounded in dialogue, a philosophy based on the simultaneous existence of least two opinions, two people exchanging thoughts. In that spirit, *Either/Or* is presented as a collection of found manuscripts, letters, lectures, and diaries written by two invented characters—one, called A, an aestheticist and seducer, the other, called B, his ethical and religious friend—and edited by a third person, one Victor Eremita. *Either/Or* is thus rigorously divided and balanced: A against B, seducer against believer, distanced observer against active participant, Don Juan against married man, *either* against *or*. The editor takes special care to balance these two positions, and these two interlocutors, so that neither triumphs. Even though he has arranged the sequence of the two manuscripts so that A comes first, to be answered by B, the editor emphasizes that the sequence could as well be reversed. Irony and open-endedness, the two features Kierkegaard had recognized in Plato's aporetic dialogues, are thus carefully preserved. Generically, they identify *Either/Or* as what one might call a displaced Socratic dialogue. Indeed, the fact that we are getting a textual form of what might have been a live dialogue is thematized explicitly: at the end of the second part, we learn from B's response that the two friends have continually visited each other during their exchange, but that B had to revert to the form of a letter to address A, since A does not like to speak about his own life person to person.[27] It is as if Kierkegaard had taken pieces of a dialogue and rearranged them in two blocks.

Kierkegaard thus does something Hegel never would have done: he writes philosophy—but is this still philosophy?—in a dramatic form and style, or as he puts it in a draft, in the form of "esthetic writing," adding in parentheses, "the pseudonyms."[28] In the end, Kierkegaard understood that his own form was a strange mixture, esthetic without being purely literary, philosophical while reverting to invented figures and scenes. For Hegel, this surely would have looked like a regression from the self-conscious, self-certain position of (Hegelian) philosophy to an earlier (dramatic) moment in history. For Kierkegaard, by contrast, the project of bringing philosophy into close proximity with drama—indeed, of mixing them up—becomes the task at hand. In a notebook, he writes about this mixture: "I cannot repeat often enough what I so frequently have said: I am a poet, but a very special kind, for I am by nature dialectical, and as a rule dialectic is precisely what is alien to the poet."[29] *Dialectical* here means philosophy, in its original Socratic (but also Hegelian) sense, and the passage thus aims directly at the manner in which dialectics is brought into a literary form.

One crucial element in the use of the dramatic is the horizon of theater. This horizon led Kierkegaard to an intense, and mostly positive, engagement with the theater. Writing in some kind of dramatic form forces one, sooner or later, to engage the dimension of theater invariably inscribed in drama. Even though one can, in principle, distinguish a philosophy based on *dran*, that is, action or interaction among characters (such as Kierkegaard's pseudonyms), from *theatron*, that is, from visual representation, those two aspects are often intimately intertwined. This certainly was the case with Plato, leading him to his elaborate critique of theater, and it is also the case with Kierkegaard, who in *Either/Or* undertakes his own engagement with and critique of theater. Indeed, the use and value of theater becomes one of the principal differences between A and B. A, it turns out, is a passionate theater and opera lover, a predilection for which B chastises him. In a sense, what we have here is a new version of the old debate about theater: A, the aestheticist, loves the theater, while B, the ethicist, objects to it.

It is in the first part of *Either/Or* that theater receives its most extensive treatment, and it is here that we can therefore find Kierkegaard's most differentiated relation to that art form. While keeping in mind that everything A does with the theater will be subject to B's critique, we will find in A an attitude that engages the theater but also seeks to control it, incorporating it into a philosophical framework. The first thing to be said about A's interest in the theater is that it deviates from the traditional privileging of tragedy among philosophers, visible, for example, in Hegel. Even though *Either/Or* contains profound reflections on tragedy, both ancient and modern, it also includes extensive observations about various forms of comedy. This, after all, is to be expected from a philosopher intrigued by Socrates' claim about the ultimate unity of the two genres. And comedy also comes first. A responds to two major theater events: Mozart's late eighteenth-century opera buffa, *Don Giovanni* (1787), and Eugène Scribe's well-made play *First Love* (*Les Premières Amours*; 1831). In the course of writing about these two plays, A delivers an elaborate and remarkable reflection on *theatron*, on spectatorship, but also on the dramatic dimensions of the theater, including the status of the actor, masks, personification, and action.

Character or figure is the dramatic category most central to Kierkegaard's own philosophical style and therefore deserves particular attention. Like Hegel, Kierkegaard often finds his philosophically relevant figures in drama, including *Don Giovanni* and *Antigone*, and like Hegel, he uses them for his own philosophical purposes. In "The Diary of a Seducer," the most famous section of *Either/Or*'s first part, Kierkegaard casts his A as a Don Juan figure. But if A is an erotic seducer, he is also a philosophical one, precisely what Kierkegaard had once identified Socrates as being.[30] A is transfixed by his theatrical counterpart, the protagonist of Mozart's *Don Giovanni*, and it is through an exploration of that figure that A begins his extraordinary interpretation of the opera.

Kierkegaard's first approach to the character Don Giovanni is to view him as an impersonation of an abstraction—a frequent tendency of philosophical interpretations of theatrical characters. Just as Kierkegaard had identified Plato's character Socrates with theatrical irony, so his A now identifies Mozart's character Don Giovanni with sensuality. *Don Giovanni* provides a perfect occasion for working through the problem of personhood and personification, so central to Kierkegaard's own dramatic style, because this opera is based on a character who does nothing but fulfill his own desires, an extreme form of egoistical self-realization.[31] In the course of his enthusiastic praise of Mozart's opera, however, A begins to realize that Don Giovanni is a very peculiar kind of person indeed. Not only the sheer number of conquests, 1,003 in Spain alone, but also his singular motivation makes him less an individual character and more an allegory of desire.[32] As A writes, "Don Juan continually hovers between being idea—that is, power, life—and being an individual," or, in an almost tautological formulation, "Don Juan . . . is the incarnation of the flesh."[33] Incarnation of the flesh, personification of personhood—Don Giovanni becomes the theatrical allegory of personification in its purest form, flesh onstage.

This reading betrays Kierkegaard's general concerns with the interaction of music, character, and impersonation, but it is not, in the end, a surprising interpretation of the opera. The question of Don Giovanni's status as a desiring individual and deceptive mask lies at the heart of *Don Giovanni*, which, like so many of Mozart's operas, revolves around appearances, the play of light and darkness, and, above all, masks. The first act culminates in a scene in which three masked characters, the *mascherette*, plot to expose Don Giovanni as the ruthless seducer he is. At the beginning of Act II, Don Giovanni and his servant, Leporello, who is derived from the commedia dell'arte figure Alrecchino, exchange clothes, and each ends up being taken for the other in their subsequent adventures (Peter Sellars took this confusion to its logical extreme by casting identical twins for the two roles in his notorious production of the opera).[34] The character most closely associated with the mask is of course Don Giovanni himself. We first encounter him at night descending from Donna Anna's balcony hidden behind a mask; only his voice will betray him. Indeed, the plot is structured around an unmasking, the visible exposure of Don Giovanni as the murderer of Donna Anna's father. The entire opera depends on the clash between sight and sound, and it is this contrast that is also the dominant theme of A's interpretation.

But Kierkegaard wants to do more than simply offer an interpretation of Mozart's opera. Rather, the opera serves as an occasion to stage an encounter between philosophy and the theater. A is on the side of the theater—he is, after all, an opera enthusiast—but he also imposes onto the theater his own agenda, which is a form of control. He does not simply want to be drawn into the theater and overwhelmed by it, and therefore he develops strategies for resisting it. This leads him to approach the opera anew, this time not from a dramatic angle, one focused primarily on character and action, but from a theatrical one, focused on visibility.

His first strategy is to read a certain discontent with visibility into the opera itself—not without some justification. A challenges Don Giovanni's well-established relation to sight, masks, and deception by declaring that in essence he is "an inner qualification and thus cannot become visible or appear in bodily configurations and movements."[35] But Don Giovanni does not remain invisible in any simple manner. In the same sentence, A qualifies his observation, further describing the protagonist as "a picture that is continually coming into view but does not attain form." With reference to sight, this can only be captured as a paradox, a coming into view of an essentially internal quality that therefore can never take on an external form. With reference to a rival sense, hearing, the paradox is shed. A's analysis of the opera culminates with the claim, repeated ad nauseam, that Don Giovanni finds his highest expression in Mozart's music: "[Don Giovanni] dissolves, as it were, in music for us; he unfurls in a world of sounds."[36] Don Giovanni here is no longer flesh incarnate but flesh musicalized. It is in music that Don Giovanni becomes the true figure for the erotic.

Behind this move from theater (and thus seeing) to music stands a normative nineteenth-century hierarchy of the arts that places music on the top and theater on the bottom. A repeats a doctrine often associated with Arthur Schopenhauer, which is that music is the only direct and unmediated expression of desire (or "will") because it does not need the type of personification—Schopenhauer would call it "individuation"—on which theatrical representation depends. But Kierkegaard does not simply repeat Schopenhauer's antivisual identification of desire (will) and music. Nor does he see music, as Schopenhauer did, as a way of circumventing representation altogether. For Kierkegaard, the status of Don Giovanni as a theatrical person is transposed into music, but in this transposition, neither Don Giovanni's status as personification nor his visible presence onstage is entirely erased. This is the case even though much of what he says sounds antivisual, including the provocative conclusion he derives from his argument about Don Giovanni and music, namely, that we should "shut the eyes when listening to music."[37] What happens in the act of closing the eyes? What kind of negation does this refusal to see evince? Kierkegaard wants the spectacle, the theater, to be there in front of him, even if it is unseen; he is not arguing for a nonstaged performance of the opera in the manner of an oratorio. And even though A reports that he sometimes listened to *Don Giovanni* from outside the closed door, he always goes back to the theater, is drawn to the theater, even if he sometime closes his eyes. In other words, the act of closing the eyes takes place in the midst of a *theatron*, a place of seeing; it is an interruption of vision that is internal to the theater.[38] The closing of the eyes is a perfect example of the contentious engagement between philosopher and theater that is the hallmark of theatrical philosophy.

What A develops here is a particular manner of going to the theater, a mode of reception appropriate to the act of reflection. This reception theory and practice is Kierkegaard's central strategy for controlling theatricality. A leaves the theater as it is—Kierkegaard is no theater reformer, after all, nor does he advocate the closing of theaters—and places all agency with the viewer. A describes how he keeps moving around in the theater, trying out different seats, close to the front at one point, further back later on, and even outside in the corridor.[39] This testing of different positions with respect to the spectacle resonates with Kierkegaard's *Repetition*, in which Constantin Constantius returns to Berlin after a long absence and tries to recapture his earlier experiences there, including that of watching a farce by Johann Nestroy, *Der Talisman* (1840), at the Königstädter Theater.[40] He had found that boxes five and six on the left were the ones most congenial for his purposes and is dismayed when these boxes are not available now and he is forced to sit on the right.[41] This, more than anything, prompts his main insight that "there is no repetition at all."[42] Reception is more important than production because it promises to give agency to the audience and thus, ultimately, to the reflecting philosopher who tries to come to terms with the theater.

The fact that Kierkegaard both is drawn to the theater and also feels that he must control it becomes even clearer when A takes on a second theatrical performance, Eugène Scribe's *First Love*. In this case, sight is not as completely displaced as it had been in *Don Giovanni*—perhaps because there is no music to displace it to—although it is still subjected to critique and revision. Like *Don Giovanni*, *First Love* revolves around assumed and mistaken identities, presented in one of those fantastically complicated plots that would make Scribe the target of modernist polemics— and had made him one of the most influential playwrights of the nineteenth century. In contrast to his habit of going to see *Don Giovanni* with his eyes closed, A now insists (like a good theater historian) that the "theatrical performance . . . is a very important factor in my interpretation," and he concludes that "the performance is itself the play."[43] Theatrical spectacle has suddenly acquired central importance. A particularly admires how *First Love* stages layer upon layer of mistaken identities, exploiting the interstices of masks and resemblances as they occur in the visible space of the stage.

However, despite this emphasis on theatrical performance, A does not let this play rest in the domain of seeing. The whole point of this play, A claims, is that the confusions of masks and identities are not cleared up, that the play does not end, as *Don Giovanni* does, with a final unmasking. The lesson to be learned is that one cannot trust one's own eyes, and this lesson requires that we assume an entirely new attitude toward the stage. More particularly, it requires a new way of watching theater. A writes: "If I were to show a stranger our stage, I would take him to the theater . . . and assuming that he was familiar with the play, I would say to him: . . . 'Look at Madame Heiberg; lower your eyes, for perhaps Emmeline's charm might become dangerous to you; hear the girl's sentimental languishing in the voice . . . Open your eyes—how is it possible? Repeat these movements so quickly that they become almost simultaneous in the moment.'"[44] This stranger, whom A likens to his "philosophical friend," is instructed to blink, to repeatedly open and close his eyes. It is the mode of reception appropriate for a philosopher going to see comedy. Philosophers do not simply enjoy comedy; they look and they avert their eyes, almost simultaneously, for their mode of reception is one marked by a rivalry with the desiring bodies and dangerous visions that make up the stage. But all this occurs in the middle of a theater, be it Mozart's opera buffa, Nestroy's *Der Talisman*, or Scribe's well-made play.

The term Kierkegaard uses to describe the result of this blinking, of closing and opening the eyes, is *shadow play*, a term that appears elsewhere in his writings and that he uses in its German form: *Schattenspiel*. Toward the end of the essay on Scribe, A writes: "The curtain falls; the play is over. Nothing remains but the large outline in which the fantastic *Schattenspiel* of the situation, directed by irony, discloses itself and remains afterward for contemplation. The immediately actual situation is the unreal situation; behind it appears a new situation that is no less awry, and so on."[45] Unlike the cave parable, this passage does not find a real world behind the theatrical one; there is nothing but theater. The conclusion to be drawn from this is not to denounce theatricality, but rather to control it by interrupting it. The philosopher Kierkegaard recommends looking at the stage, but he also interrupts and redirects the eye of this imaginary audience to the afterimage of the theater, the remains of the theater, which have become a fantastic shadow play. This strategy leads to a new interpretation of Plato's cave. Whereas in Plato, shadows had stood for the fake theatrical world that needed to be overcome, here shadows are actually a product of abstraction, a result from a control of theatrical appearance by a critical observer. Shadows are theater, but theater methodized.

The impression that shadow play is the product of A taking control of the theater is borne out in a middle section of part I of *Either/Or*, located between the discussion of Mozart's music and Scribe's masks, entitled "Shadow Figures." These shadow figures are not the afterimages of theatrical impressions, filtered through critical reflection, but A's very own creations. They appear in an address A gives to a fellowship called the "Symparanekromenoi," the fellowship of the dead, a kind of secret society of suffering and the tragic. This section is also the moment when Kierkegaard moves from comedy to tragedy: the shadow figures are subjects of suffering and include Antigone as well as Elvira, Don Giovanni's most tragic victim. In contrast to his intense interest in the performance of *Don Giovanni* and *First Love*, A here shows little interest in the theatrical performance of the plays that contain these figures. He recounts the plots of these tragedies, but only to focus more or less exclusively on the characters themselves, inventing new scenes for them in the process. The main dynamic is once again the struggle with theatricality. A calls these character sketches of suffering "shadow figures" because these figures cannot, in any simple way, become visible: they are at odds with the theater. Once more, Kierkegaard thinks about the limits of theatrical visibility. The main reason for this is, as A explains, that "sorrow wishes to conceal itself" and cannot be depicted though external appearance.[46] As a consequence, A seeks to create shadow figures that form an "interior picture"[47]: "I call them silhouettes [*skyggerids*, which literally means "shadow outlines"], partly to suggest at once by the name that I draw them from the dark side of life and partly because, like silhouettes, they are not immediately visible."[48]

While suffering cannot be represented in the theater in any simple way, it can be much better represented in the kinds of sketches that A himself provides: imagined scenes in whose creations his readers participate. This requires A to insist on active readers who fill in what his deliberately vague sketches leave out: "So, my dear Symparanekromenoi, come closer to me, form a circle around me as I send my tragic heroine [Antigone] out into the world, as I give the daughter of sorrow a dowry of pain as her outfit. She is my work, but still her outline is so indistinct, her form so nebulous, that each and every one of you can fall in love with her and be able to love her in your own way."[49] "Picture X," "imagine Y," "fasten your gaze on Z"— A's speech seeks to create pictures for his audience, or readers, who, as in the passage above, form a circle around him and listen to him attentively as he exercises his art of the spoken sketch.[50] These mental pictures are explicitly conceived of as alternatives to the theater, to external, visual representation. A writes: "So fasten your gaze, dear Symparanekromenoi, on this interior picture; do not let yourselves be distracted by the exterior, or, more correctly, do not produce it yourselves, for I shall continually draw it aside in order to penetrate better into the interior." A works with and against visual representation: the listeners have to fasten their gaze, but on an interior picture; at the same time they are instructed not to produce the picture outlined for them by A, who also says that he will not only sketch this picture but also take it away, producing in this double effect of showing and concealing, of picturing and unpicturing, precisely the secret, inner picture that he deems appropriate for the depiction of suffering.

A knows that he is embarking on a paradoxical enterprise, one that requires a "special eye to see it, a special vision to pursue this unerring indication of secret sorrow."[51] In search for yet another model for this kind of double-edged vision, he says that these types of pictures "must be looked at in the way one looks at the second hand of a watch; one does not see the works, but the interior movement expresses itself continually in the continually changing exterior. But this changeableness cannot be portrayed artistically, and yet this is the point of the whole thing."[52] A piles paradox upon paradox, but these paradoxes demonstrate most fully the extent to which he seeks to redirect, transform, and displace the regime of visibility. In a way, A here turns the act of blinking into a technique of producing shadow figures. Calling these sketches "shadow figures" is itself a metaphor, translating a visual form into Kierkegaard's prose. But it is a metaphor that points to Kierkegaard's own attempt at combining seeing and contemplation, drama and philosophy, his own relation to the stage as he both looks at and averts his eyes from Mozart's opera and Scribe's play. He has appropriated the theater, wrested from it the characters he chooses to dwell upon even as he reuses theater by turning it into a series of imaginary scenes that exist only in the mind's eye.

The creation of afterimages is central because the whole first part—A's engagement with the theater—itself becomes an afterimage once we move on to the second part, which consists of a reply by A's friend B, a judge and married man who presents an alternative to A's aesthetic life: the ethical life. Even though the first part of *Either/Or* has received the most attention, we cannot assign drama and theater its true place in Kierkegaard's thinking without taking into account the fact that the first part is followed by the second part. The protagonist of the second part does more than simply present an alternative life; he defines that life in direct opposition to A's aestheticism and in particular to A's interest in the theater. The ethical life is one of acts, of choices, of decisions between good and bad. The main choice and act is marriage, and it is in the course of an extended praising of marriage that B presents the contours of his ethical life. But his general categories—act, decision—have a more general validity: they speak to an active life rather than a passive one. It is by contrast to this active life that B accuses A of being a mere "observer." The aesthetic attitude means that A never really gets involved in life, observing even his own life as if from a distance. Even though A, like Don Juan, is egoistically following his every whim, B claims that A is only a "dim" personality, that following one's every mood is only an "abstract" form of personal engagement. Finally B charges that A is only a mask with no core, that the choice presented to him is to be "either a pastor—or an actor."[53] A has chosen the latter.

B mobilizes familiar tropes of antitheatricalism: on one hand, A is only an observer; on the other hand, he is an actor without a true core. In the course of the same line of argument, B also identifies the observer attitude with that of the philosopher. The philosopher, too, does not act, does not engage life, but instead only contemplates the past. What we get here, then, is a confirmation that A's attitude toward the theater is strongly aligned with that of the philosopher, that his peculiar way of watching theater, insisting on and simultaneously undoing personification, is a specifically philosophical reception of theater. The ethical alternative, by contrast, is antitheatrical. It proceeds not by contemplation but by action. B, fully engaged with life, has no time for philosophy, nor for the theater, nor even for "imaginary constructions in thought," as he puts it, no doubt thinking of A's shadow figures.[54] In this and other ways, the two stages, aesthetic and ethical, are presented as strict contrasts. Later in Kierkegaard's oeuvre, a third stage would join them: the religious. As in Hegel's dialectic, which Kierkegaard often criticized as a part of his engagement with Hegel, the early stages, in particular the first, are not erased. Even though B claims to reject A's poetic prose, dismissing A's engagement with the theater, B, too, uses poetic prose just as he uses A's set of characters, from Don Juan to Antigone, to which he even adds his own figures, such as Nero. In fact, just as A includes his diary in the "Diary of the Seducer," so B uses himself and his marriage as an example, as a character and exemplary figure in an ethical drama.

It is difficult to specify the status of this dramatic technique in the second part of B. It may simply reflect the necessity of using A's weapons against him. But even this necessity demonstrates, I would argue, that there can be no question of superseding A and therefore no clear progression from A to B. This reading is borne out in Kierkegaard's subsequent oeuvre. Even though Kierkegaard was more and more intent on writing about the last stage, the religious stage, with its famous figure of the "leap of faith," Kierkegaard continued to draw on the dramatic techniques first developed via the figure of A, using fictional personae, creating scenes, inventing figures, sketching silhouettes. So even if we pose the either/or as a question of theater or nontheater, or of drama and nondrama, drama and theater persist, albeit in altered form.

It is this altered form that I am trying to capture through the term *dramatic Platonism*, which describes a drama displaced and reused by philosophy. This philosophical drama contains both a critique of the theater and an engagement with it, integrating theater into the project of philosophy, but not without a critical edge. Philosophical drama is always a rare, unusual, and difficult enterprise. Kierkegaard's oeuvre provides a particularly rich and unusual example of this type of engagement, the result of a dramatic imagination infused with dialectical ambition. In this way, Kierkegaard became the unlikely inventor of a new form of philosophy—one that was "personal and free," as he put it, but whose most important feature was the reinvention of Plato's dramatism. It proved to be an invention with consequence. As the following sections will show, Kierkegaard managed to inaugurate a dramatic as well as theatrical way of writing philosophy.

Friedrich Nietzsche

In 1870, the twenty-six-year-old Friedrich Nietzsche was writing a tragedy based on Empedocles.[55] Nietzsche's desire to try his hand at drama was due in part to his tendency to dabble, somewhat amateurishly but not without skill, in the various arts he wrote so passionately about, including music and poetry. Many modern philosophers dreamed of being artists, and while very few actually ended up doing so, the dream remains significant. One result of such artistic desires is the fact that the poet, the musician, and the dancer often become the heroes of modern philosophical works. The more important result, however, is the creation of a philosophy that variously integrates art into its own procedures, conceiving of philosophy itself as artistic. For Nietzsche this meant infusing philosophy with eulogies of artists, from Greek tragedians to Richard Wagner and Georges Bizet; it meant becoming the philosopher who coined the battle cry of aestheticism, that the world can only be justified as an aesthetic phenomenon;[56] and most important, it meant creating a new style and mode of writing philosophy.

A continual point of reference in this endeavor was Socrates. In the summer of 1875 Nietzsche notes: "I have to admit that Socrates is so close to me that I almost always engage him in battle."[57] Socrates remained Nietzsche's dearest foe; no other figure comes even close to rivaling Socrates in importance throughout Nietzsche's life.[58] The most urgent cause of this battle with Socrates was the charge, articulated by Nietzsche in *The Birth of Tragedy from the Spirit of Music* (1872), that Socrates had killed the glorious art of Greek tragedy. Extending Diogenes Laertius' claim that Socrates had influenced Euripides and perhaps collaborated with him, Nietzsche detects Socrates' corrosive influence in Euripides' mixing of tragedy and comedy, his tendency to portray mythic personages as everyday Athenians, and his use of abstract oppositions, such as the ones used by the sophists and by Socrates alike. Nietzsche's own fantasy of Greek tragedy is something quite different: an art grounded in communal experience. The art of the chorus is based on a shared language, but also on dance and music. The chorus, therefore, occupies a position of collective unity, and the individual protagonists are viewed with skepticism since they threaten that collective unity as well as its mirror image, the unity of the assembled audience. It is almost as if Nietzsche is trying to imagine an original form of tragedy, or rather the very origin of tragedy when it was little more than choral recitation and dance and not yet drama based on dialogue among individuals.

If Euripides loosened the ties to the origins of tragedy, Socrates, in Nietzsche's view, cut them entirely. He did so by developing an art of questioning, in which he applied an abstract form of rationality to the inherited morality and traditional values on which many choral odes are based. This determination to question everything destroyed the cultural and intellectual basis on which tragedy had thrived. The *Birth of Tragedy*, which tells of the rise and fall of Greek tragedy, is itself structured like a drama, in fact like a typical nineteenth-century melodrama with protagonists and villains: Socrates is the great seducer of innocent but corruptible Greek tragedy. This melodrama would end terribly if we didn't have a savior who enters the scene at the last minute: Richard Wagner. He will save Greek tragedy by reviving the form for the modern world.

One thing is odd about Nietzsche's drama of the corruption and last-minute salvation of tragedy: it turns out that Nietzsche identifies—can't help identifying—with the villain. After all, Nietzsche himself is not a tragedian nor a musician, but a philosopher, just like Socrates. Hence Nietzsche's confession that he always fights with Socrates because he is so close to him. Nietzsche knows that in the end he is a descendant of Socrates, not of the great tragedians. And so Nietzsche also knows that in his melodrama of tragedy's death, he is part of the problem. What to do? Nietzsche begins to fantasize about a Socrates who would not be hostile to music and tragedy, but who would somehow embrace them. Such a Socrates is not entirely absent from the dialogues: it is the Socrates from the beginning of the *Phaedo*, who has been prompted by a dream to start "doing music" (*mousiken poiei*), which should be translated not as "composing music" but more generally as "making art." Socrates puts this dream into practice by turning Aesop's fables into verse. This is a modest step, to be sure, but it is a step in the right direction—the direction, in fact, of the Socrates plays, many of which legitimize themselves through reference to this episode in Plato. Nietzsche is willing to bet the entire future of tragedy on this same step: if tragedy is to return in the future, it will be in the name of a Socrates who makes music (*musiktreibender Sokrates*).[59] In this way Nietzsche tries to come to terms with the fact that he himself is not a tragedian, that instead of writing tragedies, as he had tried to do, he should write philosophy, albeit in the mode of a music-making philosopher. This way, the villain of the melodrama called "death of tragedy" can be redeemed and hailed as a savior. The future of tragedy, in other words, is not the neotragedian Richard Wagner but a music-making Socrates by the name of Friedrich Nietzsche.

Characteristically, Nietzsche thinks of theater history and its relation to philosophy in dramatic terms, that is, as struggle and conflict among representative figures: Dionysius versus Apollo, Aeschylus versus Euripides and Socrates. He also thinks of it in terms of genre. In the course of his critique of Socrates, Nietzsche comes closer than anyone before him to identifying Plato's dialogues as a peculiar form of philosophical drama. Arguing that Plato wrote in direct competition with the drama of his time, Nietzsche even places this generic struggle between Plato and drama within the Greek culture of competition.[60] But Nietzsche's insight goes further still, to the point at which he argues that Plato created an "art form that is akin to the existing art forms he [Plato] rejected."[61] Being akin to existing art forms, however, does not mean being identical to them. On the contrary, Plato's dialogues distinguish themselves by having "mixed all existing styles and forms." In a brilliant and quite accurate image, Nietzsche compares Plato's dialogues to a Noah's ark in which all Greek genres are gathered and preserved for the future. But they are preserved in a hodgepodge that erases their distinctiveness because they are now subjected to a new and different set of rules: the rules of Plato's philosophical drama. As early as 1869, Nietzsche writes, "Plato's philosophical drama belongs neither to tragedy nor to comedy: it lacks a chorus and musical, religious motifs. . . . Mainly, it is not meant for praxis, but for reading: it is a rhapsody. It is literary drama [*Literaturdrama*]."[62] This is a central insight into Plato as a dramatist. Nietzsche recognizes the enormous differences between Greek tragedy and Plato's plays, identifying in Plato's literary drama something much closer to bourgeois drama, the form that is likewise fully and deliberately literary drama. What killed tragedy, according to this logic, was not so much philosophy as a discipline, or even the activities of Socrates the philosopher, but rather the new genre that Plato had created.

Nietzsche recognizes that Plato was competing with tragedy and comedy and also that his dialogues are mixtures that impose onto existing forms and styles the demands of a new discipline called philosophy. This does not mean, however, that Nietzsche praises all aspects of Plato's artistic achievements. At one point, for example, he complains that when Plato turns spoken exchanges into dialogue, "everything is either too long or too short."[63] Later he picks up the same idea and characterizes Plato's dialogues as simply "boring" and "horribly self-satisfied and childish" (says the author of *Thus Spoke Zarathustra*).[64] Similarly, he complains that Plato's Socrates, as opposed to the one that emerges from Xenophon's texts, is too improbable, too elevated, too "overdetermined," and therefore cannot be imitated.[65] Plato has concentrated too many features in one figure. (Again, it is strange to see the author of *Zarathustra* make such a complaint—or did Nietzsche later decide that he was wrong and that Plato was right?) Nietzsche attributes this weakness to Plato's skill, or rather lack thereof, as a dramatist: "Plato is not dramatist enough to capture the image of Socrates in a single dialogue." Instead, Nietzsche complains, Plato creates an improbable composite that is constantly changing.[66] Nietzsche here gives Plato dramaturgical advice: he takes him seriously as a dramatist, even if he does not agree with the final product. For all his failures as a dramatist, however, Plato is clearly also doing something right: "I read the Apology of Socrates with inner excitement," Nietzsche notes at one point.[67] At another, he recommends that philosophy students avoid professional academic philosophers and instead immerse themselves in Plato.[68]

Nietzsche's critique of Plato's drama is rooted in a classical conception of drama typical of the nineteenth century. Plato's dramatic form, with its mixtures of genres, use of an overdetermined protagonist, and slow pace (which Kierkegaard had admired), violates Nietzsche's nineteenth-century conception of drama, as well as his own fantasy of tragedy. He dislikes everything about Socrates that smacks of comedy, including his dying words—"We owe a cock to Asclepius"—which he reads, wrongly, as proof of guilt, resentment, and a more general denial of life, when it is in fact Socrates' attempt to defeat tragedy.[69] When it comes to drama, in other words, Nietzsche is a (nineteenth-century) Aristotelian and remains focused on a classical, tragic conception of the hero. Another way of saying this is that while Nietzsche was without doubt an untimely philosophical writer, the first twentieth-century philosopher, he was also a traditionalist, at least as far as drama is concerned. He looked to classical protagonists, distinctions between genres, dramatic action, and the chorus as the non-dialogic origin of tragedy. In a sense, Nietzsche was caught between his fantasy of nondialectical choral tragedy and the protomodern, literary, mixed drama of Plato. Yet despite these nineteenth-century dramatic values, Nietzsche recognizes Plato's dramatic project and even acknowledges its effectiveness: Plato's dramas did manage to displace tragedy and anticipate modern literary drama as well as the modern novel.[70]

In the course of his career, Nietzsche became more doubtful about the tragic pole in the dichotomy between choral tragedy and Plato's intellectual drama. While in *The Birth of Tragedy* he had hailed Wagner as the rejuvenator of tragedy, he would become increasingly disenchanted with that promise. Much ink has been spilled over why exactly Nietzsche turned against Wagner. Surely one can imagine a mixture of personal and aesthetic reasons that led to Nietzsche's great anti-Wagnerian polemic, *The Case of Wagner* (1888). My own view of the matter is that Nietzsche ultimately attacked Wagner because Wagner was increasingly determined to turn what had hitherto been little more than a theatrical vision, a theater of the future, into reality. With the help of Prince Ludwig II, Wagner built his own festival theater in Bayreuth: the theater of the future was now set in stone. This single-minded determination to realize the theater of the future turned Nietzsche against Wagner and even against the theater as such. Consequently, Nietzsche's polemic against Wagner is phrased in explicitly antitheatrical terms: he denounces Wagner for having "theatricalized" music, for being an "actor" through and through, and for instituting a veritable "theatrocracy," which Nietzsche understands (somewhat differently than Plato) as the rule not of the audience but of the theater—of theatricality—over the arts.[71] In this antitheatrical polemic, Nietzsche's affinity to Plato comes to the fore. For Nietzsche, theater clearly was central as a concept, as a project, and as a fantasy, but not as an institution. For this reason, Nietzsche could not stand the actually existing Bayreuther Festspielhaus and had to flee in the midst of the theater festival even when he was still Wagner's putative friend and ally. Theater, for him, was primarily a philosophical category. He could bemoan the death of tragedy in ancient Greece, even as he could fantasize about its rebirth in the future, but in both cases death and rebirth were philosophical events. Nietzsche wrote as a dramatic philosopher; he had little interest in aligning himself with a theater impresario.

After Nietzsche dismissed Wagner as too theatrical, his primary interest shifted to dance. Dance had already played a role in his search for the origin of tragedy, since the chorus dances as well as sings. Now he turned to dance to find contemporary alternatives to Wagner. One such alternative was Georges Bizet's *Carmen*, with its dancing protagonist and its dance-oriented music. Nietzsche's excessive praise of the composer of *Carmen* has always surprised commentators, since *Carmen*—let alone Bizet's other operas—seemed to lack the gravitas of works by Nietzsche's earlier idol, Wagner. But for Nietzsche, *Carmen* represented precisely the lightness of the French as opposed to Wagner's Teutonic seriousness. Part of this new infatuation with lightness resided in the opera's emphasis on dance, which was beginning to emerge as Nietzsche's newly privileged performing art.

Thus, Nietzsche's new system of theater consisted of three elements: undialectical, choric tragedy, which was lost and, now that Nietzsche had rejected Wagner, could no longer be revived; Bizet's celebration of dance; and Plato's dialectical and literary drama, which included the enigmatic figure of the music-making Socrates. The question now was how Nietzsche's own mode of writing philosophy would fit into this system. One thing is clear: Nietzsche's fascination with different forms of drama and theatrical performance left deep traces on his own mode of writing philosophy. The most important way in which drama affected Nietzsche's philosophy was in Nietzsche's realization that he could not write philosophy under his own name, that he had to invent philosophical characters, as Plato and Kierkegaard had done. In order to accommodate those characters, some form of dramatic form would have to be invented. Given the range of his dramatic interests, this form would have to be some combination of the genres that he had spent so much time thinking and writing about: Greek tragedy, philosophical drama, and dance. If one looks at Nietzsche's work through the lens of genre, it is clear that he tried out various combinations of those three.

First came the Empedocles play. In the outline Nietzsche sketched around 1870, the philosopher Empedocles is elected king but grows to despise the people, who are suffering from a plague, and finally decides on their annihilation. He goes mad, declares the truth of reincarnation, and throws himself into Mount Etna. This Empedocles play is clearly built around the tragic death of the philosopher; like all of Nietzsche's dramatic creations, it is a character-centered work. The plague echoes Sophocles' *King Oedipus*, and indeed, in the summer of 1872, after having completed *The Birth of Tragedy*, Nietzsche sketched a philosophical Oedipus drama, in which Oedipus calls himself "the last philosopher."[72] Nietzsche was trying out different philosophical characters to anchor his dramatic experiments. But Oedipus, the most reflective and most philosophical of

Greek tragic protagonists, was still not good enough for Nietzsche, since he is a character for whom philosophy, the single-minded search for truth, has only brought grief. He has no positive, life-affirming philosophy such as the one Nietzsche envisioned. Oedipus asks for pity, and pity is precisely what Nietzsche sought to avoid. Empedocles, who has overcome his pity for the people, was more to his liking. But in the end, Nietzsche gave up on Empedocles as well and moved on to a third character, the figure on which so much of his philosophy is staked: Zarathustra.

Like his works on Oedipus and Empedocles, *Thus Spoke Zarathustra* began as drama. Many of the early fragments and schemes are dramatic; apparently, Nietzsche conceived of *Zarathustra* as a play in four acts. Up to the fall of 1883, Nietzsche envisioned the play as a tragic one, focusing on Zarathustra's death, which put it in line with the two preceding dramatic sketches.[73] The fragments themselves are either direct pronouncements by Zarathustra or short, scenic moments of dialogue that are sometimes framed by descriptive sentences in the present tense, which function as stage directions. They note key turning points in the action, important speeches, and encounters between Zarathustra and others, leading up the climax, the moment when Zarathustra, like Empedocles, speaks the truth of the eternal return and dies.

When Nietzsche began to write *Zarathustra*, this dramatic conception was largely preserved, but not entirely. In the end, what he wrote was technically no longer a drama but a text framed by a narrative voice. Nevertheless, this text remained structured around a single character and that character's action and speeches, which in turn are set in distinct scenes. Nietzsche created a mixture of narrative and drama, a mix of styles and modes, including sermons and Romanic poetry, but also Aristotle, Seneca, Emerson, and Goethe, all supercharged with an elevated rhetoric stemming from biblical prophecy. In this way, Nietzsche repeated the mixture he had recognized in Plato's drama. Nietzsche's friend Erwin Rohde immediately recognized the similarity and wrote in a letter: "Plato creates his Socrates and you your Zarathustra."[74] This (generically speaking) Platonic mixture, which originated as a play, can be called a displaced drama and may be compared to Kierkegaard's equally displaced drama of *Either/Or*. It is important, though, not to revert to the default assumption that such displaced drama becomes some kind of novelistic creation. Rather, such creations should be grouped under an expanded notion of the dramatic that goes beyond formalistic definitions of drama; what results instead is a family of forms that privilege characters and their direct speech and that place these characters in scenes to effect their interaction.

This leaves the final component of the definition of the dramatic to be determined: the theatrical horizon. Like Plato or Kierkegaard, Nietzsche proceeds with constant reference to theater; *Zarathustra* clearly competes with the theater of his time. But the type of theater that frames *Zarathustra* is not, as it had been for Plato, the elevated genre of tragedy; rather, it is the circus and the fair. When Zarathustra begins his first descent from the mountains, he enters a town that has assembled to watch a tightrope walker. Zarathustra bursts in on the scene and begins to deliver his sermons and maxims to the assembled crowd. One member of the crowd in fact mistakes Zarathustra for the tightrope walker and shouts that he should stop talking and start walking. At this moment, the language of the circus enters Zarathustra's speech. Rather than clarifying the confusion, he utters this sentence: "Man is a rope between animal and superman, a rope across an abyss," and further elaborates on this image.[75] In the midst of this elaboration, Zarathustra is interrupted by an actual performance: the tightrope walker has all of a sudden appeared on his rope. The audience loses interest in Zarathustra, who has to give way to the spectacle. But then a strange thing happens. His new rival, the tightrope walker, is in turn interrupted by a rival of his own: a clownish creature referred to as a jester (*Possenreisser*) appears on the tightrope, chases the tightrope walker, and finally jumps over him, thus outdoing and humiliating this performer. This action causes the tightrope walker to lose his balance and fall down, landing in front of Zarathustra's feet. Zarathustra takes the body, carries it away, and buries it.

This opening scene creates an intriguing interrelation between Zarathustra and the circus performer, but also more generally between Nietzsche's text and the theater. Zarathustra interrupts a performance; he is confused with the performer; he adopts a language of circus performance; and he is in turn interrupted by a second circus performance (which is then interrupted by the jester). Even though Zarathustra competes with the theater and is outdone by it, he nevertheless incorporates the theater into his own language: his sermons are phrased in the language of the theater. The image of the tightrope and the one who walks across it remains central for the rest of the work.

The language of the circus is soon joined by a second model, which would prove even more central: dance. Nietzsche's chief figure for philosophy becomes the act of dancing. He describes speaking as a kind of tomfoolery, with which humans "dance above and across everything."[76] The third part of *Zarathustra* contains an entire section called "Dancing Song" (*Tanzlied*), and Zarathustra's virtue is characterized as a "dancer's virtue," referring no doubt to Carmen as opposed to Wagner.[77] After having been mistaken for a tightrope walker at the beginning, Zarathustra ends up becoming a sort of dancer.

In order to understand why Nietzsche would use displaced drama as a mode of writing philosophy, we can analyze this form according to a Platonic dramaturgy focused on the philosophical instrumentalization of character, scene, and action. As with Plato's Socrates, much weight is given to the central protagonist, Zarathustra. Just as Socrates, as Plato's creation, is not identical with the author, so Nietzsche's Zarathustra is not simply Nietzsche. Zarathustra is a dramatic vehicle for presenting philosophy through a personage who engages in dialogue and interaction with other characters. But what kind of action is central to this character? Zarathustra's main action, like Socrates', is speech, as the title promises:

Thus Spoke Zarathustra. This phrase is repeated after every section, almost ritually, as a conclusion of the narrative frame.

This endlessly repeated phrase also serves as a summary of the action of the preceding scene: speaking is what Zarathustra has done, and his particular drama is mostly about the act of speech. In a way, this does not come as a surprise. Nietzsche is not only a thinker of the body, insisting on the body against all forms of idealism. He is also a thinker of language, introducing into philosophy a keen sense of the significance of metaphor, of rhetoric more generally, and of the insight that philosophy must be, among other things, a critical analysis of language. And since the task of Nietzsche's character is to articulate his philosophy, it is around speech that this drama revolves: how to speak philosophy, how to become a particular kind of speaker, how to say what needs to be said but cannot be said simply by Nietzsche himself.

Nietzsche focuses not only on speaking but also on being understood. The main drama of *Thus Spoke Zarathustra* lies in the differing responses to Zarathustra's speech—the effects, both intended and unintended, that the prophet's utterances have on various kinds of audiences.[78] We first find him speaking in front of the crowd gathered around the tightrope walker. But the crowd does not understand Zarathustra, and the experience of different forms of misunderstanding characterizes the subsequent sections as well. After his negative experience with the crowd, Zarathustra becomes more careful in his choice of audience, restricting himself mainly to groups of friends or followers. But even there, he is not safe from being misunderstood and finds that his followers have created grossly mistaken versions of his philosophy. As a consequence, Zarathustra withdraws again, opting to speak only to himself, and significant stretches of the work are therefore devoted to soliloquies. There is one group of listeners, however, that is seemingly safe from generating misunderstanding: Zarathustra's animals. These animals are helpers of sorts, bringing Zarathustra food when he is ill and comforting him when he is dispirited. But their primary function seems to be serving as a kind of sympathetic audience, one that will not misunderstand Zarathustra's speech. The real target audience for Zarathustra, of course, is humans. But addressing humans is a precarious business, while the animals are a safe, comforting group of listeners, an audience that does not respond and is not supposed to be transformed by the speech that both is and isn't addressed to it.

The drama around Zarathustra's speech and his listeners determines the action of the entire work, for the different speech acts and speech situations are accompanied by a relatively simple and repetitive sequence of action: Zarathustra descends from the mountains, speaks, and withdraws again, over and over again in a movement that harks back to the prisoner in Plato's cave, who ascends and descends again only to be faced, like Zarathustra, with misunderstanding and hostility. There is progress or at least a process at work here: with each repetition Zarathustra has realized something, and by the end, Zarathustra will have learned how to speak to humans.

The action of descending and ascending, of hoping to find an audience and realizing that an appreciative audience is wanting, leads to the most important development of the entire work: the emergence of Zarathustra as the prophet of Nietzsche's two philosophical doctrines, the will to power and the eternal return. At first Zarathustra hesitates to give voice to these doctrines himself and contents himself with announcing, John the Baptist–like, the coming of one who will be able to put these doctrines into words. However, the more Zarathustra recognizes the limitations of his followers, the more he doubts that any of them will be the one, the overman or meta-man, destined to declare these doctrines. At this point, Zarathustra realizes that he himself must become the prophet of the eternal return.[79] Just as Plato's dialogues shy away from simply announcing Plato's doctrines through Socrates and instead seek to produce insights indirectly, in dialogue with his interlocutors, so *Thus Spoke Zarathustra* does not simply put Nietzsche's thought into that character's mouth but describes the process by which Zarathustra becomes the subject and speaker of his philosophy. In this sense, *Zarathustra* is the drama of the emergence of a philosophical protagonist, of Zarathustra becoming the speaker of this new philosophy.

Zarathustra's two doctrines—the will to power and the eternal return—are both direct responses to Socrates and Plato. The will to power is a critique of Socrates' ethics, which holds that evil is done only through ignorance (of the good): as soon as people understand the good, they will do it. The will to power, by contrast, denies that there exists an idea of the good in the first place, and even if it existed, ignorance alone would not suffice to explain any deviation from it. Instead, the will to power imagines a universe of competing forces. The will to power is also a theory of truth: since no direct access to the world is possible, all we have is competing acts of interpretation. This competition is best described as a struggle for power, a struggle for domination over other acts of interpretation. There is no place here either for the idea of the good or for reaching it through knowledge. Ethics is not a matter of finding truth, but of gaining dominance in a kind of evolutionary process.

The other doctrine, the eternal return, is notoriously difficult to pin down. It is easier to say what it is not: it does not, despite its name, describe a cyclical universe in which everything happens over and over again. Rather, it serves as the cornerstone of the doctrine Zarathustra finally pronounces as he descends from the mountains. Nietzsche calls the doctrine of the eternal return "affirmative" because it opposes all philosophies that critique the world as mere appearance, as an imperfect rendering of an ideal. Nietzsche considered metaphysics, which he associated with Plato's theory of ideas, as nihilistic: it says no to the world, no to experience, no to the body because it presumes a real world behind the world we know. Saying yes, by contrast, means saying that there is no other world, that this world is all we have. Because this is all we have, we are stuck with what we have for all eternity: all that can happen is the endless recycling of the world. There is no other reservoir, no other realm whence something new could arrive.

It is only once we read backward from the eternal return that the dramatic form of *Thus Spoke Zarathustra* makes sense. Its repetitive plot, with Zarathustra descending from the mountains, preaching, and withdrawing again, is an illustration of a worldview in which everything returns. In addition, *Thus Spoke Zarathustra* illustrates a second consequence of the eternal return: that no messiah, no meta-man, will enter this world from elsewhere. The entire text is devoted to the heralding of such a meta-man, but then the meta-man does not come. Even the disciples, whatever they may have absorbed from Zarathustra's speeches, fall woefully short of becoming this figure. Instead, Zarathustra realizes that he has to fashion himself into that new person. It is for this reason that Nietzsche abandoned the original idea of having Zarathustra die just like Empedocles. In fact, Nietzsche had always interpreted Socrates' death, his willingness and eagerness to die, as a sign of the nihilistic, destructive, and self-negating aspect of his philosophy. Zarathustra, by contrast, was to be the anti-Socrates, the great affirmer of life. For this reason, Zarathustra cannot die; he must transform himself into the figure he had called for.

In the end, *Thus Spoke Zarathustra* is a drama of speech or, to be precise, a displaced drama of speech. Nietzsche forged a genre that would be suited to this task, creating a literary form that draws on drama as the principal genre of staging speech and speakers, but then displacing this form into a hybrid that draws on different genres for the single purpose of fashioning the speaker and the speech ideally suited to the articulation of Nietzsche's philosophy.

Given how clearly Nietzsche conceives of his own philosophy as an overturning of Socrates and Plato, this is perhaps a good occasion to address a crucial dimension of what I call dramatic Platonism: how it relates to the repeated, almost obsessive anti-Platonism propounded not only by Nietzsche but also by so many modernist thinkers and writers. I have already sought to indicate how Socrates and, to a lesser extent, Plato are profoundly ambivalent figures for Nietzsche. I say *figures* or *characters*, not philosophies, for Nietzsche seems to have no ambivalence about the philosophical positions he and most of the philosophical tradition associate with those figures. He simply rejects those positions. His most visceral objection to Platonism is that it has merged with Christianity, contributing to the dismissal of the body and of the world. "Christianity is Platonism for the masses" is his inversion of Marx's famous formulation.[80] Yet, along with a more positive view of Socrates as a music maker, Nietzsche also comes to a more nuanced assessment of Plato. This view of Plato is most fully articulated in *The Gay Science* (1882). Here Nietzsche does initially view Platonism as an illness from which he hopes to "cure" philosophy (the language of illness and cure resonates with his philosophy of the body). But then Nietzsche pauses and offers a qualification of this conception of Platonism as illness: "In sum: all philosophical idealism has hitherto been something like an illness, when it wasn't, as in the case of Plato, the cautionary thought of an exuberant and dangerous healthiness, the fear of overwhelming sensory experiences, the cunning of a cunning

Socrates.—Perhaps we moderns are simply not healthy enough to need Plato's idealism?"[81] The passage presents a curious inversion. While it remains true that idealism or Platonism should be understood as an illness, the illness of having turned against life, Nietzsche makes an exception for Socrates. He recognizes that Socrates' robust constitution was an important element of Plato's philosophical character: Socrates does not get drunk at the end of the *Symposium*, for example, nor does he flee in battle, and he admits to having strong corporeal desires himself. Such passages give Nietzsche pause and lead him to come to a different conclusion: (Plato's) Socrates himself was not part of the illness of denying and ignoring life. He knew life, the overwhelming nature of the senses, only too well and constructed his idealist philosophy in response to it, as a precaution. One might understand this view of Plato as idealism framed by an "as if": Socrates and Plato (who are collapsed in this passage) did not really think that there is a separate realm of ideas. They probably did not believe that doing evil is simply a matter of not knowing the good, either. But they knew that this type of idealized intellectualism was the only adequate philosophy in the face of a culture, such as that of Greece, focused on the senses and the body. Their idealism was an antidote to the culture that surrounded them; they needed to argue and act as if there were such a realm.

Nietzsche ends this paragraph with an even more surprising conclusion, or rather a question: are we moderns not healthy enough to need Plato's idealism? Nietzsche, the avowed anti-Platonist, seems to envision a future in which we might need Plato's idealism once again. Such a future would be one in which idealism has been dismissed and materialism put in its place. This future, I suggest, has arrived; we are in the midst of it. In fact, in the realm of philosophy, Nietzsche was its principal herald. Since Nietzsche, most major philosophies have been anti-idealist, emphasizing various forms of materiality, whether the social organization of labor, institutions, or (the great slogans of our age) experience and the body. All this anti-idealism, no doubt, has been "healthy," in Nietzsche's sense. Indeed, health has been the great product of our age. Like the Greek culture of Socrates and Plato, we find ourselves celebrating this health in the gymnasium. It was precisely to such places of bodily exercise that Socrates went in order to instill in its practitioners the antidote: idealist philosophy. We are now so overwhelmingly healthy, so focused on the body, that we have dire need of Plato.

Jean-Paul Sartre and Albert Camus

In the history of existentialism, Kierkegaard and Nietzsche are routinely seen as the movement's most significant precursors: both of them were interested in subjective experience, in characters and their actions, in the actual existence of humans rather than their hidden essence. This difference between human existence and hidden essence is what gives existentialism its name: let's no longer look for essences, but content our-selves instead with what exists in the here and now, around us, in front of our eyes, and within ourselves, our own existence. "Existence precedes essence" is the battle cry of existentialism, and this means that existence is what we are, what characterizes us, and therefore what should concern us, even and especially in our philosophy. Everything else, including the essence of things, is impossible to access and ultimately is idle specula-tion. Our subjective life and the interaction between us and others is what really matters anyway, and it is the only thing that is real—there is no out-side of the cave.

Giving up the old philosophical obsession with essence came at a steep price. In particular, it meant that philosophy no longer satisfied the desire to know first things and was no longer in the business of providing the ground on which to stand. In this sense, existentialism left its readers and followers without foundation. This, however, was not a failing; it was the main object of existentialism, which tried to capture, rather than to dis-solve, the very feeling of groundlessness, the feeling, to put it in religious terms, that God was absent or dead. Albert Camus would call this feeling of groundlessness "the absurd"; Jean-Paul Sartre would call it "nausea." If existentialism learned from Kierkegaard and Nietzsche to banish meta-physical speculations about essence, it also learned from them something much more important: the insight that a philosophy of existence implies a new relation between philosophy and theater. After all, it had been phi-losophy's insistence on essence that had motivated its opposition to the theater, very much in accordance with the logic of the cave: we can find essence only if we leave the theater behind. Once philosophy overcomes its fixation on essence, it can overcome its rejection of the theater as well. The theater's embrace of the visible world is no longer an impediment but an advantage: what better way of presenting existence than by means of the theater?

Both Camus and Sartre made extensive use of drama and theater in their philosophies of existence. They based their philosophical articula-tions on scenes and situations, and they relied on drama as a central form in which to express their philosophy. Finally both Sartre and Camus went back to Plato, the original inventor of philosophical character—one might almost say the inventor of philosophy as a question of character. In his diary, Camus even copies Nietzsche's own diary entry—"Socrates, let me admit it, is so close to me that I constantly have to fight with him."[82]

The significance of existentialism for the theater was noted to some extent in Martin Esslin's landmark study *The Theatre of the Absurd* (1961). In this book, Esslin groups together in the name of "the absurd" a large and rather heterogeneous group of playwrights, including Samuel Beckett, Eugène Ionesco, Arthur Adamov, Jean Genet, Edward Albee, Fernando Arrabal, Günter Grass, and Harold Pinter. Their drama, Esslin argued, expressed the basic assumptions and attitudes of existentialist philoso-phy by transposing them into new dramatic forms. Beckett, in particular, becomes the playwright who captured the absurd without a single philosophical speech—if one discounts Lucky's "thinking" rant in *Waiting for Godot* (1953). The two dramatists conspicuously missing from this list of playwrights are Sartre and Camus themselves. While Esslin mentions Camus's forerunner, Nietzsche, and quotes several passages from Camus's *Myth of Sisyphus,* in which the absurd is explained, Esslin is disappointed by Camus's and Sartre's drama: "While Sartre or Camus express the new content [i.e., the absurd] in the old convention, the Theatre of the Absurd goes a step further in trying to achieve a unity between its basic assumptions and the form in which these are expressed. In some senses, the *theatre* of Sartre and Camus is less adequate as an expression of the *philosophy* of Sartre and Camus—in artistic, as distinct from philosophic, terms—than the Theatre of the Absurd."[83] Esslin's theory is still the prevalent understanding of Sartre and Camus, namely, that their drama falls short of the more daring forms associated with Beckett or Ionesco, that they were radical in their philosophy but too conventional in their playwriting.

At work in this dismissal of Camus and Sartre as playwrights is a desire to keep drama and philosophy strictly apart. Here we see the return of the fear always associated with philosophical drama: that bringing philosophy onto the stage will make bad theater. Indeed, Esslin's main worry about the drama of Sartre and Camus is their reliance on philosophical language. While the playwrights of the absurd interrupt language, chopping up dialogues into fragments, clichés, and noncommunicative utterances such as Lucky's rant in *Waiting for Godot,* Sartre's and Camus's characters express themselves much too fluently when it comes to their positions, beliefs, and attitudes. A similar complaint might even be launched against Sartre and Camus as philosophers. Existentialism was the last philosophical movement not centrally based on a critical analysis of language; for that reason, it was accused of having missed the linguistic turn of philosophy. Theodor Adorno was one of those who criticized Sartre and Camus early on for their relative lack of interest in language. In an essay that was written a few years before Esslin's study and anticipates several of its points, "Trying to Understand *Endgame*" (1958), Adorno sees Beckett's play as a product of existentialist philosophy. At the same time, he also tries to distance the play from being anything like a philosophical play. "The interpretation of *Endgame* must not pursue the fantasy of expressing its meaning philosophically."[84] Like Esslin, Adorno seeks to keep drama and philosophy apart.

Esslin (and Adorno) identified the immense confluence between existentialism and drama, a confluence that made itself felt in a relatively conventional manner: playwrights drawing on the worldview articulated by philosophers. What they downplay, however, is the fact that the exchange between philosophy and drama goes both ways, that the reason Sartre and Camus had such an immense influence on drama and the reason they themselves were compelled to write plays was that drama and theater had deeply influenced their philosophy. Existentialism is one of the moments when the membrane between philosophy and drama is unusually permeable. In order to understand existentialism as well as its relation to drama, it is necessary to analyze both the influence of drama on philosophy and the influence of philosophy on drama.

Jean-Paul Sartre: The Theater of Existence

Sartre begins with subjective existence, but this does not mean that subjective existence is readily available as a foundation on which to build a philosophical system. On the contrary, he describes subjective existence as a changing and fragile entity. In his parlance, inherited from Martin Heidegger, subjective existence is a project. It is not simply given; it must be envisioned and realized, a goal that has to be achieved in a process of self-making or self-fashioning. This self-creation does not occur in a vacuum but is delimited by various constraints. The self is never alone but is embedded in the world around it, in what Sartre calls a situation. The situation influences the self and, in a sense, threatens to determine the self. The most important component of this situation is the existence of other people. Because we are never alone, we are confronted not only with the world around us but also with other people, who in turn regard us, approach us, and define us; Sartre goes so far as to say that they try to create us. For Sartre, this claim made by the world and by other humans on us is a great danger, for we are now subject to the views and whims of others, who turn us into whatever they will. For Sartre, who inherits this fear from Heidegger as well, this leads to a profound alienation, the alienation of our subjective existence from itself.

Sartre, like the protoexistentialist philosophers Kierkegaard and Nietzsche, to whom he turns with some frequency, recognized that existentialism not only allows for but also makes necessary a new relation between theater and philosophy. Gone is the fixation on essence that is then contrasted with theatrical appearance. The theater can thus be used as a model, and also as a form, through which to capture the drama of existence. Not infrequently, therefore, Sartre's main work, *Being and Nothingness* (1943), which is mostly presented in an abstract, philosophical style of argumentation inherited from Edmund Husserl and Heidegger, is interrupted by extended examples that take on a life of their own, dramatic scenes that betray the sensibility of a playwright. Indeed, for many readers, it is those scenes that are the most memorable parts of Sartre's work, allowing it to have an effect beyond that of its original audience of philosophers. There is, for example, the figure exemplifying bad faith. Sartre takes two pages to describe her: a woman who meets a man for the first time, lingers, but indefinitely postpones the decision of whether to go home with him. She remains aloof, not responding to his flirtation and innuendos, pretending that the question of whether to go home is not what is in fact happening right now. Sartre leaves us with the image of this noncommittal contact: "the hand rests inert between the warm hands of her companion—neither consenting nor resisting—a thing."[85]

Another scene related to bad faith is perhaps the most famous in the book: it seeks to capture the immense difficulty of self-fashioning. Self-fashioning, the imperative that we make ourselves what we are, as Sartre knows, is a process taken straight from the theater, from acting. The process of self-fashioning can easily become inauthentic when we turn ourselves into some preconceived function or, to use the language of the theater, a role. Sartre's chief example is that of the waiter who tries just a little too hard at being a waiter, overfulfilling his job so that he is simply "playing at *being* a waiter."[86] Sartre adds—but this addition is not even necessary since the theatrical overtones are clear already—that this role-playing waiter is a waiter only "as the actor is Hamlet, by mechanically making the *typical gestures*" associated with the role.[87] Other figures, such as one called Pierre, also populate *Being and Nothingness* and likewise enter suddenly, as if from the wings, in order to perform their philosophically relevant scenes, only to disappear again.

If a philosophy of self-fashioning and the dangers of bad faith lend themselves to these mini-scenes, Sartre's most important conception of the relation between self and other is the climax of this dramatic technique: the chapter entitled "The Look." Seeing and being seen, it turns out, are the primary constituents of Sartre's conception of the self. From the beginning, the interplay of seeing and being seen is conceived of in terms of conflict, another dramatic category. Sartre begins with a scene in a park, a simple scene as observed by an "I" of a man passing by some benches that are placed at the edge of a lawn.[88] Conflict begins as soon as Sartre considers the possibility that the man is himself a subject who sees. Now there are two points of view in conflict, two subjects with two competing claims on the visual space. This conflict becomes constitutive of the self, the result of the "permanent possibility of *being seen* by the Other."[89] In order to capture the drama of this conflict, Sartre develops the most elaborate scene of them all. In a first step, a man, driven by jealousy, is spying through a keyhole. Sartre increases the stakes and also specifies the type of visual perception at work: the subject is in the dark, separated from the visual field by the door, and so in a sense is a pure eye that is itself invisible. What occurs next is described with deliberate drama: "But all of a sudden I hear footsteps in the hall. Someone is looking at me!"[90] What happens is nothing less than an "interruption of the self." From the beginning, Sartre had described the possibility of being seen as a kind of shame, and it is this feature that the scene of the voyeur captures particularly vividly. But Sartre is not content with shame, and after several pages of commentary, he continues the scene in yet another mode: danger. Now the man not only looks but also threatens to call the police or even to take out a gun; the look becomes a "gun pointed at me."[91] After pure voyeurism and shame, the central conflict comes to the foreground again and becomes life-threatening.

Here, looking is more than just one among many ways of perceiving the world and other people; it becomes a name for the principal way of being in the world and relating to others. It is perhaps this centrality of sight that induces Sartre time and again to use a vocabulary borrowed from the theater, the place of seeing. The act of watching is compared to attending the theater, as when the voyeur's look through the keyhole affords him a view of a "spectacle."[92] And attending the theater is described several times in a chapter on "being with others," a phrase that is reminiscent of Heidegger's notion of the "Man": the inauthentic and impersonal group or crowd.[93] This crowd is exemplified by the audience of a theater, the passive, anonymous audience, which already Plato had decried with his notion of "theatrocracy," a term also used with glee by Nietzsche.[94] In fact, I can think of very few philosophers who have not condemned the passive audience. Within Sartre's theatrical universe, we therefore find the kind of double-edged use of drama and theater that is familiar to us by now: a rejection of certain elements of theatrical performance (passive audiences), coupled with an appropriation of select theatrical and dramatic categories (sight, characters, scenes) for philosophical ends.

Given the fact that Sartre's philosophy resonates so richly with drama and theater, it comes as no surprise that he would translate this philosophy into actual plays. To be sure, Sartre expressed his philosophy in other literary forms as well. One was the novel, whose capacity to focus on a single consciousness enables it to capture the conflict between self-creation and creation by others from the perspective of the individual subject, as in Sartre's great novel *Nausea* (1938).[95] In drama, by contrast, this conflict is not experienced from within but rather viewed from outside. The theater is best suited to the task of showing the pure confrontation between several agents. They are there, on the stage, at a distance, and all we can do is observe the drama of their alienated interaction, from a position that might be compared to Brecht's critical observer.

We can see this most clearly in Sartre's most famous play, *No Exit* (1944).[96] Its well-known conceit presents three characters, a woman and two men, who find themselves in the afterlife and are forced into a room from which they cannot escape. For eternity, they are doomed to be with one another, never by themselves; each will never escape from the others. This scene exemplifies what Sartre means by "situation"—that we are inevitably thrown in together with others—just as it echoes the emphasis on scene in Kierkegaard and other dramatic philosophers. Sartre takes care to dramatize the tragedy of this setup, and he does so by means of a love triangle that leaves everyone unsatisfied and desperate. But this unhappy love triangle is only the most obvious dimension of the more fundamental fact that the three characters are invariably subject to their views of one another, their acts of creating one another. The situation of *No Exit* is tragic because the three characters are particularly ill suited to one another. In this sense, *No Exit* is guilty of a certain dramatic exaggeration, the product of exemplifying the situation with particular starkness. The point, however, is that all situations are in principle like the one depicted in the play: whether ill suited or not, the confrontation of different people will always threaten subjective existence and incorporate it into some social situation that will spell the beginning of its alienation. Sartre's philosophy could be described as the tragedy of the second-person perspective. This second-person perspective finds its proper form on a stage with three characters that are bound to their mutual existence forever.

No Exit emphasizes the visual dimension of the situation, Sartre's interest in the eye, in seeing and being seen. After all, the theater has always been concerned with making things visible, with forcing the invisible onto a stage and thereby exposing it to the eager eyes of the audience. In *No Exit*, Sartre exploits this visual theatricality in two ways. The first is through the relatively simple technique of banishing mirrors or any other reflecting surface from the stage. The situation in which the three characters find themselves is such that they will never again be able to see themselves in a mirror; from now on, they will be entirely dependent on the perceptions of others. Not only are they constantly exposed to the gazes of one another, but these gazes are all they have when it comes to perceiving themselves. They are doomed to the second-person perspective. The other technique concerns the visions these characters have of their earlier lives. Perceptions are not only generated in the here and now but also remembered from the past, and consequently the characters see themselves in their earlier incarnations, endlessly replaying scenes from their past lives in their mind's eye. But as the play goes on, these visions grow fainter; more and more, the three characters are reduced to the present tense and its regime of mutual perception. Sartre thus manages to capture two aspects of his philosophy through the theater: the situational, social nature of the theater, which confronts characters without ever leaving them alone, and the primacy of the visual, which exposes characters to the eyes of others onstage but also to those of the audience. In the theater there is no escape from the domain of the visual, and for this reason it becomes the perfect vehicle for a philosophy in which subjective existence is dependent on others: theater is other people.

While most dramatic philosophers embrace a philosophy of figures and acts but feel more ambivalent about the use of theatrical representation, Sartre embraces drama and theater in equal measure. His philosophy depends on people and scenes, and he therefore translates this philosophy into drama. At the same time, what is of central interest to him in this dramatic setup is the act of seeing; it foregrounds the visual aspect of theater, seeing and being seen.

Even as his plays became famous signature pieces of existentialist drama, Sartre had another significant influence on theater as well: his advocacy of a novelist by the name of Jean Genet, who was then in the process of becoming a dramatist. The established philosopher devoted a long philosophical work to the unknown writer, *Saint Genet* (1953), which recognized in Genet's novels a dramatic and theatrical sensibility that was to be proved right by Genet's subsequent success in the theater. *Actor and Martyr* is the subtitle of this book, which among other things praises the artificiality of the world Genet creates in his novels and plays, the obviously theatrical scenarios that are everywhere focused on role play, on the taking of positions, on a metatheatricality that is as thrilling but also as dangerous as it is in Pirandello. Sartre's work, which helped launch Genet's career, has triggered a whole host of philosophical commentary, which includes Jacques Derrida's *Glas* (1981), a work written in two columns, one of which is devoted to Genet and the other to Hegel. In this intriguing and difficult work, Derrida undertook his own juxtaposition, if not confluence, of drama and philosophy.[97] Sartre's formulation of existentialism, his own dramas, and his writings on theater testify to the resources drama and theater can provide for the philosopher and the resources philosophy can provide for the playwright.

Albert Camus: The Myth of Caligula

No philosopher of the twentieth century was more affected by the dramatic and theatrical philosophy of Kierkegaard and Nietzsche than Albert Camus, whose writings are littered with references to these two predecessors. And yet it is difficult to specify precisely how Kierkegaard and Nietzsche could be seen as the founding fathers of Camus's philosophy of the absurd. Indeed, there has always been a question of whether Camus should count as a proper philosopher in the first place and therefore whether he read Kierkegaard and Nietzsche properly as philosophers. Camus's sometime friend and sometime foe, Sartre, was always condescending to Camus the philosopher, even as he praised him as a writer. Camus, Sartre felt, had understood neither Kierkegaard nor Nietzsche, and his interpretation of the two philosophers therefore had no philosophical value. The charge, although not without a certain justification, raises the question of the status of Camus's own work: if it is not as a philosopher that we should read him, then as what instead? Sartre's charge also begs the question of whether Kierkegaard and Nietzsche themselves were philosophers in a traditional sense, for indeed they had been confronted with accusations very similar to that now faced by Camus. If they were not proper philosophers, then what were they?

The answer to the latter question I have been trying to give is that Kierkegaard and Nietzsche, and now Camus as well, should be seen as specifically dramatic philosophers, that is, as philosophers who recognized the philosophical potential of drama and theater. The reemergence of Plato's dramatic heritage through these figures also produced a radical change in the nature of philosophy, so those who reject Kierkegaard, Nietzsche, or Camus as philosophers are in a sense not entirely wrong. If philosophy means exploring the essence of man and nature, as is suggested in the cave parable, then theatrical philosophy, the use of models and forms derived from the theater, can only be seen as misguided, trivial, or even dangerous. Essence has always been defined against appearance, and any essentialist philosophy therefore has had to define itself against the theater. Camus may well have misunderstood certain doctrinal points in Kierkegaard's theology or Nietzsche's philosophy of language, but he properly understood—and perhaps understood better than Sartre—the dramatic and theatrical dimension of their work and sought to incorporate that dimension into his own writing. He took a particular interest in Kierkegaard's and Nietzsche's main protagonists, Don Juan and Zarathustra, as well as in their predecessor, Socrates. But the recognition of these figures as philosophical agents was only one part of his endeavors, which would entail a full-fledged dramatization as well as theatricalization of philosophy.

For Camus, it all began in the theater. As a young man in Algiers between 1935 and 1939, he served as the leading figure of two amateur theatrical companies, Théâtre du Travail and Théâtre de l'Équipe, which put on productions from the highbrow canon, including plays by Ben Jonson, Maxim Gorki, and J. M. Synge, as well as adaptations of novels by André Malraux and Dostoevsky. Camus provided adaptations and served as actor, producer, and director, learning the theater trade from the bottom up. Once Camus had moved to Paris and established himself as a writer and philosopher there, he wrote four original plays, as well as a number of adaptations, and he continued to be involved with the theater; Sartre had originally wanted Camus to play Garcin in the premiere of *No Exit*. Camus was influenced by the experiments of modern drama and the new theatrical techniques and resources of the early twentieth century. This turned out to be his central advantage over Kierkegaard and Nietzsche, who had to make do with eighteenth- and nineteenth-century theater. It also explains why Camus—like Sartre—was more confident in expressing his dramatic philosophy in actual plays rather than in choosing the quasi-dramatic forms of Kierkegaard and Nietzsche. Unlike Kierkegaard and Nietzsche, Sartre and Camus could draw on the development sketched in the preceding chapter, the emergence of Platonic modern drama.

Camus remained a man of the theater, writing stage plays and adaptations until his untimely death in a car accident at the age of forty-six. But he had also become a philosopher, specifically one who made the theater the basis of his thought. Camus's most important philosophical statement of his philosophy of the absurd, *The Myth of Sisyphus* (1942), is also his most dramatic. Like Kierkegaard and Nietzsche, Camus thinks through characters; indeed, the first character he uses in his philosophical work is none other than Don Juan, previously used by Kierkegaard and Shaw. And like Kierkegaard, Camus seeks to understand Don Juan not so much as a sexual predator but as a character who has pursued a certain attitude toward life to an extreme. Don Juan has gone all the way and overcome all obstacles with a single-minded determination that is almost not human. He is a man in the grip, if not of an idea, at least of an imperative, a single principle.

It is Camus's great insight, one claimed also by Kierkegaard, to have seen that Don Juan's single-mindedness makes him, in the end, not simply an egoist but rather the dramatic embodiment of an idea. Camus calls this idea an "ethics of quantity,"[98] the pursuit of as many woman as possible, irrespective of their particular qualities.[99] All women are the same to him, they all deserve to be loved, and Don Juan will devote his entire existence to the task of loving them, one after the other. Camus also recognized that this devotion to quantity means that Don Juan himself does not have any particular features and quirks, that his entire existence is somehow consumed by his pursuits. Don Juan has no personality, no individual taste, nothing that is not determined by his single purpose. He is ready to do anything and to be anyone as long as he has his way; there is nothing else. "He has chosen to be nothing," Camus writes.[100] Camus knew that Don Juan is a creature born on the stage, a character who populates the theater in the many dramatic adaptations of the story, and he emphasizes Don Juan's "taste for theater."[101] Like Kierkegaard (and Shaw), Camus recognized that Don Juan is a theatrical figure in a pure sense, a figure without core, a mere mask—in short, a figure who serves to highlight the theatricality of the theater itself. It is perhaps not surprising that shortly before his death, Camus was contemplating a new play based on none other than Don Juan.[102] To this end, he had begun to translate Tirso de Molina's original version of Don Juan into French; there is also a diary entry from 1940 in which Camus sketched the contours of his Don Juan play, complete with structure and central lines of dialogue.[103] With this sketch, Camus sought to translate Don Juan from the domain of theatrical philosophy back into theater.

It is only fitting that after discussing Don Juan as a theatrical character and one who represents theater, Camus goes on to speak about the figure whom Don Juan represents: the actor. The actor as such is the abstract principle of which Don Juan is the particular instance. For Camus, the actor is the closest we come to experiencing the absurd. In the hands of actors, roles come to life and die within a few hours on a few square feet of planks—"never has the absurd been so well . . . illustrated," Camus exclaims.[104] The actor knows and experiences every night just how ephemeral and precarious our lives are, that they perish all too soon, a moment of glory and then it is all over. The actor's advantage is precisely this: knowing the absurd. Here we are reminded of how highly Camus values self-consciousness, as had Heidegger before him. Heidegger had coined the phrase "being unto death" to express the original existentialist attitude toward life. Camus recognized that the theater was the perfect illustration of this attitude. This recognition can also be turned around: if the theater illustrates existentialism, then existentialism has incorporated the theater, privileging the theater to express the central tenets of its philosophy. The theater is not one illustration, one example among many. For Camus, it captures the very essence—or perhaps one should say the lack thereof—of existentialism.

The centrality of the theater for existentialism comes into view when we turn to Camus's second point: actors experience the ephemerality of life more intensely than others. Camus calls the actor the "mime of the ephemeral" and adds that actors know that they exist only in the realm of appearance; that is their proper domain. The antitheatrical prejudice has come full circle. Accused of dealing only in appearances, the theater was dismissed from a philosophy devoted to essence. But once philosophy changed its focus to existence, the theater suddenly became a privileged domain. The best way of being a philosopher was being a man of the theater.

Embracing the theatrical, Camus also focuses on all that is associated with the dramatic, such as actor, action, and act. The theme of the act runs through the entire *Myth of Sisyphus*, beginning with its famous first line: "There is only one truly serious philosophical problem, and that is suicide."[105] For Camus, suicide brings to the fore the connection between thought and action. Suicide, he says, is not a question of sociology. "Suicide has never been dealt with except as a social phenomenon. On the contrary, the question is, from the beginning, the relationship between individual thought and suicide. An act like this is prepared within the silence of the heart, just like a great work of art."[106] Suicide is an act, but one that is intimately connected to thought, because nothing stands between the thought and the act except the willingness to perform it.

By opening the essay with the problem of suicide, Camus makes it clear from the outset that the relation between thought and act is a serious one, a life-and-death question. Philosophy is a problem not only of knowing but also of acting, of deciding about existence. Is suicide the proper response to the absurd? Camus leaves this possibility open. Over the course of his essay, however, he undertakes a subtle but far-reaching translation: the question of this one act (suicide) becomes a question of (theatrical) acting. Camus recognizes the profound ambiguity that surrounds the notion of acting. On one hand, acting is a serious business, the most serious, perhaps, leading to the absolute act of suicide (or murder). On the other hand, acting is also associated with a place of entertainment, the theater. Indeed, the word Camus uses is *geste* (gesture), which resonates with theatrical acting.

Beginning with the act in the first sense, with suicide, Camus more and more shifts to acting in the second sense, to theatrical acting. This is the other reason for his fascination with Don Juan. Don Juan is the pure actor in the sense that he has no inner core; he is all mask and pretense. But Don Juan is also a figure who acts, who is defined by the determination with which he translates his desire into action: Don Juan sees things through to the end. The same is true of the actor. The actor acts constantly and also consciously, knowing full well the hollowness and ephemeral nature of the world—in short, knowing the absurdity of existence. Yet the actor acts and does nothing but act until the lights are switched off.

With this elaboration of action, Camus takes us to the core of theater. He recognizes that the theater is a great model for a philosophy that emphasizes appearance and pretense. But it is an equally good model for a philosophy that says that appearance is a serious matter. Acting captures both of these claims at once. It cuts across the line that divides the theater from reality, saying that theatrical appearance and reality are related, that thinking of our existence in theatrical terms does not mean that our existence is mere play, but rather that it is bound up with the act. Here Camus goes beyond the traditional antitheatrical prejudice that associates theater only with appearance. For Camus, the theater is the place where appearance becomes dramatic, that is, a question of acting, of acting out principles, such as the one driving Don Juan, and more specifically acting in the face of recognition of the absurd. Actors don't stop acting because they know the hollowness and ephemerality of their world; they embrace that recognition and act despite of it and, in fact, because of it. It is the ephemerality and hollowness that allow them to act and to be actors in the first place. In this way the theater becomes the place of acting in full knowledge of the absurd.

Toward the end of *Myth of Sisyphus*, Camus turns to the writer who has captured the absurd most successfully in literary form: Franz Kafka. Preceding the chapter on Kafka is a chapter entitled "Philosophy and the Novel," in which Camus claims that the greatest novelists, such as Sade, Melville, Dostoevsky, and Kafka, are all philosophical novelists.[107] These remarks remind us that Camus, like Sartre, wrote philosophical novels as well as philosophical plays and that *The Stranger* and *Nausea*, even more than *Caligula* and *No Exit*, would become the best-known works of existentialism. But Camus does not distinguish between philosophical plays and philosophical novels. He sees both as hybrid genres, so much so that he even reads the philosophical novel in dramatic terms. This becomes clear in the very pages that discuss the philosophical novel, in which he emphasizes that novel's dramatic nature, declaring that philosophical novels "embody a drama of the intelligence" and repeating almost the exact phrase a page later when he observes that the "work of art embodies an intellectual drama."[108] For Camus at least, these intellectual discussions occurring in the novel are still, in essence, dramatic, even when they are incorporated into novelistic forms.

Given how much Camus depends on the theater to articulate the philosophy of the absurd, and how much this philosophy is derived from his experience as actor, theater manager, and playwright, it is not surprising that Camus would want to translate his thoroughly theatrical philosophy back into actual theater. He did so with a play written roughly at the same time as *Myth of Sisyphus*, the 1945 work *Caligula*. Like Nietzsche's *Zarathustra*, it is built around a single protagonist, Caligula, who serves to dramatize the central tenets of Camus's philosophy. The dramatization of a dramatic (and theatrical) philosophy is a rather complicated, but also fascinating, process that deserves to be examined in some detail. Caligula embodies Camus's philosophy at least to the extent that he has recognized the absurd (later, it will turn out that he embodies this philosophy badly). The play opens when Caligula has disappeared from court only to return a changed man: he has had a moment of recognition, the recognition that "men die; and they are not happy."[109] This is the recognition of the absurd. Recognizing the absurd is not just an intellectual matter; it causes a physical reaction, a feeling of nausea, and it leaves a bad taste in the mouth. Not everyone is able to acknowledge the absurd, however. In fact, everyone else either fails to notice the absurd or chooses to ignore it.

There are only two other characters who have insight into the absurd, the poet Scipio and his friend Cherea, and for this reason they are Caligula's main antagonists. The poet has an intuitive sense of the absurd, which enables him to compose poems that Caligula loves. Cherea, by contrast, has a philosophical sense of the absurd, but he suppresses and denies this knowledge, choosing comfort and safety instead. These two characters end up killing Caligula by stabbing him in the face. They do so because he has become a tyrant, to be sure. But their deeper reason for murdering Caligula is that he confronts them with the absurd on a daily basis. The only way to get rid of the absurd is to get rid of Caligula.

The play thus offers three attitudes toward the absurd: a poetic one, a philosophical one, and a third, represented by Caligula. From the beginning, Caligula is described as a man of ideas and ideals, and when he returns from his moment of recognition, he declares that from now on he will be guided by logic: "I have resolved to be logical."[110] There is no higher authority to judge good and bad, and in the face of death, all actions are equal. "I shall make this age of ours a kingly gift—the gift of equality," he declares, and then begins to act out this principle with unflinching determination.[111] We see him rape and kill his underlings at random, but he also saves their lives, even and especially when they are guilty of treason. It is precisely the unpredictable way in which he acts that characterizes, according to him, the logic of the absurd, which is that all actions are the same.

As emperor, Caligula is in a unique position to act on his insight: his logic is sustained by power. Everyone else would be hindered by laws, rivals, fears, and other constraints. It has always been tempting to see in Caligula an example of tyranny, and this was the reason for the play's success with audiences in postwar Europe. But Camus stressed on several occasions that he did not mean to see in Caligula the type of fascist dictator his audiences had in mind when they applauded the play. The excessive violence came from a difference source: the insight into the absurd and the readiness and ability to act out its logic to the end. "He is converting his philosophy into corpses," Cherea declares.[112] If Caligula is a tyrant, he is a tyrant of the absurd.

The emperor's palace is thus the place where the absurd can be pursued to its limit, but it is not the only such place. The other one is the theater. For philosophers who know how to use it, the theater can become something of a laboratory, a place where thoughts and their consequences can be tried out and pursued to their limit or logical extreme. (This is what Brecht proposed at more or less the time when Camus was writing both *Myth of Sisyphus* and *Caligula*). Camus's play can be said to test different attitudes toward the absurd. Emperor and artist are therefore in similar positions, which is one reason the poet Scipio feels a kinship with Caligula without being able to follow him to the last consequence. The kinship between artist and emperor in fact becomes the play's major theme. At one point Caligula declares, "I am the only true artist Rome has known— the only one, believe me—to match his inspiration with his deeds," and for similar reasons he will finally banish all poets for failing just that, for failing to enact their inspirations through bloody deeds.[113] Even Scipio, who understands Caligula, a point that is repeated several times, finally turns on his master when he, together with Cherea, stabs Caligula at the end of the play. Caligula recognizes the potential parallels between artist and emperor. He says to Scipio: "The great mistake you people make is not to take the drama seriously enough. If you did, you'd know that any man can play lead in the divine comedy and become a god."[114] Caligula has determined to become a playwright to the world around him and to govern Rome in the manner of a director—"I invite you to the most gorgeous of shows,"[115] he declares toward the end of the first act—and the rest of the play is the enactment of this vision.

The play as a whole reinforces the parallel between artist and emperor. In Act II, Caligula forces the assembled nobles into a laughing contest, dictating their reaction to a supposedly funny story he has been telling them. They oblige, but only mechanically, puppet-like; the stage direction specifies that they "behave like marionettes in a puppet play."[116] More extravagantly, Act III opens with Caligula playing Venus in a show, frightening his underlings by threatening to have them killed, only to reveal that it is an idle threat. Similar fears are evoked in Act IV, when Caligula once again puts on a show, this time wearing a ballet dancer's skirt and his head garlanded with flowers. This show gives way to a second, when he has poets line up and perform their creations, only to interrupt them with a whistle during the first line, finding them all wanting except for Scipio. Caligula turns Rome into a stage, which means that the play constantly veers toward metatheater, toward scenes of theater-within-theater.

These metatheatrical scenes, however, are not the most dangerous moments in the play. Camus evokes, but does not simply subscribe to, the violent tendency of metatheater, from Plato's cave and Calderón's *Life Is a Dream* to Pirandello and Genet. In *Caligula*, the metatheatrical scenes frighten the nobles, especially when Caligula dictates their reactions, but they are, in the end, harmless—just theater. Things become bloody only when Caligula plays theater for real, when he re-creates Rome as a stage modeled on the absurd—when theatrical acting becomes serious acting. The main point here is that for Caligula, there is no difference between theatrical acting and serious acting, or the difference does not matter to him; because he has supreme power, he can play at divine tragedy both onstage and offstage. Again and again, the play thus returns to the seam between theatrical acting and serious acting, approaching this seam from both sides, observing what happens when this line is crossed or blurred. Indeed, during the play's two central confrontations, first between Scipio and Caligula and then between Cherea and Caligula, the power struggles revolve around the question of whether the two opponents are playacting or being honest.

What kind of attitude does the play as a whole take toward Caligula? Camus himself does not simply subscribe to Caligula's dictum that all actions are equal. In *Myth of Sisyphus*, he writes: "The absurd does not liberate; it binds. It does not authorize all actions."[117] *Caligula*, as well as its protagonist, shows what happens when the insight into the absurd is taken as license for everything. True, Caligula does feel bound to the absurd. He not only recognizes it but also cherishes it; he wants to be true to it, no matter what. But this truth is not the whole truth. Caligula does not recognize that being bound to the absurd does not liberate him from everything else. His logical attitude toward the absurd is therefore not the right one. This does not mean that his two antagonists, Scipio and Cherea, fare any better. They may be less dangerous, but they have betrayed the absurd and do not have the courage of their convictions. Only Caligula does, even if his particular understanding—and practice—of the absurd turns out to be mistaken. By transforming his philosophy into a drama, Camus can test its consequences, including the difference between theatrical and serious acting. If only Caligula had recognized this difference himself, he might have become a great director and playwright; instead he became a tyrant.

Kenneth Burke

Kierkegaard, Nietzsche, Sartre, and Camus—these names form an existentialist-inflected history of theatrical philosophy, but they are not its endpoint. In the twentieth century, theatrical philosophy reached a critical mass, which meant that there were many attempts not only to continue this tradition but also to write its history. Two very different philosophers have worked toward such a theatrical history of philosophy and therefore proved crucial for my own thinking: the American writer and intellectual Kenneth Burke and the French philosopher Gilles Deleuze. With their work, theatrical philosophy can be said to have reached historical awareness: now we have not just scattered philosophers incorporating dramatic and theatrical techniques into their philosophies but attempts to write a dramatic history of philosophy as well.

Like Kierkegaard and Nietzsche, Burke wrote outside academic philosophy and has remained a relatively unknown, or at least understudied, figure, even as tributes to him appear with some frequency, testifying to the subterranean influence of his work.[118] Unlike Kierkegaard and Nietzsche, who favored late eighteenth- and nineteenth-century theater, but like Sartre and Camus, Burke had the benefit of modern drama—Ibsen is a frequent point of reference—and witnessed at first hand the explosion of dramatic possibilities in drama and theater in the first half of the twentieth century. The extreme expansion of what drama was and could be no doubt encouraged his own extension of drama to the core of philosophy. Burke's "dramatism," as he termed it, comes quite close to what I have been calling "the dramatic" in my own discussion of dramatic Platonism.

Burke's engagement with theater began with an interest in Greek tragedy, continued with a theatrical theory of language as well as a theatrical sociology of human interaction, and culminated with the use of drama as the measure by which to analyze various schools of philosophy. The first book-length study to be devoted to what Burke would later call dramatism was his *The Philosophy of Literary Form* (1941). Here, in the midst of a reading of poetry, Burke interrupts himself to observe that "the general perspective that is interwoven with our methodology of analysis might be summarily characterized as a *theory of drama*" (Burke's emphasis).[119] By this, Burke means not the analysis of different dramatic forms or the plays of various periods but a theory of drama as the origin of all art. Burke continues the passage above: "We propose to take *ritual drama* as the Ur-form, the 'hub,' with all other aspects of *human* action treated as spokes radiating from this hub" (Burke's emphasis). True to this interest in origins, Burke's references include the emergence of Greek drama from the goat song to many other forms of ritual, an interest driven in part by James Frazer's influential *The Golden Bough* (1922).[120] Burke writes as an anthropologist interested in the functional aspect of ritual and ritual theater. He even defends ritual fertility and rain dances as being embedded in a structure of agricultural efficacy: "even the most superstition-ridden tribe must have had many very accurate ways of sizing up real obstacles and opportunities in the world, for otherwise it could not have maintained itself."[121] However, it becomes increasingly clear that Burke is less interested in the rituals of particular tribes than in the schemata derived from the work of early anthropologists, such as Frazer, that model general patterns of human behavior; ritual, after all, is supposed to allow Burke to analyze "all other aspects of human action."[122]

This anthropological approach to drama is one step toward what Burke would come to call dramatism. This term's articulation occurred in *A Grammar of Motives* (1945), in which Burke turns it—very significantly for my purposes—into a method of reading the entire history of philosophy in theatrical terms.[123] We can take this text as the culmination of philosophy's dramatic turn because here the entire history of philosophy is examined through a dramatic lens. Unabashedly, Burke presents what he had previously referred to only in a footnote, his so-called dramatistic pentad, which consists of five terms or categories: *agent*, *agency*, *act*, *purpose*, and *scene*. The first four of these offer different perspectives on action, the primary dramatic category. The fifth one—scene—describes the setting or field within which action occurs. Even though this dramatistic scheme seems to be geared toward the analysis of drama, Burke uses it to offer a theatrical history of philosophy.

Once drama is firmly installed at the center of philosophy, Burke classifies and analyzes each and every philosopher worth mentioning—Plato, Aristotle, Hobbes, Spinoza, Berkeley, Hume, Leibniz, Kant, Hegel, Marx, James, Santayana, and the list goes on—according to which of the five dramatistic terms each philosopher privileges. Those philosophers who foreground the scene are materialists, for example, while those putting emphasis on agency are pragmatists. In this manner, all prominent philosophical concepts are translated into dramatic terms. The notion of the subject in idealism, for example, becomes the theatrical agent, while the material conditions in Marxism become the scene. This exercise in translation can also serve to highlight the contradictions within a given philosophical system. In a reading of the *Communist Manifesto*, for example, Burke demonstrates that there is a tension between the privileging of the material conditions, that is, the scene, and the hope that this scene will be transformed by some revolutionary act.[124]

Burke is not so much interested in developing a dramatic philosophy as in using a dramatic scheme for writing its history. This also means that he is for the most part surprisingly little interested in the particular tradition of dramatic philosophy. Yet Burke's own dramatism belongs in that history: it is, after all, a dramatic form of doing philosophy, if only in a historical mode. For this reason, Burke frequently touches on figures relevant for my own history of dramatic philosophy, including Plato. As early as 1941, in *Philosophy of Literary Form*, he had written, "The relation between 'drama' and the 'dialectic' is obvious. Plato's dialectic was appropriately written in the mode of ritual drama."[125] From this view, Burke derives his mode of writing history: "In equating 'dramatic' with 'dialectical,' we automatically have also our perspective for the analysis of history, which is a 'dramatic' process, involving dialectical opposition."[126] We are approaching here one of the central connections between philosophy and theater, namely, the kinship between dialectics and drama. Both insist on a multiplicity of voices, and both trust that this multiplicity will generate transformation and change: the drama of history is the transformation that ensues from the encounter of irreducible positions. By reading the history of philosophy dramatically, or dramatistically, Burke thus restores dialectical philosophy to theater, from which it was originally derived. But even as he does so, Burke begins to distance himself from the theater. In this, he resembles Kierkegaard, who closed his eyes to practice philosophical blinking, and Nietzsche, when he turned against Wagner. Burke recognizes this dynamic: "Every philosophy is in some respect or other *a step away* from drama. But to understand its structure, we must remember always that it is, by the same token, a step away from *drama*" (Burke's emphasis).[127] Even in distancing itself from the theater, then, philosophy reinforces the ties between them.

One consequence of a dramatistic approach to philosophy is that the question of the agent, and hence of personification, moves to the center. Since the center of his analysis is action, and since "the basic unit of action is the human body in purposive motion," dramatism is a scheme that relies on the human agent, human agency, the human act, and human purpose.[128] This is indeed what we should expect from a philosophical methodology derived from the theater, an art form that depends on live human performers. Theatrical philosophy is thus prone to inventing philosophical characters or figures, including Plato's Socrates, Hegel's Napoleon, and Nietzsche's Zarathustra. When philosophy relies on personalization, it tends toward allegory and prosopopoeia, reading characters as personifications of abstract entities. Should we understand Socrates as a portrait of Plato's teacher or as the personification of philosophy? And is Nietzsche's Zarathustra a stand-in for Nietzsche, for the meta-man, or for neither of them?

Personification also points to a tension within Burke's dramatistic pentad. While four of its terms—*act, action, agency,* and *purpose*—are tied to the human and therefore to the personalizing tendency of dramatism, the fifth term, *scene*, exceeds personification. It can be seen as a kind of internal limit to personification. The problem with this internal limit is that it does not represent the impersonal except as the limit of the personal: it cannot name the nonpersonal other than in terms of the ground or scene on which the personal drama of human acts, actions, agencies, and purposes unfolds. Hence, Burke makes the discovery that there are two uses of the term *scene*, one within drama and one without: "Thus we have two kinds of scene: one designating a function *within* the pentad, another designating a function *outside* the pentad; for a term as highly generalized as the 'dramatistic' calls for the 'non-dramatist' as its sole contextual counterpart."[129] Scene is a kind of limit case: it can be understood in theatrical terms, but it can also function as a word for what is outside drama, the nondramatist. The problem that arises now is that this doubleness of scene cuts both ways: it points to the limit of dramatism, but it also points to a kind of internalized limit, because the scene is one of the five dramatistic terms around which Burke's reading is built. The result of this double limit is nothing less than the collapse of dramatism, and Burke recognizes this very clearly: "In the case of our pentad, for instance, after having stressed the need for the functioning of all five terms in rounded vocabularies of motives, we summed up our position as 'dramatistical'— whereupon of a sudden we discovered that our terms had *collapsed* into a new title that had, as its only logical ground, the 'non-dramatistic'" (my emphasis).[130] Dramatism cannot remain a neat, self-enclosed system, because the nondramatic has entered through the Trojan horse of the double scene. The scene outside the pentad may appear to be nothing but a second scene, but this homology is misleading, for the scene outside is nothing like the scene inside; instead, it is the necessary context or counterpart that makes it possible for the scene inside to appear as scene. This dependence of the scene on something that can no longer be called simply scene interrupts the neat workings of dramatism.

Burke draws a radical conclusion from the collapse he is forced to recognize in his dramatistical pentad: "The 'dramatistic' itself must have as its context a grounding in the 'non-dramatist.' . . . So there is a point at which the dramatist perspective, defined in terms of its contextual opposite, *must 'abolish itself' in the very act of its enunciation*" (my emphasis).[131] At the end of his dramatism, Burke thus announces the "dissolution of drama." This dissolution does not mean that his dramatistic pentad is wrong. It only means that it is in the process of breaking down, that at the moment of its enunciation it must "abolish itself." This can be understood as a plea that dramatism be always aware of its own limits, in particular of its tendency to personalize the nonpersonal, what Burke at a different moment called the "agentification" of scene."[132] For the nonpersonal is also radically dissociated from the dichotomy between actor and scene: it lies entirely outside the theater and outside the pentad. Indeed, the pentad even depends on this nonpersonal that is beyond its horizon. The nonscenic scene is the limit of dramatism, and Burke calls upon us never to forget this limit, even if this means that we must be always in the process of abolishing dramatism.

Burke's pentad is derived from Aristotle's *Poetics*. In the middle of his dramatistic history of philosophy, when discussing Aristotle's philosophy, Burke cannot but recognize this connection. In Aristotle, Burke says, "the dramatist nature of this vocabulary [a philosophical vocabulary based on the category of the act] is well revealed in the fact that it was so well suited to the discussion of drama," and he mentions Aristotle's preference for action over character. He then proceeds to translate each of his five dramatistic terms into Aristotle's six elements of drama. Later Burke comes back to the prominence of Aristotle in his scheme when he observes that even though Aristotle had given up on Plato's dramatic form, he attributed an essentially dramatic understanding to the universe.[133] Perhaps it was this effectively Aristotelian origin and nature of Burke's dramatism that made his scheme ill equipped for a dramatic history of philosophy, which ultimately requires a poetics of a very different sort—a Platonic one. Such a Platonic poetics would include a critique of person, scene, and action; it would be attuned to the impersonal and the abstract as well as to the embodied and scenically grounded. Burke experienced this only negatively, as a hitch in his dramatism. He was too much of an Aristotelian and not enough of a Platonist to transform his Aristotelian dramatism into a Platonic one.

Gilles Deleuze

Gilles Deleuze has come to be known as the author of a sprawling oeuvre that draws on a vast range of sources, from biology to geology and from psychiatry to literature and philosophy. To look for a hidden center in a work that explicitly rejects any talk of center would probably be foolish. Yet I will seek to tease out what seems to me a driving concern in Deleuze's writing from his early work onward: the relation between philosophy and theater. Deleuze is the twentieth-century philosopher who comes closest to recognizing a specifically theatrical strain within modern philosophy—as opposed to Burke's emphasis on drama and dramatism.

The relation between theater and philosophy is an important theme in Deleuze's first major, though still underappreciated, work, *Différence et répétition* (first published in 1968 but not translated into English until 1994). It is a densely written work directed against most hitherto existing philosophies. At the heart of this project is the attempt to critique all philosophies based on the opposition between identity and difference. Such a philosophy can be found throughout the entire philosophical tradition, from Plato and Aristotle to Descartes, but Deleuze sees it exemplified most fully in Hegel. The principle of identity—and its opposite, difference—imposes onto the world a stable matrix of essences: either you are X or, if you are not X, you are non-X. Instead of this rigid scheme, Deleuze favors a worldview based on flux. He develops such a view by replacing the scheme of identity and difference with one based on repetition. For this to happen, the notion of repetition has to be wrested from its subservience to identity so that it no longer means repetition of the same, but rather repetition with a difference. Only now can repetition become a force for change, development, and diversification, anticipating Deleuze's later philosophy of schizophrenic drifts, nomadic wanderings, and rhizomatic webs. One reason for choosing Hegel as target is that he had come close to Deleuze's own project: his, too, was a philosophy of change and development, and what drove this change was a form of difference, that is, the force of negation. But this Hegelian negation, for Deleuze, is precisely an example of difference being pressed into the service of a higher identity rather than into proliferating repetitions. The repetition-with-a-difference Deleuze envisions, by contrast, is a difference that displaces identity, creating series of repetitions that are not bound to a principle of identity. Deleuze derives his new notion of repetition from a staggeringly wide range of domains including biology, philosophy, and mathematics, but it remains abstract, reading at times almost like the Hegel it is trying to dislodge.

Deleuze enlists a number of allies in his attempt to think of repetition and difference outside the pair of identity and difference, including Leibniz, Hume, and Bergson. The most surprising ally, however, is Plato. Deleuze agrees with most modern philosophers that "the task of modern philosophy has been defined as the overturning of Platonism."[134] Based on his later philosophical work, Deleuze is often seen as an important representative of modern anti-Platonist materialism, the herald of a new form of empiricism. In *Difference and Repetition*, however, things are not so simple. Deleuze adds to the sentence above the following proviso: "That this overturning conserves much of the characteristics of Plato is not only inevitable but even to be hoped for." Overturning Platonism, then, is also a way of returning to Plato. Even though Deleuze does not discuss Plato's dramatic form, a strange omission in a book that moves to the theater with some frequency, his reading of specific dialogues stresses their dialogic and ironic style, as well as the resistance they pose to the desire to extract from them a single, abstract "Platonist" doctrine. In the course of a reading of the *Sophist*, for example, Deleuze even asks whether we shouldn't think of Plato as the first to have overturned Platonism.[135]

While Plato occupies a crucial but ambivalent role, Deleuze spends most of his book with two less fraught allies: Kierkegaard and Nietzsche. Deleuze does not discuss Kierkegaard in detail but invokes him time and again at crucial moments, praising his imaginative text *Repetition* (1843) as a literary and philosophical approach that manages to free repetition from identity. The other reference point is Nietzsche's doctrine of the eternal return. Here, too, Deleuze takes care to emphasize that eternal return does not signify the return of the same, but rather allows for the emergence of differences.

It is in the course of appreciating Kierkegaard and Nietzsche as philosophers of repetition that Deleuze encounters the dramatic nature of their philosophy. First he notices that they present their respective conceptions of difference through a figure or character, what Deleuze calls "heroes of repetition": Abraham (in *Fear and Trembling*, Kierkegaard had written different versions of Abraham being called to sacrifice his son) and Zarathustra.[136] This makes their philosophy "an idea of a man of the theater, the idea of a director [*metteur en scène*]."[137] But how is it that philosophers can also be men of the theater, and how will their philosophy relate to the theater? Here Deleuze excludes two possible relations: first, undertaking "philosophical reflection[s] about the theater," specifically, "in the manner of Hegel," and second, creating a "philosophical theater." For Deleuze, both possibilities are of limited interest. Instead, he presents a third option: "They [Kierkegaard and Nietzsche] invent in philosophy an incredible equivalent of the theater, and in doing so they found this theater of the future and at the same time a new philosophy."[138] The theater is not an object of philosophical study, as it had been since Aristotle. Nor does Deleuze envision a philosophical theater of the kind many adapters of Plato's drama wanted to create. Rather, he sees Kierkegaard and Nietzsche as thinkers who "live the problem of masks," who create theaters of the future that are also philosophies. *Zarathustra*, for example, is "conceived entirely within philosophy but also entirely for the scene. Everything in it is sonority, visuality, subject to movement, motion, and dance."[139] Deleuze even notes that Zarathustra began as a dramatization of Empedocles. Finally, Deleuze recognizes that neither Kierkegaard nor Nietzsche was finally interested in seeing their vision of a theatrical philosophy realized on the stage. Their theater was a theater of the future, a theater of philosophy, a *theatrum philosophicum*, as Michel Foucault put it in his rave review of Deleuze's book.[140]

Given the importance of Hegel for the tradition of theatrical philosophy from Kierkegaard onward, it is useful to understand precisely why Deleuze considers Hegel's own use of drama of limited value. Even as Hegel tended to reduce the theater to the status of an object of philosophical inquiry, he also attempted to give the theater a role in his philosophy. World history unfolds in so many theatrical scenes and protagonists, such as the figure of Napoleon, but those historical scenes are driven by the history of the spirit.

But while Hegel is important because he uses the theater in his philosophy, he does so in the wrong way; specifically, he uses theater to *represent* concepts. *Representation* is the second bad term in Deleuze's book, one that is intimately tied to the first (*identity*): in the act of representation, that which is being represented is accorded prior status, which is then confirmed in the act of representation itself. In this way, representation is always geared toward the principle of identity: in the act of representation you assert the identity (and hence original status) of what you represent. The very distinction between representation and what is being represented subscribes to the principle of identity: representation does not touch, let alone dislodge, the identity of what is being represented, but in fact affirms it.

For Deleuze this conception gets everything wrong about theater. Theater precisely does not, or should not, represent ideas. Such a theater of representation of ideas is only a pseudotheater, a "faux theater, faux drama, faux movement," as Deleuze puts it.[141] True theater means "masks" behind which lurk no essences, a language of pure "gestures."[142] All these belong not to the domain of representation but rather to repetition. By repetition he may be thinking of the rehearsal process (in French, the word for "rehearsal" is *répétition*), but more important is his program to think of the theater more generally as an art devoted to a form of repetition that is no longer tied to identity (the representation of a concept, or of a dramatic script) and that instead opens an infinite series of repetitions. Deleuze envisions an empty theatrical space that is "filled, determined by signs and masks and within which the actor plays a role which refers to other roles."[143] Along with identity and representation, repetition also does away with the fixation on essence. In this theatrical scenario, masks no longer hide essences but only conceal more masks; roles refer not to preestablished characters but to other roles. Theater here is no longer a vehicle for representation, but a technique for creating endless series of repetitions.

The conception of theater Deleuze develops remains vague, but it can be made concrete by relating it to an actual theater maker who played a crucial role in Deleuze's thinking: Antonin Artaud. For Deleuze and other theatrical philosophers, we can always specify their often schematic conceptions of theater by relating them back to the existing theaters by which they were variously inspired and repulsed. In the case of Plato, this occurred with Greek tragedy and comedy; in the case of Kierkegaard, with eighteenth-century opera and nineteenth-century drama; in the case of Nietzsche, with his turn against Wagner and his embrace of *Carmen*. There are essentially two ideas about theater that Deleuze gets from Artaud: a conception of theater without representation and a theater of repetition. Deleuze echoes Artaud when he speaks of a theater of "pure forces, dynamic traces in space that act upon the spirit without mediation."[144] By the same token, Deleuze is fascinated by "Artaud's cries" that cannot be comprehended.[145] But most of all he is intrigued by Artaud's Theater of Cruelty, which he understands as an attempt to rigorously try to envision a theater that instead of representation would be based on a "gravitational movement . . . that touches the organism directly," a theater "without author, without actors, and without subjects."[146] The person who recognized the importance of this kind of antirepresentational theater in Deleuze's book was Foucault, whose review, entitled "Theatrum Philosophicum," advances the claim that in this theater we "encounter, without any trace of representation (copying or imitating), the dance of masks, the cries of bodies, and the gesturing of hands and fingers."[147] The rejection of representation also touches on how Deleuze imagines the relation between theater and philosophy. Unsurprisingly, he hopes to find a theater that does not represent ideas but rather "incarnates an Idea," thinking perhaps of Kierkegaard's reading of Don Giovanni.[148] For Deleuze, Artaud becomes the hero of "a thinking without image," and this also means without representation.[149]

At the same time, Artaud vehemently rejected mechanical repetition (repetition of the identical, as Deleuze would say) and instead envisioned a theater of endlessly morphing series of repetitions. It was this rejection of mechanical repetition that underpinned his notorious and often misunderstood attack on dramatic literature and indeed on all writing: "Written poetry is worth reading once, and then it should be destroyed."[150] Dramatic masterpieces have the effect of centering theater on a point of fixity, and for this reason they must be abolished. Instead, Artaud envisioned a scenic writing in the manner of hieroglyphics that would not obey the literary principle of identity; instead it would be subject to theatrical differences. The best vehicle for producing theatrical differences is gestures. While literature is petrified and dead, the theater takes the form of "gestures . . . which can never be reproduced twice."[151] Very much in the spirit of Deleuze, Artaud wants to purge the theater of all its mediating and representational dimensions, using theater to somehow "touch life" directly.[152] To be sure, Artaud did not supply Deleuze with a thriving theater practice; Artaud himself was more of a visionary, articulating his conception of a theater of repetition in manifestos and letters and only occasionally on the actual stage.[153] This is a fate Artaud's theater shares with the theaters used by philosophers for their various purposes.[154] Perhaps the kinship between Deleuze and Artaud was based on the fact that Artaud, too, was less interested in founding theaters than in creating the theater's philosophical equivalent.

In Deleuze's subsequent work, theater was accorded a less favorable role, even though he and his new collaborator, Félix Guattari, proceeded to refer frequently to drama and theater. In particular, however, they now fixated on a very particular play and figure: Oedipus. Theater as represented by Oedipus became an object of critique. Freud's Oedipal psychoanalysis, the two authors recognized, not only drew on plays such as King Oedipus and Hamlet but also envisioned a psychoanalytic theater of identification (with figures) and representation (of a complex, for example); it was a theater that depicted a purely personal drama, a "private" and "intimate theater."[155] Against Freud, Deleuze and Guattari now seek to posit the impersonal, depersonalized figure of the schizophrenic, along with a Marxian conception of production. The unconscious, they say, is not a theater at all, as Freud had assumed, but a factory. The new master trope of this anti-Oedipal philosophy therefore becomes the machine. Seen from the perspective of the machine, the theater (of representation) forces machines into the wings, while they reign supreme in the factory.[156] The lesser and more negative function of theater in this conception is registered in how the two authors view Artaud, who continues to be an important figure, but for different reasons: he ceases to function as a theater visionary and instead becomes the quintessential anti-Oedipal schizophrenic.

The (negative) identification of theater as a space of Oedipal representation did not last, however. In 1991 Deleuze and Guattari published *What Is Philosophy?* which harks back to *Difference and Repetition* and its theatrical vocabulary. In particular, this new book foregrounds the category of the philosophical figure, what the two authors call "conceptual personae."[157]

The earlier "heroes of repetition" reappear, including Kierkegaard's Don Juan and Nietzsche's Zarathustra, who are now joined by Nikolaus von Cusa's figure of the idiot and Stéphane Mallarmé's Igitur.[158] The primary and most important conceptual persona, however, the one *What Is Philosophy?* comes back to with frequency, is Plato's Socrates: "Socrates is the principal conceptual persona of Platonism," they declare emphatically.[159] To this end, Deleuze and Guattari speak of a "Platonic theater that produces a proliferation of conceptual personae by endowing them with the powers of the comic and the tragic."[160] In his late work, Deleuze returns to his earlier approach and captures one of the central insights of dramatic Platonism.

Deleuze and Guattari are representative anti-Platonic philosophers, who even speak of their project as an overturning of Platonism. At the same time, they acknowledge that Plato himself was no Platonist, that Plato himself was the first to overturn Platonism. This recognition also allows them to get an inkling of Plato's own dramatic practice, thus bringing us to the brink of what I call dramatic Platonism. Dramatic Platonism argues that it was Plato's dramaturgy that effectively "overturned" Platonism, that Plato's dramatic technique would help mediate between Platonism and anti-Platonism, creating a third approach in the process. What kept Deleuze and Guattari from connecting the two gestures of their thought—their own theatrical approach to philosophy and their interest in Plato's dramatic technique—was, without doubt, their deeply ingrained opposition to Platonism in all of its forms. This opposition informs most prevalent philosophies of the late nineteenth and twentieth centuries, but it is this opposition, the automatic repetition of the anti-Platonist gesture, that must be overcome in order to bring the dramatic Plato into view. To this task is the next and final chapter of this book dedicated.

5

The New Platonists

The influence of Plato on modern philosophy is pervasive and, for that reason, difficult to pinpoint. But what is certain is that for the last 130 years, Plato was not so much the acknowledged master to whom all philosophers paid homage as the straw man against whom they sought to define themselves as modern philosophers. In particular, they defined themselves against different versions of idealism, including the belief in the independent existence of ideas—concrete universals—but also in the ultimate coincidence of the true, the beautiful, and the good. Both these forms of idealism can be derived from Plato. However, the Plato I have been presenting in this book, the dramatic Plato, has little to do with these forms of idealism. Few of the authors of Socrates plays and none of the philosophers who continued Plato's project of a dramatic philosophy were idealists in that sense. On the contrary, they often presented themselves as anti-Platonists because they wanted to distance themselves from idealism, the theory of forms for which the name Plato had come to stand. In order to find that other, dramatic Plato, it has thus been necessary to go beyond the equation of Plato and idealism. The "dramatic" component of that coinage emphasizes precisely what idealism seeks to leave behind, namely, the material, scenic, and corporeal elements of Plato. By writing dramatically, Plato presented us with constant reminders of the tangible, the personal, and the concrete. Only once this dramatic understanding of Plato has been established can we return to the theory of forms and understand it in new ways—in a dramatic context. When seen within this context, the theory of forms is no longer a stand-alone metaphysical construct, but rather a critique and reform of traditional drama; it establishes a tension within drama between the scenically grounded individual characters and the process of abstraction for which the term *form* serves as a convenient shorthand.

Yet there is a sense in which this book would be incomplete without a fuller engagement with self-declared Platonists. For this reason, I turn now to a number of contemporary philosophers who, despite the overwhelming anti-Platonist tendency of late nineteenth- and twentieth-century philosophy, have, against all odds, held on to some principles of Platonism. Among those Platonists are several who in very different ways have touched on the dramatic dimension of Plato, including Iris Murdoch, Martha Nussbaum, and Alain Badiou. They were driven to recognize this dramatic dimension in part by the pressures of a materialist age. It makes sense that these Platonists would tend toward dramatic Platonism, which negotiates between materialism and idealism. Put differently, dramatic Platonism can be understood as a materialist form of Platonism.

Iris Murdoch

Few philosophers have thrown in their lot with Plato as confidently and consistently as Iris Murdoch. Conceived of in the second half of the twentieth century, when anti-Platonism was taken for granted by most influential philosophical schools and tendencies, Murdoch's Platonism was first and foremost an oppositional posture, a critique of the philosophical currents of her time. Her Platonism took many forms and had many consequences, but its chief ingredient was the belief that beauty is a symbol for the good. Because of that vital link between aesthetics and ethics, she was attuned to the literary dimensions of Plato, prompting her to write novels and plays as well as do philosophy.

With her Platonism, Murdoch sought to critique three doctrines in particular: relativism, language philosophy, and existentialism. Of these three, relativism is the most important and also the one that Plato himself had attacked with the greatest fervor. Plato saw in relativism a tendency toward philosophical defeatism: if philosophy contents itself with the observation that the world is in constant flux, then it can say nothing certain about the world. Against this epistemological relativism (relativism with respect to knowledge), Plato had insisted on the existence of abstract categories as reference points for philosophical inquiry. For Murdoch, relativism was most problematic not in epistemology but in moral philosophy, her primary field of interest, where it was championed by G. E. Moore. (In Tom Stoppard's antirelativist play *Jumpers*, the idealist protagonist by the name of Moore is maddened by being confused with his eponymous philosophical opponent.) Moore himself had started with a dissertation heavily indebted to the British idealist F. H. Bradley but then turned sharply against idealism, spending the rest of his life arguing against any anchoring idea of goodness.

Murdoch's insistence on the idea of goodness against the anti-idealism of Moore was connected to a second form of relativism, one that goes to the heart of twentieth-century philosophy: language philosophy, or what Murdoch called "linguistic monism." In the twentieth century, earlier philosophers were accused of having ignored or not having paid enough attention to the medium in which philosophy invariably occurred:

language. Far from cheerfully assuming that whatever difficulties language presented for philosophy could be overcome, modern philosophers insisted that those difficulties had to become the primary subject of philosophical inquiry itself. From Martin Heidegger ("language is the house of being")[1] and Rudolf Carnap ("overcoming metaphysics through logical analysis of language")[2] to Ludwig Wittgenstein ("the limits of my language mean the limits of my world"),[3] language became, for the first time, what philosophy needed to focus on above all else. The early twentieth century also saw the emergence of linguistics as well as of structuralism (and then poststructuralism), which likewise insisted that the classical fields of philosophy, including ethics, aesthetics, and epistemology, needed to be rethought on the basis of an inquiry into language. Closer to Murdoch's own philosophical context, Moore's moral relativism was also rooted in this type of language philosophy. There can be no unified conception of the good, for instance, because the word *good* is used differently in different situations.

From Murdoch's perspective, a language philosophy that shows us to be invariably caught in a web of language from which we cannot escape amounted to a new type of relativism, what one might call linguistic relativism. For a Platonist, this finding would not come as a surprise. Linguistic relativism, after all, is a perfect description for the figure against whom Socrates had established his own philosophy: the sophist. In dialogue after dialogue, sophists show themselves to be cunning manipulators of language who also claim that words are infinitely malleable and have no firm referent. Since we are all caught in an unreliable web of language and since there is no hope of attaining any sort of truth, we may as well make the best of it and seek to manipulate language to suit our own purposes. This conclusion was as unacceptable to Murdoch as it had been to Plato. For her, the more language philosophers stressed our inability to come to clear judgments because of the shiftiness of language, the more they threatened to lay the groundwork for a linguistic relativism and therefore for a sophistic use of language. Poststructuralist philosophers such as Jacques Derrida were even more guilty of this than the likes of Moore. If language philosophy meant relativism, Murdoch argued, then philosophy needed to be taken beyond the confines of language. Platonism, the positing of ideas, was the best way of doing so.

The third position, existentialism, was one Murdoch encountered the earliest in her life. Existentialism might have offered her an alternative to linguistic relativism because it was only peripherally part of the linguistic turn. But Murdoch did not go that route and instead positioned her Platonism against it. The limitation of existentialism, for Murdoch, was its restriction to the subject, the fact that it was based on the individual. Murdoch's main concern was ethical, and her ethics required going beyond the personal, the individual. She articulated this in idealist terms, as an ascent toward goodness. As in Plato's idealist—and therefore antipersonal, or at least depersonalizing—set pieces such as Diotima's speech in the *Symposium*, Murdoch conceived of this ascent as a restraint of individual desires and to some extent a denial of them. Her ethical idealism, therefore, required a critique of the subjective, something resonant with Christian denial.

Murdoch joined a long line of Platonists, from Ficino to Wilde, who emphasized the significance of art for Plato—and, in the case of Murdoch, connected art to some conception of the good. For Murdoch, the importance of art lay in the fact that it could serve as a symbol of the good. This is so because art as Murdoch conceived of it is primarily antipersonal or, in the parlance of modernism, impersonal or depersonalized. Art, she held, is the most powerful experience we have of being taken outside ourselves. And since the good requires leaving behind individual desires and desire for individual bodies, as in Diotima's speech, art is the best training for goodness. Murdoch's modernist conception of art as an impersonal symbol of the good was not a popular claim when it was made and was even less popular in the 1980s and 1990s, when aesthetics came more and more under attack as a retrograde piety hiding class interests and other forms of political conservatism. Murdoch's own traditionalism, her reliance on Christianity both in her life and her writing, seemed to confirm these suspicions. However, since the end of the nineties, a renewed interest in aesthetics has made itself felt, for example, in Elaine Scarry's *On Beauty and Being Just* (1999), in whose argument Murdoch plays a crucial role. Scarry, too, connects beauty to the good when she argues that beauty bears a structural resemblance to justice and can therefore serve as justice's training ground.[4]

Murdoch not only emphasized the importance of art for ethics but also recognized an artistic dimension in philosophy itself. For all her critique of existentialism, for example, Murdoch acknowledged its artistic and, more specifically, dramatic aspiration. Even Sartre's novels, she claimed, are inherently theatrical to the point that they "could be staged with hardly an alteration."[5] In a BBC conversation with Bryan Magee, she highlights the dramatic element in the history of philosophy, from Hegel to Sartre, speaking of a "rather dramatic form of the thought in the philosophy itself, that there is some kind of drama which can be exhibited."[6] In the published form of this interview, Murdoch claims that "Sartre emphasizes the more dramatic aspects of the philosophy of Hegel," adding the more general conclusion that "'Ideas' often seem more at home in the theatre."[7]

But when it comes to connecting philosophy and art, there is one figure who is more important for Murdoch than either Hegel or Sartre, and that is Plato. Murdoch here continues a history of a specifically aesthetic Platonism that extends as far back as Ficino and then reaches a high point with Pater and Wilde, a tradition that finds in Plato inspiration for art despite the philosopher's putative critique of it. Art now becomes a way of giving shape and form to otherwise intangible ideas. The formulation of a Platonist aesthetics usually goes hand in hand with some recognition of Plato as an artist and therefore with some appreciation of him as a dramatist. This is certainly the case with Murdoch. In a series of texts, including *The Fire and the Sun* (1977) but also her final, grand summary, *Metaphysics as a Guide to Morals* (1992), she keeps coming back to Plato the artist and insists that through his art of drama, Plato never abandoned the concrete in favor of abstract ideas.[8] His art is everywhere filled with characters, scenes, and actions, which the reader never forgets.

Given this interest in Plato's drama, it does not come as a surprise that Murdoch herself would choose to write plays in addition to novels. Very much in the spirit of Plato's own mixed forms and the fact that he can be seen as an ancestor of both modern drama and the modern novel, Murdoch does not make too much of the difference between the two genres, sometimes translating between the two, as she did, for example, with *The Severed Head*, which she wrote both as novel (1961) and as drama (1964).[9] But while Murdoch does not emphasize the difference between novels and plays, she does emphasize the difference between her literary works and her Platonist philosophy. In her conversation with Magee, for instance, Murdoch declares: "I feel in myself such an absolute horror of putting theories as such into my novels."[10] Murdoch extends this critique even to Plato himself, claiming that the literary quality of the *Symposium* is but an exception. Given that throughout her career Murdoch had insisted on the crucial function of art for a Platonic ethics and recognized Plato's own literary accomplishments, this sudden attempt to keep philosophy and literature strictly apart demands an explanation.

One reason for this implausible attempt to separate philosophy and literature is no doubt the long-standing prejudice against both the drama of ideas and the novel of ideas. Indeed, Murdoch's talk of "horror" is specifically tied to the idea of putting theories "as such" into the novels. But even if we admit that Murdoch is not guilty of spoiling her novels by inserting theories "as such," these theories still inform her novels and plays in many ways. A. S. Byatt has been most perceptive in this regard, writing, "Nietzsche saw Plato's dialogues as the first form of the novel, and there is a sense in which all Iris Murdoch's novels contain Platonic dialogues."[11] Byatt's point is borne out in Murdoch's novels and plays. *The Bell* (1958) uses a religious community as a point of departure for its own mystical abstractions, but these abstractions are counterbalanced by a distancing irony that is the saving grace of this work. *The Black Prince* (1973), even though its characters revel in half-baked ideas, is saved by a pervading sense of satire. When it comes to drama, Murdoch continues the tradition among philosophical writers of undercutting philosophizing characters, a technique she recognizes in the plays of George Bernard Shaw.[12]

Despite Murdoch's conviction that literature and philosophy should be kept apart, her own work testifies to a thorough entanglement, if not complete merging, of the two. This is especially the case with a work that occupies a middle ground, one that might be readily associated with Plato: the philosophical dialogue. Her *Acastos: Two Platonic Dialogues* (1986) consists of two carefully composed dialogues that pay close attention to dramatic categories such as character, action, and scene. Indeed, so fully dramatic are these dialogues that they have actually been staged. And since they revolve around the character Socrates, they also belong, although Murdoch may not realize it, to the tradition of the Socrates play.

The first of the two dialogues, "Art and Eros: A Dialogue About Art" (1980), deserves particular attention. It is set in fifth-century Athens and in 1970s England, and this double setting is indicated in the costumes and language of the characters. Murdoch here dramatizes her insistence on Plato's continuing significance. The primary topic of discussion in the dialogue is the value of art, and most of the arguments are based on the *Republic*. But since the argument is supposed to have present-day relevance, Murdoch adds a position that would have been unthinkable to Plato: a radical pro-art position that comes close to the aestheticist doctrine of art for art's sake espoused by Wilde, in addition to a simple anti-art position. But more important than these two extreme positions are the ones taken by the dialogue's two central characters: Socrates and Plato. Like many authors of Socrates plays before her, Murdoch introduces Plato as a character into her play. Neither Plato nor Socrates is simply against art; rather, Murdoch distributes some of her own convictions between them, siding firmly with neither one.

The difference between Plato and Socrates is manifested dramatically in their behavior as much as in their theories. Murdoch shows Plato to be Socrates' most talented student, but he does not tend to get involved in the discussion and instead hovers at its edge, listening to the arguments of others but also forming his own distinct opinions about them. Part of this isolation from the dialogic atmosphere is that he writes down what others say, violating Socrates' own indictment of writing. Socrates, by contrast, functions as a benevolent moderator who sympathizes with all positions and hopes that his students will get along. He opposes extreme statements and favors compromise, contenting himself with second-best options. Herself poised between them, Murdoch can have it both ways, retaining from Plato the desire for the absolute while relying on Socrates' common sense to keep that desire from becoming too monomaniacal. This division of labor between Socrates and Plato is rather conventional and echoes the decisions made by many other authors of Socrates plays, who side with the more open-minded Socrates against the dogmatic Plato. But then Murdoch does something unusual: she projects this difference onto the question of art in philosophy. The discursive Socrates is presented as an ideal philosopher who listens to different positions, questions their premises, pursues arguments, and stimulates inquiry. Plato, by contrast, is a very strange kind of philosopher: not only does he often withdraw from debates, but it turns out that in addition to being a philosopher he is also a poet.

Plato's poetic leanings come to the fore when he develops a somewhat unusual version of the cave parable. In the *Republic*, Socrates had offered that parable to demonstrate a point about knowledge and education; in Murdoch's dialogue, the cave is in the service of an argument about art. Plato says:

This darkness is sex, power, desire, inspiration, *energy* for good or evil. Many people live their whole lives in that sort of darkness, seeing nothing but flickering shadows and illusions, like images thrown on a screen. . . . All these people are like—like living in a cave. They see only shadows, they don't see the real world or the light of the sun. But then sometimes some people can get out of the cave. . . . When they get out they're *amazed*, they see real things in the sunlight . . . and you begin . . . to see the difference between truth and falsehood in the clear light of truth itself.[13]

The development of the cave parable occurs over almost two pages, but the interjections of his companions have little effect on Plato, who pursues this image with his usual single-minded determination. When Plato finally pauses, Acastos says, "I like your picture—very much—though I can't understand it." "Neither can he," Deximenes quips, and Plato does not object.[14] A little later, Plato is still trying to explain the cave. Socrates had conceded that we often prefer illusion to the hard task of thinking and that half-truths may be the comforting place where we stop trying to reach true knowledge. But why do we, or some of us, still try the difficult ascent from the cave? Plato ventures: "We try because our home is elsewhere and it draws us like a magnet." But now Socrates, who had just commented on the image of the cave, has had enough and interjects: "This too is a poetic image and may be a comforting one," implicitly critiquing Plato for being an image maker.[15] This judgment is echoed by Callistos, who concludes: "We are philosophers and Plato is a poet."[16] But Plato does not accept these charges. At the end of the dialogue he declares that he will burn his poems, reminiscent of the scene when Plato burns his tragedy upon encountering Socrates—only now it is Socrates, ever the compromising teacher, who wants to keep the peace and tells Plato to preserve his poems. Plato is a philosopher who uses poetic images and a poet who insists on the category of truth.

The entire debate about the poetic image of the cave occurs in the context of a discussion about theater. Of all forms of art, the theater is the most controversial. To develop this theme, Murdoch turns not to the *Republic* but to the *Symposium*. Like the *Symposium*, "Art and Eros: A Dialogue About Art" takes place just after everyone has returned from the theater, and it is with respect to the theater, its uses and dangers, that the topic of art is first introduced. Callistos, throughout the dialogue, plays with a theatrical mask, which he periodically puts on to recite the choral hymn to Zeus from the beginning of Aeschylus' *Agamemnon*. Most important, however, is Alcibiades, who had played a central role both for Plato and for subsequent writers of Socrates plays. Murdoch includes in her own dialogue the most vivid theatrical set piece from the *Symposium*, Alcibiades' drunken entrance. But Murdoch also asserts her independence by introducing a new dynamic, made possible because in her dialogue Plato himself is a character: Plato competes with Alcibiades for Socrates' attention.

Introducing Plato as a character not only allows for the creation of dramatic rivalries with Alcibiades but also has important consequences for the character Socrates, who now has to grapple with the presence of the authorial Plato. In confronting Socrates with Plato, Murdoch downplays the fact that Socrates, as presented in Plato's dialogues, is always Plato's creature, a character invented by the playwright. And in suggesting that Plato himself dislikes dialogue and tends toward monologue, Murdoch ignores that it was Plato, not Socrates, who invented philosophy as drama—with Socrates as its main but not only character. Perhaps this split mirrors the alleged split in Murdoch's own oeuvre between literature (novel and drama) and philosophy, a desire to philosophize about art and a separate desire to capture philosophy in literary form.

Martha Nussbaum

Like Byatt and many other readers of Murdoch, Martha Nussbaum is keenly attuned to the intricate connections between Murdoch's philosophy and her literary works. She, too, objects to Murdoch's declaration that the two are not connected, concluding that Murdoch's "novels have a rich vein of philosophy running through them; many focus on philosophical issues that are also central to her theoretical work."[17] And she recognizes the centrality of Plato not only for Murdoch's philosophical work but also for her novels and plays. For example, Nussbaum sees Plato's account of love at work in *The Black Prince* and reads the entire novel through a Platonist lens, which is to say through the interplay of the concrete and the abstract. The novel, Nussbaum explains, fulfills a philosophical function precisely because it does not "flee the real," refusing to "obscure our sight with generalities," while at the same time not contenting itself with realism and the everyday. Murdoch's literature is thoroughly Platonic, but she keeps her Platonist metaphysics grounded in characters, situations, scenes, and actions.

The tendency of Platonism to abandon the concrete world of persons and things and to flee to generalities is the central concern of Nussbaum's own philosophy and of her reading of Plato. Nussbaum responds to the threat of abstraction by attending to emotions, which are the subject of her most important philosophical statement to date, *Upheavals of Thought: The Intelligence of Emotions* (2001). Emotions have been sidelined at best and dismissed as detrimental to philosophy at worst, but this philosophical prejudice runs counter to our lived experience, in which emotions and thoughts are intermingled, sometimes to the point of being indistinguishable. While the title of the book, *Upheavals of Thought*, seems to continue the philosophical prejudice against emotion by acknowledging the upheavals thoughts must go through when they are informed by emotions, the subtitle, *The Intelligence of Emotions*, makes it clear that such upheavals are not necessarily a bad thing, that they are simply the form that the intelligence of emotions takes. Indeed, Nussbaum goes further, claiming that emotions actually contain judgments about the world; in this way, they function as a deliberative process, one that philosophy must not ignore.

Any attempt to critique the philosophical prejudice against emotions will sooner or later have to grapple with Plato's Socrates, with whom is associated an intellectual ethics—that is, an ethics based on the power of the intellect to control unruly emotions. Socrates prizes rational argument above all, and he pokes fun at interlocutors, such as Thrasymachus in the first book of the *Republic*, whose minds are clouded by emotions such as anger and hurt pride. It speaks to the quality of Nussbaum's thinking, however, that she does not present her philosophy as a simple anti-Platonist reversal, as so many other philosophers since Nietzsche have done. Rather, her philosophy engages in a critical dialogue with Plato. Among the emotions she singles out, compassion occupies an important position, for example, but the book culminates in an extended and wide-ranging meditation on love. As Nussbaum knows, love poses the greatest challenge to her argument about the intelligence of emotions since it is so firmly associated with the erratic and irrational.

In thinking about love, Nussbaum turns to the *Symposium*. Here Plato acknowledges the unruly nature of love and offers as a solution the process of ascent whereby love is gradually purified, leaving behind its attachment to particular bodies and engaging instead the idea of the good. So central is the figure of ascent to Nussbaum that she takes it as the topic and title of her last chapter, "Ascents of Love." Indeed, her entire book, as she explains, can be seen as a ladder culminating in this concluding meditation on Diotima's metaphor. But as the chapter title suggests, Nussbaum cannot subscribe to Plato's conception of the ascent entirely. In the course of the chapter, she revises Plato in two ways, first by replacing his one ascent with many, and then by questioning the metaphor of the ascent itself. This metaphor, Nussbaum warns, entails the considerable risk of losing touch with the ground of the real: "By lifting us above ourselves, they [ideals] risk the cry of disgust when we discover our daily reality. . . . What seems required, then, is an idealism that also shows mercy and love to the real."[18]

In her search for such an idealism, Nussbaum turns to art, especially literature and music. Taking her point of departure from Plato, she moves through a number of writers in the Platonist tradition, such as St. Augustine and Dante, and ends with modern writers such as Walt Whitman and James Joyce, who are devoted to the everyday and the real. Implied in this trajectory is one of the most common, but also most problematic, assumptions about the history of art: that it pursues an increasingly successful discovery of the real. In the realm of art history, this assumption underpins the influential work of Ernst Gombrich; in literature, it was articulated with particular brilliance in Erich Auerbach's *Mimesis* (1946), subtitled *Representation of Reality in Western Literature*.[19] In much the same way, Nussbaum constructs a trajectory from the earlier Platonists, who are still too bound up with ideas and generalities, to the modernists, who truly grasp the real. The story that Nussbaum tells about realism is conventional enough; its interest lies in how it reveals her ambivalence about philosophical abstraction.

But even as Nussbaum criticizes Plato and Platonists for scorning the real, she holds on to the notion of idealism and hence to the ladder as it structures her own book, an idealism "that shows mercy and love to the real." It is almost as if Nussbaum agrees with Diotima's ladder but does not want to be banished at the top forever, so she refuses to throw away the ladder, as Wittgenstein would have it, once she has climbed all the way up. Instead, she wants to climb up and down, gaining the uplift promised by ideas yet not losing touch with the real by staying up there for too long. We are asked "to climb the ladder and yet, at times, to turn it over, looking at a real person in bed or on a chamber pot."[20] But increasingly, this image of going—and looking—up and down becomes confusing. Since the problem with the (Platonic) ladder is that you invariably lose touch with the real once you climb up, the difficulty lies with the ladder itself, not just our use of it. Why bother ascending at all if the ascent causes problems for which the only remedy is the modernist literature of the everyday—precisely the modernist literature that refuses the ladder? Indeed, Nussbaum herself described the trajectory of Joyce as a descent rather than an ascent, an "upside-down ladder."[21] One wonders whether we should not simply stick to Joyce and use his great novel to make our peace with the real, thus staying on the horizontal plane on which we belong anyway.

The problem here is perhaps once again the division of labor between Platonist philosophy and modernist literature, with philosophy articulating idealism and literature putting us in touch with the real again. Against this division, I am proposing an entanglement of philosophy and literature in what I describe as dramatic Platonism. Such an entanglement is what Plato accomplishes through the overall dramatic construction of the *Symposium*. After Diotima's speech, we are brought back to the world of egoistic love, love of bodies, with the dramatic entrance of Alcibiades, the greatest egomaniac of ancient Greece, and his declaration of love not for beauty or the good as such, but for Socrates. If we understand the intention of Plato's idealism to be an effect produced by reading the *Symposium* or hearing it recited, then surely that intention cannot be that we forget about earthly love. On the contrary, that final scene with Alcibiades and Socrates lingers powerfully in one's imagination, tempering the one-directional idealism of Diotima. This is all the more so since Diotima is never even present on the (imaginary) stage, depending instead on Socrates as a witness for her thought to be made present in the dialogue. The dialogue as a whole leaves readers oscillating between Diotima's speech and Alcibiades' insistence on a love for bodies. This entanglement of idea and the tangible lies at the heart of dramatic Platonism, a form of idealism (if we still want to use this loaded and, to some extent, misleading term) that is everywhere grounded in drama, an idealism that is but one moment in a sequence of dramatic events that need to be understood in their entirety. Plato's plays remind us that philosophy is something practiced by real humans, with real emotions and real desires. The fact that Plato created vivid scenes of human frailty demonstrates that he never wanted us to forget this, whatever else his philosophical ambitions—call them idealist—might have been.

Whereas *Upheavals of Thought* emphasizes the critique of Plato, Nussbaum's earlier book *The Fragility of Goodness* (1986) comes much closer to appreciating Plato as a playwright. *Fragility* is devoted to the concept of luck as it emerges in Greek tragedy and philosophy. Once more Plato plays a pivotal, but also problematic, role in the story. Where Greek tragedians accept forms of luck as central to the human experience, Plato's Socrates seems singularly devoted to its defeat by means of philosophical rationality. Yet Nussbaum argues that Plato's dialogues also contain elements of contingency that counterbalance that project. Beginning with the *Protagoras* and its belief in practical reasoning, and continuing with the *Republic* and its perfectionism, Nussbaum ends with a reading of *Phaedrus* as a dialogue that questions some of Plato's earlier rationalist positions, for example, acknowledging a certain form of madness in philosophy. For Nussbaum, this acknowledgment is a recantation of Plato's earlier condemnation of the poets, an admission that their expertise in contingency, in the fragility of human existence, cannot and should not be banished from any ideal city nor from the project of philosophy.

The centerpiece of Nussbaum's mediation on Plato's dramatic technique is a short interlude entitled "Plato's anti-tragic theater." Nussbaum describes eloquently how Plato wrote in competition with the tragic playwrights as well as Homer. Open-ended plots draw in readers (spectators) and allow them to make up their own minds about the arguments being made by various opponents, and the dramatic structure shows what I would call the scene of philosophy, namely, how and why a philosophical discussion arises out of real-life situations (however fictionally rendered).[22] Nussbaum's reading of Plato's use of dialogue touches on several elements of dramatic Platonism. Perhaps only the lingering, dramatic effects of Alcibiades do not quite come into view here; a fuller dramatic reading would further deemphasize Socrates' rationalist arguments and highlight Plato's continuing connection with the material world, dramatically rendered, in which his dialogues are set and to which they always return.

Since Nussbaum's account is informed by a dramatic interest in the dialogue form, it is not surprising that, like Murdoch, she would try out that form herself. Like Murdoch's *Acastos*, Nussbaum's *Emotions as Judgments of Value: A Philosophical Dialogue* (1998) has in fact been performed.[23] It should be added that it was by no means Nussbaum's first foray into drama. Early in her life she had been an actress, working for summer stock companies, including the Ypsilanti Greek Theater, which was devoted to Greek drama. In a recent interview, Nussbaum emphasized how central her experience in theater has been for her philosophical work. Nor has this experience come to an end; to prepare for lectures, she is now taking singing lessons.[24]

In the preamble to the dialogue, Nussbaum states that initially the dialogue was an attempt to represent central arguments from *Upheavals of Thought*. The dialogue form was not supposed to contribute anything substantial to the argument of the book, which was already finished and fixed. What it did contribute from the beginning, however, was an autobiographical note: in this dialogue, Nussbaum reuses some of her own experiences, exploring the way in which emotions have informed her own thinking. One might consider this autobiographical dimension as being in the tradition of philosophical self-experiments from St. Augustine and Descartes to Rousseau and Wittgenstein. At the same time, Nussbaum's dialogic self-experiment is also informed by twentieth-century thinking about the psyche, in particular psychoanalysis and its emphasis on the nuclear family and the various structures it generates. It should be added that she does not present herself in her own voice but, like many authors of dialogues including Plato and Wilde, creates an authorial persona. The main dialogue revolves around the fictional philosopher's parents, and it presents a working through of the family dynamic between intellectual father, nonintellectual mother, and philosopher daughter. This family scene is framed by a public lecture delivered by the fictional philosopher on the topic of *Upheavals of Thought*, a lecture that is interrupted by the hallucinatory appearance of the philosopher's dead parents, who reenact what appear to be the family's most common and fundamental conflicts from times past.

If these family dynamics are a far cry from Plato's dialogues, the dialogue's topic is not: in her imaginary conversations with her parents, the philosopher has to defend not only her thesis concerning the emotions—which is Nussbaum's thesis from *Upheavals of Thought*—but also the enterprise of philosophy itself. The mother is dismissive of all bookish knowledge and finds it particularly absurd that the daughter is treating the emotions in such a hyperrational, philosophical manner. The mother has long criticized this tendency in the daughter. The mother's position has the appeal of common sense, but it is also motivated by jealousy: bookish, intellectual talk is what draws the father and daughter together, while excluding the mother. The father, by contrast, appreciates the daughter's philosophical discourse, but he also objects to the role accorded to the emotions—albeit for the opposite reason. To him, the emotions are too muddled and unreliable to be worthy of philosophical inquiry, and so the daughter has to defend her position once more.

Underlying this debate is a whole complex of feeling, deeply embedded in the family triangle. Guilt, jealousy, identification, desire, rejection, accusation, love—they all flare up and are brought into the open. Especially gripping are the accusations made by the mother about the daughter's behavior when the mother was dying. The daughter, we learn, could not be with the mother in her last hours since she was away giving a lecture. And even though she was clearly stricken by her mother's death, the daughter still managed to write on the airplane, turning even this experience into more material for a book. The father, though generally less accusatory, makes a similar point: the daughter managed to finish her Ph.D. only a year after the father's death, clearly exhibiting resources and strengths that seem to be at odds with the debilitating effects the father expected would accompany proper mourning. These accusations cut to the heart of the daughter's philosophy of emotions. Is the daughter exploiting and instrumentalizing her emotions, and thus her family's tragedies, for her philosophy?

The best answer to this question is perhaps another question: would that be such a bad thing? If indeed Nussbaum's theory is right, then philosophers should turn to and in that sense exploit their own intimate experiences, perhaps thinly disguised in fiction, as their most important philosophical resource. In fact, the dialogue proves that this can be an important and productive part of doing philosophy. Nussbaum admits in the preface that originally she had thought of the dialogue as a mere appendix to the book, but now, after having written the dialogue, she finds that it played a much more important role than what she would have deemed possible: in allowing her own experiences to become part of her philosophical writing, the dialogue actually led her to revise the book itself, thus becoming an integral part of the philosophical process.

Nussbaum's dialogue resembles Plato's dialogues but also departs from them. Nussbaum's dialogue stages the confrontation between philosophy and emotions and then proceeds to integrate them. What it does not do is introduce into philosophy the external and contingent elements of which she speaks in her book. The dialogue is all relevant and all geared toward the philosopher: a highly charged family drama in which everything is significant, an utterly private phantasmagoria that leaves no room for an outsider to intrude. This stands in contrast to the Socratic dialogues, in which the philosopher is always confronted from the outside by a Thrasymachus, Protagoras, or Gorgias who is either inducted into the proper mode of doing philosophy—or, more often, leaves it behind.

Alain Badiou

Murdoch and Nussbaum approach dramatic Platonism from different positions: Murdoch from a critique of language philosophy and relativism, insisting on a metaphysics of ideas that is centered on the connection between the idea of beauty and the idea of the good, Nussbaum as part of a program that accords intelligence to emotions and envisions the work of emotions as some kind of Platonist ascent, albeit one that remains tied to everyday, lived experience. A third philosopher, Alain Badiou, approaches dramatic Platonism from yet another tradition, one that both Murdoch and Nussbaum reject: Continental philosophy. Yet he is as determined as they are to counter the anti-Platonist gestures of twentieth-century philosophy with a new Platonism of his own.

Among the living philosophers, few stand more clearly at the intersection of theater and philosophy than Alain Badiou, whose significance for the study of theater cannot be overestimated.[25] Badiou presents an intriguing combination of the two principal ways in which philosophy has used drama and theater. He is deeply engaged with theater, as demonstrated by his extensive writings on it as well as the role he accords to theater in his philosophy. And in line with the dramatistic model, Badiou writes: "For me philosophical theatricality means this, that the essence of philosophy . . . is an act."[26] But most important is Badiou's call for a return to Plato, which even includes the demand that "we can, we must write for our contemporaries *Republics* and *Symposiums*."[27] Badiou brings together the theatrical model and the dramatistic model and traces both of them back to Plato.

The main reason for Badiou's investment in Plato is the continuation of philosophy as an independent discipline. The integrity of philosophy has been under threat through the last 150 years, when philosopher after philosopher has declared the end of metaphysics and therefore the end of classical philosophy. Nietzsche's attack on Platonism makes him the most famous of those seeking to end philosophy, but Badiou also includes Marx, Heidegger, Wittgenstein, and Derrida among their number.[28] Declaring the end of (Platonist) metaphysics, Badiou argues, comes at too steep a price: it means ceding philosophy to its enemies, the sophists and other relativists, and giving up what has distinguished philosophy from sophistry, namely, the category of truth.[29] Badiou, it should be added, is not an idealist in the sense of asserting the existence of concrete universals (as, for example, Murdoch does). For him, reversing anti-Platonism is a way of staying true to the project of philosophy itself, "philosophy as it was instituted by Plato."[30] Once philosophy gives up truth, it reverts to sophistry, relativism, mere descriptions of an ever-changing world. Badiou identifies with Plato when he watches modern anti-Platonist philosophy tear down Plato's bulwark against relativism. Philosophical self-critique is all well and good, but modern anti-Platonism has thrown out the baby with the bathwater, ensuring the death of philosophy in the process.

The philosopher who represents, for Badiou, an intriguing version of this anti-Platonist tendency is none other than Deleuze. Drawing on Nietzsche among others, Deleuze positioned his own philosophy of the multiple against Plato, making anti-Platonism the center of his method. In many ways, Deleuze is the perfect example of what happens when you declare Platonist metaphysics to be over: all that is left to do is to celebrate contingency, immanence, heterogeneity, and endless series of differences, reveling in the sheer groundlessness of all thinking. "Deleuze is the cheerful thinker of the confusion of the world," Badiou writes; Deleuze offers "an immense description, a collection of today's diversity."[31] This reading dovetails with my discussion of Deleuze as the thinker of bodies, of endlessly differing repetitions, of machines and matter in its myriad forms, a Dionysian thinker of the multiple who identified his own writing with the project of a "reversal of Platonism."

Badiou goes on to a second claim: that in reversing Plato, Deleuze has left Platonism more or less intact. Yes, Badiou says, Deleuze enjoys his endless series of differences, but behind this immense mobilization of difference lurks the same old distinction between appearance and essence. Using the language of the cave, one might say that this is exactly the distinction first made in Plato's cave parable, the only difference being that Deleuze enjoys the multiple appearances of shadows on the wall and feels little desire to turn around and leave the cave. Deleuze does not dismantle the Platonist distinction between appearance and essence but merely changes the values assigned to them, favoring the ever-changing world of appearance over the Platonic ascent to the realm of forms. The same argument can be made with respect to other anti-Platonists, since it speaks to a danger almost invariably associated with reversal: reversing Platonism leaves the distinction between cave and upper world in place and only reverses the values associated with it. As I argued earlier, modern philosophy has never stopped paying homage to the theater of the cave, even if it has tended to do so by means of reversal. Deleuze is a good example of this rule since his philosophy of contingency was deeply engaged with the theater, especially in *Difference and Repetition*, which celebrates the theater as an art form prone to disrupting the principle of identity and difference on which idealist philosophy had staked so much.

Without discussing this theatrical dimension, Badiou adds a surprising third step to his argument: Deleuze starts out as a Platonist in reverse, but he ends up being a Platonist in disguise. It turns out that behind Deleuze's fascination with the multiple lurks a Platonic conception of the one. Badiou lists many passages in which Deleuze relates multiplicities to a transcendent notion of unity and oneness. There is a singularity to Deleuze's notion of being, for example. Here Badiou argues that Deleuze's philosophy is a "classical" one, and this means that it is a "metaphysics of Being and of foundation."[32] This is also true of Deleuze's other central category, borrowed from Bergson: time. Time is the foundation of Deleuze's philosophy; it guarantees that the world of wild differences can nevertheless yield a conception of truth. Although not everyone will want to follow Badiou all the way to this identification of Deleuze as a Platonist in search of truth, his bravura reading of Deleuze is not to be dismissed out of hand; it registers above all Badiou's own Platonist philosophy, which here manifests itself as a reinterpretation of one of Plato's greatest foes.

If anti-Platonism is one target for Badiou's approach, the other is language philosophy. Like Murdoch, with whom he otherwise shares very little, Badiou recognizes the focus on language as one of the dominant strains within twentieth-century philosophy and one of the chief opponents of any kind of Platonism. For Badiou, the main problem with language philosophy is that it replaces the question of truth with the question of meaning. Posed against a (Deleuzian) philosophy of the body and a (Wittgensteinian) philosophy of language, Badiou summarizes the cornerstones of his philosophy in the recent book *Logics of Worlds* (2006) with the following formula: "There are only bodies and languages."[33] Even as he thus recognizes the achievements of a philosophy of the body and of language, Badiou supplements that assertion with a crucial addition: "There are only bodies and languages, except that there are truths." The body-language doctrine, Badiou argues, can be traced back to the sophists and their (relativistic) declaration that "man is the measure of all things."

Badiou understands truth to work against such anthropomorphic relativism. Truth is what takes you outside the human realm; it "dislocates," as Badiou puts it with respect to truth in the *Republic*.[34] At another moment he says that "truths exist as exceptions to what there is," as interruptions in the continuity of bodies and languages.[35] What Badiou formulates here is a theory of exception: truth is an exception to bodies and languages, and it takes exception to their exclusive existence.

So far, Badiou's resuscitation of Plato takes place within the frame of the first paradigm of the cave: modern philosophy is anti-Platonist in that it has abandoned truth and thus the possibility of the world above, contenting itself with the theater of shadows and words below. Only the most astute anti-Platonists, such as Deleuze, pay grudging homage to Plato by being not Platonists in reverse but Platonists in disguise. But it takes a reader such as Badiou to ferret out the Platonist overtones in the celebration of shadows, bodies, and languages current in much twentieth-century philosophy.

Folded into this critique of anti-Platonism, however, we find Badiou availing himself of the second, dramatistic paradigm, the understanding of philosophy as a (dramatistic) act. The key term here is *event*, which Badiou first developed in his book *Being and Event* (1988) and further elaborated in *Logics of Worlds* as well as in several other texts.[36] For example, when, in the quote above, Badiou speaks of truth as an exception, he has in mind his notion of the event as an exceptional occurrence. Badiou offers us four routes toward the event: love, politics, mathematics, and art. The second, politics, is perhaps the most intuitive and is also the one that reveals Badiou's political convictions: a history of true events is nothing other than the history of revolts and revolutions, beginning with Spartacus and extending to the Cultural Revolution in China. Here *event* can be translated as meaning "revolutionary event"; periods of reaction, by contrast, are not true events, but merely negative attempts to dilute the revolutionary effects of true events.

Among the four domains, mathematics is the most difficult, but it is also, for Badiou, the most crucial. Trained as a mathematician, Badiou has always sought to remind philosophy of its connection to mathematics. In this regard, too, Badiou follows Plato, who identified mathematics as a stepping-stone in the ascent from the cave to the realm of truth. Badiou believes that today's philosophy has reversed Plato's preference for mathematics over poetry by installing poetry at the center of (Continental) language philosophy, most prominently so in the work of Heidegger (but also in much poststructuralism).[37] Badiou seeks to rectify this situation. From mathematics, Badiou takes his theory of multiples. Unlike Plato, with his insistence (at least in his middle period) on concrete universals, single ideas that are themselves sustained by the transcendent idea of the good, Badiou furnishes his worlds with multiples theorized with the help of set theory as developed by the mathematician Georg Cantor in the late nineteenth century. Badiou's notion of the situation, which harbors multiples, finds its mathematical grounding here, as does the argument why we can speculate about possible worlds, not just one. Badiou's often technical use of mathematics has puzzled many readers (including this one), but suffice it to say that Badiou proposes an ontology of multiplicity that does without recourse to oneness and transcendence and remains instead on a plane of immanence.

Even though Badiou seeks to install mathematics at the center of philosophy and thus to reverse the dominance of poetry—and literature more generally—over philosophy, he does not want to give up on literature altogether. Indeed, the poem remains another path toward the event. It is notable how closely Badiou follows Heidegger's reverence for poetry, his belief that through poetry the true language of being takes place above and beyond the degraded language of communication and everyday life. But where Heidegger finds in poetry the language of being, Badiou finds there the trace of an event. Avoiding Heidegger's quasi-religious language of revelation, Badiou thinks of the poem as the moment when "what there is" is being interrupted, when something new and strange enters a situation and radically alters it; an exceptional poem bears the traces of an event that has taken place.

The difference from Heidegger is visible most clearly in Badiou's reverence for the modernists Mallarmé and Beckett. Badiou's admiration for Mallarmé stems in part from the poet's own regard for numbers and from his quasi-technical understanding of poetry as an "operation."[38] The most important poem, for Badiou, is the experimental "A Throw of the Dice," in which Mallarmé arranges words on a page in a manner reminiscent of falling dice. By deviating from the regular poetic line, Mallarmé turns every word into an event, just as the poem itself revolves around an event (a shipwreck). But even more central is the event that gives the poem its name. A throw of the dice creates an event; it distills what we might call an event to its essence. When we throw dice, we have defined the situation, a bet, into which an event will intrude by making a decision. After the throw, nothing will be the same; the event will have fundamentally altered the situation.

Not only does Mallarmé represent an event with and through his poem, but he does so, according to Badiou, by crucially relying on absence, negation, and the void. The shipwreck, in that sense, is only the ruse of an external event, not its essence, which resides in a peculiar quality of absence. In Badiou's parlance, an event takes place "on the edge of the void" in close proximity to nothing (the title of his main book, *Being and Event*, echoes Sartre's *Being and Nothingness* [1943]).[39] Badiou's ontology is one not of plenitude but of a precarious relation to absence. Such absence is a recurring concern for Mallarmé, whose poems reflect a fascination with silence and, for the first time in modern poetry, with the blank space between the words. For Badiou, Mallarmé is thus the poet of subtraction and isolation, the representative of a modernism that seeks to reduce mimesis and expression, the traditional domain of poetry, to a minimum.[40] The eccentric arrangement of words on the page in "A Throw of the Dice" might indeed be seen as a poetic rendering of Badiou's conception of multiples arranged on the edge of the void.

Situation, event, a throw of the dice—the terms of Badiou's discussion of Mallarmé have one thing in common: they are at home in the theater. Even though Badiou, following Heidegger, discusses Mallarmé under the general rubric of the poem, the more important category is in fact drama. In *Being and Event*, he stresses at the outset that "A Throw of the Dice" is *"dramatic"* (his emphasis) and that Mallarmé "is the thinker of the event-drama."[41] In *A Handbook of Inaesthetics* (1998) he details more fully what kind of theater is at work in this extraordinary poet. Trying to specify what use Mallarmé makes of the theater, Badiou approaches a category that almost all philosophers interested in the theater encounter sooner or later: antitheatricality. Mallarmé, the writer of the event-drama, is part of modernist antitheatricalism and might even be construed as an enemy of the theater. This question of theatricality and antitheatricality is related to how Badiou approaches dance. Noting the frequent opposition between dance and theater, Badiou sees an antitheatrical turn in the work of the later Nietzsche, who attacks Wagner with an antitheatrical polemic and praises instead, via Zarathustra, the superiority of dance. Mallarmé, with his interest in dance, seems to go a similar route—but not quite. Badiou sees Mallarmé as parting company with Nietzsche in that he installs a purified, idealized theater at the center of his dramatic poetry. Badiou avoids a conception of theater as mimesis and reads Mallarmé's monologue *The Afternoon of a Faun* (1865) as just such an antimimetic dramatization of the idea. This is another way of recognizing that Mallarmé has managed to install antitheatricality at the center of his theater, creating an event-drama in the manner of Plato.[42]

Thus behind Badiou's philosophy of the poem, we find a conception of Platonic theater. What are the contours of that conception? First of all, it asserts the centrality of the theater for thought. In his recent *The Century* (2005; translated into English in 2007) Badiou observes that "the twentieth century is the century of the theatre as art."[43] In particular, Badiou is interested in the figure of the director, who has emerged as "a thinker of representation as such, who carries out a very complex investigation into the relationships between text, acting, space, and public." Badiou places the modern director at the center of theater because he wants to formulate an understanding of theater that emphasizes its connection to philosophy or, more precisely, to thought. The director, as he specifies in another short text on theater, assembles components, including text, acting, set design, and music, but assembles them in a unique manner: this is why the theater can be called an event. The theatrical assemblage occurs only in the present, night after night, there, on the stage. Further, Badiou argues that due to this unique form of assemblage, the theater is capable of producing ideas. "This event—when it really is theater, the art of the theater—is an event of thought. This means that the assemblage of components directly produces ideas."[44] Since philosophical truth has the character of an event, it is the theater, the most eventful of the arts, that plays a central role in its formulation.

Badiou's most important text on theater to date is "Rhapsody for the Theatre," published in 1990 (and translated into English in 2008).[45] Badiou begins with what he calls an analytic of theater, a list of its essential components in the manner of Aristotle. These seven ingredients are place, text, director, actor, décor, costumes, and public. Though unremarkable at first, they actually contain a view of theater that goes against the grain of current trends within theater studies in several respects. The most provocative claim is probably Badiou's insistence on the text as a reference point, thus excluding mime and dance from the domain of theater—a position that goes against the widespread suspicion in theater and performance studies circles of the dramatic text as somehow traditionalist. His theory of the relation between text and performance is anything but traditional, however. Rejecting all formalist definitions of drama, he considers any type of text a "theater text" once it has been staged; a theater text thus is a text that has been or will have been staged. The second element of this definition is the incompleteness of the theater text: it needs to be staged in order to be completed. Combined with the first element, this results in an interesting definition of the process of staging a text: in doing so, directors, actors, and designers effectively declare a text to be incomplete. In other words, a theater text is a text whose incompleteness has been or will have been demonstrated by directors and actors.

This understanding of theater texts and their relation to the stage also has bearing on another element of the theater, the actor. Of course, Badiou follows most theories of theater in that the incorporation of the theater, the use of the actors' bodies, is crucial. At the same time, he emphasizes the precarious status of the actor's body: the body is not a given or a foundation, and this is so precisely because of its dynamic relation to the text—"The actor's is a borrowed body, a precarious body, but also, therefore, a glorious body . . . a body eaten by the words of the text."[46] At a time when it is assumed that theater is an art of the body and that this fact is not in need of further exploration, Badiou's understanding of a theatrical body as completing a theater text, and of a theater text as making a body precarious, is an important corrective. The talk of the "borrowed" body of the actor has one further consequence that also deviates from all approaches that think of theater as a search for the authentic body. In the theater, Badiou suggests, there is no such thing as an authentic body.

Badiou's analytic of the theater, his list of the theater's essential components and their interaction, leaves us with a view of theater that can serve as a corrective to various misconceptions current in theater studies, including the suspicion of the dramatic text and a view of actors as bodies onstage. But this analytic does not yet lead to the theater Badiou has in mind. In order for this to happen, the seven elements of his analytic have to be assembled in a particular way. And this assemblage must be guided by another set of principles.

The first of those principles is the theater's relation to the state. Badiou's conception of theater as event identifies the theater as the most political art form, the one most closely tied to the state. This, of course, is especially true in France, with its tradition of a national theater and generous state subsidies. Things couldn't be more different in the United States. But even if we allow for national difference, the essential relation of the theater to the state posited by Badiou has relevance for us to the extent that it rests on a particular view of the spectator, the audience. This audience is an assembled public and thus resembles a political assembly.[47] Here and elsewhere Badiou contrasts the theater audience with viewers of film, who are anonymous, stay in the dark, and are not activated by a sense of the liveness of the theater (this preference for theater over film might be seen as yet another contrast with Deleuze, whose earlier interest in theater had given way to an engagement with film). In order to preserve this character of the live assembly, Badiou also demands that theaters keep the practice of intermission, the moment when the audience can see and experience itself as audience rather than disappear, as it does with film, in the anonymity of the dark.

The most important dimension of theater, however, is the relation between theater and philosophy. Badiou's most provocative thesis is "All theatre is theatre of Ideas."[48] In the theater, ideas have to struggle against another principle, desire. It is because of this struggle that philosophy since Plato has been suspicious of theater as a rival: "Theatre would be: philosophy seized by debauchery, the Idea on the auction block of sex, the intelligible dressed up in costume at the fair."[49] Badiou seems to be echoing Plato's suspicions, and in a sense he might be said to confirm them, but it must be remembered that these formulations are really voiced in a kind of free-indirect discourse: Badiou himself approves of intermingling idea and desire, philosophy and psychoanalysis.

We can now see the contours of Badiou's theatrical philosophy. The poem is for him an "event-drama," and this emphasis on the event ultimately leads him to think of the theater as the art form—or assemblage of existing art forms—that is the most directly tied to ideas. Like many theatrical philosophers before him, including Plato, Ficino, Diderot, Voltaire, Kierkegaard, Nietzsche, Camus, Sartre, Murdoch, and Nussbaum, Badiou also translated his dramatic philosophy into actual drama. His plays have not appeared in English even though they have acquired a (small) following in France. They are wide-ranging and witty, turning philosophical concepts into scenes and characters, including the figure of Ahmed, an Algerian immigrant around whom four of Badiou's plays revolve. These plays testify to the fact that Badiou's philosophy not only is dramatic but also actually veers toward theatrical performance. Badiou's work is an occasion for rethinking the relation between philosophy and theater; it also is itself an exemplar of this relation, a reminder of how fruitful the encounter between theater and philosophy can be.

Epilogue
Dramatic Platonism

In this book, the concept of dramatic Platonism has served a number of historical and analytical purposes. In chapter 1, it provided the lens though which to focus on Plato's use of drama. In chapter 2, it functioned as a tool for excavating the mostly forgotten tradition of the Socrates play. In chapter 3, it worked as a frame through which to explain the radical innovations of modern drama. In chapter 4, it directed our attention to the "dramatic turn" and "theatrical turn" of philosophy, identifying the reentry of drama and theater into the history of philosophy. And in chapter 5, it connected this dramatic and theatrical philosophy back to Plato by attending to contemporary Platonists with an interest in drama. Taken together, these chapters have sought to supply a new perspective on the histories of theater and philosophy, allowing us to see familiar figures in a new light, but also helping us to locate new objects, new connections, and a new question (what is the relation between philosophy and drama?), as well as a new problem (how to integrate drama and philosophy?). By way of a conclusion, I will outline, in a schematic manner, some of the theoretical consequences of dramatic Platonism for contemporary thought.

Corporealism

The twentieth century witnessed an extraordinary flourishing of writing about the body, an interest that reached its climax in the last decades of the twentieth century across different fields in the humanities. Foucault's interest in the disciplined body, Deleuze's fascination with what Artaud called the body without organs, the wide-ranging interest in corporeal practices within gender and sexuality studies—these are some of the more recent manifestations of a wider phenomenon I call corporealism. The three-volume series called *Fragments for a History of the Human Body*, published by Zone Books, might be seen as one of its most characteristic manifestations in the late 1980s, while its high-water mark was reached in the early nineties with Jean-Luc Nancy's *Corpus*.[1] But corporealism can be traced back all the way to Nietzsche's celebration of the body. In this history of the body, we can also include the analysis of the working body in motion inspired by Taylorism, concerns about sensory overload in the modern metropolis, and an anthropological fascination with so-called primitive rituals.

Dramatic Platonism does not seek to overturn the conviction that the body is the foundational entity of research in the humanities, but it does seek to place the study of the body within a new frame. For this project, it takes a cue from Plato's own literary practice. His dialogues pay minute attention to the body—its needs, its desires—much in keeping with the fact that drama more generally is an art of the body. The training of actors, theories of gestures, different forms of gymnastics, and the choreography of bodies onstage—all these are ingredients of the theater's immense attention to the corporeal. At the same time, Plato and, in his wake, dramatic Platonism do not leave theatrical bodies alone. Dramatic Platonism does something to and with bodies: it seeks to detach them from the ground on which they stand and undermine their self-sufficient complacency. In the cave parable, Plato expressed this somewhat melodramatically as an unchaining and turning around, and also as a shock, an interruption, an encounter with something other than the body (idea or form), a type of radical (and, in the metaphoric world of the parable, "celestial") alterity. Something happens to bodies in Plato's dramaturgy, and Plato uses all his literary, dramatic, and philosophical resources to capture the experience of this happening. One language with which Plato described this experience was the theory of forms. This theory gave an answer to the question of why and how this process of bodies coming unchained (interrupted, turned around) might take place. In its most radical form, which Plato later complicated, the theory of forms generalized this process of coming unchained by claiming that bodies were in fact less real than they seemed and that ideal forms enjoyed a superior status. What better way of making sure that bodies would never again seem grounded and solid than relegating them to a secondary, derivative position? But the theory of forms can be understood as something other than a positive metaphysics that posits the independent existence of concrete universals; instead, it can be understood as a way of describing the process of unchaining bodies. This second meaning is the one most relevant for us today. What matters about forms (or ideas) is their effect on the status of the body.

This unchaining or uprooting of bodies can serve as a starting point for a critique of corporealism. For this purpose, it is useful to revisit the domain in which corporealism has been especially prominent: theater. Instead of considering the theater as an art form in which the body reigns supreme, as is often done, dramatic Platonism describes the theater— whether imagined or real—as precisely the place where bodies come unhinged all the time. The theater, after all, would be an odd place to insist on the grounding of bodies, since it takes bodies and places them on ontologically slippery ground. In the theater, everything is up for grabs; you can't trust your eyes, and nothing is what it seems; bodies and things are put on boards that might signify the world, as Friedrich Schiller has it, but which are not, in and of themselves, that world. In the theater, material entities are not simply there; rather, they are made use of. In the end, the history of acting is a program not for discovering the body as what it is but for changing it, for molding it into something that will be of use on the stage.

If the uprooting of bodies is inevitable in the theater, it is nevertheless a process (or state) that can be revealed or concealed, hindered or furthered. Illusionist realism, for example, is in the business of covering up the gap between theatrical bodies and real ones, of rechaining bodies to the ground. Dramatists who work in the vein of dramatic Platonism, by contrast, recognize and further this unchaining of bodies; they greet theatrical bodies with enthusiasm and use them for their own purposes. But like Plato, they often do so under the rubric of ideas or forms: the idea or form is what ultimately effects the unchaining of bodies. Far from being a marginal phenomenon, the theater of ideas, broadly understood, can be said to have recognized a central feature of theater and to have made use of it more fully than other traditions. Viewing theater through the lens of dramatic Platonism thus provides us with a model for a critique of corporealism—on its home territory.

Relativism

In addition to this critique of corporealism, dramatic Platonism aims at a second target, relativism. Relativism can take different forms: epistemological relativism, moral relativism, linguistic relativism. Plato was concerned about all three, primarily because he feared the abuses to which relativism could lead. And so he developed philosophy as the assertion that there *must be* an absolute point of reference for knowledge, otherwise arguments would be won by the stronger and knowledge would become subject to power. There *must be* a single idea of the good, otherwise value is at the mercy of willful manipulation. Words *must be* grounded in reality, otherwise we cannot trust them and our thinking will be based on slippery ground. This is one of the arguments in the *Parmenides* for holding on to a version of the theory of forms despite all the problems and contradictions this theory brings with it. The theory of forms turns out to be crucial for the survival of philosophy itself.

Today, as at the time of Plato, we are at a moment in the history of thought that is dominated by relativisms of an epistemological, moral, and linguistic kind. Linguistic relativism has become the most powerful attitude within philosophy proper, whether articulated by Nietzsche, Wittgenstein, J. L. Austin, or various proponents of poststructuralism. It should be added that not all proponents of language philosophy are relativists. Rudolf Carnap and others sought to ground their epistemologies in a controlled edifice of language, with basic sentences ("protocol sentences") providing the foundation for more elaborate forms of description. The relation between language and the world was crucial for this endeavor. The failure of these efforts encouraged those, such as the later Wittgenstein, who formulated a philosophy of language that focused on the actual use of language, dismissing all efforts to turn the muddle of language into a more rational and controlled system. Even the late Wittgenstein, however, still grounded language games in forms of life, that is, forms of extralinguistic social reality. But this grounding became less important for a tradition of language philosophy that sometimes used the late Wittgenstein but more often availed itself of alternative theories of language derived from structuralism, rhetoric, and literary criticism. Here, too, the assumption was that a sophisticated understanding of language would demolish all hitherto established philosophical certainties, reducing lofty philosophical abstractions to the unruly formulations in which they were expressed. Language, now viewed as essentially uncontrollable, was said to destabilize any foundational philosophical discourse. Not infrequently, poststructuralism merged this linguistic relativism with corporealism: the material side of language, "the materiality of the signifier," was held responsible for the slipperiness of language. In this view of language as the Achilles' heel of metaphysics, poststructuralists could look back to Nietzsche as an important precursor, the first to have connected an anti-Platonist philosophy of the body to a materialist view of language.

This view of language was always faced with the problem that in most people's experience, language functions rather well even though it may not always be reliable. Functioning language as we all know it, including successful acts of theorizing and philosophizing, had to be explained as an exception to the rule, as a special case, as so many marginal phenomena blocking our view of the fundamental instability of language. Yes, language sometimes works, we would be told, but this is a mere side effect. And in any case, most examples of functioning language are exaggerated: the closer you look, the more you can see the malfunctioning of language. Philosophy, or what remained of it, would do exactly that: pay minute attention to the destabilizing logic of language, tracking its every slip and infelicity. The inability to control its own meaning became the tragedy of philosophy, leading to recurring predictions of the death of philosophy itself.

While Plato's Greece rarely doubted its own cultural superiority, today our most potent form of relativism is cultural relativism, both on the political left and on the political right. A reaction to pervasive cultural chauvinism, cultural relativism refuses evaluative judgments about cultures and instead merely describes what differentiates them from one another. Difference is the keyword here, and the moral imperative that is attached to this term is respect: respecting the other culture for its difference becomes the basic attitude recommended by cultural relativism. Respecting differences is certainly not a bad thing and should be encouraged everywhere; its premise, however, needs to be examined critically, for difference here becomes a foundational term, the ontology of this worldview. The problem with this ontology is that it must insist on differences and nothing but differences, described as the natural state of culture. This insistence on difference makes any dynamic, changing conception of identity difficult to grasp. At the same time, anything that smacks of fusion, the possibility of overlaps, coherences, and alliances, is subject to suspicion, for it threatens to downgrade or even bracket the assumption of stable, quasi-natural, and insurmountable differences.

Culturalism is particularly strong on the left, where anticolonial struggles and the desire to combat all forms of chauvinism and racism have led to the rise of a doctrine whose imperative might be summarized as "respecting the other" (or Other). But a form of culturalism has arisen on the right as well, where its most prominent advocate is Samuel Huntington.[2] Huntington divides the world into different cultural zones, organized mostly by religion; no political or cultural alliance is possible across these borders. To be sure, Huntington's primary concern is not an ethics of respect but the limits of geopolitical alliances. The upshot is the same, however: whether you respect the other because you revere difference or leave the other alone because you think he/she is too different, in both cases it is the same insurmountable and immutable difference that reigns supreme. There is no doubt that I would prefer respect to this skepticism— it's not that respect is a bad thing—but what I want to emphasize is that both are based on similar assumptions. The left thinks it's bad to try to overcome difference (it would imply a lack of respect for difference); the right thinks it wouldn't work anyway.

Dramatic Platonism does not simply reject this culturalism; after all, Plato's own dialogues frequently feature foreigners as interlocutors, and Plato's critique of Athens aimed at its feeling of superiority over its neighbors. At the same time, dramatic Platonism is not content with a culturalism of difference. It recognizes, with Plato, that a descriptive culturalism, however well-meaning it may be, can easily be abused, for example, for a project such as Huntington's. Differences must be taken as a point of departure for procedures that can envision, and value positively, forms of alliance, convergence, and assimilation. In order to mobilize such a process, the ontology of difference has to be called into question by a hypothetical form of universalism. The point here is not to posit an ontology of universals. Rather, it is to imagine a projective universal, a universalism to come—the possibility that differences can be bridged (or fused or aligned). Universals are never a given but only a form of mobilization. This, I would posit, was the original function of Plato's own theory of forms. Plato's dialogues show us the process by which differences are sent on a trajectory of assimilation, if not of identity. Dramatic Platonism pursues a similar project with respect to culturalism. Despite the fear that invoking universalism will be decried as bad, we have to invoke it, we have to act as if universalism is possible, just as the *Parmenides* asks us to act as if there were ideas, otherwise we will be stuck in a static culturalism forever.

Truth

The category most frequently attacked by relativists is that of truth. In the face of so much uncertainty, whether based on language or cultural difference, the very invocation of truth has come to be seen not only as hopelessly naive but also as outright suspect. I am not intent on formulating at this late date a new theory of truth. I am working with an effect-oriented notion, namely, that truth is what unsettles the complacency of corporealism (including linguistic corporealism) and cultural relativism—something along the lines of Badiou's theory of truth as exception. To this I add an imperative: we have to assume the possibility of truth (as exception) in order to break the dominance of difference (including the difference of bodies) and to allow for a reorientation of differences into some kind of alliance. Truth for Plato was what allowed him to critique the linguistic relativists of his time, the sophists; it was what inaugurated the project of philosophy, and this means a mode of interaction and discourse that would, if not overcome differences (the difference between bodies, between persons), at least make those differences seem less solid, less set in stone. Without this reorienting— but also, and importantly, disorienting—effect, philosophy would cease to exist and would lapse back into sophistry, into a relativism that would give rise to a rhetoric of power. Truth, the universal, the idea— these terms cannot and should not be filled with content. That has been the mistake of most forms of idealism—a mistake first committed, then recognized, and finally corrected by Plato himself.

Today we are at a moment when Plato's project of philosophy has lost much of its status. The most important philosophers of the last 150 years, from Nietzsche through Wittgenstein to Derrida, have declared the end of philosophy as we know it. Corporealism, linguistic relativism, and cultural relativism reign supreme. It is time to revive Plato—not the discredited Plato of idealism, but a different one, the Plato of dramatic Platonism. This Platonism does not simply dismiss corporealism, linguistic relativism, and cultural relativism; rather, it points to the ways in which this doxa of our time might be questioned and rethought. Indeed, it is this act of pointing that is dramatic Platonism's most fundamental gesture. Pointing is the gesture of a body, of a body becoming language; it is a corporeal sign that ends in thin air, a gesture into nothing that draws the eyes toward it and toward the nothing to which it points. It is a Platonic gesture, or rather Platonism as gesture. This gesture is best captured in Jacques-Louis David's painting *The Death of Socrates*: a pointing that urges the assembled bodies to reorient themselves, to look not at the dying Socrates but at that to which he points. There is nothing Socrates points to, yet his pointing finger forces the bodies we see in the painting to change their attitude, to turn around. This is the function of truth, of the idea, of the universal: a pointing that causes bodies to look beyond themselves without knowing what this beyond might be.

Appendix 1
Socrates Titles

Year of First Publication	Title	Author	Confirmed Publication Information
167	*Dialogues of the Dead*	Lucian	Greek.
1469	*De Amore*	Ficino	Latin.
1533	*Of that knowlage, whiche maketh a wise man. A disputacion Platonike*	Sir Thomas Elyot	Fletestrete, in the house of Thomas Berthelet, 1549.
1605	*Timon of Athens*	Shakespeare and Middleton	1623 Folio.
1630	*L'Alcibide fanciullo*	Antonío Rocco	Published anonymously in 1951.
1640	*Life of Socrates*	François Charpentier	
1649	*Der sterbende Sokrates*	Chrístían Hoffmann von Hoffmannswaldau	Breßlau, 1679.
1675	*Alcibiades. A Tragedy*	Thomas Otway	Premiered 1675, The Duke's Company, London.
1680	*La pazienza di Socrate con due moglie*	Nicolò Minato (libretto), Antoni Draghi (music)	Prag.

1681	*Plato Redivivus. Or, A Dialogue Concerning Government*	Henry Neville	London: Printed for *S.I.* and Sold by *R. Dew.*
1700	*Dialogues des Morts. Socrate et Alcibiade*	François de Salignac de la Mothe-Fénelon	Paris; anon.
1711	*The Memorable Things of Socrates.* A translation of Charpentier's *Life of Socrates.*	Edward Bysshe	London, J. Batley, at the Dove in Pater-noster Row, 1722.
1713	*Cato: A tragedy*	Joseph Addison	London: J. Tonson, at Shakespear's Head against Catherine-Street in the Strand, 1713.
1716	*Socrates Triumphant; or, the Danger of Being Wise in a Commonwealth of Fools*	Anonymous	London: Printed for the author, and sold by J. Browne, 1716.
1717	*A Portraiture of Socrates in blank verse (dramatic poem)*	Sam Catherall	Oxford. L. Lichfield, 1717.
1721	*Der geduldige Sokrates.* After Minato	Johann Ulrich von König	Premiered in Hamburg, 28 January, 1721.
1731	*A Dialogue on Beauty in the Manner of Plato*	George Stubbes	London: W. Wilkins, in Lombard Street, 1731.
1731	*Alcibiade. Comédie en trois actes*	Philippe Poisson	Paris, 1731.
1741	*Der sterbende Sokrates*	Nathaniel Baumgarten	Berlin, 1746.
1745	*Dialogue on Devotion*	Thomas Amory	London: printed for J. Waugh and S. Chaulkin, bookseller in Tunton, 1746; second edition.
1746	*The heathen martyr: or the death of Socrates, an historical tragedy*	George Adams	London: printed for the author, 1746.

1749	*The Life of Socrates*	John Gilbert Cooper	London: R. Dodsley at Tully's Head in Pall-mall,1749.
1756	*Gespräch des Sokrates mit Timoclea, von der scheinbaren und wahren Schönheit*	Christoph Martin Wieland	
1758	*Socrates. A Dramatic Poem*	Amyas Bushe	London: R. and J. Dodsley in Pall-Mall, 1758.
1758	*La Mort de Socrate.* Fragment	Denis Diderot	unpublished.
1759	*Socrate. Ouvrage dramatique*	Voltaire	Amsterdam; n.p.
1760	*Sketch for Alcibiades-Socrates play*	Gotthold Ephraim Lessing	unpublished.
1763	*La Mort de Socrate. Tragédie en trois actes, et en vers*	Louis Billardon de Sauvigny	Paris: Prault le jeune, Libraire, Quai de Conti, vis-à-vis la descente du Pont-Neuf, à la Charité, 1763.
1764	*Socrate*	Simon Nícolas Henri Linguet	Amsterdam, chez Marc-Michel Rey.
1767	*The Banquet* (English translation with commentary on dramatic convention)	Floyer Sydenham	London: Printed for W. Sandby, in Fleet-Street.
1767	*Phaedon oder über die Unsterblichkeit der Seele, in drey Gesprächen*	Moses Mendelssohn	Berlin, bey Friedrich Nicolai, 1767.
Before 1770	*The Death of Socrates*	Thomas Cradock	Baltimore, MD; unpublished.
1775	*Socrate Immaginario. Commedia per musica*	Galiani et Lorenzi; music by Giovanni Paisiello	Permiered in Naples, Teatro Nuovo, 1775.
1775	English translation of *Wieland's Socrates and Timoclea*	n.a.	London, printed for S. Leacroft, at the Globe, Charing Cross, 1775.

1781	*Alcibiades*	August Gottlieb Meissner	Leipzig, 1781. Dresden, bei Johann Gottlob Immanuel Breitkopf, 1785; second edition.
1789	*Socrate. Tragédie en cinq actes et en vers*	François Pastoret de Calian	Not available.
1790	*Le Procès de Socrate, ou le régime des anciens temps. Comédie en trois actes et en prose*	Jean-Marie Collot d'Herbois	Premiered at the Théâtre de Monsier, 9 November, 1790; published in Paris: Chez la veuve Duchesne, & Fils, 1791.
1795	*Sokrates, Sohn des Sophroniscus. Ein dramatisches Gemälde*	Wilhelm Friedrich Heller	Frankfurt: Esslinger, 1795.
1796	*Socrate*	Anonymous	Florence: Luigi Carlieri, Librajo in Via de' Guicciardini, 1796.
1798	*Death of Socrates. A Dialogue in a suit of scenes*	Charles Stearns	Leominster: John Prentiss, & co., 1798.
1804	*Socrate. Tragedia*	Luigi Scevola	Milan: Pirotta e Maspero, 1804.
1806	*Socrates. A dramatic poem written on the model of the ancient Greek tragedy*	Andrew Becket	London: Longman, Hurst, Rees, Orne, & Brown, Paternoster-Row, 1811.
1807	*The Life of Socrates*	n. a.	Augusta, GA: printed at the Chronicle Office, 1907.
1808	*La Mort de Socrate*	Jacques-Henri Bernardin de Saint-Pierre	Paris, Chez Méquignon-Marvis, Librarie, 1818.
1809	*La maison de Socrate le sage. Comédie en cinq actes, en prose*	Louis-Sébastien Mercier	Paris, Duminil-Lesueur, 1809.
1814	*Socrates. A tragedy in five acts*	Anonymous	Paris, printed by Sétier, 1822.

1818	*The Banquet. Translation*	Percy Bysshe Shelley	Manuscript; partial publication by Mary Shelley in 1840. First full publication in privately printed edition of 100 by Sir John C. E. Shelley-Rolls in 1931. Manuscript in the Bodleian Library, The Bodleian record, II (1946), 144-145.
1828	*Socrates. A Dramatic Poem*	Henry Montague Grover	London: Longman, Rees, Orme, Brown, and Green, Paternos-ter-Row,1828.
1835	*Sokrates. Tragødie*	Adam Gottlob Oehlenschläger	Kopenhagen: Forfatterens Forlag, 1835. German version 1839.
1840	*Socrates. A Tragedy in Five Acts*	Francis Foster Barham	London: William Edward Painter, 1842.
1843	*In Vino Veritas. A Recollection*	Søren Kierkegaard	Kopenhagen: Hilarius bookbinder, printed for the author, 1845.
1858	*Sokrates*	Ludwig Eckardt	Jena: Hochhausen's Verlag, 1858.
1872	*Alcibiade*	Felice Cavallotti	Milan: C. Barbini, 1874.
1884	*Xanthippe*	Fritz Mauthner	Dresden und Leipzig: Verlag von Heinrich Minden, 1884.
1885	*Socrate et sa femme. Comédie en un act*	Théodore de Banville	Premiered at the Comédie-Française, December 2, 1885. Published in Paris: Calmann Lévy, éditeur Ancienne Maison Michel Lévy Frères, 1885.
1888	*Sokrates*	Ernst Hermann	Not available.
1894	*La Mort de Socrate, pièce en 4 actes en vers*	Charles Richet	Premiered at the Odéon, 1894.

1903	*Der Sturmgeselle Sokrates. Komödie in vier Akten*	Hermann Sudermann	Stuttgart und Berlin: J. G. Gotta'sche Buchhandlung Nachfolger, 1903.
1903	*Hellas (Socrates)*	August Strindberg	Unpublished; Premiered in Hannover, 1922.
1905	*Historiska Miniatyrer (Historical Miniatures)*	August Strindberg	Stockholm: Albert Bonniers förlag, 1905.
1908	*The New Plato. Or Socrates redivivus*	Thomas L. Masson	New York: Moffat, Yard, & Company, 1908.
1911	*Symposium, ritualistic readings*	Stefan George and his cricle	Munich, Römerstraße 16, Kugelzimmer.
1917–19	*Der Gerettete Alkibiades*	Georg Kaiser	Potsdam: Gustav Kiepenheuer Verlag, 1920.
1918	*Socrate*	Erik Satie	Premiered at the home of Jane Bathori; first public performance 1920.
1918	*Socrates. A poem play*	Willis G. Sears	Omaha, Neb.: Festner Printing Co., printed for the author.
1921	*Eupalinos ou l'architecte*	Paul Valéry	Architectures 1921 (September).
1921	*L'Ame et la danse*	Paul Valéry	La Revue Française, 1921 (December).
1924–1925	*Symposium*	Nikos Kazantzakis	First publication Athens, 1971, edited by Emmanuel H. Kasdaglis, published by Heleni Kazantzaki.
1925	*The Death of Socrates. A Dramatic Scene, founded upon two of Plato's Dialogues, the 'Crito' and the 'Phaedo'; adapted for the stage*	Laurence Housman	London: Sidgwick & Jackson Ltd., 1925.

1926	*Platone: poema drammatico in 4 atti*	Guido Spotorno	Bari: F. Casini & figlio.
1927	*Socrate. Tragedia*	Federico Valerio Ratti	Florence: Vallecchio Editore, 1927.
1927	*Die grosse Hebammenkunst. Komödie*	Robert Walter	Leipzig: P. Reclam Jun., 1927.
1930	*Prozess Sokrates*	Hans Kyser	Berlin: Reimar Hobbing, 1930.
1930	*Der Tod des Sokrates. Ein Sendespiel in 4 Scenen*	Hans Kyser	Unpublished manuscript; Vertriebsstelle des Verbandes Deutscher Bühnenschriftsteller, 1930.
1930	*Socrates. A Play in Six Scenes*	Clifford Bax	London: Victor Gollancz, 1930.
1932	*Der Verführer. Drama in Fünf Akten*	Helene Scheu-Riesz	Wien: Universal-Edition, 1932.
1938	*Sokrates und Xanthippe. Ein frohes Spiel*	Heinz Steguweit	Berlin: Langen/Müller.
1939	*Der verwundete Sokrates*	Bertolt Brecht	Kalendergeschichten, Berlin: Gebrüder Weiss, 1949.
1941	*Sokrates. Drama in vier Akten, der antiken Chronik nachgebildet*	John Knittel	Zürich-Leipzig: Orell Füssli Verlag, 1941.
1943	*Der tapfere Herr S. Komödie*	Hans Hömberg	Premiered at Kleines Haus, 21 January, 1943. Unpublished.
1943	*Two Plato Settings*	Martha Alter	New York: Galaxy Music, 1943.
1943	*Xanthippe. Eine betrübte Comödie*	Wolfgang Goetz	
1951	*Barefoot in Athens*	Maxwell Anderson	Premiered at the Martin Beck Theater, 1951; New York: William Sloane Associates, 1951.

1953	Sokrates. Roman, Drama, Essay	Manès Sperber	Manuscript from 1953. Zürich: Europa Verlag, 1988.
1954	Serenade (after Plato's 'Symposium')	Leonard Bernstein	
1957	Socrates. A Drama in Three Acts	Lister Sinclair	Agincourt: The Book Society of Canada, 1957.
1960	Die Verteidigung der Xanthippe	Stefan Andres	Munich: R. Piper & Co., 1960.
1964	Ctésippe	Jean Bloch-Michel	Paris: Gallimard, 1964.
1964	Alkibides. Three acts and an epilogue	Nikos Toutountzakes	Athens: 1964.
1965	The Drinking Party	Jonathan Miller	London: BBC, 1965.
1966	Socrates Tried. Drama Reconstruction	Doros Alastos	Nicosia, Cyprus: Zavallis Press, 1966.
1966	Kümmert Euch Nicht Um Sokrates	Josef Pieper	Munich: Kösel Verlag, 1966.
1966	Het Proces Socrates	Joseph van Hoeck	Antwerp: Uitgeverij de Sikkel N.V., 1966.
1967	Alcibiades. A Play of Athens in the Great Age	Charles Wharton Stork	Syracuse: Syracuse University Press, 1967.
1969	Socrate (by Satie) Transcribed for piano	John Cage	Paris: M. Eschig, 1984.
1970	Shadowplay, op. 30	Alexander Goehr	Mainz: Schott, 1970
1970	Der Fall Sokrates	Wilhelm Wolfgang Schütz	Zurich: Peter Schifferli Verlag, Die Arche, 1970.
1970	The Drinking Party	Paul Shyre	Typescript; New York: Library of the Performing Arts, 1970.
1971	Socrates Savunuyor, Iki Perdelik Tragedya	Turano A. Oflazoglu	

1972	*Sócrates*	Enrique Llovet	Madrid: Escelicer, S. A., 1972.
1975	*Conversations with Socrates*	Edvard Radzinsky	Premiered at the Mayakovsky Theatre, Moscow, April 4, 1975. English translation by Alma H. Law premiered at the Jean Cocteau Repertory Theatre on September 19, 1986.
1979	*Az Állam*	Maróti Lajos	Budapest, Szépirodalmi Könyvkiadó, 1980.
1980	*Art and Eros. A Dialogue about Art*	Iris Murdoch	London: Chatto & Windus, 1986.
1982–1989	*Symposium. Opera in two acts, op. 33*	Libretto by Gerrit Komrij	
1984	*Bloody Poetry*	Howard Brenton	London: Samuel French, 1985.
1985	*Socrate L'Anarchico. Drama in due atti*	Marcello Ricci	Arrone (Terni): Editrice Thyrus, 1985.
1986	*Socrate et le Fils D'Anytos. Pièce in cinq actes*	Henri Bressolette	Montpellier, 1986.
1987	*Ankläger des Sokrates. Roman aus dem alten Athen*	Diego Viga	Halle: Mitteldeutscher Verlag, 1987.
1992	*Xanthippe. Schöne Braut des Sokrates*	Maria Regina Kaiser	Hamburg: Hoffmann und Campe, 1992.
1994	*Elephant Memories*	Ping Chong	

1996	*Plato's Euthyphro, Apology, and Crito. Arranged for Dramatic Presentation from the Jowett translation with Choruses*	Sarah Watson Emery	Lanham, MD: University Press of America, 1996.
1997	*Socrate chez Mikey. Petit précis de philosophie et l'usage des amateurs de Disneyland Paris et tous les autres*	Eric Schilling	Paris: Michalon, 1997.
1998	*Hedwig and the Angry Inch*	Written and directed by John Cameron Mitchell; music, lyrics, and original score by Stephen Trask	Premiered at the Jane Street Theater on February 14, 1998.
1998	*Le Dernier Jour de Socrate*	Livret de Jean Claude Carrière	Premiered at the l'Opéra Comique in Paris, 1998. Éditions Mario Bois.
1999	*La rêve de Diotime. Scène dramatique*	Pierre Bartholomée	Premiered at the Théâtre de la Monnaie, Brussels, 1999.
2002	*Plato's Retreat. A Play in Two Acts*	Sean O'Connell	Edmonton, Alberta: Phi-Psi Publishers, 2002.
2005	*Socrate dans Walt Disney Studios, ou Le Démon de la Philosophie*	Éric Shilling	Nantes: Éditions Pleins Feux, 2005.
2008	*The Last Days of Socrates*	Steve Hatzai	Premiered in Philadelphia, at the American Philosophical Society's Franklin Hall, August 31, 2008.

Appendix 2
Charting the Socrates Play

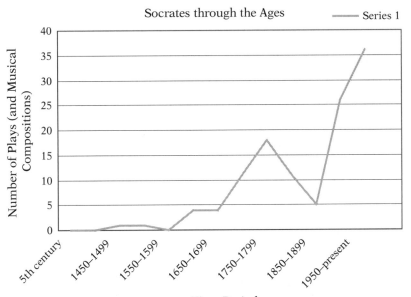

Socrates through the Ages

Series 1

Time Period	Number of Sources
5th century	0
6th century	0
1450–1499	1
1500–1549	1
1550–1599	0
1600–1649	4
1650–1699	4
1700–1749	11
1750–1799	18
1800–1849	11
1850–1899	5
1900–1949	26
1950–present	36

Notes

Chapter 1

1. Diogenes Laertius, "Plato," in *Lives of Eminent Philosophers*, trans. R. D. Hicks (Cambridge: Harvard University Press, 1972), vol. 1, 3:6. I freely admit to having embellished this scene.

2. Plato, of course, was not the only one to write Socratic dialogues. Several former students of Socrates wrote them, including Xenophon, whose dialogues are preserved. Charles Kahn has discussed in detail the fragments of dialogues written by other former students. Charles H. Kahn, *Plato and the Socratic Dialogue* (Cambridge: Cambridge University Press, 1996).

3. Aristotle, *Poetics*, ed. and trans. Stephen Halliwell (Cambridge: Harvard University Press, 1995), 27–141; 1447b, 9–10.

4. Diogenes Laertius, "Plato," 3:6, 3:9, 3:56.

5. Ibid., 3:18.

6. Diogenes Laertius, "Socrates," in *Lives of Eminent Philosophers*, trans. R. D. Hicks (Cambridge: Harvard University Press, 1972), vol. 1, 2:18, 2:33.

7. Claudius Aelianus, *Varia Historia*, trans. Diane Ostrom Johnson (Lewiston: Edwin Mellen Press, 1997), 40.

8. Plato, *Republic: Books VI–X*, trans. Paul Shorey (Cambridge: Harvard University Press, 1935), 514ff. The manipulation of objects that cast shadows is compared by Socrates to *"tois thaumatopoiois,"* which might be translated as "creators of puppet shows."

9. In a brilliant reading, Andrea Wilson Nightingale has reconstructed the history of the term *theoria* as originating in the practice of making a pilgrimage to a festival. She then uses this newly enriched notion of *theoria* for a reading of Plato's cave, in which it calls attention to the upward movement of the freed prisoner in his quest for seeing and insight. Andrea Wilson Nightingale, *Spectacles of Truth in Classical Greek Philosophy:*

Theoria in Its Cultural Context (Cambridge: Cambridge University Press, 2004).

10. This approach is exemplified by F. M. Cornford, who simply eliminated the dialogic element in his translation of *Parmenides*, explaining that the dramatic form was incidental to the philosophical argument. F. M. Cornford, *Plato and Parmenides* (London: Routledge, 1993). Against this reading of Plato's dialogues as thinly disguised treatises, a second school emerged that was determined to read them as dialogues. This second school, on whose findings I build in my attempt to connect Plato to modern drama, reached a first high-water mark in Friedrich Schleiermacher's famous introductions to his translation of Plato. Friedrich Schleiermacher, *Platon, Sämtliche Werke*, ed. Ernesto Grassi, 6 vols. (Hamburg: Rowohlt, 1957); *Schleiermacher's Introductions to the Dialogues of Plato*, trans. William Dobson (Cambridge: J. & J. J. Deighton, 1836).

11. Jonas Barish, *The Antitheatrical Prejudice* (Berkeley: University of California Press, 1981).

12. Even though Plato is usually ignored by theater scholars or misunderstood as a simple enemy of theater from whom nothing can be learned except a "prejudice," there are some exceptions to this rule. Among the studies that have referred to the cave and to Plato more generally are Samuel Weber's *Theatricality as Medium* (New York: Fordham University Press, 2004), which offers a particularly incisive understanding of the scene and of place. Also interested in the scene is Paul A. Kottman, *A Politics of the Scene* (Stanford: Stanford University Press, 2008), which likewise refers back to Plato and seeks to formulate a Platonic notion of mimesis before moving on to Hobbes and Shakespeare, the book's primary focus. Finally, I am looking forward to Freddie Rokem's *Philosophers and Thespians: Thinking Performance*, forthcoming from Stanford University Press, which also takes its point of departure from Plato. The quality of these studies is the best proof of how fruitful it is for theater scholars to engage Plato, and how central Plato is for the study of theater.

13. Many commentators have noted this connection, including Martha Nussbaum, in *The Fragility of Goodness: Luck and Ethics in Greek Tragedy and Philosophy* (Cambridge: Cambridge University Press, 1986), 122–35; I comment on this interpretation in chapter 5. Other incisive commentaries include Andrea Wilson Nightingale, *Genres in Dialogue: Plato and the Construct of Philosophy* (Cambridge: Cambridge University Press, 1995), 60–92.

14. Plato, *Laws: Books VII–XII*, trans. R. G. Bury (Cambridge: Harvard University Press, 1926), 817b.

15. Plato, *Phaedo*, in *Euthyphro, Apology, Crito, Phaedo, Phaedrus*, trans. Harold North Fowler (Cambridge: Harvard University Press, 1914), 193–403, 64a: "Those who pursue philosophy aright study nothing but dying and being dead."

16. Emily Wilson, in her excellent book *Death of Socrates* (Cambridge: Harvard University Press, 2007), has traced the afterlife of Socrates across

different genres and art forms, including painting, the novel, and drama. Indeed, she is one of the very few to have recognized the dramatic tradition engendered by Plato.

17. Diogenes Laertius objects to dividing Plato's dialogues into dramatic and narrative ones because this distinction is relevant to theater but not to philosophy. Diogenes Laertius, "Plato," 3:50.

18. Plato, *Laws: Books I–VI*, 658c-e.

19. For a strong argument associating tragedy with democracy, see Rush Rehm, *Greek Tragic Theatre* (London: Routledge, 1992). Somewhat more cautious is S. Sara Monoson, *Plato's Democratic Entanglements: Athenian Politics and the Practice of Philosophy* (Princeton: Princeton University Press, 2000).

20. Plato, *Phaedo*, 117d.

21. Ibid., 115a.

22. Ibid., 84e, 117e.

23. Ibid., 84d.

24. Ibid., 91a-b.

25. Ibid., 81e, 82e.

26. Some commentators interested in Plato's literary devices have recognized the importance of drama as a connection of abstract arguments to everyday life. Among them is Diskin Clay, *Platonic Questions: Dialogues with the Silent Philosopher* (Philadelphia: University of Pennsylvania Press, 2000), 89. Ruby Blondell, in *The Play of Character in Plato's Dialogues* (Cambridge: Cambridge University Press, 2002), 48ff., argues that drama becomes the form through which Plato explores the limits of transcendence. James A. Arieti, in *Interpreting Plato: The Dialogues as Drama* (Savage, MD: Rowman & Littlefield, 1991), goes furthest in identifying Plato's dialogues as dramas.

27. Plato, *Phaedo*, 58e.

28. Charles Kahn is among those who have recognized Plato's affinity to comedy and his interest in the follies of love and the everyday. Kahn, *Plato and the Socratic Dialogue*, 68ff.

29. Henri Bergson, "Laughter," in *Comedy*, ed. Wylie Sypher (New York: Doubleday, 1956), 61–192.

30. Hans Blumenberg, *Das Lachen der Thrakerin: Eine Urgeschichte der Theorie* (Frankfurt am Main: Suhrkamp, 1987).

31. Plato, *Apology*, 19c.

32. The literary theorist Mikhail Bakhtin took these features of Socrates to turn him into a precursor of the type of protagonist populating the modern novel. M. M. Bakhtin, "Epic and Novel," in *The Dialogic Imagination: Four Essays*, ed. Michael Holquist, trans. Caryl Emerson and Michael Holquist (Austin: University of Texas Press, 1981), 24–25.

33. As I am writing this chapter (the summer of 2007), I have just seen one such performance at the Kitchen, an established off-Broadway venue, where the *Symposium* has received a production by the Target Margin Theater under the direction of David Herskovits; even the *New York Times* deigned to give it a relatively positive review. Charles Isherwood,

"Checking In with Glimmer Twins, Plato and Aristotle," *New York Times*, June 18, 2007.

34. Freddie Rokem, in a wonderful article on the *Symposium*, which it was my pleasure to publish in *Theatre Survey* while serving as editor of that journal, emphasizes the competition between Socrates and the two playwrights. Freddie Rokem, "The Philosopher and the Two Playwrights: Socrates, Agathon, and Aristophanes in Plato's *Symposium*," *Theatre Survey* 49:2 (November 2008): 239–52.

35. Plato, *Symposium*, in *Lysis, Symposium, Gorgias*, trans. W. R. M. Lamb (Cambridge: Harvard University Press, 1925), 73–245, 174a.

36. Ibid., 219b-c. Pièrre Hadot discusses how Alcibiades, in talking about Socrates instead of Eros, as the other guests had done, places Socrates in the position of Eros. Pièrre Hadot, *Philosophy as a Way of Life: Spiritual Exercises from Socrates to Foucault*, ed. Arnold I. Davidson, trans. Michael Case (Oxford: Blackwell, 1995), 160.

37. Plato, *Gorgias*, 481d, 482a-b. A similar superimposition of erotic love, friendship, and love of wisdom occurs in *Lysis*, in which a discussion of friendship, though it does not reach a conclusion, is related to philosophy (213d). More important, the discussion of friendship at the end of the dialogue results, if not in a hard-and-fast definition of friendship, in friendship itself. Socrates says that he now counts himself a friend of the much younger interlocutors (223b). Once more, the dramatic interaction among characters triumphs: the scene has produced friendship.

38. Plato, *Symposium*, 215b. Among commentators who have seen the Socratic dialogues as aligned to the satyr play is Sarah Kofman, *Socrates: Fictions of a Philosopher*, trans. Catherine Porter (Ithaca: Cornell University Press, 1998), 28.

39. Plato, *Philebus*, in *The Statesman, Philebus, Ion*, trans. Harold N. Fowler (Cambridge: Harvard University Press, 1925), 48a.

40. Ibid., 50a.

41. Mixing tragic and comic elements was also the specialty of Euripides, a reason, no doubt, why Diogenes speculated that Euripides collaborated with Socrates and Plato.

42. For a discussion of these modes, see especially Nightingale, *Genres in Dialogue*; Kathy Eden, *Friends Hold All Things in Common: Tradition, Intellectual Property, and the* Adages *of Erasmus* (New Haven: Yale University Press, 2001).

43. Bakhtin, *Dialogic Imagination*, 24–25.

44. Diogenes Laertius, "Plato," 3:48.

45. Ibid., 3:37; 52.

46. Throughout this book, I consider Socrates as a character, not as a portrait of a historical personage. In making this choice, I side with those, such as Charles Kahn in *Plato and the Socratic Dialogue*, who consider Plato's entire oeuvre, with the possible exception of the *Apology*, as part of Plato's vision of Socrates.

47. Diogenes Laertius, "Plato," 3:48; translation modified by me.

48. Diogenes Laertius reports that Plato read aloud *Phaedo* and that everyone in the audience left except for Aristotle. Diogenes Laertius, "Plato," 3:37.

49. Plato, of course, did not respond to Aristotle, who wrote after him. But he and Aristotle were both responding to those features of tragedy and comedy that characterized contemporary theater in Athens, and which Aristotle then theorized.

50. Aristotle, *Poetics*, 1454b8–9.

51. Presenting Socrates as a figure whose life is as unique as his philosophy also explains the fascination throughout the classical world with Socrates' life and death, and hence with philosophical death and suicide more generally. Recently, Simon Critchley has written a short history of philosophy in the form of miniportraits of philosophers, with an emphasis on their attitude toward death as well as their actual mode of dying. Simon Critchley, *The Book of Dead Philosophers* (New York: Vintage, 2008).

52. Hadot, in *Philosophy as a Way of Life*, has argued forcefully for the classical conception of philosophy as a way of life.

53. Among those who have analyzed this phenomenon is Alexander Nehamas, *The Art of Living: Socratic Reflections from Plato to Aristotle* (Berkeley: University of California Press, 2000).

54. Plato, *The Statesman*, in *The Statesman, Philebus, Ion*, trans. Harold N. Fowler (Cambridge: Harvard University Press, 1925), 257c.

55. Plato, *Republic: Books I–V*, trans. Paul Shorey (Cambridge: Harvard University Press 1930), 358c.

56. In the *Oeconomicus*, Xenophon uses Socrates to present some of his own ideas and in the process presents Socrates as a dogmatic, opinionated philosopher. This is in contrast to the early Platonic dialogues, in which Socrates professes to know nothing.

57. Walter Ong argues that Aristotle's conception of a tightly constructed plot is itself a product of a literary culture, while the looser structure of epic poetry is a result of an oral one. Greek drama, in this argument, is the first "literary" genre in that sense, i.e., a genre that has incorporated the new values of literacy. When seen from this perspective, Plato's even more "literary" plays merely push an already literary drama to its ultimate conclusion. Walter J. Ong, *Orality and Literacy: The Technologization of the Word* (London: Methuen, 1982), 142ff.

58. Aristotle, *Poetics*, 1452a15–35.

59. Ibid., 1449b25–30.

60. Ibid., 1450b15–20, 1453b1–13.

61. Plato, *Laws: Books I–VI*, 701a.

62. Gilbert Ryle even argues that certain dialogues, especially *Phaedo* and *Symposium*, were performed as part of competitions similar to those of other forms of drama. Gilbert Ryle, *Plato's Progress* (Cambridge: Cambridge University Press, 1966), ch. 2.

63. Plato, *Theaetetus*, in *Theaetetus, Sophist*, trans. Harold North Fowler (Cambridge: Harvard University Press, 1921), 1–257, 143b-c.

64. Plato, *Republic: Books I–V*, 393a–d.

65. An example of this fear of interruption and a premature end is to be found in Plato, *Protagoras*, in *Laches, Protagoras, Meno, Euthydemus*, trans. W. R. M. Lamb (Cambridge: Harvard University Press, 1924), 85–257, 333c.

66. Plato, *Republic: Books I–V*, 327a and following.

67. Plato, *Lysis*, in *Lysis, Symposium, Gorgias*, trans. W. R. M. Lamb (Cambridge: Harvard University Press, 1925), 223a.

68. Plato, *Greater Hippias*, in *Cratylus, Parmenides, Greater Hippias, Lesser Hippias*, trans. H. N. Howler (Cambridge: Harvard University Press, 1926), 333–423, 295b.

69. Kenneth M. Sayre emphasizes that the primary audience of Plato's dialogues was the Academy and pays attention to their interest in audience and reception. Kenneth M. Sayre, *Plato's Literary Garden: How to Read a Platonic Dialogue* (Notre Dame: University of Notre Dame, 1995).

70. Eric A. Havelock, *Preface to Plato* (Cambridge: Harvard University Press, 1963); Eric A. Havelock, *The Muse Learns to Write: Reflections on Orality and Literacy from Antiquity to the Present* (New Haven: Yale University Press, 1986).

71. Ong, *Orality*, 80. Ong draws on Havelock, *Preface to Plato*. The over-determined question of writing and orality also explains why Plato's dialogues would spend so much time discussing the transmission and circulation of speech and writing. Whenever the drama is not presented directly but reported by a speaker, there is much ado about how precisely he has learned about a particular conversation. Had he been present? How does he remember? And if he had not been present himself, how did he learn about it through a third party? The justification, in the *Theaetetus*, that the written account had been double-checked repeatedly with Socrates himself is perhaps the most elaborate but by no means the only moment when the preservation, transmission, and circulation of what was once a live conversation becomes a topic a great concern in the play itself.

72. This argument also has implications for the admittedly vexed relation of Plato to Athenian democracy. As Sara Monoson' has shown in *Plato's Democratic Entanglements*, the widespread image of Plato as the simple enemy of democracy is wrong. My reading of the performance dimension of Plato's dialogues contributes to this argument. Plato rejected the pseudoparticipatory "rule of the audience" in large theaters and preferred the much more active participation of participant observers, bringing him closer to radical democrats such as Brecht than to the theatrical aesthetics of fascism, which is precisely geared toward passive mass audiences.

73. Socrates deals with Heracleitus most explicitly when it comes to the relativism of words, in the *Cratylus*, 402a; 411b–c. In the latter passage, Socrates observes wittily: "The present philosophers . . . get dizzy as they turn round and round in their search for the nature of things, and then the things seem to them to turn round and round and be in motion."

74. Ludwig Wittgenstein, *Bemerkungen über die Grundlagen der Mathematik*, ed. G. E. M. Ascombe, Rush Rhees, and G. H. von Wright (Frankfurt am Main: Suhrkamp, 1989).

Chapter 2

1. Marsilio Ficino, *Commentary on Plato's* Symposium *on Love*, trans. Sears Jayne (Dallas: Spring Publications, 1985).

2. The discrepancy in the date, 1468 in Ficino's *De Amore* and 1474 in Mussini's title, can be traced back to Ficino himself, who uses different dates in different texts.

3. Alfred North Whitehead, *Process and Reality* (New York: Macmillan, 2009), 39.

4. One of the few exceptions is the wonderful reception history of Socrates by Emily Wilson, *The Death of Socrates* (Cambridge: Harvard University Press, 2007), which discusses a number of dramatic adaptations, in addition to paintings and other representations of the dying Socrates.

5. Amyas Bushe, *Socrates: A Dramatic Poem* (London: R. and J. Dodsley, 1758), 6.

6. Ibid., vi.

7. Henry Montague Grover, *Socrates: A Dramatic Poem* (London: Longman, Rees, Orme, Brown, and Green, 1828), ix.

8. Ibid., viii.

9. Ibid., 162.

10. Jean-Marie Collot, *Le Procès de Socrate, ou le régime des anciens temps: Comédie en trois actes et en prose* (Paris: Chez la veuve Duchesne & Fils, 1791), v. Collot's name originally was Collot d'Herbois; he opportunistically dropped the aristocratic title at the outset of the revolution.

11. Antonio Rocco, *L'Alcibiade fanciullo a scola* (manuscript dates from 1630; published anonymously in 1651).

12. Marquis de Sade, *La philosophie dans le boudoir: Les institutuers immoraux* (Paris: Christian Bourgois Éditeur, 1972), 267. Also see Martin Puchner, "Sade's Theatrical Passions," *Yale Journal of Criticism* 18, 1 (Spring 2005): 111–25.

13. Diogenes Laertius, "Socrates," in *Lives of Eminent Philosophers*, trans. R. D. Hicks (Cambridge: Harvard University Press, 1972), vol. 1, 2:26.

14. *The Banquet*, trans. Percy Bysshe Shelley, prefaced by *Discourse on the Manners of the Ancient Greeks Relative to the Subject of Love*. Manuscript in the Bodleian Library; partial publication by Mary Shelley in 1840, first full publication in privately printed edition of 100 by Sir John C. E. Shelley-Rolls in 1931. *Bodleian Record* 2 (1946): 144–45; James A. Notopoulos, *The Platonism of Shelley: A Study of Platonism and the Poetic Mind* (New York: Octagon Books, 1969), 388.

15. Joseph Pieper, *Kümmert euch nicht um Sokrates: Drei Fernsehspiele* (Munich: Kösel-Verlag, 1966).

16. "Origin of Love," in *Hedwig and the Angry Inch*, written and directed by John Cameron Mitchell, music, lyrics, and original score by Stephen Trask. Premiered at the Jane Street Theater on February 14, 1998.

17. Maxwell Anderson, *Barefoot in Athens* (New York: William Sloane Associates, 1951). The play premiered at the Martin Beck Theater, for a two-month run, in 1951. Adaptation to TV film in George Schaefer's *Showcase Theatre* series, broadcast on November 11, 1966; Peter Ustinov won an Emmy for his performance as Socrates; also starring Christopher Walken as Lamprocles.

18. Karl Popper, *The Open Society and Its Enemies* (London: Routledge, 1945).

19. Manès Sperber, *Sokrates: Roman, Drama, Essay* (Zürich: Europa Verlag, 1988). Manuscript dates from 1953.

20. Plato, *Republic: Book I–V*, trans. Paul Shorey (Cambridge: Harvard University Press, 1930), 607b.

21. Michael Steveni, "The Root of Art Education: Literary Sources," *Journal of Aesthetic Education* 15, 1 (January 1981): 83–92.

22. George Stubbes, *A Dialogue on Beauty in the Manner of Plato* (London: W. Wilkins, 1731), iii.

23. Plato, *Phaedo*, in *Euthyphro, Apology, Crito, Phaedo, Phaedrus*, trans. Harold North Fowler (Cambridge: Harvard University Press, 1914), 60d.

24. Francis Foster Barham, *Socrates: A Tragedy in Five Acts* (London: William Edward Painter, 1842), 71.

25. Plato, *Phaedrus*, in *Euthyphro, Apology, Crito, Phaedo, Phaedrus*, trans. Harold North Fowler (Cambridge: Harvard University Press, 1914), 244a-b.

26. Martha C. Nussbaum is among the commentators who have called attention to this scene and thus to the interaction between setting and philosophy. Martha C. Nussbaum, *The Fragility of Goodness: Luck and Ethics in Greek Tragedy and Philosophy* (Cambridge: Cambridge University Press, 1986), 200ff.

27. Erik Satie, *Socrate: drama symphonique en 3 parties avec voix* (Paris: M. Eschig, 1988); originally published in 1918. Later transcribed for two pianos by John Cage, to which Merce Cunningham created choreography, naming the piece *Idyllic Song*. Erik Satie, *Socrate: drama symphonique en 3 parties, arrangé pour 2 pianos par John Cage* (Paris: M. Eschig, 1984).

28. Plato, *Epistle VII*, in *Timaeus, Critias, Cleitophon, Menexenus, Epistles*, trans. R. G. Bury (Cambridge: Harvard University Press, 1929), 332d.

29. More recently, the political philosopher Leo Strauss was a powerful advocate of this reading for Plato's hidden meaning, and like Socrates, he seems to have inspired some more antidemocratic politicians such as Paul Wolfowitz and William Kristol. But, as every teacher knows, and as Socrates argued in the *Apology*, it seems unfair to be held respon-

sible for the follies of one's students. See, for example, Leo Strauss, *Socrates and Aristophanes* (New York: Basic Books, 1966); Leo Strauss, *Studies in Platonic Political Philosophy* (Chicago: University of Chicago Press, 1983).

30. Biographical sketch based on Malcolm Cook, "Bernardin de Saint-Pierre," in *Dictionary of Literary Biography*, vol. 313: *Writers of the French Enlightenment I*, ed. Samia I. Specer (Detroit: Gale, 2005), 52–59.

31. Plato, *Phaedo*, 59b; Plato, *Apology* in *Euthyphro, Apology, Crito, Phaedo, Phaedrus*, trans. Harold North Fowler (Cambridge: Harvard University Press, 1914), 34a, 38b.

32. Jacques-Henri Bernardin de Saint-Pierre, *La Mort de Socrate*, in *Oeuvres Complètes*, ed. L. Aimé-Martin (Paris: Chez Méquignon-Marvis, 1818 [orig. pub. 1808]), 12:242.

33. Lionel Abel, *Tragedy and Metatheatre: Essays on Dramatic Form* (New York: Holmes & Meier, 2003).

34. Howard Brenton, *Bloody Poetry* (London: Samuel French, 1985), 41ff.

35. Alexander Goehr, *Shadowplay: Music Theatre for Actor, Tenor, and Five Instruments*, op. 30 (Mainz: Schott, 1970).

36. This dramatic approach dovetails with the understanding of classical philosophy reconstructed by the French classicist Pièrre Hadot as a question not of doctrine but of the conduct of one's life. Pièrre Hadot, *Philosophy as a Way of Life: Spiritual Exercises from Socrates to Foucault*, ed. Arnold I. Davidson, trans. Michael Case (Oxford: Blackwell, 1995), 160. A similar train of thought was developed by Michel Foucault in his last lectures at the Collège de France, with particular attention to Socrates. Michel Foucault, *The Hermeneutics of the Subject: Lectures at the Collège de France 1981–1982*, ed. Frédéric Gros, trans. Graham Burchell (New York: Picador, 2005); Michel Foucault, *Le Gouvernement de Soi et des Autres: Cours au Collège de France, 1982–1983*, ed. Frédéric Gros under the direction of François Ewald and Alessandro Fontana (Paris: Gallimard, 2008); Michel Foucault, *Le Courage de la Vérité: Le Gouvernement de Soi et des Autres II: Cours au Collège de France, 1984*, ed. Frédéric Gros under the direction of François Ewald and Alessandro Fontana (Paris: Gallimard, 2009).

37. François Charpentier, "The Life of Socrates," in *The Memorable Things of Socrates. Written by Xenophon. In Five Books. Translated into English. The Second Edition. To which are prefix'd the Life of Socrates, from the French of Monsieur Charpentier, A Member of the French Academy. And the Life of Xenophon, collected from several Authors; with some Account of the Writings. Also complete Tables are added*. By Edward Bysshe, Gent. (London: J. Batley, 1722 [first printing, 1711; orig. French pub. 1640]), 47.

38. Those plays centered on Alcibiades include *Alcibiade: comédie en trois actes* (1731) by Philippe Poisson; *Alcibiades* (1781) by August Gottlieb Meissner, a sketch of a play based on the relation between Alcibiades and

Socrates by the most important eighteenth-century German playwright and theorist, Gotthold Ephraim Lessing; *Alcibiades Delivered* (1920) by the influential Expressionist playwright Georg Kaiser; and Nikos Toutoun-tayakes' *Alkivides: theatro* (1964).

39. Plutarch writes: "It is said, and with good reason, that the favour and affection which Socrates showed him [Alcibiades] contributed not a little to his reputation." Plutarch, *Lives: Alcibiades and Coriolanus, Lysander and Sulla*, trans. Bernadotte Perrin (Cambridge: Loeb Classics Library, 1916), 2.

40. Thomas Otway, *Alcibiades: A tragedy, acted at the Theatre Royal, by Their Majesties' servants* (London: R. Bentley and S. Magnes, 1687).

41. Plato, *Symposium*, in *Lysis, Symposium, Gorgias*, trans. W. R. M. Lamb (Cambridge: Harvard University Press, 1925), 220d-e.

42. Prominent among those who painted the death of Socrates are Charles-Alphonse Dufresnoy (1650), François Boucher (1762), François-Louis-Joseph Watteau (1789), Giambettino Cignaroli (1706–70), and Christoffer Wilhelm Eckersberg (1783–1853).

43. John Gilbert Cooper, *The Life of Socrates, Collected from the Memorabilia of Xenophon and the Dialogues of Plato* (London: R. Dodsley, 1749), 55.

44. George Adams, *The Heathen Martyr: or, the Death of Socrates, An Historical Tragedy* (London: Author, 1746).

45. The attack came from George Colman. This and the biographical information on Adams is based on Anna Chahoud, "Adams, George (b. 1697/8)," *Oxford Dictionary of National Biography* (Oxford: Oxford University Press, 2004), http://www.oxforddnb.com/fiew.article/115, accessed October 17, 2006.

46. Adams, *Heathen Martyr*, 34; 32.

47. Ibid., 37.

48. Ibid., 39.

49. Ibid., 40.

50. Ibid., 51.

51. Andrew Becket, *Socrates; A dramatic poem written on the model of the ancient Greek tragedy. New edition with (now first printed) an advertisement, containing an apology for the author and the work* (London: Longman, Hurst, Rees, Orme, & Brown, 1811 [orig. pub. 1806]).

52. Information based on "Andrew Becket," http://198.82.142.160/spenser/AuthorRecord.php?&method=GET&recordid=33227, accessed May 27, 2007.

53. Becket writes: "I know not of any Drama on the Death of Socrates," and adds in a footnote, "This is the more extraordinary, as his life was glorious, (if glory consist in virtue) and his death the same,—if fortitude,—I had almost said *Christian* fortitude—can render it so" (Becket, *Socrates*, v).

54. Ibid., 45.

55. Ibid., iv.

56. Ibid., iii.

57. Louis Billardon de Sauvigny, *La Mort de Socrate: Tragédie en trois actes, et en vers. Représentée pour la premiere fois sur le Théâtre François, au mois de Mai 1763* (Paris: Prault le jeune, 1763), iv.

58. V.A., *Socrate* (Florence: Luigi Carlieri, 1796), v, iii.

59. Ibid., v.

60. The original edition is listed as Voltaire and James Thomson, *Socrate, ouvrage dramatique, traduit de l'anglais de feu Mr. Tompson* (Amsterdam: n.p., 1759). The preface claims that the first edition was printed in 1755, but in all likelihood the 1759 edition is the first. Even though this title does not identify the work as a tragedy, Voltaire does so in his preface.

61. As George Steiner put it, "The problem of tragedy is shaped by the divided heritage of the classic and Elizabethan past." George Steiner, *The Death of Tragedy* (New York: Knopf, 1961), 33.

62. Voltaire, "Dix-Huitième Lettres sur la Tragedie," in *Lettres écrites de Londres sur les Anglois et autres sujects* (Basel: W. Bowyer, 1734), 158. I follow the first English translation: *Letters Concerning the English Nation* (London: T. Pridden, 1776), 140–41.

63. Quotations from the preface are translated by me based on the original text as it appears in Rose May Davis, "Thomson and Voltaire's *Socrate*," *PMLA* 49, 2 (June 1934): 560–65.

64. Voltaire, *Socrates: A Tragedy of Three Acts* (London: R. and J. Dodsley), A2.

65. The second play worth mentioning is *Midsummer Night's Dream* (1594). While it does not contain a philosopher, it has incorporated Renaissance Platonism. But by and large, Shakespeare did not think of drama as the primary vehicle for his Platonist philosophy, for which he reserved his other great passion instead: the sonnet.

66. Samuel Johnson, *Johnson's Life of Addison* (London: George Bell & Sons, 1893), 56.

67. Joseph Addison, *Cato, a Tragedy. As it is acted at the Theatre-Royal in Drury Lane by Her Majesty's servants* (London: J. Tonson, 1713), 31.

68. Voltaire, *Lettres*, 91; 92.

69. Jean-Jacques Rousseau, "Parallèle de Socrate et de Caton," in *Jean-Jacques entre Socrate et Caton*, ed. Claude Pichois and René Pintard (Paris: Corti, 1972).

70. This, in any case, is what is claimed by Thomas Tickell in his preface to *The Miscellaneous Works, in verse and prose, of the late right Honourable Joseph Addison. With some account of the life and writings of the author* (London: J. and R. Tonson, 1726), xx; cited in M. M. Kelsall, "The Meaning of Addison's Cato," *Review of English Studies* 17 (1966): 152. Tickell reminds readers that even though such a topic might seem "unpromising," Addison attacks the "intrigues and adventures, to which the romantic taste has confined modern Tragedy," and, after the example of his predecessors in Greece, would have employed the drama "to wear out of our minds everything that is mean, or little; to cherish and cultivate that humanity

which is the ornament of our nature; to soften insolence, to soothe afflic-
tion, and to subdue our minds to the dispensations of Providence."

71. Fredric M. Litto, "Addison's Cato in the Colonies," *William and
Mary Quarterly* 23 (1966): 440, 447.

72. *The Poetic Writings of Thomas Cradock, 1718-1770*, ed. David Curtis
Skaggs (Newark: University of Delaware Press, 1983), 52.

73. Ibid., 74.

74. Thomas Cradock, *The Death of Socrates*, in *Poetic Writings*, 201–75,
quote from 212 n. 7. The text is based on the manuscript.

75. Information based on entry on Francis Foster Barham in *Oxford
Dictionary of National Biography*, http://www.oxforddnb.com.monstera.
cc.columbia.edu:2048/view/article/1373, accessed April 23, 2009.

76. Barham, *Socrates*, iv.

77. Ibid., iii.

78. Ibid., iv.

79. D. A. F. Sade, *Oeuvres Complètes* (Paris: Jean-Jacques Pauvert,
1970), 32:26.

80. Robert Walter, *Die Grosse Hebammenkunst: Komödie in drei Akten*,
in *Robert Walters Ausgewähltes Werk, Komödien* (Hannover: Adolf Spon-
holz Verlag, 1947 [orig. pub. 1927]), 295–377.

81. Charles Wharton Stork, *Alcibiades: A Play of Athens in the Great Age*
(Syracuse: Syracuse University Press, 1967), 65.

82. Lister Sinclair, *Socrates: A Drama in Three Acts* (Agincourt: Book
Society of Canada, 1957), 7.

83. Ibid., 25.

84. The late nineteenth-century writer Théodore de Banville, a theorist
of the group of poets known as the Parnassians, had even written a play
about Aristophanes, yet his own Socrates comedy, *Socrates and His Wife*
(1885), does not mention Aristophanes at all. Théodore de Banville, *Socrate et sa femme. Comédie en un acte*, 3rd ed. (Paris: Calmann Lévy, 1886
[orig. pub. 1885]).

85. Philippe Poisson, *Alcibiade: Comédie en trois actes et en vers* (Paris:
Le Breton, 1731).

86. Philippe Poisson, *Alcibiade: Comédie en trois actes et en vers*, in
Chef-d'oeuvres de Philippe Poisson (Paris: Petite Bibliothèque des Théâtres,
1784), 12.

87. Louis-Sébastien Mercier, *La maison de Socrate le sage: comédie en
cinq actes, en prose* (Paris: Duminil-Lesueur, 1809), 25.

88. Banville, *Socrate et sa femme*.

89. Ibid., 23.

90. Georg Philipp Telemann, *Der Geduldige Sokrates* (Hamburg, 1721).
Recording by the vocal soloists of the Summer Music festival in Hitzacker,
1965, South-West German Chamber Orchestra, Günter Weissenborn,
conductor.

91. Giovanni Paisiello, *Socrate immaginario*, libretto by F. Galiani and
G. B. Lorenzi, premiered in Naples, Teatro Nuovo, 1775; CD release,
edited by De Stefano, Bongiovanni, 2001.

92. Biographical details derived from "Collot d'Herbois, Jean-Marie," *Encyclopaedia Britannica*, http://search.eb.com/eb/article-9024794, accessed April 23, 2009.

Chapter 3

1. See Lionel Abel, *Tragedy and Metatheatre: Essays on Dramatic Form* (New York: Holmes & Meier, 2003).

2. Elinor Fuchs, "Clown Shows: Anti-Theatricalist Theatricalism in Four Twentieth-Century Plays," in *Against Theatre: Creative Destructions on the Modernist Stage*, ed. Alan Ackerman and Martin Puchner (New York: Palgrave, 2006).

3. One notable exception is a recent, excellent book by Toril Moi on Henrik Ibsen, often seen as the founder of modern drama. Moi describes Ibsen's modernism, and modernism more generally, as a battle against idealism. Idealism thus enters the picture, but only negatively as a foil. Toril Moi, *Henrik Ibsen and the Birth of Modernism: Art, Theater, Philosophy* (Oxford: Oxford University Press, 2006). See also Martin Puchner, "Staging Death," *London Review of Books* 29, 3 (February 2007). Otherwise, only scattered remarks by critics of modern drama have approached the centrality of ideas. An example is Robert Brustein's *Theatre of Revolt*, in which Brustein recognizes the conflict between "idea and action" to be a central dynamic of modern drama, without honing in on this problem as such. Robert Brustein, *Theatre of Revolt: Studies in Modern Drama from Ibsen to Genet* (Chicago: Ivan R. Dee, 1991), 14.

4. I. A. Richards, *Why So, Socrates? A Dramatic Version of Plato's Dialogues Euthyphro Apology Crito Phaedo* (Cambridge: Cambridge University Press, 1964).

5. Manès Sperber, *Sokrates: Roman, Drama, Essay* (Zürich: Europa Verlag, 1988). Manuscript dates from 1953.

6. Jonathan Miller, director, *The Drinking Party*, BBC, 1965; David Herskovits, director, *The Dinner Party*, created by the company, adapted from Plato's *Symposium*, Target Margin Theater, 2007.

7. August Strindberg, *Det sjunkande Hellas* (1870). Date established by Gunnar Ollén, *Strindbergs Dramatik* (Stockholm: Egnellska Boktryckeriet, 1961), 522.

8. August Strindberg, *Hellas (Socrates)*, trans. Arvid Paulson, in *World Historical Plays by August Strindberg*, The Library of Scandinavian Literature, Erik J. Friis, gen. ed. (New York: Twayne Publishers, 1970), 6:166–232.

9. August Strindberg, *Historical Miniatures*, trans. Claud Field (London: George Allen, 1913 [orig. pub. 1905]).

10. Strindberg, *Hellas*, 172.

11. Ibid., 184.

12. Ibid., 223.

13. Ibid., 175.

14. For an incisive reading of Nietzsche's influence on modern drama, including Strindberg, see David Kornhaber's 2009 Columbia dissertation.

15. Georg Kaiser, *Der Gerettete Alkibiades: Stück in Drei Teilen* (Potsdam: Gustav Kiepenheuer Verlag, 1920).

16. Ibid., 37.

17. Georg Kaiser, "Das Drama Platons," in *Werke*, ed. Walther Huder (Frankfurt: Propyläen Verlag, 1971), 4:544–45.

18. Ibid., 545.

19. Georg Kaiser, "Der Kopf ist stärker als das Blut: Ein Gespräch zwischen Georg Kaiser und Hermann Kasack," *Der Monat* 41 (February 1952): 527–29.

20. Ibid., 527, 528.

21. Ibid.

22. Ibid., 529.

23. Bertolt Brecht, "Der verwundete Sokrates," in *Gesammelte Werke II, Prosa I* (Frankfurt am Main: Suhrkamp Verlag, 1967), 286–303.

24. Oscar Wilde, "The Portrait of Mr. W. H.," in *The Artist as Critic: Critical Writings of Oscar Wilde*, ed. Richard Ellmann (Chicago: University of Chicago Press, 1982), 183–84.

25. The pedagogical and homosexual Platonism at Oxford has been very well documented and discussed by Linda Dowling in *Hellenism and Homosexuality in Victorian Oxford* (Ithaca: Cornell University Press, 1994).

26. *The Complete Letters of Oscar Wilde*, ed. Merlin Holland and Rupert Hart-Davis (New York, Henry Holt, 2000), 702.

27. Quoted in Dowling, *Hellenism*, 1.

28. Michel Foucault, *Le Courage de la Vérité: Le Gouvernement de Soi et des Autres II: Cours au Collège de France, 1984*, ed. Frédéric Gros under the direction of François Ewald and Alessandro Fontana (Paris: Gallimard, 2009); Michel Foucault, *Le Gouvernement de Soi et des Autres: Cours au Collège de France, 1982–1983*, ed. Frédéric Gros under the direction of François Ewald and Alessandro Fontana (Paris: Gallimard, 2008).

29. For the relation between realism and reform, see Amanda Claybaugh, *The Novel of Purpose: Literature and Social Reform in the Anglo-American World* (Ithaca: Cornell University Press, 2007).

30. Walter Pater, *Plato and Platonism* (New York: Barnes & Noble Books, 2005), 51.

31. Oscar Wilde, "The Decay of Lying," in *The Artist as Critic: Critical Writings of Oscar Wilde*, ed. Richard Ellmann (Chicago: University of Chicago Press, 1982), 301.

32. Judith Butler, *Gender Trouble* (New York: Routledge, 1990).

33. Oscar Wilde, "The Critic as Artist," in *The Artist as Critic: Critical Writings of Oscar Wilde*, ed. Richard Ellmann (Chicago: University of Chicago Press, 1982), 391.

34. Oscar Wilde, *The Portrait of Dorian Gray*, in *Complete Works of Oscar Wilde* (London: Collins, 1989), 41.

35. Quoted in Ellmann, *Oscar Wilde*, 46.

36. Oscar Wilde, "The Soul of Man Under Socialism," in *The Artist as Critic: Critical Writings of Oscar Wilde*, ed. Richard Ellmann (Chicago: University of Chicago Press, 1982), 255–89.

37. Wilde, *The Picture of Dorian Gray*, 74–75.

38. See Ellmann, *Oscar Wilde*, 369.

39. Quoted in ibid., 421 n. 21.

40. Oscar Wilde, *The Importance of Being Earnest*, in *Complete Works of Oscar Wilde* (1998), 321–84, 325.

41. *Salomé*, with Al Pacino, Kevin Anderson, and Jessica Chastain, at the Wadsworth Theatre, Los Angeles, April 14 to May 14, 2006.

42. Alfred Douglas, "Salomé: A Critical Review," *The Spirit Lamp: An Aesthetic, Literary and Critical Magazine* 4, 1 (May 1893): 26. I would like

to thank Sharon Marcus for drawing my attention to this review, and for many illuminating discussions about Wilde.

43. Oscar Wilde, *Salomé: A Tragedy in One Act: Translated from the French of Oscar Wilde*, in *The Complete Works of Oscar Wilde* (New York: Doubleday, 1923), 9:105–6.

44. Ibid., 9:128–29.

45. Ibid., 9:119.

46. Ibid., 9:136. The French original is even clearer about the gesture of refusal implicit in this tautology: "Non. La lune ressemble à la lune, c'est tout" (9:33).

47. Ibid., 9:163.

48. Ibid., 9:183.

49. Song of Solomon, 4:2–3, in *The Holy Bible*, New Revised Standard Version (Oxford: Oxford University Press, 1989), 693.

50. Gilbert Keith Chesterton, *George Bernard Shaw* (New York: J. Lane, 1909), 201.

51. Ibid., 242.

52. Eric Bentley, *The Playwright as Thinker: A Study of Drama in Modern Times* (New York: Harcourt, Brace, Jovanovich, 1987), 76.

53. George Bernard Shaw, *Back to Methuselah: A Metabiological Pentateuch*, rev. ed. (Oxford: Oxford University Press, 1947).

54. Michael Frayn, *Copenhagen* (London: Methuen, 1998).

55. George Bernard Shaw, *Man and Superman*, in *Plays by George Bernard Shaw* (New York: Signet, 1960), 243.

56. Quoted in Eric Bentley, *Bernard Shaw* (Norfolk, Conn.: New Directions, 1947), 188–89.

57. George Bernard Shaw, *Bernard Shaw:* Man and Superman *and* Saint Joan: *A Casebook*, ed. A. M. Gibbs (London: Macmillan, 1992), 25, 26.

58. George Bernard Shaw, *Pygmalion* (New York: Dover, 1994).

59. *Times* letter by Shaw, Shaw Collection, British Library, box 20.

60. Shaw, *Man and Superman*, 333.

61. Ibid., 334.

62. *Shaw's Music*, ed. Dan H. Laurence (London: Max Reinhardt, 1981), 1:57.

63. Shaw, *Man and Superman*, 340.

64. Ibid., 338.

65. *Times* letter by Shaw, Shaw Collection, British Library, box 20.

66. George Bernard Shaw, *Shakes versus Shav*, in *George Bernard Shaw: Last Plays*, ed. Dan H. Laurence (London: Penguin, 1974), 183–90.

67. Laurence Housman, *The Death of Socrates: A Dramatic Scene, Founded upon Two of Plato's Dialogues, the "Crito" and the "Phaedo"; Adapted for the Stage* (London: Sidgwick & Jackson, 1925).

68. Ibid., vi.

69. Abel, *Tragedy and Metatheatre*.

70. Luigi Pirandello, *On Humor*, trans. Antonio Illiano and Daniel P. Testa (Chapel Hill: University of North Carolina Press, 1974), 24.

71. Adriano Tilgher, *Relativisti Contemporanei* (Rome: Libreria di Scienze e Lettere, 1921).

72. Pirandello, *On Humor*, 137; also see the commentary on this passage in Mary Ann Frese Witt, *The Search for Modern Tragedy: Aesthetic Fascism in Italy and France* (Ithaca: Cornell University Press, 2001), 95.

73. Tilgher, *Relativisti*, 66. Also see the incisive commentary on this connection in Witt, *The Search*, 96ff.

74. Cited in Gaspare Giudice, *Luigi Pirandello: A Biography*, trans. Alastair Hamilton (London: Oxford University Press, 1975), 145–46.

75. In the preface to the new edition of his work, Abel writes: "I see tragedy as dealing with the real world and metatheatre as dealing with the world of the imagination" (Abel, *Tragedy and Metatheatre*, v).

76. Elinor Fuchs, "Clown Shows: Anti-Theatricalist Theatricalism in Four Twentieth-Century Plays," in *Against Theatre: Creative Destructions on the Modernist Stage*, ed. Alan Ackerman and Martin Puchner (New York: Palgrave, 2006), 39–57.

77. Ibid., 28.

78. Among the very few commentators to have connected Brecht to Plato is William E. Gruber in "'Non-Aristotelian' Theater: Brecht's and Plato's Theories of Artistic Imitation," *Comparative Drama* 21, 3 (Fall 1986): 199–213. In *Stage Fright: Modernism, Anti-Theatricality and Drama* (Baltimore: Johns Hopkins University Press, 2002) I also developed a Platonist reading of Brecht.

79. Walter Benjamin, *Versuche über Brecht*, ed. Rolf Tiedemann (Frankfurt am Main: Suhrkamp, 1971), 34.

80. Bertolt Brecht, "Der Messingkauf," in *Gesammelte Werke* (Frankfurt am Main: Suhrkamp, 1967), 16:499–657.

81. Ibid., 511.

82. Ibid., 512.

83. Ibid., 640.

84. Ibid., 541ff.

85. The philosopher says that reality "muß . . . durchschaut werden." Ibid., 520.

86. Ibid., 531.

87. Ibid., 526.

88. First introduction of the term in ibid., 508; it is elaborated in 638ff.

89. Ibid., 560.

90. Ibid., 649.

91. Information based on John J. White, *Brecht's Dramatic Theory* (Rochester, N.Y.: Camden House, 2004), 248. White is one of the few commentators on Brecht to include the *Messingkauf* dialogues in his discussion of Brecht's dramatic theory.

92. Brecht, *Messingkauf*, 644.

93. For an incisive commentary on "crude thinking," see Fredric Jameson, *Brecht and Method* (London: Verso, 1998), 25ff.

94. The 2002 New York premiere of *The Invention of Love* was reviewed in the pages of the *New York Review of Books* by Daniel Mendelsohn. This triggered several rounds of increasingly hostile letters between Stoppard and Mendelsohn, which amounted to a debate about the fate of ideas in Stoppard's theater. The question, as I would paraphrase it, involves whether Stoppard creates comic stage philosophers and whether this means that his plays are, for all their philosophical fire power, anti-intellectual. While *Invention of Love*, like almost all of Stoppard's plays, raises the question of ideas in the theater, it is not the best or most successful play to answer this question for Stoppard's oeuvre; it is not the best play to adjudicate the question of whether Stoppard uses tragic (and comic) stage philosophers (such as, allegedly, Housman) for the purpose of discrediting ideas since

its governing opposition is that of the theatrical dandy and the academic, which is not quite the same as (though perhaps tantalizingly close to) the opposition of artist and intellectual or theater and ideas. Daniel Mendelsohn, "The Tale of Two Housmans," *New York Review of Books*, August 10, 2000; Tom Stoppard, reply by Daniel Mendelsohn, "'The Invention of Love': An Exchange," *New York Review of Books*, September 21, 2000; Tom Stoppard, reply by Daniel Mendelsohn, "On 'The Invention of Love': Another Exchange," *New York Review of Books*, October 19, 2000).

95. Tom Stoppard, *Jumpers* (New York: Grove, 1972), 43.

96. Ibid., 44.

97. One of the reviewers remarked that the actor playing Moore, Michael Hordern, had made a career of the "absent-minded professor," whom he recognizes as a "standard figure." J. W. Lambert, review of first production, *Drama*, Summer 1972, 16–17, in Tom Stoppard, *Casebook*, 121.

98. A. J. Ayer, "Love Among the Logical Positivists," *Sunday Times*, April 9, 1972, 16.

99. That *Jumpers* proceeds by teasing out the theatricality of philosophy and by translating philosophical arguments into theater has been missed by those philosophers who consider Moore's lecture to be the only philosophical element of the play and who therefore denounce the play's treatment of philosophy as superficial, a judgment made by Jonathan Bennett in "Philosophy and Mr. Stoppard," *Philosophy* 50 (January 1975): 5–18. This opinion was countered, in the same journal, by Roy W. Perrett, who recognized that the play's contribution to philosophy should not be reduced to Moore's lecture, and instead locates this contribution in its rich treatment of what Perrett calls the "appearance-reality theme" and its dramatic treatment in *Jumpers* in the form of a philosophical farce. Roy W. Perrett, "Philosophy as Farce, or Farce as Philosophy," *Philosophy* 59 (October 1984): 373–81.

100. Tom Stoppard, interview with R. Hudson, S. Itzin, S. and Trussler, "Ambushes for the Audience: Towards a High Comedy of Ideas," *Theatre Quarterly* 4, 4 (May-July 1974): 12. In *Rosencrantz and Guildenstern Are Dead, Jumpers, Travesties: A Casebook*, ed. T. Bareham (London: Macmillan, 1990), 118.

101. Stoppard, *Jumpers*, 83.

102. Ibid., 83.

103. Ibid., 85.

Chapter 4

1. This was the case with the Socrates play of the German exile writer Manès Sperber. Clearly Sperber could not decide which genre was best suited to this material, and in the end he left the whole thing unfinished.

2. M. M. Bakhtin, *The Dialogic Imagination: Four Essays*, ed. Michael Holquist, trans. Caryl Emerson and Michael Holquist (Austin: University of Texas Press, 1981), 263, 275.

3. One of the few theater scholars to have taken Bakhtin to task for his instrumentalization of dramatic categories for his theory of the novel is Marvin Carlson, in "Theater and Dialogism," in *Critical Theory and Performance*, ed. Janelle G. Reinelt and Joseph R. Roach (Ann Arbor: University of Michigan Press, 1992), 313–23.

4. Bakhtin, *The Dialogic Imagination*, 25.

5. Søren Kierkegaard, "Petition to the King," in *Letters and Documents*, vol. 25 of *Kierkegaard's Writings*, ed. and trans. Howard V. Hong and Edna H. Hong (Princeton: Princeton University Press, 1978), 24.

6. Søren Kierkegaard, *The Concept of Irony with Continual Reference to Socrates*, vol. 2 of *Kierkegaard's Writings*, ed. and trans. Howard V. Hong and Edna H. Hong (Princeton: Princeton University Press, 1989).

7. Ibid., 125. Kierkegaard wrote his dissertation under the direct influence of Hegel, but he censors Hegel for not appreciating enough the literary side of Plato. Kierkegaard, *Concept of Irony*, 222. Adorno is among those who tried to keep the literary and philosophical sides of Kierkegaard apart. Theodor W. Adorno, *Kierkegaard: Konstruktion des Ästhetischen* (Frankfurt am Main: Suhrkamp, 1974).

8. Kierkegaard, *Concept of Irony*, 28.

9. Ibid., 127.

10. Ibid., 254.

11. Ibid., 152.

12. Ibid., 257.

13. Ibid., 75, 257.

14. Ibid., 55.

15. Ibid., 41.

16. Ibid., 271.

17. Ibid., 129, 145.

18. Ibid., 52.

19. Kierkegaard's remarkable use of personae also derived from a widespread trend of anonymous and pseudonymous reviewing and publishing in Denmark (and elsewhere). Kierkegaard wrote for the small literary elite of Copenhagen—most of his books, all self-published, sold a few hundred copies at best—which meant that the true identity of the author was generally known. For a discussion of the literary scene around Kierkegaard, see Joakim Garff, *Søren Kierkegaard: A Biography*, trans. Bruce H. Kirmmse (Princeton: Princeton University Press, 2005).

20. Søren Kierkegaard, "'In Vino Veritas': A Recollection," in *Stages on Life's Way*, vol. 11 of *Kierkegaard's Writings*, ed. and trans. Howard V. Hong and Edna H. Hong (Princeton: Princeton University Press, 1988), 1–86.

21. Georg Wilhelm Friedrich Hegel, *Phänomenologie des Geistes*, ed. Eva Moldenhauer and Karl Markus Michel (Frankfurt am Main: Suhrkamp, 1986), 322, 348.

22. Hegel writes: "Daß die Weltgeschichte dieser Entwicklungsgang und das wirkliche Werden des Geistes ist, unter dem wechselnden Schauspiele ihrer Geschichten—dies ist die wahrhafte *Theodizee*, die Rechtfertigung Gottes in der Geschichte." G. W. F. Hegel, *Vorlesungen über die Philosophie der Geschichte* (Frankfurt am Main: Suhrkamp, 1970), 540. The second quote reads: "Der Geist ist aber auf dem Theater, auf dem wir ihn betrachten, in der Weltgeschichte, in seiner konkretesten Wirklichkeit" (29).

23. In his excellent book *Tragödie im Sittlichen*, Christoph Menke has detailed the role of tragedy for Hegel and used its important role for a reading against the grain, a reading intent on showing the lingering effects of tragedy for a philosophy that has putatively superseded it. Christoph Menke, *Tragödie im Sittlichen: Gerechtigkeit und Freiheit nach Hegel* (Frankfurt am Main: Suhrkamp, 1996).

24. George Steiner, *Antigones* (New Haven: Yale University Press, 1996), 21.

25. Sarah Kofman, *Socrates: Fictions of a Philosopher*, trans. Catherine Porter (Ithaca: Cornell University Press, 1998), 39.

26. Søren Kierkegaard, *Either/Or*, Part I, vol. 3 of *Kierkegaard's Writings*, ed. and trans. Howard V. Hong and Edna H. Hong (Princeton: Princeton University Press, 1978); Søren Kierkegaard, *Either/Or*, Part II, vol. 4 of *Kierkegaard's Writings*, ed. and trans. Howard V. Hong and Edna H. Hong (Princeton: Princeton University Press, 1978).

27. Kierkegaard, *Either/Or*, Part II, 332.

28. Ibid., 441.

29. Ibid., 438.

30. Kierkegaard, *Concept of Irony*, 188.

31. Shoshana Felman identifies this theatrical quality also in Don Juan's language, the language of performative theatricality. Shoshana Felman, *Le scandale du corps parlant: Don Juan avec Austin, ou, la séduction en deux langues* (Paris: Éditions du Seuil, 1980).

32. Other commentators have made similar observations as well. Julia Kristeva, *Histoires d'amour* (Paris: Denoil, 1983); Slavoi Zizek and Mladen Dolar, *Opera's Second Death* (London: Routledge, 2001); Sarah Kofman and Jean-Yves Masson, *Don Juan, ou, Le refus de la dette* (Paris: Galilée, 1991).

33. Søren Kierkegaard, *Either/Or*, Part I, 92, 88. The identification of Don Giovanni as an idea has been discussed by Barnard Williams, "Don Juan as an Idea," in *The Don Giovanni Moment: Essays on the Legacy of an Opera*, ed. Lydia Goehr and Daniel Herwitz (New York: Columbia University Press, 2006), 107–18.

34. Wolfgang Amadeus Mozart, *Don Giovanni*, directed by Peter Sellars (London: Decca, 1991).

35. Kierkegaard, *Either/Or*, Part I, 106.

36. Ibid., 134.

37. Ibid., 120.

38. For this reason, Kierkegaard does not belong, in any simple manner, to the iconoclastic tradition of philosophy Martin Jay has identified in *Downcast Eyes: The Denigration of Vision in Twentieth-Century French Thought* (Berkeley: University of California Press, 1993).

39. Kierkegaard, *Either/Or*, Part I, 120.

40. Søren Kierkegaard, *Fear and Trembling/Repetition*, vol. 6 of *Kierkegaard's Writings*, ed. and trans. Howard V. Hong and Edna H. Hong (Princeton: Princeton University Press, 1983).

41. Kierkegaard, *Fear and Trembling/Repetition*, 165, 168.

42. Ibid., 169.

43. Kierkegaard, *Either/Or*, Part I, 239.

44. Ibid., 278.

45. Ibid., 277.

46. Ibid., 169ff.

47. Ibid., 173.

48. Ibid., 172–73.

49. Ibid., 153.

50. A is doing something that resonates with Elaine Scarry's theory of reading as articulated in *Dreaming by the Book* (New York: Farrar, Straus, and Giroux, 1999).

51. Kierkegaard, *Either/Or*, Part I, 175.

52. Ibid., 178.

53. Kierkegaard, *Either/Or*, Part II, 165.

54. Ibid., 163.

55. Friedrich Nietzsche, "Chronik zu Nietzsches Leben," in *Kritische Studienausgabe*, ed. Giorgio Colli and Mazzino Montinari (Munich:

Deutscher Taschenbuch Verlag, 1980), 15:27–28. All references to Nietzsche are based on this edition.

56. Nietzsche, *Die Geburt der Tragödie,* in *Kritische Studienausgabe,* 1:152.

57. Nietzsche, *Nachlaß 1875–1879,* in *Kritische Studienausgabe,* 8:97.

58. The importance of Socrates for Nietzsche can be judged by the frequency of his references to Socrates, which can be found in Nietzsche, *Gesamtregister,* in *Kritische Studienausgabe,* 15:354.

59. Nietzsche, *Geburt,* 1:102, 111.

60. Nietzsche, "Homer's Wettkampf," in *Kritische Studienausgabe,* 2:277-286..

61. Nietzsche, *Geburt,* 1:93.

62. Nietzsche, *Nachlaß 1869–1874,* 7:42.

63. Nietzsche, *Der Wanderer und sein Schatten,* 2:539.

64. Nietzsche, *Götzen-Dämmerung,* in *Kritische Studienausgabe,* 6:155.

65. Nietzsche, *Nachlaß 1875–1879,* 8:95.

66. Ibid., 327.

67. Ibid., 505.

68. Nietzsche, *Nachlaß 1869–1874,* 7:484.

69. Nietzsche, *Die fröhliche Wissenschaft,* book IV, paragraph 340, in *Kritische Studienausgabe,* 3:569–70.

70. This argument was later developed by Bakhtin, who considered Plato as a precursor of the novel and not of modern drama. Bakhtin, *Dialogic Imagination,* 25.

71. For a more detailed analysis of Nietzsche's antitheatrical polemic, see my *Stage Fright: Modernism, Anti-Theatricality, and Drama* (Baltimore: Johns Hopkins University Press, 2002), 31–40.

72. Nietzsche, *Nachlaß 1869–1874,* 7:460.

73. For a discussion of Zarathustra's death, see David Farrell Krell, *Postponements: Woman, Sensuality, and Death in Nietzsche* (Bloomington: Indiana University Press, 1986).

74. Quoted in Philippe Lacoue-Labarthe, *Typography: Mimesis, Philosophy, Politics,* ed. Christopher Fynsk (Stanford: Stanford University Press, 1989), 48.

75. Nietzsche, *Also sprach Zarathustra,* in *Kritische Studienausgabe,* 4:16.

76. Ibid., 272.

77. Ibid., 290.

78. Peter Sloterdijk writes: "It is no coincidence that this herald of immoralism [Zarathustra] is at the same time a rediscoverer of prophetic speech." Peter Sloterdijk, *Thinker on Stage: Nietzsche's Materialism,* trans. Jamie Owen Daniel (Minneapolis: University of Minnesota Press, 1989), 40.

79. Also see Laurence Lampert, *Nietzsche's Teaching: An Interpretation of* Thus Spoke Zarathustra (Yale: Yale University Press, 1986), 245ff.

80. Nietzsche, *Jenseits von Gut und Böse,* in *Kritische Studienausgabe,* 5:12.

81. Nietzsche, *Die fröhliche Wissenschaft,* 3:624.

82. Albert Camus, *Carnets: janvier 1942–mars 1951* (Paris: Gallimard, 1964), 79.

83. Martin Esslin, *The Theatre of the Absurd* (New York: Anchor Books, 1961), xx.

84. Theodor Adorno, "Versuch das Endspiel zu verstehen," in *Noten zur Literatur*, ed. Rolf Tiedemann (Frankfurt: Suhrkamp, 1974), 283.

85. Jean-Paul Sartre, *Being and Nothingness: A Phenomenological Essay on Ontology*, trans. Hazel E. Barnes (New York: Washington Square Press, 1992 [orig. French pub. 1943, first trans. 1956]), 97.

86. Ibid., 102.

87. Ibid., 103.

88. Ibid., 341.

89. Ibid., 344.

90. Ibid., 349.

91. Ibid., 354.

92. Ibid., 347.

93. Ibid., 535.

94. Ibid., 551.

95. Jean-Paul Sartre, *Nausea*, trans. Lloyd Alexander (New York: New Directions, 1964 [orig. French pub. 1938]).

96. Jean-Paul Sartre, *No Exit and Three Other Plays* (New York: Vintage Books, 1989).

97. More recently, Henry Turner has continued this tradition with his book *Shakespeare's Double Helix*, whose two columns, printed on facing pages, juxtapose a reading of Shakespeare's *A Midsummer Night's Dream* with a discussion of science. Henry S. Turner, *Shakespeare's Double Helix* (London: Continuum, 2007).

98. Albert Camus, *Le mythe de Sisyphe: Essai sur l'absurde* (Paris: Gallimard, 1942), 102. All translations from this text are mine.

99. Albert Camus, *Le mythe de Sisyphe: Essai sur l'absurde* (Paris: Gallimard, 1942), 102. All translations from this text are mine.

100. Ibid., 104.

101. Ibid., 100.

102. See E. Freeman, *The Theatre of Albert Camus: A Critical Study* (London: Methuen, 1971), 148.

103. Albert Camus, *Carnets: mai 1935–février 1942* (Paris: Gallimard, 1962), 214–15.

104. Camus, *Mythe*, 110.

105. Ibid., 17.

106. Ibid., 18.

107. Ibid., 101.

108. Ibid., 134, 135.

109. Albert Camus, *Caligula and Three Other Plays*, trans. Stuart Gilbert (New York: Vintage Books, 1958), 8.

110. Ibid., 13.

111. Ibid., 17.

112. Ibid., 21.

113. Ibid., 65.

114. Ibid., 44–45.

115. Ibid., 17.

116. Ibid., 25.

117. Camus, *Mythe*, 96.

118. Hayden White's influential *Metahistory* takes its four master tropes from Burke. Hayden White, *Metahistory: The Historical Imagination in Nineteenth-Century Europe* (Baltimore: Johns Hopkins University Press,

1973). In the area of drama, one of Burke's few champions has been Bert O. States, with his inspiring study *Irony and Drama: A Poetics* (Ithaca: Cornell University Press, 1971). In particular, States is attuned to the ways in which Burke translates the philosophical mode of dialectic into drama.

119. Kenneth Burke, *The Philosophy of Literary Form: Studies in Symbolic Action* (Berkeley: University of California Press, 1973), 103.

120. James George Frazer, *The Golden Bough: A Study in Magic and Religion* (New York: Macmillan, 1922).

121. Burke, *Philosophy of Literary Form*, 108.

122. One of Burke's favorite patterns is the scapegoat, which connects his interest in Greek tragedy to that in history (for example, the beheading of kings) and all the way to a sociology of different punitive systems. We are not surprised to hear that Burke ultimately did not care about possible objections raised against the historical accuracy of his theory of ritual and ritual theater, for what he was really after was "a calculus—a vocabulary, or a set of coordinates, that serves best for the integration of all phenomena studied by the social sciences" (105). And so, step by step, Burke abstracts from his immediate object of analysis, the ritual origin of Greek tragedy, and moves to a general theory that ends up encompassing not only all of human interaction but the study of nature as well. Burke writes: "The broad outlines of our position might be codified thus: 1) We have the drama and the scene of the drama. The drama is enacted against a background. 2) The description of the scene is the rôle of the physical sciences; the description of the drama is the rôle of the social sciences" (114). It is in the course of this radical expansion of the dramatic "hub" that Burke first mentions, in a footnote, what he later called the "dramatist pentad," a theatrical scheme of universal applicability. In note 25, Burke writes: "Instead of the situation-strategy pair, I now use five terms: act, scene, agent, agency, purpose" (106).

123. Kenneth Burke, *A Grammar of Motives* (Berkeley: University of California Press, 1969), 200ff.

124. For a more detailed analysis of Burke's reading of Marx, see my *Poetry of the Revolution: Marx, Manifestos, and the Avant-Gardes* (Princeton: Princeton University Press, 2006), 23ff.

125. Burke, *Philosophy of Literary Form*, 107.

126. Ibid., 109.

127. Burke, *Grammar of Motives*, 230.

128. Ibid., 61.

129. Ibid., 440.

130. Ibid.

131. Ibid., 441.

132. Ibid.,128.

133. Ibid., 253–54.

134. Gilles Deleuze, *Différence et répétition* (Paris: Presses Universitaires de France, 1968), 82. All translations from this text are mine.

135. Ibid., 93.

136. Ibid., 13.

137. Ibid., 16.

138. Ibid., 17.

139. Ibid., 18.

140. Michel Foucault, "Theatrum Philosophicum," in *Mimesis, Masochism, and Mime: The Politics of Theatricality in Contemporary French Thought*, ed. Timothy Murray (Michigan: University of Michigan Press, 1997), 216–38.

141. Deleuze, *Différence*, 18.

142. Ibid., 19.

143. Ibid.

144. Ibid.

145. Ibid., 264.

146. Ibid., 282.

147. Foucault, "Theatrum Philosophicum," 220.

148. Deleuze, *Différence*, 282.

149. Ibid., 192.

150. Antonin Artaud, *Oeuvres Complètes* (Paris: Gallimard, 1956), 4:93–94.

151. Ibid., 4:94.

152. Ibid., 5:18.

153. For a more detailed discussion of Artaud's manifesto theater, see my *Poetry of the Revolution*, 196ff.

154. Surprisingly Artaud evoked the fact that Wagner's theater remains a chimera until he found a powerful patron in order to engage in a similar fund-raising effort.

155. Gilles Deleuze and Félix Guattari, *Anti-Oedipus: Capitalism and Schizophrenia*, trans. Robert Hurley, Mark Seem, and Helen R. Lane (Minneapolis: University of Minnesota Press, 1983), 49, 271.

156. Ibid., 307.

157. Gilles Deleuze and Félix Guattari, *What Is Philosophy?* trans. Hugh Tomlinson and Graham Burchell (New York: Columbia University Press, 1994), 61ff.

158. Ibid., 66, 64.

159. Ibid., 63.

160. Ibid., 10.

Chapter 5

1. Martin Heidegger, *Über den Humanismus* (Frankfurt am Main: Klostermann, 1949), 5.

2. Rudolf Carnap, "Überwindung der Metaphysik durch logische Analyse der Sprache," *Erkenntnis* 2 (1931): 219–41.

3. Ludwig Wittgenstein, *Tractatus Logico-Philosophicus*, in *Werkausgabe* (Frankfurt am Main: Suhrkamp, 1989), 1:67.

4. Elaine Scarry, *On Beauty and Being Just* (Princeton: Princeton University Press, 1999), 112ff.

5. Iris Murdoch, *Sartre: Romantic Rationalist* (New Haven: Yale University Press, 1953), 75.

6. Iris Murdoch, "Literature and Philosophy: A Conversation with Bryan Magee," originally shown on BBC Television, October 28, 1977, accessed on YouTube, April 29, 2009, at http://www.youtube.com/watch?v=ahDWiS-X_nM.

7. Iris Murdoch, *Existentialists and Mystics: Writings on Philosophy and Literature* (New York: Penguin, 1998).

8. Murdoch approvingly quotes Stanley Rosen's critique of Heidegger's commentary on Plato: "In my opinion Heidegger goes wrong because he is not sufficiently attentive to the silence of Plato. Still more specifically, he never confronts the significance of Socratic irony or the dramatic form of the dialogues." Iris Murdoch, *Metaphysics as a Guide to Morals* (New York: Penguin Books, 1993), 181. The Stanley Rosen quote is from his

book *The Quarrel Between Philosophy and Poetry: Studies in Ancient Thought* (New York: Routledge, 1988), 132.

9. Murdoch's tendency to portray psychoanalysts as Jews (as, for example, in *The Severed Head*) whose ideas are then confronted by a Christian framework mixes racial and religious categories that at least resonate with Christian anti-Semitism.

10. Murdoch, "Literature and Philosophy," 19.

11. A. S. Byatt, "Introduction," in Iris Murdoch, *The Bell* (London: Penguin, 1999), viii.

12. Murdoch, "Literature and Philosophy," 21, 18.

13. Iris Murdoch, "Art and Eros: A Dialogue About Art," in *Acastos: Two Platonic Dialogues* (London: Chatto & Windus, 1986), 55–56.

14. Ibid., 58.

15. Ibid., 61.

16. Ibid., 47.

17. Martha C. Nussbaum, "Introduction," in Iris Murdoch, *The Black Prince* (London: Penguin, 2003), x.

18. Martha C. Nussbaum, *Upheavals of Thought: The Intelligence of Emotions* (Cambridge: Cambridge University Press, 2001), 712.

19. Ernst Hans Grombrich, *Art and Illusion: A Study in the Psychology of Pictorial Representation* (London: Pantheon, 1960); Erich Auerbach, *Mimesis: The Representation of Reality in Western Literature* (Bern: A. Francke Verlag, 1946).

20. Nussbaum, *Upheavals of Thought*, 713.

21. Ibid., 712.

22. Martha C. Nussbaum, *The Fragility of Goodness: Luck and Ethics in Greek Tragedy and Philosophy* (Cambridge: Cambridge University Press, 2001), 127.

23. Martha C. Nussbaum, "Emotions as Judgments of Value: A Philosophical Dialogue," *Comparative Criticism* 20 (1998): 33–62.

24. "The Capability of Philosophy: An Interview with Martha C. Nussbaum," conducted by Jeffrey Williams, *Minnesota Review*, Winter/Spring 2009, 69.

25. One of the first, and few, theater scholars to be interested in Badiou was Janelle Reinelt, who wrote "Theatre and Politics: Encountering Badiou," *Performance Research* 9, 4 (2004): 87–94.

26. Alain Badiou, *Conditions* (Paris: Éditions du Seuil, 1992), 103 n. 15.

27. Ibid., 77.

28. Ibid., 30ff. Also see Alain Badiou, *L'antiphilosophie de Wittgenstein* (Caen: Nous, 2009).

29. Badiou, *Conditions*, 75.

30. Ibid., 77.

31. Alain Badiou, *Deleuze: Le clamour de l'Etre* (Paris: Hachette, 1997), 18, 26. All translations from this text are mine.

32. Ibid., 83.

33. Alain Badiou, *Logiques des Mondes* (Paris: Éditions du Seuil, 2006). For my review of this book, "Nothing but the Truths," see *Bookforum*, April–May 2009.

34. Badiou, *Conditions*, 318.

35. Badiou, *Logiques des Mondes*, 12.

36. Alain Badiou, *Being and Event*, trans. Olivier Feltham (London: Continuum, 2005).

37. Badiou, *Conditions*, 157ff.

38. Badiou, *Handbook of Inaesthetics*, trans. Alberto Toscano (Stanford: Stanford University Press, 2005), 20.

39. Badiou, *Being and Event*, 192.

40. Badiou, *Conditions*, 108.

41. Badiou, *Being and Event*, 191.

42. Martin Puchner, *Stage Fright: Modernism, Anti-Theatricality, and Drama* (Baltimore: Johns Hopkins University Press, 2002). It has been one of the pleasures of encountering Badiou's work to see his reading of theater, from Mallarmé via Brecht to Beckett, dovetail with my own (anti-) theatrical history of a Platonist theater. In *Handbook of Inaesthetics*, for example, he identifies, in passing, Brecht's anti-Aristotelian theater as "ultimately Platonic," noting that Brecht "theatrically reactivated Plato's anti-theatrical measures" (6). Beckett is cited as having achieved another reactivation of Plato.

43. Alain Badiou, *The Century* (Cambridge: Polity Press, 2007), 40.

44. Badiou, *Handbook*, 72.

45. As editor of *Theatre Survey*, I commissioned a translation of this work into English; it appeared in its entirety in the fall 2008 issue of *Theatre Survey* and can be accessed via Cambridge Journals Online. Alain Badiou, "Rhapsody for the Theatre," trans. Bruno Bosteels, *Theatre Survey* 49, 2 (November 2008): 187–238.

46. Badiou, "Rhapsody," 214.

47. This view of the audience as mirroring a political assembly has been criticized by Jacques Rancière, who argues that spectators absorb a theater event individually, and not necessarily according to the dictates of directors and dramatists. "The Emancipated Spectator," *Artforum* 45, 7 (March 2007): 271–79. Rancière, too, takes his point of departure from Plato, measuring different conceptions of the spectator against Plato's cave parable.

48. Badiou, "Rhapsody," 206.

49. Ibid., 227.

Epilogue

1. *Fragments for a History of the Human Body*, ed. Michel Feher with Ramona Naddaff and Nadia Tazi (New York: Zone Books, 1989); Jean-Luc Nancy, *Corpus* (Paris: Éditions Métailié, 1992) and *Corpus*, trans. Richard A. Rand (New York: Fordham University Press, 2008).

2. Samuel P. Huntington, *The Clash of Civilizations and the Remaking of the World Order* (New York: Simon & Schuster, 1996).

Bibliography

Abel, Lionel. *Tragedy and Metatheatre: Essays on Dramatic Form*. With an introduction by Martin Puchner. New York: Holmes & Meier, 2003.

Addison, Joseph. *Cato, a Tragedy. As it is acted at the Theatre-Royal in Drury Lane by Her Majesty's servants*. London: J. Tonson, at Shakespear's Head against Catherine-Street in the Strand, 1713.

Adorno, Theodor W. *Kierkegaard: Konstruktion des Ästhetischen*. Frankfurt am Main: Suhrkamp, 1974.

———."Versuch das *Endspiel* zu verstehen." In *Noten zur Literatur*. Edited by Rolf Tiedemann. Frankfurt am Main: Suhrkamp, 1974.

Aelianus, Claudius. *Varia Historia*. Translated, with an introduction and notes, by Diane Ostrom Johnson. Lewiston, NY: Edwin Mellen Press, 1997.

Arieti, James A. *Interpreting Plato: The Dialogues as Drama*. Savage, MD: Rowman & Littlefield, 1991.

Aristotle, *Poetics*. Edited and translated by Stephen Halliwell. Cambridge: Harvard University Press, 1995: 27–141.

Artaud, Antonin. *Œuvres Complètes*, vol. 4–5. Paris: Gallimard, 1956.

Auerbach, Erich. *Mimesis: The Representation of Reality in Western Literature*. Bern: A. Francke Verlag, 1946.

Ayer, A. J. "Love Among the Logical Positivists." *The Sunday Times*, 9 April 1972.

Badiou, Alain. *Being and Event*. Translated by Olivier Feltham. London: Continuum, 2005.

———. *The Century*. Cambridge: Polity Press, 2007.

———. *Conditions*. Preface by François Wahl. Paris: Éditions du Seuil, 1992.

———. *Deleuze: Le clamour de l'Etre*. Paris: Hachette, 1997.

———. *Handbook of Inaesthetics*. Translated by Alberto Toscano. Stanford: Stanford University Press, 2005.

———. *L'antiphilosophie de Wittgenstein*. Caen: Nous, 2009.

———. *Logiques des Mondes*. Paris: Éditions du Seuil, 2006.

———. *Rhapsody for the Theatre*. Edited by Martin Puchner, translated by Bruno Bosteels. *Theatre Survey* 49:2 (November 2008): 187–238.

Bakhtin, M. M. *The Dialogic Imagination: Four Essays*. Edited by Michael Holquist, translated by Caryl Emerson and Michael Holquist. Austin: University of Texas Press, 1981.

Barish, Jonas. *The Antitheatrical Prejudice*. Berkeley: University of California Press, 1981.

Benjamin, Walter. *Versuche über Brecht*. Edited and with an afterword by Rolf Tiedemann. Frankfurt am Main: Suhrkamp, 1971.

Bennett, Jonathan. "Philosophy and Mr Stoppard." *Philosophy* 50 (January 1975): 5–18.

Bentley, Eric. *Bernard Shaw*. Northfolk, CT: New Directions, 1947.

———. *The Playwright as Thinker: A Study of Drama in Modern Times*. New York: Harcourt, Brace, Jovanovich, 1987.

Bergson, Henri. "Laughter." In *Comedy: An* Essay on Comedy *by George Meredith*, Laughter *by Henri Bergson*. Edited, with an introduction and appendix, by Wylie Sypher. New York: Doubleday, 1956.

Blondell, Ruby. *The Play of Character in Plato's Dialogues*. Cambridge: Cambridge University Press, 2002.

Blumenberg, Hans. *Das Lachen der Thrakerin: Eine Urgeschichte der Theorie*. Frankfurt am Main: Suhrkamp, 1987.

Brecht, Bertolt. "Der Messingkauf." In *Gesammelte Werke*, vol. 16. Frankfurt am Main: Suhrkamp, 1967.

Brustein, Robert. *Theatre of Revolt: Studies in Modern Drama from Ibsen to Genet*. Chicago: Ivan R. Dee, 1991.

Burke, Kenneth. *A Grammar of Motives*. Berkeley: University of California Press, 1969.

———. *The Philosophy of Literary Form: Studies in Symbolic Action*. Berkeley: University of California Press, 1973.

Butler, Judith. *Gender Trouble*. New York: Routledge, 1990.

Byatt, A. S. "Introduction." In *The Bell*. By Iris Murdoch. London: Penguin, 1999.

Camus, Albert. *Caligula & Three Other Plays*. Translated from the French by Stuart Gilbert. New York: Vintage Books, 1958.

———. *Carnets: janvier 1942–mars 1951*. Paris: Gallimard, 1964.

———. *Carnets: mai 1935–février 1942*. Paris: Gallimard, 1962.

———. *Le mythe de Sisyphe: Essai sur l'absurde*. Paris: Gallimard, 1942.

Carlson, Marvin. "Theater and Dialogism." In *Critical Theory and Performance*. Edited by Janelle G. Reinelt and Joseph R. Roach. Ann Arbor: University of Michigan Press, 1992.

Carnap, Rudolf. "Überwindung der Metaphysik durch logische Analyse der Sprache." *Erkenntnis* 2 (1931): 219–41.

Chesterton, Gilbert Keith. *George Bernard Shaw*. New York: J. Lane Company, 1909.

Clay, Diskin. *Platonic Questions: Dialogues with the Silent Philosopher*. Philadelphia: University of Pennsylvania Press, 2000.

Claybaugh, Amanda. *The Novel of Purpose: Literature and Social Reform in the Anglo-American World*. Ithaca: Cornell University Press, 2007.

Cornford, F. M. *Plato and Parmenides*. London: Routledge, 1993.

Craddock, Thomas. *The Poetic Writings of Thomas Cradock, 1718–1770*. Edited with an introduction by David Curtis Skaggs. Newark: University of Delaware Press, 1983.

Critchley, Simon. *The Book of Dead Philosophers*. New York: Vintage, 2008.

Deleuze, Gilles. *Différence et répétition*. Paris: Presses Universitaires de France, 1968.

Deleuze, Gilles, and Félix Guattari. *Anti-Oedipus: Capitalism and Schizophrenia*. Translated from the French by Robert Hurley, Mark Seem, and Helen R. Lane. Minneapolis: University of Minnesota Press, 1983.

———. *What Is Philosophy?* Translated by Hugh Tomlinson and Graham Burchell. New York: Columbia University Press, 1994.

Douglas, Alfred. "Salomé: A Critical Review." *The Spirit Lamp: An Aesthetic, Literary and Critical Magazine* 4:1 (May 1893): 20–27.

Dowling, Linda. *Hellenism and Homosexuality in Victorian Oxford*. Ithaca: Cornell University Press, 1994.

Eden, Kathy. *Friends Hold All Things in Common: Tradition, Intellectual Property, and the* Adages *of Erasmus*. New Haven: Yale University Press, 2001.

Ellmann, Richard. *Oscar Wilde*. New York: Alfred A. Knopf, 1987.

Esslin, Martin. *The Theatre of the Absurd*. New York: Anchor Books, 1961.

Feher, Michel, with Ramona Naddaff and Nadia Tazi, editors. *Fragments for a History of the Human Body*. New York: Zone Books, 1989.

Felman, Shoshana. *Le scandale du corps parlant: Don Juan avec Austin, ou, la séduction en deux langues*. Paris: Editions de Seuil, 1980.

Ficino, Marsilio. *Commentary on Plato's* Symposium *on Love*. English translation by Sears Jayne. Dallas: Spring Publications, 1985.

Foucault, Michel. *Le Courage de la Vérité: Le Gouvernement de Soi et des Autres II: Cours au Collège de France, 1984*. Edited by Frédéric Gros under the direction of François Ewald and Alessandro Fontana. Paris: Gallimard, 2009.

———. *Le Gouvernement de Soi et des Autres: Cours au Collège de France, 1982–1983*. Edited by Frédéric Gros under the direction of François Ewald and Alessandro Fontana. Paris: Gallimard, 2008.

———. *The Hermeneutics of the Subject: Lectures at the Collège de France 1981–1982*. Edited by Frédéric Gros, translated by Graham Burchell. New York: Picador, 2005.

———. "Theatrum Philosophicum." In *Mimesis, Masochism, & Mime: The Politics of Theatricality in Contemporary French Thought*. Edited by Timothy Murray. Michigan: University of Michigan Press, 1997.

Frayn, Michael. *Copenhagen*. London: Methuen, 1998.

Frazer, James George. *The Golden Bough: A Study in Magic and Religion*. New York: Macmillan, 1922.

Freeman, E. *The Theatre of Albert Camus: A Critical Study*. London: Methuen, 1971.

Fuchs, Elinor. "Clown Shows: Anti-Theatricalist Theatricalism in Four Twentieth-Century Plays." In *Against Theatre: Creative Destructions on the Modernist Stage*. Edited by Alan Ackerman and Martin Puchner. New York: Palgrave, 2006.

Garff, Joakim. *Søren Kierkegaard: A Biography*. Translated by Bruce H. Kirmmse. Princeton: Princeton University Press, 2005.

Giudice, Gaspare. *Luigi Pirandello: A Biography*. Translated by Alastair Hamilton. London: Oxford University Press, 1975.

Goehr, Lydia, and Daniel Herwitz, editors. *The Don Giovanni Moment: Essays on the Legacy of an Opera*. New York: Columbia University Press, 2006.

Grombrich, Ernst Hans. *Art and Illusion: A Study in the Psychology of Pictorial Representation*. London: Pantheon, 1960.

Gruber, William E. "'Non-Aristotelian' Theater: Brecht's and Plato's Theories of Artistic Imitation." *Comparative Drama* 21:3 (Fall 1986): 199–213.

Hadot, Pièrre. *Philosophy as a Way of Life: Spiritual Exercises from Socrates to Foucault*. Edited and with an introduction by Arnold I. Davidson, translated by Michael Case. Oxford: Blackwell Publishing, 1995.

Havelock, Eric A. *Preface to Plato*. Cambridge: Harvard University Press, 1963.

———. *The Muse Learns to Write: Reflections on Orality and Literacy from Antiquity to the Present*. New Haven: Yale University Press, 1986.

Hegel, Georg Wilhelm Friedrich. *Phänomenologie des Geistes*. Edited by Eva Moldenhauer and Karl Markus Michel. Frankfurt am Main: Suhrkamp, 1986.

———. *Vorlesungen über die Philosophie der Geschichte*. Frankfurt am Main: Surkamp, 1970.

Heidegger, Martin. *Über den Humanismus*. Frankfurt am Main: Klostermann, 1949.

Holland, Merlin, and Rupert Hart-Davis, editors. *The Complete Letters of Oscar Wilde*. New York: Henry Holt, 2000.

Huntington, Samuel P. *The Clash of Civilizations and the Remaking of the World Order*. New York: Simon & Schuster, 1996.

Isherwood, Charles. "Checking in with Glimmer Twins, Plato and Aristotle." *New York Times*, 18 June 2007.

Jameson, Fredric. *Brecht and Method*. London: Verso, 1998.

Jay, Martin. *Downcast Eyes: The Denigration of Vision in Twentieth-Century French Thought*. Berkeley: University of California Press, 1993.

Johnson, Samuel. *Johnson's Life of Addison*. With introduction and notes by F. Ryland. London: George Bell & Sons, York Str., Covent Garden, 1893.

Kaiser, Georg. "Das Drama Platons." In *Werke*, vol. 4, edited by Walther Huder. Frankfurt: Propyläen Verlag, 1971.

Kahn, Charles L. *Plato and the Socratic Dialogue*. Cambridge: Cambridge University Press, 1996.

Kierkegaard, Søren. *The Concept of Irony with Continual Reference to Socrates*. Edited and translated with introduction and notes by Howard V. Hong and Edna H. Hong. Princeton: Princeton University Press, 1989.

———. *Either/Or*. Part I. Edited and translated by Howard V. Hong and Edna H. Hong. Princeton: Princeton University Press, 1978.

———. *Either/Or*. Part II. Edited and translated by Howard V. Hong and Edna H. Hong. Princeton: Princeton University Press, 1978.

———. *Fear and Trembling, Repetition*. In *Kierkegaard's Writings, VI*. Edited and translated by Howard V. Hong and Edna H. Hong. Princeton: Princeton University Press, 1983.

———. *Letters and Document: Kierkegaard's Writings, XXV*. Edited and translated by Howard V. Hong and Edna H. Hong. Princeton: Princeton University Press, 1978.

———. *Stages on Life's Way*. In *Kierkegaard's Writings, XI*. Edited and translated by Howard V. Hong and Edna H. Hong. Princeton: Princeton University Press, 1988.

Kofman, Sarah, and Jean-Yves Masson. *Don Juan, ou, Le refus de la dette*. Paris: Galilée, 1991.

Kofman, Sarah. *Socrates: Fictions of a Philosopher*. Translated by Catherine Porter. Ithaca: Cornell University Press, 1998.

Kottman, Paul A. *A Politics of the Scene*. Stanford: Stanford University Press, 2008.

Krell, David Farrell. *Postponements: Woman, Sensuality, and Death in Nietzsche*. Bloomington: Indiana University Press, 1986.

Lacoue-Labarthe, Philippe. *Typography: Mimesis, Philosophy, Politics*. Edited by Christopher Fynsk with an introduction by Jacques Derrida. Stanford: Stanford University Press, 1989.

Laertius, Diogenes. *Lives of Eminent Philosophers*. With an English translation by R. D. Hicks, vol. 1. Cambridge: Harvard University Press, 1972.

Lampert, Laurence. *Nietzsche's Teaching: An Interpretation of* Thus Spoke Zarathustra. Yale: Yale University Press, 1986.

Laurence, Dan H., ed. *Shaw's Music*. vol. 1. London: Max Reinhardt, Bodley Head, 1981.

Mendelsohn, Daniel. "The Tale of Two Housmans." *New York Review of Books* 47:13 (August 2000).

Menke, Christoph. *Tragödie im Sittlichen: Gerechtigkeit und Freiheit nach Hegel*. Frankfurt am Main: Suhrkamp, 1996.

Moi, Toril. *Henrik Ibsen and the Birth of Modernism: Art, Theater, Philosophy*. Oxford: Oxford University Press, 2006.

Monoson, S. Sara. *Plato's Democratic Entanglements: Athenian Politics and the Practice of Philosophy*. Princeton: Princeton University Press, 2000.

Murdoch, Iris. *Acastos: Two Platonic Dialogues*. London: Chatto & Windus, 1986.

———. *Existentialists and Mystics: Writings on Philosophy and Literature*. New York: Penguin, 1998.

———. "Literature and Philosophy: A Conversation with Bryan Magee." Originally shown on BBC Television, 28 October 1977.

———. *Metaphysics as a Guide to Morals*. New York: Penguin Books, 1993.

———. *Sartre: Romantic Rationalist*. New Haven: Yale University Press, 1953.

Nancy, Jean-Luc. *Corpus*. Paris: Éditions Métailié, 1992.

———.*Corpus*. Translated into English by Richard A. Rand. New York: Fordham University Press, 2008.

Nehamas, Alexander. *The Art of Living: Socratic Reflections from Plato to Aristotle*. Berkeley: University of California Press, 2000.

Nietzsche, Friedrich. *Kritische Studienausgabe*. Edited by Giorgio Colli and Mazzino Montinari, 15 vols. Munich: Deutscher Taschenbuch Verlag, 1980.

Nightingale, Andrea Wilson. *Genres in Dialogue: Plato and the Construct of Philosophy*. Cambridge: Cambridge University Press, 1995.

———. *Spectacles of Truth in Classical Greek Philosophy: Theoria in Its Cultural Context*. Cambridge: Cambridge University Press, 2004.

Nussbaum, Martha C. "The Capability of Philosophy: An Interview with Martha C. Nussbaum," conducted by Jeffrey Williams, *The Minnesota Review* (Winter/Spring 2009): 71–72:63–86.

———. "Emotions as Judgments of Value: A Philosophical Dialogue." In *Philosophical Dialogues*. Edited by E. S. Shaffer. *Comparative Criticism* 20 (1998): 33–62.

———. *The Fragility of Goodness: Luck and Ethics in Greek Tragedy and Philosophy*. Cambridge: Cambridge University Press, 1986.

———. "Introduction." In *The Black Prince*, by Iris Murdoch. London: Penguin, 2003.

———. *Upheavals of Thought: The Intelligence of Emotions*. Cambridge: Cambridge University Press, 2001.

Ong, Walter J. *Orality and Literacy: The Technologization of the Word*. London: Methuen, 1982.

Pater, Walter. *Plato and Platonism*. With an introduction by Martin Golding. New York: Barnes & Noble Books, 2005.

Perrett, Roy W. "Philosophy as Farce, or Farce as Philosophy." *Philosophy* 59 (October 1984): 373–81.

Pirandello, Luigi. *On Humor*. Introduced, translated, and annotated by Antonio Illiano and Daniel P. Testa. Chapel Hill: University of North Carolina Press, 1974.

Plato. *Cratylus, Parmenides, Greater Hippias, Lesser Hippias*. With an English translation by H. N. Fowler. Cambridge: Harvard University Press, 1926.

———. *Euthyphro, Apology, Crito, Phaedo, Phaedrus*. With an English translation by Harold North Fowler. Cambridge: Harvard University Press, 1914.

———. *Laches, Protagoras, Meno, Euthydemus*. With an English translation by W. R. M. Lamb. Cambridge: Harvard University Press, 1924.

———. *Laws: Books VII–XII*. With an English translation by R. G. Bury. Cambridge: Harvard University Press, 1926.

———. *Lysis, Symposium, Gorgias*. With an English translation by W. R. M. Lamb. Cambridge: Harvard University Press, 1925.

———. *Republic: Books I–V*. With an English translation by Paul Shorey. Cambridge: Harvard University Press, 1930.

———. *Republic: Books VI–X*. With an English translation by Paul Shorey. Cambridge: Harvard University Press, 1935.

———. *The Statesman*. In *The Statesman, Philebus, Ion*. With a translation by Harold N. Fowler. Cambridge: Harvard University Press, 1925.

———. *Theaetetus, Sophist*. With a translation by Harold North Fowler. Cambridge: Harvard University Press, 1921.

———.*Timaeus, Critias, Cleitophon, Menexenus, Epistles*. With a translation by R. G. Bury. Cambridge: Harvard University Press, 1929.

Plutarch. *Lives: Alcibiades and Coriolanus, Lysander and Sulla*. Translated by Bernadotte Perrin. Cambridge: Loeb Classics Library, 1916.

Popper, Karl. *The Open Society and Its Enemies*. London: Routledge, 1945.

Puchner, Martin. "Nothing but the Truths." *Bookforum* (April-May 2009): 34.

———. *Poetry of the Revolution: Marx, Manifestos, and the Avant-Gardes*. Princeton: Princeton University Press, 2006.

———. "Sade's Theatrical Passions." *The Yale Journal of Criticism* 18:1 (Spring 2005): 111–25.

———. *Stage Fright: Modernism, Anti-Theatricality, and Drama*. Baltimore: Johns Hopkins University Press, 2002.

———. "Staging Death." *London Review of Books* 29:3 (February 2007): 21–22.

Rancière, Jacques. "The Emancipated Spectator." *Artforum* 45:7 (March 2007): 271–79.

Rehm, Rush. *Greek Tragic Theatre*. London: Routledge, 1992.

Reinelt, Janelle. "Theatre and Politics: Encountering Badiou." *Performance Research*, special issue on Civility, 9:4 (2004): 87–94.

Rokem, Freddie. *Philosophers and Thespians: Thinking Performance*. Stanford: Stanford Univeristy Press, forthcoming.

———. "The Philosopher and the Two Playwrights: Socrates, Agathon, and Aristophanes in Plato's *Symposium*." *Theatre Survey* 49:2 (November 2008): 239–52.

Rosen, Stanley. *The Quarrel Between Philosophy and Poetry: Studies in Ancient Thought*. New York: Routledge, 1988.

Ryle, Gilbert. *Plato's Progress*. Cambridge: Cambridge University Press, 1966.

Sade, Marquis de. *La philosophie dans le boudoir: Les instituteurs immoraux*. With a preface by Glibert Lely. Paris: Christian Bourgois Éditeur, 1972.

———. *Œuvres Complètes*, XXXII. Théâtre I. Paris: Jean-Jacques Pauvert, 1970.

Sartre, Jean-Paul. *Being and Nothingness: A Phenomenological Essay on Ontology*. Translated and with an introduction by Hazel E. Barnes. New York: Washington Square Press, 1992.

———. *Nausea*. Translated from the French by Lloyd Alexander, introduction by Hayden Carruth. New York: New Directions, 1964.

———. No Exit *and Three Other Plays*. New York: Vintage Books, 1989.

Sayre, Kenneth M. *Plato's Literary Garden: How to Read a Platonic Dialogue*. Notre Dame: University of Notre Dame, 1995.

Scarry, Elaine *On Beauty and Being Just*. Princeton: Princeton University Press, 1999.

———. *Dreaming by the Book*. New York: Farrar, Straus, and Giroux, 1999.

Schleiermacher, Friedrich. *Platon*, Sämtliche Werke, 6 vols. Edited by Ernesto Grassi. Hamburg: Rowohlt, 1957.

———. *Schleiermacher's Introductions to the Dialogues of Plato,*. Translated by William Dobson. Cambridge: J. & J. J. Deighton, 1836.

Shaw, Bernard. *Back to Methuselah: A Metabiological Pentateuch*. Revised edition with a postscript. Oxford: Oxford University Press, 1947.

———. *Bernard Shaw:* Man and Superman *and* Saint Joan*: A Casebook*. Edited by A. M. Gibbs. London: Macmillan, 1992.

———. *George Bernard Shaw: Last Plays*. Under the editorial supervision of Dan H. Laurence. London: Penguin Books, 1974.

———. *Plays by George Bernard Shaw: Mrs. Warren's Profession, Arms and the Man, Candida, Man and Superman*. With a Foreword by Eric Bentley. New York: Signet, 1960.

———. *Pygmalion*. New York: Dover, 1994.

———. *Shakes versus Shav*. In *George Bernard Shaw: Last Plays*. Under the editorial supervision of Dan H. Laurence. London: Penguin Books, 1974.

Sloterdijk, Peter. *Thinker on Stage: Nietzsche's Materialism*. Translated by Jamie Owen Daniel, foreword by Jochen Schulte-Sasse. Minneapolis: University of Minnesota Press, 1989.

States, Bert O. *Irony and Drama: A Poetics*. Ithaca: Cornell University Press, 1971.

Steiner, George. *Antigones*. New Haven: Yale University Press, 1996.

———. *The Death of Tragedy*. New York, Knopf, 1961.

Strauss, Leo. *Studies in Platonic Political Philosophy*. With an introduction by Thomas L. Pangle. Chicago: University of Chicago Press, 1983.

Steveni, Michael. "The Root of Art Education: Literary Sources." *Journal of Aesthetic Education* 15:1 (January 1981).

Stoppard, Tom. *Jumpers*. New York: Grove, 1972.

———. "'The Invention of Love': An exchange." *New York Review of Books* 47:14 (September 2000).

———. "On 'The Invention of Love': Another Exchange." *New York Review of Books* 47:16 (October 2000).

———. *Rosencrantz and Guildenstern Are Dead, Jumpers, Travesties: A Casebook*. Edited by T. Bareham. London: Macmillan, 1990.

Tilgher, Adriano. *Relativisti Contemporanei*. Rome: Libreria di Scienze e Lettere, 1921.

Turner, Henry S. *Shakespeare's Double Helix*. London: Continuum, 2007.

Voltaire. "Dix-Huitième Lettres sur la Tragedie." In *Lettres écrites de Londres sur les Anglois et autres sujects*. Basel: W. Bowyer, 1734.

Weber, Samuel. *Theatricality as Medium*. New York: Fordham University Press, 2004.

White, Hayden. *Metahistory: The Historical Imagination in Nineteenth-Century Europe*. Baltimore: Johns Hopkins University Press, 1973.

White, John J. *Brecht's Dramatic Theory*. Rochester, NY: Camden House, 2004.

Whitehead, Alfred North. *Process and Reality*. New York: Macmillan, 2009.

Wilde, Oscar. *The Artist as Critic: Critical Writings of Oscar Wilde*. Edited by Richard Ellmann. Chicago: University of Chicago Press, 1982.

———. *The Complete Letters of Oscar Wilde*. Edited by Merlin Holland and Rupert Hart-Davis. New York, Henry Holt, 2000.

———. *Complete Works of Oscar Wilde*. With an introduction by Vyvyan Holland. London: Collins, 1989.

———. *Salomé: drame en un acte* in *Salome and Other Plays*. With an introduction by Arthur Symons. *The Complete Works of Oscar Wilde*, vol. 9. New York: Doubleday, 1923.

Wilson, Emily. *The Death of Socrates*. Cambridge: Harvard University Press, 2007.

Witt, Mary Ann Frese. *The Search for Modern Tragedy: Aesthetic Fascism in Italy and France*. Ithaca: Cornell University Press, 2001.

Wittgenstein, Ludwig. *Bemerkungen über die Grundlagen der Mathematik. Werkausgabe 6*. Edited by G. E. M. Ascombe, Rush Rheese, and G. H. von Wright. Frankfurt am Main: Suhrkamp, 1989.

———. *Tractatus Logico-Philosophicus*, in *Werkausgabe*, vol. 1. Frankfurt am Main: Suhrkamp, 1989.

Index